Revolution and Counterrevolution in America: *A Marxist Perspective*

Revolution and Counterrevolution in America

A Marxist Perspective

John Peterson

Marxist Books
New York

Revolution and Counterrevolution in America
A Marxist Perspective
John Peterson

First edition
Published 2026

marxistbooks.com

Cover design by Gage Tijerina and Tim LaSalle

Layout by Ramneet Manrai and Wesley Allen

Proofread by Charlotte Papin, Josh Lucker,
Steve Iverson, Mark Rahman and Jon Lange

ISBN: 979 8 234 06848 4

UK distribution
Wellred Books Britain,
wellredbooks.co.uk
contact@wellredbooks.co.uk

US distribution
Marxist Books,
marxistbooks.com
sales@marxistbooks.com

Contents

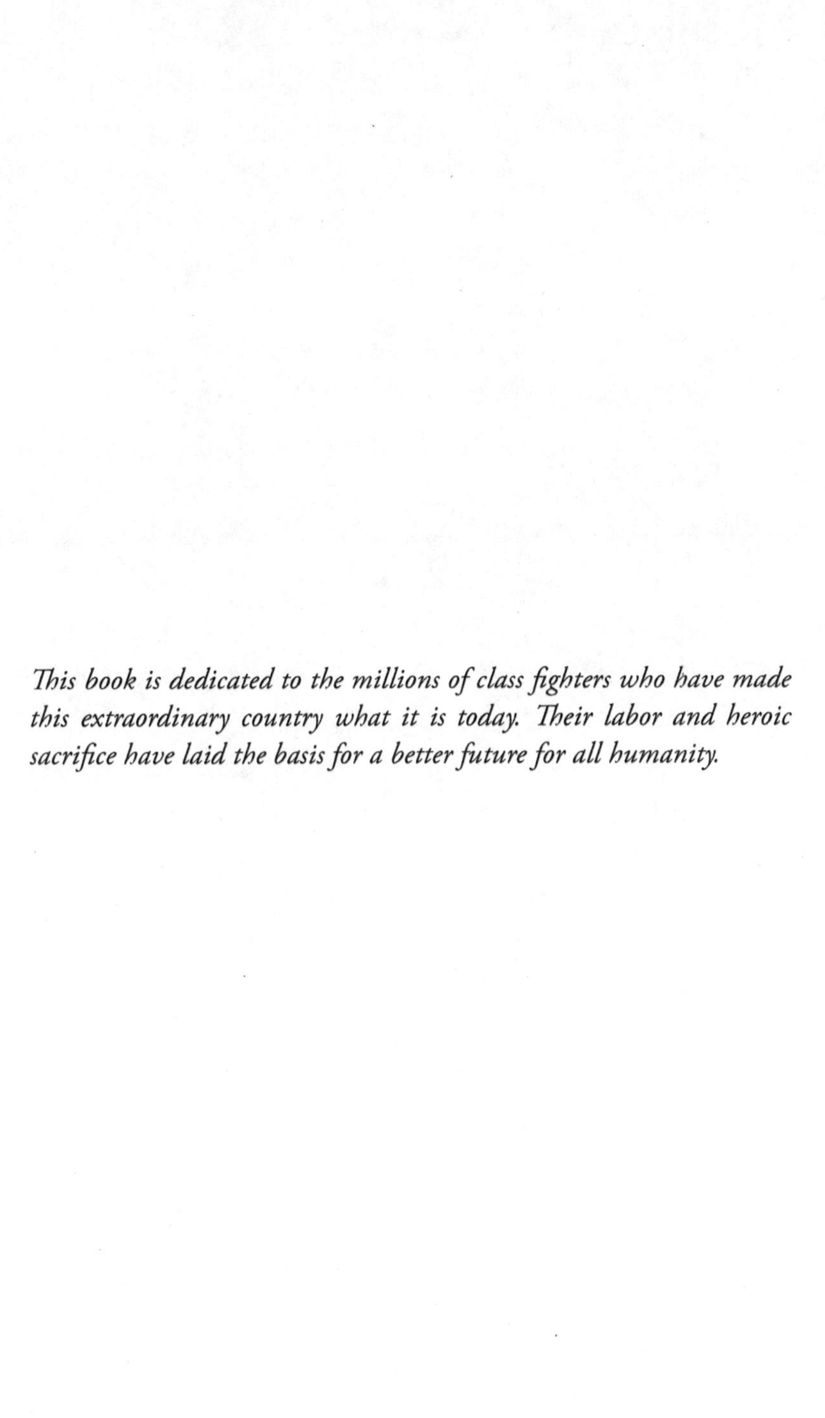

This book is dedicated to the millions of class fighters who have made this extraordinary country what it is today. Their labor and heroic sacrifice have laid the basis for a better future for all humanity.

Acknowledgements

Producing this volume in time for the 250th anniversary of the First American Revolution was truly a team effort.

I am deeply indebted to Steve Iverson, Mark Rahman, Jon Lange, and, in particular, Josh Lucker, for their tenacious proofing, editorial suggestions, additional research, and help tracking down citations. It isn't easy to find verified primary documents from the 17th and 18th centuries—I owe you a pair of beers at McSorley's Old Ale House!

Huge thanks to Fred Weston and Josh Holroyd for their careful read-through and thoughtful suggestions, especially regarding America's complex political economy.

A big thank-you is due to Ramneet Manrai and Bea Brown for giving everything an extra pass—the devil is in the details, and things always slip through the cracks!

Thanks also to Gage Tijerina, Tim LaSalle, and Wesley Allen for the dynamic cover design, which perfectly captures the spirit of this work.

As for the thankless job of laying out hundreds of pages, notes, and citations, thank you again to Ramneet Manrai and Wesley Allen, as well as to Quinn Hansen, whose technical prowess helped streamline the process.

I would also like to thank Ted Grant, Alan Woods, Ana Muñoz, Fred Weston, Rob Sewell, Jorge Martín, and Phil Mitchinson for their many years of patient explanation, encouragement, and unquenchable revolutionary optimism.

Last but certainly not least, my heartfelt thanks to Charlotte Papin, who expertly shepherded this project through to completion. There were many plates to spin, and none of them fell.

1. Revolutions have always in history been followed by counterrevolutions. Counterrevolutions have always thrown society back, but never as far back as the starting point of the revolution. The succession of revolutions and counterrevolutions is the product of certain fundamental features in the mechanics of class society, the only society in which revolutions and counterrevolutions are possible.

2. Revolution is impossible without the participation of the masses. This participation is in its turn possible only when the oppressed masses connect their hopes for a better future with the idea of revolution. In a sense the hopes engendered by the revolution are always exaggerated. This is due to the mechanics of class society, the terrible plight of the overwhelming majority of the popular masses, the objective need of concentrating the greatest hopes and efforts in order to insure even the most modest progress, and so on.

3. But from these same conditions comes one of the most important—and moreover, one of the most common—elements of the counterrevolution. The conquests gained in the struggle do not correspond, and in the nature of things cannot directly correspond, with the expectations of the broad backward masses awakened for the first time in the course of the revolution. The disillusionment of these masses, their return to routine and futility, is as much an integral part of the post-revolutionary period as is the passage into the camp of "law and order" of those "satisfied" classes or layers of classes that had participated in the revolution.

4. Closely bound up with these processes, parallel processes of a different and, to a large measure, of an opposite character take place in the camp of the ruling classes. The awakening of the broad backward masses upsets the ruling classes from their accustomed equilibrium, deprives them of direct support as well as confidence, and thus enables the revolution to seize a great deal more than it is later able to hold.

5. The disillusionment of a considerable section of the oppressed masses in the immediate conquests of the revolution and—directly connected with this—the decline of the political energy and activity of the revolutionary class engender a revival of confidence among counterrevolutionary classes—both among those overthrown by the revolution but not shattered completely, as well as among those which aided the revolution at a certain phase, but were thrown back into the camp of reaction by the further development of the revolution.

—Leon Trotsky, "Theses on Revolution and Counterrevolution," 1926

Introduction

The history of the United States is a history of violence, oppression, speculation, theft, enslavement, and war. Over several centuries, the continent's population was progressively subjected to the coercive pressures of the world capitalist market.

By hook or by crook, the primary producers were deprived of their means of production and compelled to produce commodities for exchange rather than for their own use. Over time, the vast majority of the population was transformed into propertyless wage laborers, while unfathomable riches accumulated in the hands of a tiny minority.

This isn't to say that this was the conscious policy of an omnipotent and omniscient ruling class. There were plenty of booms, busts, and unintended consequences flowing from their actions. This was simply the logic capitalism carried to its inevitable conclusion; once it grabs a gear, it takes on a life of its own.

But there is far more to American history than this. It is also a history of mass resistance, sacrifice, and revolutionary expropriation. Indigenous peoples, slaves, indentured servants, and others forced here by economic necessity didn't accept the imposition of chattel or wage slavery without a fight.

As the country's productive forces developed, so did the class struggle. This dialectical contest between progress and reaction is evident throughout history and will persist until the socialist revolution lays the basis for the end of class distinctions and ushers in stateless, moneyless communism.

Revolutionary promise

The US was quite literally born in revolution, with the Declaration of Independence serving as its birth certificate:

> We hold these truths to be self-evident, that all men are created equal, that they are endowed by their Creator with certain unalienable Rights, that among these are Life, Liberty, and the pursuit of Happiness.
>
> That to secure these rights, Governments are instituted among Men, deriving their just powers from the consent of the governed;
>
> That whenever any Form of Government becomes destructive of these ends, it is the Right of the People to alter or to abolish it, and to institute new Government, laying its foundation on such principles and organizing its powers in such form, as to them shall seem most likely to effect their Safety and Happiness.[1]

Penned by Thomas Jefferson—a slave-owning child of the Enlightenment—the Declaration is riddled with inconsistencies, especially when it comes to the rights of slaves, Native peoples, and women. Nonetheless, in its essence, it is a bold defense of a people's *self-evident and unalienable right to revolution*—a right communists defend and embrace with both arms.

By directly challenging the legitimacy of monarchical rule and establishing popular sovereignty as the foundation of legitimate government, the Declaration gave idealized expression to the political, economic, and social aspirations of the American nation—even if a significant minority of the population still identified with Britain and the monarchy.

However, the First Revolution was bookended by another, very different document: the US Constitution. Whereas the

Declaration spoke to the "Safety and Happiness" of *all* people, the Constitution, by contrast, was concerned with achieving this for the emerging bourgeoisie and Southern slaveocracy. It enshrined bourgeois property relations while simultaneously acquiescing to the continuation of chattel slavery.

Compromise was the only way to assure the creation of a semi-centralized federal state with the power to levy the taxes and troops needed to put down popular uprisings and slave rebellions, and to bring the Native peoples to heel.

But the blurred lines required to secure the Constitution's adoption ultimately necessitated a Second Revolution. Likewise, the messy outcome of the Civil War made the tragedy of Reconstruction all but inevitable.

Why we need dialectical materialism

Revolutionary periods of open class and civil war arise from converging economic, political, social, and often, military crises. Like earthquakes and volcanoes, the accumulated contradictions and pressures eventually reach a tipping point, unleash the colossal pent-up energy, and burst through the status quo's limits of tolerance.

The power of the masses is like floodwaters behind a dam; as pressure builds, even small cracks can rupture the entire structure. Likewise, shifts in the masses' outlook can be dramatic, as their understanding suddenly aligns with reality.

Instead of submitting to the political institutions and armed bodies of men of their erstwhile masters, the masses create their own. From reformism to revolution, from class collaboration to class independence, sudden shifts in mass consciousness can take even the most committed revolutionaries by surprise.

Revolutions are untidy, nonlinear processes accompanied inevitably by counterrevolution. In the heat of revolutionary battle, these poles of the class struggle can overlap and bleed into each other. It's not always a simple question of "good guys" versus "bad guys." Simplistic, ahistorical moralism is not only insufficient, but can lead to reactionary conclusions. To cut through the confusion, we must always keep the long view of history in mind and identify the fundamental class interests expressed by the warring factions—even when those on the right side of history commit questionable acts in the abstract.

As Trotsky explained in "Their Morals and Ours":

> From the Marxist point of view, . . . the end is justified if it leads to increasing the power of humanity over nature and to the abolition of the power of one person over another.[2]

All three revolutionary episodes examined in this book facilitated the development of the productive forces.

Marxists are not crude economic determinists. However, we understand that, in the final analysis, the economy is the foundation upon which the superstructure of society—ideology, religion, philosophy, intellectual life, political parties and currents, legal statutes, societal and cultural norms, aesthetics, and so on—rests. These all interact with and condition one another, and at nodal turning points in history, quantity is converted into quality, and vice versa.

In a remarkable letter to Joseph Blöch, Engels elucidated his and Marx's thinking on the dialectics of history, determinism, the role of the individual, and more, which is worth quoting at length:

> According to the Materialist Conception of History, the factor which is in the last instance decisive in history is the production and reproduction of actual life. More than this, neither Marx nor I ever claimed. If now someone distorts the meaning so that the economic factor is the *only* decisive one, this man has changed the above proposition into an abstract, absurd phrase that says nothing.
>
> The economic situation is the base, but the different parts of the structure—the political forms of the class struggle and its results, the constitutions established by the victorious class after the battle is won, forms of law and even the reflections of all these real struggles in the brains of the participants, political theories, juridical, philosophical,

religious opinions, and their further development into dogmatic systems—all this exercises also its influence on the development of the historical struggles and in cases determines their form.

It is under the mutual influence of all these factors that, rejecting the infinitesimal number of accidental occurrences (i.e., of things and events whose inner connection is so remote or so impossible to prove that we regard it as absent and can neglect it), the economic movement finally asserts itself as necessary. Otherwise, the application of the theory to any period of history would be easier than the solution of any simple equation.

We ourselves make our history, but primarily under presuppositions and conditions which are very well determined. But even the political tradition, nay, even the tradition that man creates in his head, plays an important part even if not the decisive one . . .

In the second place, history forms itself in such a way that the ultimate result springs always from the conflicts of many individual wills, each of which in its turn is produced by a quantity of special conditions of life; there are thus innumerable forces which cross each other, an infinite group of parallelograms of forces, from which is derived one resultant—the historical event—which in its turn again can be considered as the product of an active power, as a whole unconsciously and involuntarily, because that which each individual wishes is prevented by every other, and that which results from it is a thing which no one has wished. In this way, history runs its course like a natural process and has substantially the same laws of motion.

But, because of the fact that the individual wills—each of which wishes that to which it is impelled by its own physical constitution or exterior circumstances, i.e., in the last analysis, all economic circumstances (either its own personal circumstances or the general conditions of society)—do not reach that which they seek but are fused in one general media in a common resultant, by this fact one cannot conclude that they are equal to zero. On the contrary, each contributes to produce the resultant, and is contained in it.[3]

In other words, if we are to understand the inner essence of the most complex and unpredictable of social phenomena, we must *consciously and actively* apply the dialectical materialist method. Only in this way can we recognize the essential patterns and follow the inner logic and lawfulness of revolutions and their counterrevolutionary counterparts.

The importance of such an approach was further developed by Trotsky in his magnificent autobiography, *My Life:*

> Later, the feeling of the supremacy of the general over the particular became an integral part of my literary and political work. The dull empiricism, the unashamed, cringing worship of the fact which is so often only imaginary, and falsely interpreted at that, were odious to me. Beyond the facts, I looked for laws. Naturally, this led me more than once into hasty and incorrect generalizations, especially in my younger years when my knowledge, book-acquired, and my experience in life were still inadequate. But in every sphere, barring none, I felt that I could move and act only when I held in my hand the thread of the general.[4]

If we fail to do this, we risk drowning in an ocean of disconnected facts and figures.

What is a revolution?

In the final analysis, social revolutions are driven by changes in society's economic foundations. As Marx elucidated in his *Contribution to the Critique of Political Economy*:

> At a certain stage of development, the material productive forces of society come into conflict with the existing relations of production, or—this merely expresses the same thing in legal terms—with the property relations within the framework of which they have operated hitherto. From forms of development of the productive forces, these relations turn into their fetters.
>
> Then begins an era of social revolution. The changes in the economic foundation lead sooner or later to the transformation of the whole immense superstructure. No social order is ever destroyed before all the

> productive forces for which it is sufficient have been developed, and new superior relations of production never replace older ones before the material conditions for their existence have matured within the framework of the old society.[5]

As the leader of the greatest event in human history, let's see what Lenin has to add:

> The passing of state power from one *class* to another is the first, the principal, the basic sign of a *revolution,* both in the strictly scientific and in the practical political meaning of that term.[6]

And in his incomparably vivid way, Trotsky described revolution as "the inspired frenzy of history."

These basic definitions provide us with an excellent starting point for our analysis. Time and again throughout history, we've seen that when deep divisions emerge at the summit of society, the masses sense an opportunity and rise up from below to seize their destinies. They forcefully put their stamp on the course of history, even if they don't have a clearly worked out plan or a leadership up to the tasks posed by events.

As Trotsky eloquently puts it in the prologue to his *History of the Russian Revolution*:

> The most indubitable feature of a revolution is the direct interference of the masses in historical events. In ordinary times, the state, be it monarchical or democratic, elevates itself above the nation, and history is made by specialists in that line of business—kings, ministers, bureaucrats, parliamentarians, journalists.
>
> But at those crucial moments when the old order becomes no longer endurable to the masses, they break over the barriers excluding them from the political arena, sweep aside their traditional representatives, and create by their own interference the initial groundwork for a new régime . . .
>
> The history of a revolution is, for us, first of all a history of the forcible entrance of the masses into the realm of rulership over their own destiny.[7]

Revolutions are fought collectively by flesh-and-blood individuals in a battle of living forces, with different layers of the population confronting each other and the arrayed forces of the status quo. In 1915, Lenin identified the key components that make up a revolutionary situation:

> What, generally speaking, are the symptoms of a revolutionary situation? We shall certainly not be mistaken if we indicate the following three major symptoms:
>
> 1. When it is impossible for the ruling classes to maintain their rule without any change, when there is a crisis, in one form or another, among the "upper classes," a crisis in the policy of the ruling class, leading to a fissure through which the discontent and indignation of the oppressed classes burst forth. For a revolution to take place, it is usually insufficient for "the lower classes not to want" to live in the old way; it is also necessary that "the upper classes should be unable" to live in the old way.
> 2. When the suffering and want of the oppressed classes have grown more acute than usual;
> 3. When, as a consequence of the above causes, there is a considerable increase in the activity of the masses, who uncomplainingly allow themselves to be robbed in "peacetime," but, in turbulent times, are drawn both by all the circumstances of the crisis and by the "upper classes" themselves into independent historical action.[8]

To be sure, when push comes to shove, even the most bitter ruling-class rivals will close ranks if they are threatened with overthrow by the exploited and oppressed. However, classes are not homogeneous, and different layers within them can be at odds with each other at different times.

Marxists, therefore, distinguish between *political* revolutions, which result in a transfer of power from one layer of the ruling class to another, while maintaining the old property forms, and *social* revolutions, which result in a fundamental change in property relations and a new ruling class.

We must also take into account the *inter-* and *intra-*class dynamics, contradictions, and tensions as we trace the changing balance of class and property relations in a given society.

A review of the historical record reveals that revolutions are not as infrequent as the ruling class would have us believe. However, *successful* revolutions have been extremely rare. In fact, just as most strikes end in failure, most revolutions have gone down in defeat. A fortuitous alignment of objective and subjective factors—above all, the presence of a farsighted leadership ready and willing to push beyond the limits imposed by capitalism—is required to ensure success.

Even in defeat, however, profound lessons can be learned by the direct participants, as well as by the Marxists. By synthesizing the working class's efforts to change society into theory, we can avoid making the same mistakes in the future.

It is with all of this in mind that the historical periods discussed in this book qualify as revolutionary. As we will see, the interests of different classes coincided then diverged, with economic and political struggles spilling over into open armed conflict and civil war.

Why this book?

Over 100,000 books have been published on the First American Revolution, with over 10,000 focusing just on George Washington. Over 16,000 biographies have been dedicated to Abraham Lincoln, yielding place only to Jesus Christ and William Shakespeare. And although Reconstruction has received far less attention, there are several excellent tomes on the period by the likes of W.E.B. DuBois and Eric Foner.

In short, many quality histories are available on all three of these periods, including some that examine the economic and class dynamics from a more or less consistently Marxist framework. So why the need for another?

For starters, there is no single work that brings together these interrelated periods and generalizes their many lessons from an *active, revolutionary communist standpoint*. We are not academic

Marxists; we are American Bolsheviks. In our ideas and actions, we aim to embody the spirit and practice, not only of Sam Adams and John Brown, but also of Lenin and Trotsky.

The only real purpose of this modest volume, therefore, is to raise our collective political level and concentrate our minds on the dynamics of revolution and counterrevolution that have shaped this country. And the point of this is to build the RCA more rapidly and efficiently ahead of the approaching socialist revolution.

Like any other science, history does not stand above or aloof from the class contradictions suffusing society. The same basic material can be interpreted in a dizzying variety of ways. In the words of the great historical novelist and political commentator, Gore Vidal:

> All we have is a mass of more or less agreed-upon facts about the illustrious dead, and each generation tends to rearrange those facts according to what the times require.[9]

This book approaches American history from an unapologetically Marxist perspective. Despite our class bias, however, we strive to take an all-sided approach as we work through the data. We don't cherry-pick facts, figures, and quotes to prove an *a priori* schema. Rather, we present those that best illuminate the conclusions drawn through a thoroughgoing analysis of these contradictory processes. In Trotsky's words:

> Marxist thought is concrete, that is, it looks upon all the decisive or important factors in any given question, not only from the point of view of their reciprocal relations, but also from that of their development.
>
> It never dissolves the momentary situation within the general perspective, but by means of the general perspective makes possible an analysis of the momentary situation in all its peculiarities.
>
> Politics has its point of departure in *precisely* this sort of concrete analysis.[10]

Through a series of successive approximations, we arrive at an ever more nuanced understanding—all in preparation for *intervening* in similar processes as they unfold around us today.

A Marxist historian must, at a minimum, make skillful use of dialectical materialism to analyze how class and property relations evolve within a given society, paying particular attention to the nodal tipping points. But the most compelling histories do more than this: they bring revolutionary history to life by providing both concrete examples and illuminating anecdotes. All this while demonstrating how the struggles of the past shed light on the class battles of today.

Revolution and Counterrevolution in America is written in three parts, coinciding with the defining chapters of the class war that preceded the momentous struggles of the 20th and 21st centuries. These experiences helped forge the American nation-state, character, and identity, laying the foundations for the class struggles we are engaged in today.

It unfolds roughly in chronological order, jumping forward and backward as appropriate to elaborate on particular themes. Due to its big-picture focus on the reciprocal relationship between revolution and counterrevolution, it necessarily omits many episodes and individuals. In the future, we aim to produce a multi-volume revolutionary history of the United States that will go into far greater detail and cover an even wider array of episodes, individuals, and struggles by the oppressed and exploited masses.

In the meantime, it is our sincere hope that this compact work will help attune the new generation of communists to the rhythms, inner contradictions, and tensions of a revolutionary epoch. We also hope it will encourage them to dig deep into the rich history that lies just beneath the surface of the mythologized America we were taught about in school.

The 250th anniversary of the Declaration of Independence is the perfect occasion to explore the inspiring class-struggle traditions, not only of the American Revolution, but also of the Civil War and Reconstruction. Every country has its own history and traditions, and as we approach the Third American Revolution, communists must be well versed in the priceless revolutionary heritage of this uniquely contradictory country.

As this volume shows, and as is detailed in *Colossus: The Rise and Decline of US Imperialism*, the US ruling class's *modus operandi* from the beginning has been to exterminate, subjugate, expand, and humiliate in the pursuit of land, loot, natural resources, labor, profit, and power. First in the Americas and then worldwide, it has indiscriminately laid waste to one country after another in a calculated frenzy of racist mass murder and mayhem.

No wonder the modern United States is seen as a bastion of reaction and counterrevolution. But everything eventually turns into its opposite. For this reason, we are firmly convinced that its most glorious revolutionary moments lie, not in the past, but in the not-too-distant future.

John Peterson
May 1, 2026

"The history of modern, civilized America opened with one of those great, really liberating, really revolutionary wars of which there have been so few compared to the vast number of wars of conquest which, like the present imperialist war, were caused by squabbles among kings, landowners or capitalists over the division of usurped lands or ill-gotten gains. That was the war the American people waged against the British robbers who oppressed America and held her in colonial slavery, in the same way as these 'civilized' bloodsuckers are still oppressing and holding in colonial slavery hundreds of millions of people in India, Egypt, and all parts of the world."

— Vladimir Lenin, "Letter to American Workers"
August 20, 1918

Part One: The American Revolution

The American Revolution means different things to different people. For some, it's the Fourth of July, fireworks, and hot dogs. For others, it's George Washington crossing the Delaware, the Gadsden flag, and the Minutemen.

In recent decades, the tide of historiography has begun to shift, and the role of the masses and economic relations underpinning the revolutionary process have received more attention. However, most historians, and even some self-described Marxists, still present a one-sided, caricatured version of this momentous event. Some even deny that it was a "real" revolution at all. They argue it was little more than a power struggle between two groups of white property owners. In their telling, the colonial upstarts merely took over the reins of power from the British Crown with a few cosmetic adjustments.

Superficially, there is some truth to this assertion. However, as historical materialists, our task is to delve beneath the surface by unraveling the inner contradictions, fundamental processes, economic transformations, and class struggles that ultimately motivated and drove the revolution.

Flowing from Trotsky's definition, the decisive entry of the masses onto the stage of history indubitably stamped this process as revolutionary. Whether they were clear about what they were doing or not, the normally passive masses awoke to political and social consciousness and seized their destiny in an attempt to change society.

What unfolded in Britain's North American colonies was complex and contradictory. It was not purely an anti-colonial war for national liberation, democracy, and republicanism. Nor was it simply a war over land and the expropriation of Indigenous peoples. It was all of this and more—a profound, though incomplete, political and social revolution.

In short, if the American Civil War was the country's Second Revolution, the First Revolution was its first Civil War. The "loyalists" who fought to remain in the British Empire were as "American" as the self-declared "patriots."* And for much of the conflict, many colonists still saw themselves primarily as British subjects—no less "English" than most of the troops they were fighting.

Revolutionary inspiration

For over two centuries, the American colonies' successful overthrow of British rule has resonated with the world's freedom fighters and oppressed. For eight hard years, a rag-tag army fought against the world's most powerful empire—and won. The world had well and truly been turned upside down.

The "Liberator" Simón Bolívar, was considered by many to be the "George Washington" of South America. In a letter to Washington's wartime comrade, the Marquis de Lafayette, he referred to the first American president as "that great citizen, first son of the New World" and "the noble protector of social reforms."[1]

---

* The meaning and usage of "patriot" has changed over time. It was used as a derogatory term for rebels by the British in the 17th century but the American colonists who struggled against British rule embraced it. By 1775 it had become synonymous with the independence movement.

Vietnam's Ho Chi Minh, who spent time in the US before World War I, invoked Jefferson when proclaiming Vietnamese independence in 1945:

> All men are created equal; they are endowed by their Creator with certain unalienable Rights; among these are Life, Liberty, and the pursuit of Happiness.
>
> This immortal statement was made in the Declaration of Independence of the United States of America in 1776. In a broader sense, this means: All the peoples on the earth are equal from birth, all the peoples have a right to live, to be happy and free.[2]

India's first post-independence prime minister, Jawaharlal Nehru, also evoked American history as an inspiration:

> Five years ago, a professor of an American university visited me in Delhi, and gave me a gift which I have treasured greatly. That was a mould in brass of Abraham Lincoln's right hand. It is a beautiful hand, strong and firm, and yet gentle. It has been kept ever since on my study table, and I look at it every day and it gives me strength . . .
>
> Between the United States and India there had existed friendly and cordial relations even before India gained her independence. No Indian can forget that in the days of our struggle for freedom, we received from your country a full measure of sympathy and support. Our two Republics share a common faith in democratic institutions and the democratic way of life, and are dedicated to the cause of peace and freedom. We admire the many qualities that have made this country great and more especially the humanity and dynamism of its people and the great principles to which the fathers of the American Revolution gave utterance. We wish to learn from you and we plead for your friendship and your cooperation and sympathy in the great task that we have undertaken in our own country.[3]

Julius Nyerere of Tanzania also appealed to the American revolutionary tradition, declaring:

> America is a society whose faults are the more glaring because of its admirable openness, because of the principles on which the nation was founded and because of the power which comes from its wealth and its size. It is an inspiration, and a warning, to the world. Poor nations aspire to emulate it, or else they fear it—and sometimes both.
>
> For America is judged by the standards set out in imperishable language in the Declaration of Independence of 1776—which is one of the greatest documents of all time. And America now has a degree of wealth and power which could enable the ideals of its founding fathers to be translated into reality. It should now be possible for all Americans to live in dignity in a society which gives to all its citizens equal freedom and security and equal rights and responsibilities. Certainly, it should now be possible for America to "observe good faith and justice toward all nations" without having to fear for its own independence . . .
>
> Americans fought a war for their independence. They fought a civil war to maintain their unity despite the diverse social and cultural origins of Americans. The poor and oppressed of the world therefore expect Americans to understand and support the struggles of other peoples to be free and united, even if freedom and unity cannot be won peacefully. We expect that America will be the last nation, not the first, to try to thwart, pervert or destroy the real independence of other nations.[4]

Even Fidel Castro was a fan of America's revolutionary history. On a visit to the US in 1959, he laid a wreath at Lincoln's Memorial and visited George Washington's home at Mount Vernon. Years before the Cuban Revolution, in his defiant "History Will Absolve Me!" speech against the Batista dictatorship, he too, invoked America's revolutionary past:

> It is well known that in England during the seventeenth century two kings, Charles I and James II, were dethroned for acts of despotism. These events coincided with the birth of liberal political philosophy, which was the ideological foundation for a new social class then struggling to break the bonds of feudalism. Against the tyrannies based on divine right, the new philosophy upheld the principle of the social contract and

> of the consent of the governed, and constituted the foundation of the English Revolution of 1688 and the American and French revolutions of 1775 and 1789.
>
> These great events opened up the liberation process of the Spanish colonies in America—the last link being Cuba. On this philosophy our political and constitutional thought was nourished and from it evolved the first Constitution of Guáimaro to that of 1940, the latter showing the influence of present-day socialistic trends when it consecrated the principle of the social function of property and the inalienable right of man to a decent living, the efficacy of these principles having been blocked by great vested interests.
>
> The right to rebel against tyranny was consecrated definitively at that time, and was converted into an essential postulate of political freedom.[5]

This depth of inspiration is precisely why the ruling class has stripped the American Revolution of its real class content. Instead, they offer a warmed-over and superficial "Great Man" account of these events.

They do not want us to remember that, as in all social revolutions, it was the masses who fought and died for a better world and pushed the process forward at every stage. Nor do they want us to remember the significant infringements on the private property, power, and privileges of the ruling class that were unleashed by the revolution.

Indigenous America

To make sense of the genesis of the First Revolution, we must first understand the demographic, geographic, and economic conditions that set the stage for the "Glorious Cause," beginning with the Indigenous inhabitants of the Western Hemisphere.

Before the arrival of Europeans in the late 15th century, the Americas were home to a vast and diverse array of Indigenous peoples who had inhabited North, Central, and South America for at least 15,000 years, and possibly much longer. Estimates of the Americas' precontact population range from 50 to 100 million people, with some arguing for as many as 145 million. In the regions that would become the United States and Canada, between 5 and 18 million people lived in hundreds of distinct nations and cultures.

Indigenous peoples were not the "ignorant, heathen savages"* portrayed in many European accounts. Although the level of development of the productive forces lagged well behind Europe, original inhabitants of North and South America had developed sophisticated societies and technologies adapted to their environments, with rich cultural traditions that had evolved over millennia. They displayed remarkable diversity in their social structures, political organization, economic systems, spiritual beliefs, languages, and material cultures, ranging from egalitarian bands to complex chiefdoms and even imperial states with centralized authority and class stratification, as exemplified by the Aztecs and Incas.

Rather than being static sets of people as mapped by the first European explorers, these societies dynamically divided, combined, and evolved through migration, war, and technological change over thousands of years, often in response to changing climates, flora, and fauna. In North America alone, linguists have identified over 300 languages in more than 50 language families—comparable to all of Asia and Europe combined.

In the future Southwestern US, peoples influenced by the great civilizations of Mesoamerica lived, including the Ancestral Puebloans and Hohokams. At Chaco Canyon and Mesa Verde, they built densely populated urban centers with massive multistory stone buildings erected without mortar. They established a regional

---

* The terms "savage" and "savagery" have historically been weaponized by European colonialists and imperialists to justify their exploitation of weaker and less economically developed nations and peoples. However, the term was also used by early anthropologists to refer to a stage first passed through by human societies thousands of years ago. As Engels outlines in *The Origins of the Family, Private Property, and the State*, savagery refers to "the period in which man's appropriation of products in their natural state predominates; the products of human art are chiefly instruments which assist this appropriation." This 19th century usage does not inherently carry the same negative cultural or genetic assumptions.

system connected by hundreds of miles of engineered roads and trade networks extending to Central America, as well as complex irrigation canals that required advanced hydraulic knowledge.

Complex hunter-gatherer societies such as the Tlingit and Coast Salish thrived along the Pacific Northwest coast, from Alaska through British Columbia and into northern California, relying on the region's abundant marine resources. They built seafaring canoes and developed specialized food harvesting methods for rivers and the ocean. They established permanent villages and evolved sophisticated societies without relying on intensive agriculture.

California had the most densely populated area on the continent outside Mexico, with estimates ranging from 300,000 to over one million people who spoke more than 100 different languages. In coastal, interior, and valley regions, peoples including the Chumash and the Miwok adapted to the region's varied environments and abundant resources, and they mass-harvested acorns. They formed hereditary chiefdoms, built large plank canoes for ocean travel and fishing, and created elaborate rock art and shell-bead money, which they traded throughout California and beyond.

Before European contact, the Great Plains—spanning present-day central North America—supported both nomadic hunter-gatherers and semisedentary agricultural peoples. Many lived in earth-lodge villages, grew crops such as corn, beans, and squash, and hunted bison on foot, using techniques like buffalo jumps—driving herds over cliffs. The arrival of horses and firearms in the 17th and 18th centuries, introduced to the region by the Spanish, dramatically altered life on the Plains for many groups, including the Sioux, Cheyenne, and Comanche.

The equally vast Eastern Woodlands, stretching from the Atlantic coast to the Mississippi River, and from the Great Lakes to the Gulf of Mexico, supported countless Indigenous nations with complex agricultural societies, supplemented by hunting, fishing, and gathering.

Within the Midwest, part of the broader Eastern Woodlands, the Mississippian culture established a hierarchical society supported by maize agriculture. From approximately 800 to 1600 CE, its people flourished and built the largest pre-Columbian city north of Mexico at Cahokia, Illinois, near present-day St. Louis. At its peak, an estimated 10,000 to 20,000 people called it home—more than London at that time. The builders organized an extensive urban plan with over 120 earthen mounds, plazas, and a wooden astronomical observatory.

Further northeast, the Haudenosaunee, or Iroquois Confederacy, stood as one of the most powerful and resilient political organizations in precontact North America. Between 1142 and 1500 CE, five nations—the Mohawk, Oneida, Onondaga, Cayuga, and Seneca—united, with the Tuscarora joining later as the sixth.

As Lewis Henry Morgan described in *Ancient Society*, the Confederacy operated under the "Great Law of Peace," a complex pre-state constitution that established a federal-type system with careful checks and balances, democratic decision-making, and rights for both men and women. Women exercised significant political power, including the right to nominate and depose chiefs:

> Liberty, equality, and fraternity, though never formulated, were cardinal principles of the gens. These facts are material, because the gens was the unit of a social and governmental system, the foundation upon which Indian society was organized. A structure composed of such units would of necessity bear the impress of their character, for as the unit so the compound. It serves to explain that sense of independence and personal dignity universally an attribute of Indian character.[6]

How much the Haudenosaunee influenced American democracy remains unclear. But Benjamin Franklin and other Founders certainly knew of and admired the confederacy's federal structure, in which autonomous nations united for common defense and diplomacy while maintaining internal sovereignty.

Karl Marx and Frederick Engels also drew deep inspiration from the Iroquois social structure, as demonstrated by its central role in *The Origin of the Family, Private Property and the State*. They considered the Iroquois to be a classic example of what they called "primitive communism"—"primitive," insofar as the economic basis was on a far lower level than what would be unleashed by capitalism, and "communist" insofar as there were no classes or state. Engels picked up where Morgan left off:

> And this gentile constitution is wonderful in all its childlike simplicity! Everything runs smoothly without soldiers, gendarmes or police; without nobles, kings, governors, prefects or judges; without prisons; without trials . . .
>
> Those concerned decide, and in most cases centuries-old custom has already settled everything. There can be no poor and needy—the communistic household and gens know their obligations towards the aged, the sick and those disabled in war. All are free and equal—including the women. There is as yet no room for slaves, nor, as a rule, for the subjugation of alien tribes.
>
> The gens has a council, the democratic assembly of all adult male and female members of the gens, all with equal voice . . . In short, it was the sovereign power in the gens . . .
>
> The sachem's authority within the gens was of a paternal and purely moral character. He had no means of coercion at his command.
>
> The gens can depose the sachem and war chief at will. This again is carried out jointly by the men and women.[7]

Other Eastern Woodlands peoples included Algonquian-speaking nations such as the Powhatan, Pequot, Narragansett, and Wampanoag; the Cherokee in the Southeast; and the Muskogean peoples, including the Creek, Chickasaw, and Choctaw. Many of these societies also lived in permanent villages, practiced intensive agriculture, and engaged in long-distance trade networks, long before the Europeans arrived.

Far from living in an "untamed wilderness," Indigenous Americans actively managed their environments through controlled burning and the selective harvesting and transplanting of useful plants. In fact, they domesticated more plant species than any other region of the world, fundamentally transforming global agriculture and cuisine.

The "Three Sisters"—corn, beans, and squash—as well as potatoes, tomatoes, peppers, cacao, vanilla, peanuts, sunflowers, tobacco, cotton, and many other crops, were all domesticated in the Americas and account for a substantial portion of modern global food production.

With the arrival of Europeans, everything changed as they initiated the greatest demographic catastrophe in human history. Smallpox, measles, typhus, influenza, and plague ravaged Indigenous populations, who lacked immunity to these and other diseases. Mortality rates often ranged from 50 per cent to 90 per cent, and many populations disappeared forever. By the time Europeans colonized the thirteen colonies in earnest, disease had decimated many Native societies or caused their collapse.

Beyond disease—often spread deliberately—European colonization brought systematic violence, enslavement, and, of course, the theft of land, precious metals, and anything else of value. The *encomienda*[*] and *mita*[†] systems in Spanish America enslaved millions. The fur trade and later industries disrupted internal trade flows, creating new dependencies and frictions. Missionaries worked to destroy Indigenous spiritual practices and replace them with Christianity. European-style education systems forcibly removed

---

* The term *encomienda* translates to "entrustment." Emerging from late medieval Iberian practices (especially in the context of the Reconquista), this system of exploitation was later widely implemented during Spanish colonization in the Americas (and, in related forms, in Spain's Asian colonies). Individual colonists were granted *encomiendas*, entitling them to extract tribute and coerced labor from Indigenous communities. In practice, this labor was often funneled into mines and plantations—conditions effectively indistinguishable from slavery in practice.

† Under the Inca Empire, the *mit'a* (often rendered in Spanish as *mita*) was a form of labor tribute owed to the Inca state, organized in rotating turns. In return, the state provided material support and public works, including road maintenance, construction projects, and large-scale irrigation systems. Spanish colonial authorities adopted the institution's basic idea of a labor draft, but they repurposed it in a far more coercive and lethal direction. The colonial mita became an intensified form of *corvée* labor used above all to supply Indigenous workers for silver mining (most notoriously in Potosí), effectively subsidizing private mining interests and the colonial state.

children from their families to "civilize" them, beating them for speaking their languages or practicing their traditions.

Let's be clear from the outset: The displacement of the Indigenous population was not merely an accidental or unintended side effect of American expansion; it was a central goal of colonial and early American capitalist development.

Despite this genocidal assault, Native peoples survived, adapted, and resisted colonization for centuries. They were not hapless victims, but active participants in the conflicts between European powers and in the American Revolution. They pursued their own interests, alliances, and foreign policies to preserve their lands and sovereignty.

The American melting pot

The arrival of colonists from England, Scotland, Ireland, Germany, the Netherlands, France, Sweden, Finland, and beyond—each bringing with them unique cultures and traditions—added even more complexity to the American tapestry of peoples.

Europeans of all classes crossed the Atlantic for a new life: soldiers, artisans, farmers, millers, bakers, mechanics, lawyers, craftsmen, traders, trappers, merchants, bankers, preachers, fishermen, smugglers, rich, poor, religious refugees, criminals, and others seeking opportunity.

Added to this was a mishmash of religions, mainly Protestants of various stripes, including Puritans, Anglicans, Presbyterians, and Baptists, as well as Quakers, Catholics, Jews, and even atheists. Later, with the arrival of slaves from Africa and the Caribbean, came Islam and an additional galaxy of religions and cultures.

Historian Colin Woodard argues that the persistent regionalism seen in North America actually reflects 11 regional cultures—or even "nations"—that transcend the borders of the US states and Canadian provinces.[8] Several of these formed during the colonial period. Understanding these dynamics can help explain the differences that shaped the Revolution and Civil War, and which still influence American politics today.

First is what Woodard calls "Yankeedom," better known as New England. It was founded by Pilgrims in Plymouth and Puritans in Massachusetts Bay who were fleeing religious and political persecution under James I and Charles I. As many as 20,000 Puritans settled in New England in the decade before the English Revolution broke out in 1640.*

Charles I lost his head in 1649, but in 1660, counterrevolutionary forces put his son, Charles II, on the throne, sending another wave of religious dissenters to New England's shores. They left a clear imprint on the region. To this day, cities like Boston and New Haven are full of streets named after revolutionaries who signed Charles I's death warrant.

Characterized by their focus on civic participation, education, moral improvement, and town-meeting democracy, they established common schools and relatively egalitarian communities—at least for white male property owners—emphasizing the common good over individual liberty. There's a reason the state is called the "Commonwealth of Massachusetts."

Inspired by a sermon delivered by John Winthrop in 1630, they saw themselves as ordained by God to build a model religious society.

---

* A political struggle between the rising bourgeoisie, led by Parliament, and the aristocracy and bishops, led by King Charles I. The conflict, which often expressed itself in religious terms, was settled through two civil wars in the 1640s. Parliament was divided between two political factions. On one side, the Presbyterians, representing the big bourgeoisie and those rural landowners whose interests were bound up with it, sought a compromise with the King. On the other, Oliver Cromwell's Independents, representing the lower gentry and the petty bourgeoisie, came to favor abolition of the monarchy.
To break the power of the crown, Parliament's Presbyterian majority was forced to rely on Cromwell's New Model Army. After decisively defeating Charles I, the army purged the Presbyterians from Parliament, opening the way for the trial and execution of the King in 1649 and the establishment of a revolutionary dictatorship under Cromwell.
The army itself was divided along class lines between upper ranking "Grandees," who supported the Independents, and rank-and-file soldiers, who supported the more radical Levellers. The conflict between them ended with the eradication of the Levellers. Following Cromwell's death, the Grandees restored the monarchy, putting Charles II on the throne in 1660.

They envisioned a "city upon a hill." This vision, however, came at the expense of the "heathen" Indians, who were believed to live in spiritual darkness under Satan's influence.

They saw the devastation of the region's Indigenous population as divine providence to make room for the English. Winthrop even developed legal and theological justifications for taking their lands. Using the concept of *vacuum domicilium* ("empty land"), he concluded that lands not used "properly"—according to English property rights and agricultural norms—were fair game for expropriation. As early as 1620, a party of Pilgrims led by Myles Standish had looted Indian graves in search of valuables, a sign of the colonists' total disdain for the local inhabitants.

This early version of "Manifest Destiny" saw violent clashes with local Indians—not over religion, but over land. One example is the Pequot War, in which as many as 700 Natives were burned alive or killed as they tried to escape their village after it was set alight by Captain John Underhill. Survivors were then hunted down and sold into slavery in the Caribbean and Bermuda. To carry out what was considered God's work, the 1638 Treaty of Hartford banned further use of the word "Pequot."

Then there was King Philip's War, which raged from 1675 to 1678, and is considered the deadliest conflict in American history relative to the population of the time. After enduring decades of encroachment and disrespect, the Wampanoags and other Indian nations united to fight back against the colonists. The conflict was disastrous for both sides. About half of New England's Indigenous population was killed, sold into slavery, or forced westward. After the Wampanoag leader Metacom was killed, his head was displayed on a pike in Plymouth for 25 years.

From this contradictory region came some of the most radical leaders of the American Revolution, including Sam and John Adams, Paul Revere, James Otis, Jr., and John Hancock. Inspired by Puritan traditions of resistance to tyranny, their republican vision emphasized civic virtue and suspicion of concentrated power.

The tradition of town-meeting democracy and public debate proved crucial both before and during the Revolution.

Next comes New York City and the Hudson Valley, which Woodard calls "New Netherland." Originally settled by the Dutch, this small yet influential region developed a distinctly cosmopolitan, commercially oriented culture. Founded as a trading post in 1624, New Amsterdam attracted those seeking opportunities to enrich themselves in the New World. Wealthy Dutch families like the Van Rensselaers oversaw huge estates in the Hudson Valley.

After the English claimed the city under threat of naval bombardment in 1664, it was renamed New York in honor of the Duke of York. The Dutch, who had their bourgeois revolution earlier than anyone, brought traditions of religious tolerance, free trade, and a merchant-dominated social structure. Even after the English conquest, this commercial, pluralistic culture persisted, making New York the most ethnically diverse and economically dynamic of the colonies.

Out of New York emerged the Schuyler and Livingston families, John Jay, Gouverneur Morris, the New Jersey–born Aaron Burr, and, via the Caribbean, Alexander Hamilton. New York's Founding Fathers were mainly political conservatives. They supported independence but were wary of social upheaval. Coming from New York City, they championed strong property rights and centralized authority. The city and state's strategic location, along with a large Loyalist population, put New York in a unique position during the Revolution.

In Pennsylvania, Delaware, and New Jersey, we find the "Midlands." Founded by Quakers and others seeking religious freedom—including Mennonites and Moravians—the Midlands fostered tolerance, pragmatism, and suspicion of government overreach. William Penn's "holy experiment" emphasized individual conscience, peaceful coexistence, and political moderation.

The Quakers—committed pacifists loath to swear allegiance to anyone but God—brought complex dynamics to the Revolution. The Declaration of Independence and the US Constitution were both birthed in the Pennsylvania State House, now called Independence Hall.

Out of Philadelphia came Robert Morris, the "financier of the Revolution," and Benjamin Rush. The city was also home to the incomparable Benjamin Franklin and Thomas Paine, via Boston and England, respectively.

"New Sweden" ended up as a mere footnote to history, but it is worth mentioning in the context of New Netherland and the Midlands. A trading colony near present-day Wilmington, Delaware, it lasted just 17 years before Peter Stuyvesant conquered it in 1655. Nonetheless, it had a lasting impact on American culture. It was settled largely by Swedes and Finns who brought slash-and-burn agriculture, the log cabin, and an ethos of rugged self-reliance that would flow westward for centuries.

The "Tidewater" region of coastal Virginia and the lowland Carolina coast was settled by aspiring English aristocrats, their attendant commoners, and indentured servants. Many, deprived of inheritance by English law, sought to recreate the gentlemanly society of rural England in the New World. The result was a sharply stratified region dominated by a landed elite, with marked class distinctions and an emphasis on tradition and hierarchy. This foundation led to a distinct system of plantation slavery and an ideology justifying it as a natural, benevolent social order.

As elsewhere, Indians were also targeted for extermination in Virginia. In 1623, English colonists killed or incapacitated 200 members of the Powhatan Confederacy after serving them poisoned wine during a peace negotiation.

Many titans of the Revolution and Constitution hailed from Virginia, including George Washington, Thomas Jefferson, James Madison, Patrick Henry, and George Mason. They combined Enlightenment philosophical sophistication with experience governing a complex society, as well as a strong commitment to property rights—including the slave system that made their aristocratic lifestyle possible.

In what was then the frontier—from western Pennsylvania and Virginia through the Carolina backcountry—arose "Greater Appalachia." Between 1717 and 1775, approximately 250,000 Scots-Irish immigrants arrived in the colonies. Settled primarily by Presbyterians from Ulster, as well as Highlanders and others from the war-torn "borderlands" of Britain, they brought with them an outlook shaped by centuries of conflict and instability. Naturally rebellious and fiercely independent, they were disdainful of authority and outside meddling, and intensely loyal to family and their clan-like kinship networks.

Fighting the elements and the Indians alike, they hacked into the wilderness to establish hard-scrabble farms as far from the authorities as possible. Forged in a culture of honor and self-reliance, they were ready to fight to the death whenever necessary, but were nonetheless opposed to senseless foreign entanglements. Though few big-name leaders of the revolution came from this region, they would provide some of its most enthusiastic fighters.

Finally, there's the "Deep South" of South Carolina and the Georgia Low Country. Established by English plantation owners from Barbados seeking to expand their holdings, this was a horrifying mini slave empire from the very beginning. Its hallmarks were the absolute rights of property owners, minimal government, and the maintenance of rigid racial hierarchies. With Charleston as its richest and most aristocratic city, the region was dominated by a tiny elite of wealthy planters* who ruled over a majority enslaved population with an iron fist.

Outnumbered by their slaves by as much as ten to one on some plantations, South Carolina resembled the Caribbean sugar islands more than other mainland colonies. To keep their chattels in check, they relied on well-armed militias, slave patrols, and unhinged cruelty.

---

* Owners of slaves and plantations dedicated to large-scale production of cash crops—like cotton, tobacco, and sugar. Although they planted no crops themselves, they were the dominant economic and political force in the antebellum South.

The Stono Rebellion of 1739 saw a small army of escaped slaves recently arrived from Africa march south in the hopes of reaching Spanish Florida and freedom. After violently represssing the uprising, the state enacted the Negro Act of 1740, one of the harshest slave codes in North America. It severely restricted the movement of slaves and legally codified extreme punishments. It banned gatherings of more than two slaves without supervision, certain types of clothing, and even the use of drums, which were used to communicate between plantations, as in Africa. Teaching a slave to read and write was also outlawed.

Georgia was carved out of this region in 1733, the last of the original thirteen colonies. Founded by James Oglethorpe, it was seen as a buffer to protect the Carolinas from Spanish Florida. It was populated largely by the "worthy poor"—debtors and other petty criminals deemed deserving of receiving a second chance.

John and Edward Rutledge, Henry and John Laurens, and Charles Pinckney all came from South Carolina. So did the radical merchant, Christopher Gadsden, the originator of the iconic flag, with its coiled rattlesnake and "Don't Tread on Me" motto. While defending their own freedom *vis-à-vis* British impositions, they had no compunctions about denying it to their human chattels. Their fiery tenacity at the Constitutional Convention would ensure that slavery was not only protected but, in many ways, strengthened in the new American republic that resulted.

This, then, was the human material that made up the revolutionary generation. Suspicious of external authority, Indians, Catholics, and above all, each other, it was an explosive mix. Coming from a variety of places for various reasons, they and their ancestors were the initial seeds of the American population. Among them were some of Europe's most adventurous and open-minded people—as well as its most land-hungry and rapacious.

In an article titled "Europe and America," written in 1926, Trotsky gave his own brief but brilliant history of the early United States:

It is with capitalism that history has carried out the greatest number of experiments, first of all and in the most varied manner in Europe. But the most colossal and "successful" attempt appears on the North American continent.

Just think of it: America was discovered near the close of the 15th century, after Europe had already passed through a rich history. During the 16th, 17th, and even 18th centuries, and in large part throughout the 19th, the United States was a distant, self-sufficient world, an immense, godforsaken backwoods area nourished with the crumbs of European civilization.

In this interim, a country of "unlimited possibilities" was taking shape and developing, for here nature had created all the conditions for a mighty economic expansion. Europe cast across the ocean wave upon wave of the most awakened and most tempered elements from among its population, elements best qualified for developing productive forces. All the European movements of religious-revolutionary as well as political-revolutionary character—what did all these signify? They signified the struggle of the most progressive elements, first of the petty bourgeoisie and then of the working class, against feudal and clerical rubbish which impeded the development of the productive forces.

Everything that Europe cast out crossed the ocean. The flower of European nations, her most active elements, all those who wished to make their own way at any cost, fell into an environment where this historic rubbish did not exist, but where virgin nature with its inexhaustible abundance reigned. Such is the basis of America's development, America's technology, America's wealth.[9]

Indentured servants and convicts

Not all who came to America arrived of their own volition, or with full control over their persons. In addition to chattel slaves, which we will discuss in the next section, many arrived as bonded laborers, either as indentured servants or as convicts.

Colonial landowners and merchants needed someone to clear land, grow and harvest crops, build structures, and perform countless other tasks to establish towns, ports, and commercial networks. However, workers were expensive and in short supply. Those who could afford the transatlantic passage could probably acquire land and work for themselves, rather than for wages.

According to estimates by historian David Galenson, between the 1630s and 1770s, one-half to two-thirds of white immigrants to the British Colonies arrived as indentured servants.[10] Indenture was a form of temporary bonded servitude in which individuals sold their labor for four to seven years in exchange for passage to the New World.

Desperate to escape Europe's poverty and stagnation, many homeless and penniless individuals, especially the young, took the plunge. They "voluntarily" gave up self-ownership and became commodities for a set time. Enterprising captains and merchants covered the costs of transporting servants to America, then sold their labor contracts to colonial employers at a markup.

After their contracts ended, indentured servants received "freedom dues," typically clothing, tools, seeds, and sometimes livestock, cash, or even land. Many went on to become independent farmers or craftsmen, though many others remained landless laborers.

The experience of indentured servitude was often indistinguishable from outright slavery, and survival was far from guaranteed. During their period of bondage, the master controlled nearly every aspect of the servant's life, and could buy, sell, or transfer their contracts.

Servants were vulnerable to physical or sexual assault, could not marry without permission, and could have their terms extended for "bad behavior" or attempting to escape. Before patrols and rewards for runaway slaves became commonplace, similar systems were developed to capture escaped indentured servants.

Conditions varied depending on the master, region, and work required, but, as with colonial life generally, servitude was often harsh. Masters sought maximum return on investment. They imposed long, physically demanding hours, and provided minimal food, clothing, and shelter. Overwork, malnutrition, and abuse killed many before their contracts were up, sparing the master the cost of "freedom dues."

Mortality was especially high in the Chesapeake colonies, plagued by malaria, dysentery, and waterborne diseases. In Virginia and Maryland, about 40 per cent died before gaining freedom.

Not all servants came voluntarily. In 1717, Parliament passed the Transportation Act, allowing courts to sentence convicted felons to bonded labor in the American colonies for seven years to life as an alternative to execution or imprisonment. Between 1718 and 1775, an estimated 50,000 convicted criminals were transported on this basis.

Capitalism was rapidly sinking roots in the British Isles, as millions were dispossessed of their lands and forced to seek work in the rising manufacturing centers. "Transportation" out of Britain not only supplied cheap labor for the colonial enterprise, but also provided authorities with an escape valve to relieve the pressure in overcrowded cities and prisons.

Convicts, like indentured servants, were effectively sold to ship captains contracted by the government. On arrival, captains sold the contracts to local planters and property owners for profit.

Given the incentives, any excuse to transport "criminals" was good enough. To be sure, some notorious murderers and other hardened individuals were exiled to America. But you could also be deported into forced labor for poaching game, cutting down trees, stealing food, vagrancy, or expressing political dissent. Some were even "spirited away"—a euphemism for being kidnapped or blatantly tricked into servitude—a fate that befell not a few children and young people from urban slums.

The malarial Chesapeake region of Virginia and Maryland, with its booming tobacco economy, was a major destination, receiving as many as 80 per cent of such transports. Transported convicts were often stigmatized and treated even worse than those who had willingly entered labor contracts.

Usually serving longer terms than indentured servants, transported convicts were also unlikely to receive any form of "freedom dues" when their sentence was up. Nonetheless, given the opportunities open to ambitious survivors, some were able to acquire land or learn trades, and a handful even flourished in ways that would have been impossible back in Britain.

Benjamin Franklin and others expressed displeasure at Britain's policy of sending convicts to the colonies. In his 1751 essay, "Rattle Snakes for Felons," Franklin satirically proposed that the colonies reciprocate Britain's "generosity" by sending rattlesnakes to England for release in the gardens of the nobility.[11]

Compulsory transportation of British felons to the American colonies only ended with the Revolution in 1775. In 1788, Britain began offloading convicts to its new favorite penal colony, Australia.

Slavery in its foundations

Last, but certainly not least, we must examine the foundational role of chattel slavery in American history. As compared to the forms of bonded labor described above, enslaved Africans and their descendants were considered the permanent property of their owners. Although manumission was always an option, the vast majority were far more likely to be bought, sold, or bequeathed, with no legal rights or recognition of their humanity.

According to the Trans-Atlantic Slave Trade Database, between the 16th and 19th centuries an estimated 12.5 million Africans were forcibly transported across the Atlantic Ocean. Around 10.7 million survived the horrors of the Middle Passage and arrived in the Americas, with most ending up in the Caribbean or South America. They came from diverse regions of West and Central Africa, representing many ethnic, linguistic, cultural, and religious groups. Groups like the Yoruba, Igbo, Akan, and Kongo made lasting contributions to American food, music, language, and art.

As Marx explained as early as 1847, the exploitation of slave labor played an essential role in the accumulation and expansion of capital in the Americas:

> *Slavery* is an economic category like any other . . . Direct slavery is just as much the pivot of bourgeois industry as machinery, credits, etc. Without slavery, you have no cotton; without cotton, you have no modern industry. It is slavery that gave the colonies their value; it is the colonies that created world trade, and it is world trade that is the precondition of large-scale industry. Thus, slavery is an economic category of the greatest importance.
>
> Without slavery, North America, the most progressive of countries, would be transformed into a patriarchal country. Wipe North America off the map of the world, and you will have anarchy—the complete decay of modern commerce and civilization. Cause slavery to disappear, and you will have wiped America off the map of nations.
>
> Thus, slavery, because it is an economic category, has always existed among the institutions of the peoples. Modern nations have been able only to disguise slavery in their own countries, but they have imposed it without disguise upon the New World.[12]

The first African slaves arrived in Jamestown, Virginia, 1619. As the *New York Times* explains:

> Sometime in 1619, a Portuguese slave ship, the *São João Bautista*, traveled across the Atlantic Ocean with a hull filled with human cargo: captive Africans from Angola, in southwestern Africa. The men, women and children, most likely from the kingdoms of Ndongo and Kongo, endured the horrific journey, bound for a life of enslavement in Mexico. Almost half the captives had died by the time the ship was seized by two English pirate ships; the remaining Africans were taken to Point Comfort, a port near Jamestown, the capital of the English colony of Virginia, which the Virginia Company of London had established 12 years earlier. The colonist John Rolfe wrote to Sir Edwin Sandys, of the Virginia Company, that in August 1619, a "Dutch man of war" arrived in the colony and "brought not anything but 20 and odd Negroes, which the governor and cape merchant bought for victuals." The Africans were most likely put to work in the tobacco fields that had recently been established in the area.[13]

The status of these enslaved persons was initially ambiguous, and they were treated similarly to indentured servants. By the eve of the Revolution, however, institutional slavery was deeply entrenched. Slaves made up about 20 per cent of the colonial population. The first federal census, taken in 1790, recorded almost 700,000 slaves—roughly one in every six inhabitants.

The distribution of slaves varied dramatically by region, reflecting the colonies' diverse climate, geography, patterns of settlement, and above all, economic models and labor needs.

In Tidewater and the Deep South, it was foundational. In Virginia, the largest and most populous colony, about 40 per cent—200,000 out of 500,000 people —were enslaved. In 1775, the future home state of Robert E. Lee held more slaves than all the Northern colonies combined. South Carolina was even more skewed, with a 60 per cent slave population in 1775. In some rice-growing low country parishes, the proportion reached as high as 80–90 per cent.

In the Middle Colonies, New York had the most slaves in the North, making up about 12–14 per cent of its population. New York City had one of the highest urban concentrations of enslaved people in North America. The Hudson Valley's manorial estates also relied heavily on slave labor. Pennsylvania, dominated by Quakers, had the lowest proportion, just 2–3 per cent, mostly in Philadelphia—"the birthplace of freedom."

In New England, slavery remained formally legal until after the Revolution. However, the region's unsuitability for plantation agriculture meant most slaves worked on docks or as domestic servants or artisans in towns like Boston or Newport. Even in colonial times, the regional differences that would nearly fracture the country beyond repair were already taking shape.

It is important to remember that slavery's economic impact extended well beyond the big plantations. Northern merchants made fortunes from the slave trade and from selling manufactured commodities to slaveholders. Northern bankers provided credit to slave traders and plantation owners. Northern ships crossed the Atlantic with chattels and plantation goods.

The North's mills wove cotton grown and picked by slaves into textiles, and its distilleries turned slave-produced molasses into rum. By the mid–1700s, Massachusetts alone had more than 60 rum distilleries, making it one of the most profitable industries in colonial New England. With few exceptions, virtually the entire colonial economy was intermeshed with the production, circulation, and consumption of commodities produced by slave labor.

More often than not, life as a chattel was even harsher than life as an indentured servant or transported convict. Long hours of backbreaking labor were enforced with flogging, branding, and other forms of torture and mutilation. Children were routinely sold away from their parents, and husbands were frequently separated from their wives. Female slaves faced sexual exploitation and rape by masters and overseers.

Over the centuries, slaves and free Blacks developed their own cultural forms, communication networks, and methods of resistance: from work slowdowns and feigned illness, to sabotage, theft, and escape. And when they simply couldn't take it anymore, they went into open rebellion. Between 1619 and 1860, the American colonies and states experienced an estimated 250 slave uprisings, including the Chesapeake Rebellion of 1730,* the New York Conspiracy of 1741,† and Gabriel's Rebellion of 1800 in Virginia.‡

* One of the largest enslaved uprisings in colonial North America. In 1730, a rumor spread among enslaved people in Virginia that King George II had issued an order freeing all baptized slaves in the American colonies, though no such order had been issued. Roughly 200 enslaved people gathered in Princess Anne County, elected captains, and demanded that Governor William Gooch honor what they believed was a royal edict. White planters and colonial authorities arrested some participants, while others fled toward the Great Dismal Swamp, where they were pursued by the colonial authorities and allied Indigenous groups.

† A series of fires across New York City send the population into a panic. The fires are purportedly set by slaves and poor whites as part of a plot to revolt and level the city. 172 arrested and tried for conspiracy, 34 executed.

‡ Slaves across ten counties in Virginia had been involved in planning the uprising; those trained as blacksmiths had fashioned over 100 swords for the occasion. Gabriel and 25 other slaves are killed when the plans are discovered and southern state legislatures pass harsher restrictions on slaves and free Blacks.

Nat Turner's 1831 revolt in Virginia was the most significant slave uprising of all, with some 70 enslaved and free Blacks killing around 60 whites before being suppressed by militia. The incident sparked such terror in the slaveocracy that even harsher slave codes were imposed across the South.

Their heroism notwithstanding, every one of these attempts was brutally put down by the masters and their assorted bodies of armed men. And yet, time and again, the enslaved preferred to die on their feet than to live on their knees, giving lie to the disgusting idea that slavery was a benign institution.

Bacon's Rebellion

Several factors drove the intensification of African slavery as the preferred form of bonded labor in the British colonies. Indigenous peoples were initially enslaved in significant numbers, but they proved impossible to hold in bondage or else died in captivity. As the colonies took root and matured, free labor and indentured servants became increasingly difficult to obtain. The availability of Western lands would serve as both an escape and a safety valve for generations. As Virginia's lieutenant governor, Alexander Spotswood, wrote to London in 1717:

> The inhabitants of our frontiers are composed generally of such as have been transported hither as servants, and being out of their time, settle themselves where land is to be taken up and will produce the Necessities of Life with little Labour.[14]

In the early years, various forms of bonded labor coexisted on a spectrum, as indentured servants and slaves lived and worked side-by-side in similar conditions. Between 1619 and the 1660s, the importation of slaves increased steadily, but in most colonies, it was seen as a supplement to indentured servitude.

Purchasing a laborer, whether for several years or for life, was a calculated risk. Although indentured servants were cheaper, they had to be regularly replaced. Slaves cost more up front, but they were ostensibly owned until death. Furthermore, Africans tended to have better immunity to many tropical diseases and were better able to survive the hot and humid climate of Tidewater and the Deep South. In 1662, Virginia passed a law making slave status hereditary, thus making it possible to build up a permanent, self-perpetuating labor force.

In reality, however, because conditions throughout the colonies were dangerous and insalubrious, neither category of laborer was guaranteed to last even a few years. Consequently, in the early days, employers favored indentured servants, in part due to the lower up-front cost. These workers were also more readily available directly from Europe and were generally familiar with the colonists' way of life, though not all came from England. Bacon's Rebellion in 1676 changed everything.

By the 1670s, Virginia society was riven by sharpening class divisions and rising tensions. On the one hand, big plantation owners and the clique around the royal governor controlled the rich coastal lands and dominated colonial politics. On the other, a growing population of former indentured servants, independent farmers, and landless laborers was being pushed deeper inland. Though it was cheaper, land on the frontier was of poorer quality. Settlers also faced reprisals by Indigenous tribes, who were already chafing at the colonists' expansionist pressure.

Unsurprisingly, Governor William Berkeley favored the interests of the rich planters and land speculators. He restricted the lucrative fur trade to his friends, imposed taxes that fell disproportionately on small farmers, and pursued a relatively conciliatory policy toward Native Americans to protect his cronies' trading interests. Berkeley was playing with fire—and he knew it. As he complained in a letter to London in 1673:

> How miserable that man is that Governes a People where six parts of seaven at least are Poore Endebted Discontented and Armed.[15]

The frontiersmen saw no way out but to push further west. They called for military action against all Indians to facilitate the expropriation of their lands, whether they were "hostile" or not. When Berkeley refused, Nathaniel Bacon, a young, wealthy newcomer to the colony who had been denied a position in Berkeley's inner circle, rose to the leadership of the discontented frontiersmen. As Herbert Aptheker explained:

> So it was that Bacon, newly-come to Virginia, the descendant of nobility (he was kin to Francis Bacon) and himself a tobacco planter in the Virginia frontier region, was moved to declare, in 1675: "The poverty of the Country is such that all the power and sway is got into the hands of the rich, who by extortious advantages, having the common people in their debt, have always curbed and oppressed them in all manner of ways." And further, that how to mend matters was a great puzzlement since appeal had to be made to "the very persons our complaints do accuse."[16]

On his own authority, Bacon organized indiscriminate military expeditions against Indigenous settlements. When Berkeley declared Bacon a rebel, Bacon's movement was transformed from an Indian war into a revolt against the colonial government itself.

Bacon drew support from a broad coalition of the disenfranchised and dispossessed. These included yeoman farmers, landless freemen, Black and white indentured servants, and African chattels. He marched on Jamestown in June 1676 with 500–600 armed men and forced the House of Burgesses to pass reforms expanding political rights and limiting the governor's power. When Berkeley tried to reassert control, open civil war broke out. Jamestown was burned to the ground.

For several weeks, Virginia fell under rebel control. They issued a "Declaration of the People" denouncing the tyranny and corruption of Berkeley's regime. So far, so good. But they also demanded the right to drive out the Indians—a classically American amalgam of both progressive and reactionary demands.

Just weeks later, Bacon came down with dysentery and died. Deprived of its charismatic, populist leader, the movement melted away. When British troops arrived to restore order in January 1677, they managed to suppress the remaining pockets of resistance.

Once securely back in power, Berkeley executed 23 rebels, but was eventually recalled to England for his excessive brutality.

One hundred years before the Declaration of Independence, the ember of revolution was alive and well in North America—as was its counterrevolutionary counterpart.

The rise of American racism

Bacon's Rebellion impacted the course of American history in more ways than one. As Eric Foner explains:

> The fear of civil war among whites frightened Virginia's ruling elite, who took steps to consolidate power and improve their image: for example, restoration of property qualifications for voting, reducing taxes, and adoption of a more aggressive American Indian policy.[17]

Most importantly, however, it catalyzed the transition to racial slavery, a cancerous blight that has metastasized in the centuries ever since. An interracial alliance of the laboring majority was the colonial elite's worst nightmare—and remains an incubus for the ruling class to this day.

Racism in the form of anti-Indian fear and loathing was already deeply embedded in American society. But after Bacon's menacing adventure, colonial authorities and wealthy merchants consciously fomented and enforced race-based hierarchies to divide the working class. By hardening the distinction between white indentured servants and enslaved Africans, they made slavery explicitly racial and hereditary.

To this end, poor whites were granted certain "privileges"—above all, that of not being on the lowest rung of the social ladder. Thus, they came to identify with their class enemies solely on the basis of their shared skin color. In addition, it would be easier to identify and catch runaways, as escaped Black people could not easily blend into the mostly white free population.

To set the social stage for this reconfiguration, Africans were systematically demonized as racially inferior, and slavery was cemented as a keystone of the colonial economy. As the historian Edmund Morgan put it in *American Slavery, American Freedom*:

> If freemen with disappointed hopes should make common cause with slaves of desperate hope, the results might be worse than anything Bacon had done . . . The answer to the problem, obvious if unspoken and only gradually recognized, was racism, to separate dangerous free whites from dangerous slave Blacks by a screen of racial contempt.[18]

In analyzing Bacon's Rebellion and its aftermath, historian Theodore Allen concludes the following:

> First, "the white race"—supraclass unity of European-Americans in opposition to African-Americans—did not and could not have then existed [in the Virginia colony prior to the rebellion]. Second, the invention of the white race at the beginning of the eighteenth century can in no part be ascribed to demands by European-American laboring people for privileges vis-à-vis African-Americans.[19]

Correspondence and legislation from the decades after Bacon's uprising confirm the conscious nature of this transition. Among other dehumanizing provisions, the colony's updated 1705 Slave Code decreed that:

> [A]ll servants imported and brought into this country, by sea or land, who were not christians in their native country, (except Turks and Moors in amity with her majesty, and others that can make due proof of their being free in England, or any other Christian country, before they were shipped, in order to transportation hither) shall be accounted and be slaves, and such be here bought and sold notwithstanding a conversion to Christianity afterward . . .
>
> And for a further prevention of that abominable mixture and spurious issue, which hereafter may increase in this her majesty's colony and dominion, as well by English, and other white men and women intermarrying with negroes or mulattos, as by their unlawful coition with them, *Be it enacted, by the authority aforesaid, and it is hereby enacted,* That whatsoever English, or other white man or woman, being free, shall

intermarry with a negro or mulatto man or woman, bond or free, shall, by judgment of the county court, be committed to prison, and there remain, during the space of six months, without bail or mainprize; and shall forfeit and pay ten pounds current money of Virginia, to the use of the parish, as aforesaid . . .

And if any slave resist his master, or owner, or other person, by his or her order, correcting such slave, and shall happen to be killed in such correction, it shall not be accounted felony; but the master, owner, and every such other person so giving correction, shall be free and acquit of all punishment and accusation for the same, as if such incident had never happened: And also, if any negro, mulatto, or Indian, bond or free, shall at any time, lift his or her hand, in opposition against any christian, not being negro, mulatto, or Indian, he or she so offending shall, for every such offence, proved by the oath of the party, receive on his or her bare back, thirty lashes, well laid on; cognizable by a justice of the peace for that county wherein such offence shall be committed . . .

That baptism of slaves doth not exempt them from bondage; and that all children shall be bond or free, according to the condition of their mothers, and the particular direction of this act . . .

And whereas, many times, slaves run away and lie out, hid or lurking in swamps, woods, and other obscure places, killing hogs, and committing other injuries to the inhabitants of this her majesty's colony and dominion, *Be it therefore enacted, by the authority aforesaid, and it is hereby enacted,* That in all such cases, upon intelligence given of any slaves lying out, as aforesaid, any two justices (*Quorum unus*) of the peace of the county wherein such slave is supposed to lurk or do mischief, shall be and are impowered and required to issue proclamation against all such slaves, reciting their names, and owners names, if they are known, and thereby requiring them, and every of them, forthwith to surrender themselves; and also impowering the sheriff of the said county, to take such power with him, as he shall think fit and necessary, for the effectual apprehending such out-lying slave or slaves, and go in search of them:

Which proclamation shall be published on a Sabbath day, at the door of every church and chapel, in the said county, by the parish clerk, or

> reader, of the church, immediately after divine worship: And in case any slave, against whom proclamation hath been thus issued, and once published at any church or chapel, as aforesaid, stay out, and do not immediately return home, it shall be lawful for any person or persons whatsoever, to kill and destroy such slaves by such ways and means as he, she, or they shall think fit, without accusation or impeachment of any crime for the same: And if any slave, that hath run away and lain out as aforesaid, shall be apprehended by the sheriff, or any other person, upon the application of the owner of the said slave, it shall and may be lawful for the county court, to order such punishment to the said slave, either by dismembring, or any other way, not touching his life, as they in their discretion shall think fit, for the reclaiming any such incorrigible slave, and terrifying others from the like practices.[20]

In 1710, Virginia's lieutenant governor, Alexander Spotswood, warned Virginia's colonial Assembly:

> [F]reedom wears a cap which can without a tongue, call together all those who long to shake off the fetters of slavery and as such an Insurrection would surely be attended with most dreadful consequences so I we cannot be too early in providing against it, both by putting ourselves in a better posture of defence and by making a law to prevent the consultations of those Negroes.[21]

In 1736, William Byrd II, also of Virginia, wrote Lord Egmont about the growing contradictions and dangers of the slave trade:

> They import so many Negros hither, that I Fear this Colony will some time or other be confirmd by the Name of New Guinea. I am sensible of many bad consequences of multiplying these Ethiopians amongst us. They blow up the pride, and ruin the Industry of our White People, who seing a Rank of poor Creatures below them, detest work for fear it should make them look like Slaves. Then that poverty which will ever attend upon Idleness, disposes them as much to pilfer as it dos the Portuguese, who account it much more like a Gentleman to steal, than to dirty their hands with Labour of any kind.

> Another unhappy Effect of Many Negros is the necessity of being severe. Numbers make them insolent, and then foul Means must do what fair will not. We have however nothing like the Inhumanity here that is practiced in the Islands, and God forbid we ever should. But these base Tempers require to be rid of a tort Rein, or they will be apt to throw their Rider. Yet even this is terrible to a good naturd Man, who must submit to either a Fool or a Fury. And this will be more our unhappy case, the more Negros are increast amongst us.
>
> But these private mischeifs are nothing if compard to the publick danger. We have already at least 10,000 Men of these descandants of Ham fit to bear Arms, and their Numbers increase every day as well by birth as Importation. And in case there shoud arise a Man of desperate courage amongst us, exasperated by a desperate fortune, he might with more advantage than Cataline kindle a Servile War.[22]

In his final autobiography, written after the war, Frederick Douglass described the deliberate swindle as follows:

> The slaveholders, with a craftiness peculiar to themselves, by encouraging the enmity of the poor laboring white man against the Blacks, succeeded in making the said white man almost as much a slave as the Black slave himself. The difference between the white slave and the Black slave was this: the latter belonged to one slaveholder, and the former belonged to the slaveholders collectively. The white slave had taken from him by indirection what the black slave had taken from him directly and without ceremony. Both were plundered, and by the same plunderers.
>
> The slave was robbed by his master of all his earnings, above what was required for his bare physical necessities, and the white laboring man was robbed by the slave system, of the just results of his labor, because he was flung into competition with a class of laborers who worked without wages. The slaveholders blinded them to this competition by keeping alive their prejudice against the slaves as *men*—not against them as *slaves*.
>
> They appealed to their pride, often denouncing emancipation as tending to place the white working man on an equality with negroes, and by this means they succeeded in drawing off the minds of the poor whites from

> the real fact, that by the rich slave-master, they were already regarded as but a single remove from equality with the slave. The impression was cunningly made that slavery was the only power that could prevent the laboring white man from falling to the level of the slave's poverty and degradation. To make this enmity deep and broad between the slave and the poor white man, the latter was allowed to abuse and whip the former without hindrance.[23]

Thus it was that, step by step, and decade after decade, American racism took its particularly poisonous and pernicious form, a deliberate strategy to cut across the incipient solidarity of the laboring masses. Even before independence, these measures introduced insoluble contradictions that cannot be resolved within the limits of class society.

In short, the United States was built on a foundation of unfree labor. Understanding this legacy is essential if we are to grasp the depth of the fervor for liberty and self-ownership, as well as the hatred of tyranny and oppression expressed by the masses during the Revolution, Civil War, and Reconstruction.

Economic foundations

To understand the many contradictions woven into the fabric of American history, we must start by examining the genesis of US capitalism and its regionally uneven and combined development. For Marxists, the starting point for untangling the class and property relations of any society, whether capitalist or otherwise, is the following profound passage from *Capital, Volume III:*

> The specific economic form, in which unpaid surplus-labor is pumped out of direct producers, determines the relationship of rulers and ruled, as it grows directly out of production itself and, in turn, reacts upon it as a determining element. Upon this, however, is founded the entire formation of the economic community which grows up out of the production relations themselves, thereby simultaneously its specific political form.

> It is always the direct relationship of the owners of the conditions of production to the direct producers—a relation always naturally corresponding to a definite stage in the development of the methods of labor and thereby its social productivity—which reveals the innermost secret, the hidden basis of the entire social structure and with it the political form of the relation of sovereignty and dependence, in short, the corresponding specific form of the state.[24]

By the time Britain established its North American foothold, the emergence of the world market was already well underway, having started in the so-called "Age of Discovery." Marx painted a vivid picture of this epoch in *The Communist Manifesto*:

> The discovery of America, the rounding of the Cape, opened up fresh ground for the rising bourgeoisie. The East Indian and Chinese markets, the colonization of America, trade with the colonies, the increase in the means of exchange and in commodities generally, gave to commerce, to navigation, to industry, an impulse never before known, and thereby, to the revolutionary element in the tottering feudal society, a rapid development.[25]

And as he added in Volume One of *Capital*:

> The treasures captured outside Europe by undisguised looting, enslavement, and murder, flowed back to the mother-country and were there turned into capital.[26]

In the centuries that followed, the US not only borrowed, but also perfected this ruthless economic model.

In the unplanned chaos of early American colonization, elements of both feudalism and capitalism were partially transplanted from the Old World to the New as capitalist Britain sought to establish a society in its own image. However, the Americas were never a carbon copy of Europe. Although it would eventually emerge as the capitalist country *par excellence*, economic life in the embryonic United States was initially a hybrid mix of economic forms and exhibited significant regional variation. The South was controlled by slave-owning planters exploiting slave labor. And the North was dominated by merchants selling surpluses produced mainly by independent farmers and artisans.

Before proceeding, we should define four key concepts of Marxist economic theory: uneven and combined development, primitive accumulation, merchant capital, and natural economy.

Although he was writing about tsarist Russia, Trotsky's concept of uneven and combined development—a key component of his theory of permanent revolution*—is essential if we are to make sense of the at-times bewildering blend of economic forces seen in colonial America:

> The laws of history have nothing in common with a pedantic schematism. Unevenness, the most general law of the historic process, reveals itself most sharply and complexly in the destiny of the backward countries. Under the whip of external necessity their backward culture is compelled to make leaps. From the universal law of unevenness thus derives another law which, for the lack of a better name, we may call the law of *combined development*—by which we mean a drawing together of the different stages of the journey, a combining of the separate steps, an amalgam of archaic with more contemporary forms. Without this law, to be taken of course in its whole material content, it is impossible to understand the history of Russia, and indeed of any country of the second, third or tenth cultural class.[27]

---

* A theory developed by Trotsky, based on the ideas of Marx, from whom the term "permanent revolution" originates. It can be summarized as follows: The capitalist class in backward countries is incapable of carrying out a classical bourgeois-democratic revolution because its interests are tied to the imperialists and landowners. Only the proletariat can lead a national-democratic revolution. Once in power, the working class will neither want nor be able to limit itself to a bourgeois-democratic program. Indeed, the struggle to accomplish national-democratic tasks will unleash powerful class conflicts which can only be resolved through the socialist transformation of society. Since socialism cannot be achieved within the borders of one country, the revolution must spread internationally to consolidate the revolution and defeat the counterrevolution on a world scale.

As we will see, the geography, climate, distances, class struggles, and pressures of the world capitalist market all played a role in shaping the American economy over the centuries.

Next, let's look at primitive accumulation. Contrary to its propagandized origin story, capitalism didn't come to dominate the planet through the gradual accumulation of wealth through the thrift and hard work of visionary geniuses. Whether in England, India, Italy, or anywhere else, physical force, expropriation, and economic coercion were indispensable components of this process, whether it was to dispossess the peasantry, enclose common lands, or plunder and enslave the colonies. As Marx explains in Chapter 26 of *Capital*:

> [T]he accumulation of capital presupposes surplus-value; surplus-value presupposes capitalistic production; capitalistic production presupposes the preexistence of considerable masses of capital and of labor power in the hands of producers of commodities. The whole movement, therefore, seems to turn in a vicious circle, out of which we can only get by supposing a primitive accumulation ("previous accumulation" of Adam Smith) preceding capitalistic accumulation; an accumulation not the result of the capitalistic mode of production, but its starting point.
>
> This primitive accumulation plays in Political Economy about the same part as original sin in theology. Adam bit the apple, and thereupon sin fell on the human race . . . And from this original sin dates the poverty of the great majority that, despite all its labor, has up to now nothing to sell but itself, and the wealth of the few that increases constantly although they have long ceased to work . . .
>
> In themselves money and commodities are no more capital than are the means of production and of subsistence. They want transforming into capital. But this transformation itself can only take place under certain circumstances that center in this, viz., that two very different kinds of commodity-possessors must come face to face and into contact; on the one hand, the owners of money, means of production, means of subsistence, who are eager to increase the sum of values they possess, by buying other people's labor power; on the other hand, free laborers, the sellers of their own labor power, and therefore the sellers of labor.

> Free laborers, in the double sense that neither they themselves form part and parcel of the means of production, as in the case of slaves, bondsmen, etc., nor do the means of production belong to them, as in the case of peasant-proprietors; they are, therefore, free from, unencumbered by, any means of production of their own. With this polarization of the market for commodities, the fundamental conditions of capitalist production are given. The capitalist system presupposes the complete separation of the laborers from all property in the means by which they can realize their labor. As soon as capitalist production is once on its own legs, it not only maintains this separation, but reproduces it on a continually extending scale.
>
> The process, therefore, that clears the way for the capitalist system, can be none other than the process which takes away from the laborer the possession of his means of production; a process that transforms, on the one hand, the social means of subsistence and of production into capital, on the other, the immediate producers into wage laborers. The so-called primitive accumulation, therefore, is nothing else than the historical process of divorcing the producer from the means of production. It appears as primitive, because it forms the prehistoric stage of capital and of the mode of production corresponding with it.[28]

And as he adds in Chapter 31:

> The discovery of gold and silver in America, the extirpation, enslavement, and entombment in mines of the aboriginal population, the beginning of the conquest and looting of the East Indies, the turning of Africa into a warren for the commercial hunting of black-skins, signalized the rosy dawn of the era of capitalist production. These idyllic proceedings are the chief momenta of primitive accumulation . . .[29]

However, primitive accumulation was not a one-time historical event. Rather, it was an ongoing process wherever land and labor had not been drawn into the nexus of capital. In Marx's words:

> In fact, the veiled slavery of the wage-laborers in Europe needed the unqualified slavery of the New World as its pedestal.
>
> *Tantae molis erat* [so great a task it was] to establish the "eternal natural laws" of the capitalist mode of production, to complete the process of separation between the laborers and the conditions of their labor, to transform, at one pole, the social means of production and subsistence into capital, and at the opposite pole, the mass of the population into wage laborers, into the "free laboring poor," that artificial product of modern society.[30]

And, as he famously added:

> [This process] is written in the annals of mankind in letters of blood and fire.[31]
>
> If money, according to Augier, "comes into the world with a congenital blood-stain on one cheek," capital comes dripping from head to toe, from every pore, with blood and dirt.[32]

Once the primary producers are separated from the means of production, the owners of those means enjoy near total power over those who have nothing left to sell but their ability to work. The result, as Marx explains, is that "free labor" is "free in a double sense."[33] Insofar as workers are not bonded in any way to anyone, they are "free" *to* sell their labor power for a wage. But they are also "free" *from* the means of production, putting them at the mercy of the exploiting class if they want to survive.

Next, let's examine the question of merchant capital. As Marx explained, in contrast to industrial capital, merchant capital operates strictly within the sphere of circulation. It does not typically invest in production to generate surplus value by aggregating means of production, raw materials, and workers to be exploited directly. It merely plays the role of middleman, connecting geographically distant producers and consumers, buying low to sell high, and taking a cut for itself without revolutionizing the productive process. In *Capital, Volume III*, Marx explains the simple yet contradictory nature of merchant capital:

> Hitherto we have considered merchant's capital merely from the standpoint, and within the limits, of the capitalist mode of production. However, not only commerce, but also merchant's capital, is older than the capitalist mode of production, is, in fact, historically the oldest free state of existence of capital . . .
>
> Since merchant's capital is penned in the sphere of circulation, and since its function consists exclusively of promoting the exchange of commodities, it requires no other conditions for its existence—aside from the undeveloped forms arising from direct barter—outside those necessary for the simple circulation of commodities and money. Or rather, the latter is the condition of *its* existence. No matter what the basis on which products are produced, which are thrown into circulation as commodities—whether the basis of the primitive community, of slave production, of small peasant and petty bourgeois, or the capitalist basis, the character of products as commodities is not altered, and as commodities they must pass through the process of exchange and its attendant changes of form.
>
> The extremes between which merchant's capital acts as mediator exist for it as given, just as they are given for money and for its movements. The only necessary thing is that these extremes should be on hand as commodities, regardless of whether production is wholly a production of commodities, or whether only the surplus of the independent producers' immediate needs, satisfied by their own production, is thrown on the market. Merchant's capital promotes only the movements of these extremes, of these commodities, which are preconditions of its own existence.
>
> The extent to which products enter trade and go through the merchants' hands depends on the mode of production, and reaches its maximum in the ultimate development of capitalist production, where the product is produced solely as a commodity, and not as a direct means of subsistence. On the other hand, on the basis of every mode of production, trade facilitates the production of surplus-products destined for exchange, in order to increase the enjoyments, or the wealth, of the producers (here meant are the owners of the products). Hence, commerce imparts to production a character directed more and more towards exchange-value.

The metamorphosis of commodities, their movement, consists 1) materially, of the exchange of different commodities for one another, and 2) formally, of the conversion of commodities into money by sale, and of money into commodities by purchase. And the function of merchant's capital resolves itself into these very acts of buying and selling commodities. It therefore merely promotes the exchange of commodities; yet this exchange is not to be conceived at the outset as a bare exchange of commodities between direct producers. Under slavery, feudalism and vassalage (so far as primitive communities are concerned) it is the slave-owner, the feudal lord, the tribute-collecting state, who are the owners, hence sellers, of the products. The merchant buys and sells for many. Purchases and sales are concentrated in his hands and consequently are no longer bound to the direct requirements of the buyer (as merchant).

But whatever the social organization of the spheres of production whose commodity exchange the merchant promotes, his wealth exists always in the form of money, and his money always serves as capital. Its form is always M—C—M'. Money, the independent form of exchange-value, is the point of departure, and increasing the exchange-value [is] an end in itself . . .

The less developed the production, the more wealth in money is concentrated in the hands of merchants or appears in the specific form of merchants' wealth.

Within the capitalist mode of production—*i.e.*, as soon as capital has established its sway over production and imparted to it a wholly changed and specific form—merchant's capital appears merely as a capital with a *specific* function. In all previous modes of production, and all the more, wherever production ministers to the immediate wants of the producer, merchant's capital appears to perform the function *par excellence* of capital.

There is, therefore, not the least difficulty in understanding why merchant's capital appears as the historical form of capital long before capital established its own domination over production. Its existence and development to a certain level are in themselves historical premises for the development of capitalist production 1) as premises for the

> concentration of money wealth, and 2) because the capitalist mode of production presupposes production for trade, selling on a large scale, and not to the individual customer, hence also a merchant who does not buy to satisfy his personal wants but concentrates the purchases of many buyers in his one purchase. On the other hand, all development of merchant's capital tends to give production more and more the character of production for exchange-value and to turn products more and more into commodities. Yet its development . . . is incapable by itself of promoting and explaining the transition from one mode of production to another.
>
> Within capitalist production merchant's capital is reduced from its former independent existence to a special phase in the investment of capital, and the levelling of profits reduces its rate of profit to the general average. It functions only as an agent of productive capital. The special social conditions that take shape with the development of merchant's capital, are here no longer paramount. On the contrary, wherever merchant's capital still predominates we find backward conditions. This is true even within one and the same country, in which, for instance, the specifically merchant towns present far more striking analogies with past conditions than industrial towns.[34]

As for the term "natural economy," Marx used it to describe situations in which producers' main aim is the production of use-values for direct consumption, rather than production intended primarily for market exchange.

For example, in early Medieval Europe, most lordly estates were natural economies. They were largely self-sufficient and relatively insulated from the economic vagaries of the outside world. The serf or peasant families living on the lord's lands would produce grain for bread, livestock for meat and dairy, and wool for clothing. They would also craft basic tools.

Production was oriented primarily toward subsistence and the fulfillment of feudal dues and obligations. Only small, marginal surpluses would be brought to market to exchange for salt, metal implements, or other items the household couldn't produce on its own. The dominant economic relationship was between the landlords, peasants, and the land they worked, not between buyers and sellers of commodities, including labor power, in a generalized system of commodity exchange.

Colonial political economy

After more than a century of colonization, mainland British America remained overwhelmingly agricultural. Indentured servitude continued and chattel slavery was on the rise. Only a handful of towns had populations above 10,000. Most farmers were smallholders, though landholding patterns varied by region. Early plantation capitalists had set up tobacco and other farms geared toward export, and some mid-Atlantic farmers boosted their income by supplying grain and flour to the sugar islands of the West Indies, especially after the 1720s. Nonetheless, throughout the colonial period, and well into the early 1800s, independent household production along "natural economy" lines remained widespread in much of rural North America, including among many non-slaveholding whites in the South.

The big Southern plantations were a more complicated hybrid. Marx offers the following analysis of the fundamental distinction between the smallholding peasant economy prevalent in the northern colonies and the commercial slave plantations established in many parts of the South:

> Firstly: There are the colonies proper, such as in the United States, Australia, etc. Here the mass of the farming colonists, although they bring with them a larger or smaller amount of capital from the motherland, are not capitalists, nor do they carry on capitalist production. They are more or less peasants who work themselves and whose main object, in the first place, is to produce their own livelihood, their means of subsistence. Their main product therefore does not become a commodity and is not intended for trade. They sell or exchange the excess of their products over their own consumption for imported manufactured commodities etc. The other, smaller section of the colonists who settle near the

sea, navigable rivers etc., form trading towns. There is no question of capitalist production here either.

Even if capitalist production gradually comes into being, so that the sale of his products and the profit he makes from this sale become decisive for the farmer who himself works and owns his land; so long as, compared with capital and labor, land still exists in elemental abundance providing a practically unlimited field of action, the first type of colonization will continue as well and production will therefore never be regulated according to the needs of the market—at a given market-value.

Everything the colonists of the first type produce over and above their immediate consumption, they will throw on the market and sell at any price that will bring in more than their wages. They are, and continue for a long time to be, competitors of the farmers who are already producing more or less capitalistically, and thus keep the market-price of the agricultural product constantly below its value. The farmer who therefore cultivates land of the worst kind, will be quite satisfied if he makes the average profit on the sale of his farm, i.e., if he gets back the capital invested, this is not the case in very many instances.

Here therefore we have two essentially different conditions competing with one another: capitalist production is not as yet dominant in agriculture; secondly, although landed property exists legally, in practice it only exists as yet sporadically, and strictly speaking there is only possession of land. Or although landed property exists in a legal sense, it is—in view of the elemental abundance of land relative to labor and capital—as yet unable to offer resistance to capital, to transform agriculture into a field of action which, in contrast to non-agricultural industry, offers specific resistance to the investment of capital.

In the second type of colonies—plantations—where commercial speculations figure from the start and production is intended for the world market, the capitalist mode of production exists, although only in a formal sense, since the slavery of Negroes precludes free wage-labor, which is the basis of capitalist production. But the business in which slaves are used is conducted by capitalists. The method of production which they introduce has not arisen out of slavery but is grafted on to it.

> In this case the same person is capitalist and landowner. And the elemental [profusion] existence of the land confronting capital and labor does not offer any resistance to capital investment, hence none to the competition between capitals. Neither does a class of farmers as distinct from landlords develop here. So long as these conditions endure, nothing will stand in the way of cost-price regulating market-value.[35]

However, this setup cut across the development of a more efficient division of labor, which proceeded much more slowly in the Southern than in the Northern colonies. Though the slaves' primary function was to produce cash crops for sale on the market, during their "free time," they also produced most of the use-values needed to keep the plantations running, such as food, clothing, and tools.

This left more profit for profligate spending by the slave masters, and kept their bonded laborers occupied during the down season. However, this dynamic ultimately represented an obstacle to the full development of capitalist production in the South.

In many regions, especially in the Middle Colonies and New England, colonists dispensed with primogeniture and adopted partible inheritance. However, after a few generations, the repeated subdivision of arable lands resulted in parcels too small to be economically viable. In Tidewater and the Deep South, nutrient-greedy crops like tobacco and cotton rapidly depleted the soil, leading to lower yields and an insatiable demand for "virgin" territory—usually inhabited by Indigenous peoples.

All of this contributed to rising prices for quality land, forcing the younger generations to seek opportunities elsewhere, either as laborers in urban centers or by pushing deeper into Indian lands. It also meant that in the early years, agricultural land was not being aggregated into larger, commercially oriented accumulations of land, labor, and capital.

As an island state, England's territory is clearly circumscribed by the sea. In these conditions, the rising capitalist class was able to monopolize landed property and expropriate the primary producers through political and economic violence in relatively short order.

This, in turn, allowed them to compel a majority of the population, through the pressure of the market, to submit to wage slavery. The propertyless masses had no alternative if they wanted to survive.

In a place like America, however, with its seemingly endless frontier, achieving that degree of centralized control over land and people was, in many ways, more difficult. This complicated efforts to bring the dynamics of the market economy fully to bear.

To unleash capitalist development, a shift from *extensive* expansion to *intensive* accumulation is required. Rather than simply working more land, labor, and resources with the same technique, economic and political pressures must draw producers into deeper dependence on the market. These pressures also compel capitalists, through competition, to extract more from existing land and labor by continually revolutionizing the labor process and means of production.

In the faraway thirteen colonies, Britain was compelled to rule somewhat indirectly. It achieved this through colonial administrators and alliances with local landlords and merchants who benefited from the imperial relationship. Although British soldiers had been in North America earlier, the first major deployment only came in 1754. This was driven mainly by war with France and its Indigenous allies, not by the need to police colonial society.

From early on, there had been a marked regional division of labor that went beyond the North-South divide. For example, while Virginia and Maryland grew tobacco as their primary cash crop, South Carolina and Georgia were better suited to rice and indigo, both of which were mainly destined for British and European markets. Only with the rise of "King Cotton" did that crop eventually predominate across much of the Deep South, binding the region ever more tightly to the world market and the credit networks of British and Northern finance.

New York, New Jersey, Pennsylvania, and Delaware, sometimes referred to as the "bread colonies," had more diverse populations. They had more independent farmers, artisans, and merchants than the South. The region's economy was focused on producing wheat, corn, and other grains for export to the West Indies and southern Europe. In 1775, Philadelphia was the country's largest city, with a population of roughly 40,000. It served as a major port and center of commerce, manufacturing, and finance.

Given New England's rocky soil and harsh climate, its economy was the least dependent of all on agriculture. Its strong points were fishing, shipbuilding, manufacturing, and finance. It also benefited most from the notorious "triangular trade" that carried rum to Africa, slaves to the West Indies, and molasses back to New England for distillation into more rum.

Colonial class relations also varied. A small elite—landowners, slave owners, merchants, and professionals including lawyers and British officials—controlled most of the wealth and power. Below them was a substantial "middling" layer: yeoman farmers, artisans, shopkeepers, and skilled workers. At the bottom were the free laborers, poor farmers, indentured servants, transport convicts, and slaves.

As we will see, during the protracted buildup to open rebellion, the interests of these many interlinked segments of American society would converge and then diverge, depending on the balance of forces and the immediate threats and opportunities they faced.

British mercantilism and its discontents

The American merchant class served as an economic bridge between the colonies and the rest of the British Empire. While they did play a modest role in organizing at least some production, they mainly acted as middlemen to facilitate the circulation of commodities in both directions.

After importing British-manufactured goods, such as textiles, hardware, ceramics, and tea, they distributed them throughout the colonies via networks of smaller retailers and country storekeepers, with a respectable markup for their trouble. In the other direction, they aggregated and exported colonial products such as tobacco, rice, indigo, wheat, rum, and fish to Britain, Europe, the West Indies, and Africa.

With a long view toward profit-making, merchants bought ships or chartered vessels, operated warehouses, provided credit to planters and farmers, and invested in distilleries, ironworks, and shipyards. The most successful among them accumulated substantial wealth. As at all times in history, wealth translated into social prestige and political power, making merchants key movers and shakers in the colonial economy and eventual revolutionary movement.

But merchant prosperity was precarious. Ships sank, debtors defaulted, markets crashed, and wars or political unrest could wipe out investments. Merchants balanced risk-taking with a desire for stable credit, enforceable contracts, and consistent government policy—preferences that would shape the future Constitution.

The most successful American merchants operated far beyond the thirteen colonies. In the Western Hemisphere alone, Britain already held or would soon hold many other colonies. Profitable trade could be conducted in the sugar islands of Barbados, Jamaica, Antigua, Montserrat, Nevis, and St. Kitts. Other British colonies included Bermuda, the Bahamas, Nova Scotia, Quebec, Newfoundland, Prince Edward Island, British Honduras, and the Mosquito Coast.

American merchants maintained correspondents in London, Glasgow, Bristol, Amsterdam, the West Indies, and other colonial ports. They also dealt in bills of exchange, provided ship insurance, and managed complex financial transactions across currencies. The Browns of Providence, the Hancocks of Boston, and the Willings of Philadelphia built commercial empires that spanned the Atlantic world.

Agreeing with the Roman Emperor Vespasian's pragmatic quip that "money doesn't smell," merchants cared little how their commodities were produced—by yeomen, craftsmen, small manufacturers, wage laborers, indentured servants, or slaves.

Their activities varied in different parts of the colonies. As explained above, New England's merchants dominated the region's economy. Many were self-made men who rose to the top through business savvy, not Royal grants or inheritances. Merchants in Philadelphia and New York engaged in diverse activities, including the export of fur, grain, and flour, as well as banking and insurance. New York was America's financial capital from the beginning.

In the South, the merchant class was less developed and often consisted of local agents for British merchant houses rather than independent traders. Charleston was the main exception, with its endogenous merchants focusing on the rice and indigo trade, though even there, British merchant houses maintained considerable influence.

The whole point of the colonies, however, was to provide raw materials and markets with which to enrich the British ruling class. Merchants operating in the colonies were welcome to a modest cut for their services, but everything has a limit. They had privileged access to British credit, enjoyed the protection of the British navy, and could trade throughout the empire. Many American merchant families had close ties with British merchant houses and factors.* What was there to complain about?

Starting in 1651, Parliament had passed a series of laws known collectively as the Navigation Acts. The main purpose was to establish protections for British manufacturers and merchants in competition with their Dutch, French, and Spanish rivals. However, the legislation was also intended to clip the wings of the colonials. Though it would prove more difficult than herding cats, the British authorities had long sought to establish full control over the colonies' land and labor so as to impose large-scale capitalist agriculture and wage labor.

First and foremost, the Navigation Acts established a monopoly on trade. All commerce between the colonies and other nations was to be conducted on English or colonial ships, with crews that were at least three-quarters English or colonial subjects.

The most profitable colonial products—including tobacco, sugar, cotton, and more—were designated as "enumerated goods." These could only be shipped to England or other English colonies—even if a higher profit could be made elsewhere, for example, in

---

* Mercantile agents entrusted with the possession, management, and sale of goods, acting on the behalf of another party, in this case the British, and earning a commission.

the French or Spanish Caribbean colonies. Furthermore, European goods destined for the Americas had to be shipped through British ports first—where they could be taxed—so yet another layer of middlemen could take a cut. Similar restrictions also applied to trade in the other direction.

But that's not all. Under pressure from the commercial lobbyists of the day, Parliament restricted colonial manufacturing, despite its enormous potential given the abundance of raw materials and the growing number of skilled artisans. To protect one of early British capitalism's key industries, the Woolens Act of 1699 prohibited the direct export of woolen cloth, yarn, or clothing from one colony to another, or overseas. The Hat Act of 1732 similarly restricted Americans' increasingly competitive felt-hat industry.

In addition to abundant grazing lands and beavers—the objective basis for the wool and hat industries—the colonies had rich iron ore deposits and abundant forests that could provide charcoal for smelting. To further nip the danger of competition, the Iron Act of 1750 prohibited the construction of new iron mills in the colonies. It "encouraged" the export of raw iron to England. There, it would be transformed into value-added manufactured goods. The colonists were compelled to buy these at a much higher price than if they had simply produced them in America.

Just as modern capitalists use every means to block potential rivals, the British periodically banned the export of certain technologies and the emigration of skilled artisans to the colonies, fearing they would become competitors. Parliament could offer tax and other incentives to encourage investment in British manufacturing, but colonial legislatures were prevented from doing the same.

Restrictions on the issuance of currency also hampered colonial economic development. The colonies faced chronic shortages of gold and silver coin, as there were no major precious-metal mines, and their trade deficit with Britain drained specie from America. When colonial legislatures attempted to address this by issuing paper money, Parliament passed the Currency Acts of 1751 and 1764. These restrictions prohibited the colonies from issuing paper money as legal tender, making it even more onerous for colonists to conduct business or pay local debts.

This was a sweet deal for the King and the City of London. In a system that continues in various forms to this day, colonial raw materials enriched bankers, entrepreneurs, and manufacturers in Britain, while the colonies were forced to buy manufactures, luxuries, and even basic goods like tea at inflated prices.

However, strict enforcement of these many regulations and restrictions was difficult, if not impossible. The predictable result was the creation of an extensive and highly sophisticated network of smugglers. Evasion of duties, bribery of customs officials, and falsification of ship manifests were rampant. Things got so out of hand that some historians estimate that smuggling accounted for as much as one-third of colonial trade.

As the decades passed, American merchants saw their wealth grow exponentially through both legal and illegal means. Due to the preponderance of imperial restrictions, they often speculated in Western lands rather than investing in domestic industry. Eager as they were to tap the full potential of the continent, it was only natural that they would want political power commensurate with their economic power. The seed of industrial capitalism having been planted, it grew with a logic of its own. As Lenin later explained in the epoch of fully fledged imperialism:

> The export of capital influences and greatly accelerates the development of capitalism in those countries to which it is exported. While, therefore, the export of capital may tend to a certain extent to arrest development in the capital-exporting countries, it can only do so by expanding and deepening the further development of capitalism throughout the world.[36]

The French and Indian War

The tensions were mounting. London and its American colonies were on a collision course. However, the world didn't begin nor end with the British Empire. International events would decisively impact American history—and vice versa. And this would not be the last time.

The British were not the only major players seeking to dominate North America and the world. In 1754, a skirmish between French and British troops stationed in the far-off Ohio River Valley sparked the world's first truly global war. The conflict spread, then raged for seven years across Europe, North America, the Caribbean, West Africa, India, and the Philippines. Generally referred to as the Seven Years' War, its American component is better known as the French and Indian War. By the time it was over, the colonial map of North America had been redrawn.

According to the historians Jacques Lacoursière and Robin Philpot:

> The Seven Years' War only began officially in 1756, but war had already been raging in North America for two years. People in the English colonies saw the "reduction of Canada" as a necessity. Different names are used to qualify that war depending on which side people or their ancestors were on. For Europeans and English-speaking Canadians it is known as the "Seven Years' War," for the inhabitants of New France, now Quebec, it is known as the "Guerre de la conquête" or "War of Conquest;" and for the people of New England, and eventually all of the United States, it is known as the "French and Indian War." Winston Churchill would later call it the "First World War."[37]

In *Crucible of War*, the standard volume on the subject, Fred Anderson explains that the war was global both in its geographic reach and its far-reaching consequences. It ushered in British global hegemony, ended French colonial aspirations in North America and India, elevated Prussia to major power status in Europe, and set in motion the conditions that would spark both the American and French Revolutions.[38]

On the eve of the fighting, North America was divided among several European colonial powers. Each had different strategies for exploiting and relating to the lands, resources, and Indigenous peoples under their nominal control.

The British held their thirteen American colonies, along with Nova Scotia, Newfoundland, and trading posts in the Hudson Bay. The Spanish controlled California, Texas, New Mexico, and Florida, as well as Mexico, Central America, and most of South America. The Russians had established trading posts in Alaska and as far south as Northern California, including Fort Ross, in modern-day Sonoma County, just north of San Francisco.

Then there was New France, which posed the greatest threat to British interests. Spearheaded by adventurous fur traders, the French controlled a vast arc of territory, from Quebec and the St. Lawrence River to the Great Lakes, and down the Mississippi River Valley to Louisiana and the Gulf of Mexico. This *de facto* encirclement of the British colonies effectively blocked their westward expansion.

Both empires claimed the strategically located Ohio River Valley, but neither exercised effective control over it. The region was home to various Native American nations that played the Europeans against each other in pursuit of their own interests. Virginia land speculators also had significant economic interests in territories that would later become Ohio, West Virginia, Kentucky, Indiana, Illinois, and Michigan, as well as parts of Pennsylvania and New York. They injected colonial commercial ambitions into the great-power rivalry. Everyone understood that he who controlled the Ohio Country would control the heart of the continent.

On May 28, 1754, in what is now southwestern Pennsylvania, a twenty-two-year-old Virginia militia officer led an ambush against a French reconnaissance party. The commanding officer, Joseph Coulon de Jumonville, and several of his men were killed. As Jumonville was on a diplomatic mission to warn the British to leave the area, the French considered it an assassination. The American militia officer's name was George Washington.

When word of the incident leaked out, it sparked a diplomatic crisis. Meanwhile, Washington hastily built a defensive position dubbed "Fort Necessity." On July 3, combined French and Native American forces attacked his outnumbered and beleaguered troops.

After a day of hard fighting, a quarter of his men had been killed or wounded and he was forced to capitulate.

Though he later claimed he wasn't aware of the precise wording, Washington signed terms of surrender admitting to the "assassination" of Jumonville, thus handing the French a propaganda victory. Upon returning home, some praised Washington's courage, while others criticized his judgment for choosing a poor defensive position and for provoking the French by attacking them in the first place. Either way, no one would soon forget the name George Washington.

Stung by the humiliating defeat, the British decided to double down in the Ohio Country. They sent General Edward Braddock and a contingent of British regulars to push back against the French. However, his disastrous defeat near Fort Duquesne, now present-day Pittsburgh, in July 1755, only made things worse.

So far, the war had been undeclared. In the meantime, however, the European powers had undergone yet another of their periodic realignments. After decades of enmity, France and Austria now formed an alliance against Britain and Prussia. When Prussia's Frederick the Great invaded Saxony in August 1756, the European phase of the war officially began.

The fields of Europe were strewn with death and destruction as Russia, Sweden, Saxony, and other smaller powers joined the fight against the upstart Prussians. The war spilled over into the Caribbean, West Africa, and India, with local proxies doing much of the fighting and dying. Even the Philippines saw fighting when Spain entered the war, backing France. Control over trade routes, fur, and the North Atlantic's rich fishing grounds was also at stake, transforming it into a proto-imperialist conflagration.

As always, Indigenous North Americans were forced to pick sides or attempt neutrality. The French were generally seen as the lesser evil, as they relied more on trade partnerships, alliances, and intermarriage than on the overt expropriation and expansion of Britain's American colonists. The Iroquois Confederacy, traditionally allied with the British, initially chose neutrality. This hurt Britain's chances in the war—a perceived betrayal the Crown wouldn't soon forget.

At the time, there was no guarantee of British victory, either in North America or anywhere else. In addition to the disgraceful setbacks at Forts Necessity and Duquesne, they also lost to French forces at Fort Oswego on Lake Ontario and at Fort William Henry on Lake George. In Europe, they were badly beaten at the Battle of Hastenbeck in Germany and lost the key Mediterranean outpost of Minorca. In India, the British East India Company's mercenary forces were besieged and lost their fort at Calcutta. In the Caribbean, the British were under intense pressure from French privateers.

By early 1757, Britain was losing on almost every front. French and Indian forces controlled the Ohio Valley and the Great Lakes. They had captured key forts and seemed poised to push the British colonists back to the Atlantic coast.

Robert Clive's 1757 victory at the Battle of Plassey in India marked the beginning of a turnaround. In 1758, Britain's Secretary of State, William Pitt, dramatically reorganized the war effort. He poured resources into the American theater. He sent regular British troops and offered to reimburse the colonies for their military expenses. Only then did the tide really begin to turn in King George II's favor. By 1760, the British had captured Cape Breton, Quebec, and Montreal.

Thus, after an auspicious beginning, the war ended in disaster for Louis XV. According to the Treaty of Paris of 1763, France gave up all its North American territories east of the Mississippi River, including Canada and all claims to the Ohio Valley and the Great Lakes region. Spain, which joined the war late on France's side, gave Florida to Britain. To make up for Spain's loss, France gave it a good part of its large Louisiana Territory west of the Mississippi, including New Orleans.

Effectively expelled from the mainland, France kept only a few small islands off the coast of Newfoundland. It also retained its Caribbean sugar islands. Britain, on the other hand, now had an empire "upon which the sun never set."

For Native Americans, the British victory was catastrophic. With French support gone, they now faced the British Empire and its colonists alone. After the Treaty of Paris, an alliance of Great Lakes and Ohio Valley nations led by Pontiac attacked British forts and settlements. The uprising was bloodily suppressed by 1766, but it showed that Indigenous peoples remained determined to resist British-American expansion.

The Western frontier had been defended and dramatically extended. What should be done with those lands became the burning question of the day. In this, the colonists and Indians had diametrically opposed interests. The British government was caught in the middle, unable to satisfy either side. Just as the later Mexican-American War of 1846–48 posed questions only the Civil War could resolve, the French and Indian War paved the way for the First Revolution.

Within a dozen years, Britain's most glorious colonial triumph would lead to its greatest colonial disaster. To paraphrase Fred Anderson, The war that made America also unmade the British Empire in America.

From colonial dependence to national consciousness

Life in the thirteen colonies could be exceedingly harsh. However, compared to many parts of Europe, it could also be relatively good. In the early days, abundant farmland on untilled soil supported large families. Better nutrition and less crowded living conditions led to longer life expectancy, higher birth rates, and lower infant mortality.

In addition to this endogenous demographic growth, a steady flow of voluntary and involuntary immigrants boosted America's colonial population, which doubled roughly every 25 years. By 1775, roughly one in four English-speakers in the British Empire lived in the thirteen colonies, some 2.5 million people.

For most of the colonial period, Americans considered themselves loyal subjects of the British Crown. They may have had this or that disagreement over this or that policy, but they overwhelmingly saw themselves as British—especially in relation to the French.

However, as the decades passed, a shift occurred, and the kernel of a distinct national identity began to emerge. Though originally transplanted from different corners of the Old World, the American admixture of peoples gave rise to unique social, cultural, linguistic, political, religious, and legal institutions and practices.

The process was uneven, but the colonists gradually diverged from the norms of the mother country. With no hereditary aristocracy, powerful courts, prisons, or standing army, Americans saw themselves as more industrious, self-reliant, pragmatic, independent, and egalitarian than Europeans—not to mention more zealous and aggressive.

There was also a clear class basis to the changing sentiment and growing regionalism, which deeply impacted the evolution of the "American character." For the poorest Americans, life in the colonies was a million miles from the European-inspired comforts found in the grand houses of the rich.

Town meetings in New England, the Virginia House of Burgesses, and other colonial charters established traditions of self-government and representative democracy. These traditions diverged from British parliamentary practice. Over time, many Americans identified more as a "Massachusetts man" or a "Virginian" than an Englishman.

The English language offers another interesting example. As someone once quipped, the English and the Americans are "two peoples separated by a common language." Linguistic drifting began with the fact that the original colonists came from different parts of Britain, each with their own linguistic peculiarities. As Americans adopted words from various European, Native American, and African languages, their speech patterns, vocabulary, and spelling morphed, and a wide range of regional accents evolved. These changes were eventually documented in 1828 by Noah Webster in his masterwork, *An American Dictionary of the English Language.*

On the religious front, the "Great Awakening" of the 1730s and 1740s gave rise to distinctly American religious practices. Reflecting the relative anarchy of the New World, and as a reaction against the Church of England, the movement was decentralized, egalitarian, and anti-hierarchical.

Preachers like Jonathan Edwards and George Whitefield drew massive crowds and emphasized personal religious conversion and experience over ecclesiastical orthodoxy. The proliferation of Protestant groupings—some of them influenced by the Levellers* of the English Revolution—gave rise to diverse sects, including the Free Will Baptists, Methodists, Separate Congregationalists, and New Side Presbyterians.

The organizational networks formed during the "Great Awakening," which engendered a flurry of correspondence, pamphleteering, and mass meetings to coordinate activities across colonies, would be used in the buildup to the revolution to resist British policies. By the time of the revolution, many religious leaders were on board with independence, framing the conflict as a struggle between good and evil. This is a perfect illustration of Marx's idea that history wastes nothing.

Reflecting all of this, Benjamin Franklin proposed a "Plan of Union" at a meeting of colonial delegates held in Albany, New York in 1754. With war against the French looming, this was the first serious attempt to form a unified colonial government.

Until then, colonial legislatures in the thirteen colonies were locally elected assemblies, typically consisting of an elected lower house, a Crown-appointed council, and a royal governor. They could levy local taxes, control spending, and pass local laws, though these were generally subject to gubernatorial assent and could be reviewed or disallowed by authorities in London. Franklin envisioned something far more substantial.

---

* The radical-democratic party in the English Revolution. The Levellers demanded religious freedom and the right of the people to choose their own government. Small and middling businessmen, independent craftsmen, and small farmers made up their social base. Unlike the more radical Diggers, they defended the right to private property. The party had a utopian vision of an economic system dominated by small, independent producers and enjoyed strong support among rank-and-file soldiers of the New Model Army. Cromwell leaned on the Levellers to defeat the King and the Presbyterians, before eradicating them and executing their leaders in 1649.

His Union would have had the power to raise taxes and maintain armies for common defense and for dealings with Native Americans, with overall oversight by the Crown. As part of his efforts to get everyone to buy in, Franklin published his famous "Join, or Die" cartoon—depicting the colonies as individual segments of a chopped-up snake.

In the end, both the colonies and the British authorities rejected Franklin's proposal: the colonies, because it encroached on their autonomy; the British, because of the centrifugal forces it might unleash. Nonetheless, Franklin's prescient initiative anticipated the direction of things to come.

Though imperceptible to those living through it, a new society had matured in the womb of the old. This was an American variant of Marx's brief outline of historical development in *A Contribution to the Critique of Political Economy*:

> No social order is ever destroyed before all the productive forces for which it is sufficient have been developed, and new superior relations of production never replace older ones before the material conditions for their existence have matured within the framework of the old society. Mankind thus inevitably sets itself only such tasks as it is able to solve, since closer examination will always show that the problem itself arises only when the material conditions for its solution are already present or at least in the course of formation.[39]

Once objective conditions had ripened sufficiently to allow for an independent path of development, the will to fight and the emergence of the revolutionary subjective factor accelerated. Britain and America both represented the still historically progressive system of capitalism, but they exhibited significant differences.

The British were saddled with a monarch and other legacies of feudalism, despite having had a bourgeois revolution of their own. They wanted to maintain the conservative traditions, stability, and profitability of their robust and growing empire.

Meanwhile, the Americans offered the world a fresh, audacious bourgeoisie sitting on enormous economic potential, just waiting to be unleashed. To uncork that potential—for the benefit and enrichment of the American ruling class instead of the British—they required the more efficient and stable confines of their own nation state. As historian Charles Andrews succinctly explained:

> On the one side was the immutable, stereotyped system of the mother country, based on precedent and tradition and designed to keep things comfortably as they were; on the other, a vital dynamic organism, containing the seed of a great nation, its forces untried, still to be proved. It is inconceivable that such a connection should have continued long between two such yoke-fellows, one static, the other dynamic, separated by an ocean and bound only by the ties of a legal relationship.[40]

Unsurprisingly, Adam Smith, whose *The Wealth of Nations* was published in 1776, sympathized with the colonists' instinctive yearning to break free from the artificial constraints of Britain's mercantilism:

> To prohibit a great people, however, from making all that they can of every part of their own produce, or from employing their stock and industry in the way that they judge most advantageous to themselves, is a manifest violation of the most sacred rights of mankind . . .[41]
>
> [T]he labor of the English colonists is not only likely to afford a greater and more valuable produce, but, in consequence of the moderation of their taxes, a greater proportion of this produce belongs to themselves, which they may store up and employ in putting into motion a still greater quantity of labor . . .[42]
>
> From shopkeepers, tradesmen, and attorneys, are become statesmen and legislators, and are employed in contriving a new form of government for an extensive empire, which, they flatter themselves, will become, and which, indeed, seems very likely to become, one of the greatest and most formidable that ever was in the world.[43]

When they were young and vulnerable, the young colonies had welcomed economic and military nurturing and protection. Now that they had reached adolescence, they couldn't wait to get out of the stifling parental home. As Benjamin Franklin had prophesied in his 1767 letter to Lord Kames:

> But America, an immense territory, favored by nature with all advantages of climate, soil, great navigable rivers, and lakes, etc., must become a great country, populous and mighty; and will, in less time than is generally conceived, be able to shake off any shackles that may be imposed on her.[44]

And as he expressed it in a satirical 1765 verse:

> We have an old mother that peevish is grown; She snubs us like children that scarce walk alone; She forgets we're grown up and have sense of our own.[45]

The beginnings of a distinct national identity had started to form: American patriotism coupled with free-market capitalism and aggressive territorial expansionism. As John Adams wrote decades later, in 1818:

> The American Revolution was not a common event. Its effects and consequences have already been awful over a great part of the globe. And when and where are they to cease?
>
> But what do we mean by the American Revolution? Do we mean the American War? The Revolution was effected before the War commenced. The Revolution was in the minds and hearts of the people, a change in their religious sentiments of their duties and obligations. While the king, and all in authority under him, were believed to govern in justice and mercy according to the laws and constitution derived to them from the God of nature, and transmitted to them by their ancestors, they thought themselves bound to pray for the king and queen and all the royal family, and all in authority under them, as ministers ordained of God for their good. But when they saw those powers renouncing all the principles of authority, and bent upon the destruction of all the securities of their lives, liberties, and properties, they thought it their duty to pray for the Continental Congress and all the thirteen state congresses, etc.[46]

Parliament cracks down

The defeat of the French and their Indian allies had removed the colonists' only serious external threat. Thousands of Americans had acquired military experience and fought shoulder to shoulder across colonial borders. The need for British military protection was no longer as pressing as before, further loosening one of the key bonds tying them to the empire. And it was precisely at that moment that the British felt compelled to squeeze the American colonies harder.

Immediately after the war, Britain issued the Proclamation of 1763. It prohibited colonial settlement west of the Appalachian Mountains; those lands were to be reserved for Native Americans. Unable to police the entire frontier, Parliament hoped to maintain control over resources by establishing a geographic buffer between the two populations.

Many colonists, especially land speculators and war veterans who had been promised land, saw this as a betrayal and intrusion into colonial affairs. Most colonies claimed territory inland from the Atlantic coast to at least the Mississippi River. True to their "pioneering spirit," thousands ignored the "proclamation line" and moved west anyway.

The hard-fought war had bankrupted the British treasury and nearly doubled the national debt from £75 million to £133 million. The cost of keeping garrisons in the newly acquired territories added to this. British taxpayers already bore a heavy burden, so Parliament turned to the American colonies to help pay for their own defense and administration.

As part of a policy of "salutary neglect," the colonies had long enjoyed considerable autonomy. In return, they participated in Britain's lucrative commercial empire. For generations, London had relied on exorbitant mercantile profits rather than direct taxes. The rate of taxation was so low that the average American colonist paid just one shilling per year to the Crown, while the average subject in Britain paid 25 shillings.

From the British government's perspective, asking the thankless Americans to pay their fair share seemed perfectly reasonable. After all, the Empire had bankrolled the recently concluded war to defend them and their way of life. The colonists, however, saw any change to the *status quo ante** as outrageous and unreasonable tyranny. With anti-French-and-Indian unity between the colonists and the Crown a thing of the past, a new enemy took shape in the minds of many Americans: Parliament.

To pay its debts, London needed hard cash. Harsher enforcement of the Navigation Acts and a crackdown on smuggling operations were only the first steps. In April 1764, Parliament passed the Revenue Act, more commonly known as the Sugar Act.

In practice, the new law actually reduced the existing tax on molasses imported into North America from the French West Indies. In exchange, it provided for far stricter enforcement. More customs officials with broader powers to search ships and warehouses were stationed in American ports. Instead of trying violators of the Act in sympathetic colonial courts, they would now be brought before vice-admiralty courts without juries.

Goods, including wine, coffee, and textiles, were subject to higher duties, and tighter regulations were imposed on the lumber and iron industries. All of this hit the bottom line of colonial merchants, distillers, and smugglers, while raising prices for everyone.

It was now crystal clear that the colonies would never achieve economic maturity while under British control. But it was not merely the increased prices, duties, and restrictions that inflamed colonial spirits; it was the principle itself. While they were British subjects, the colonists had no elected representatives in Parliament to advocate for or against such laws on their behalf. This was their right as free Englishmen, and if denied, they were effectively unfree. It was as simple as that. In the ever-eloquent words of Samuel Adams:

---

* Latin for "the state in which before"; the previously existing state of affairs.

> We are in short ultimately yielding large supplies to the Revenues of the Mother Country, while we are laboring for a very moderate Subsistence for ourselves. But if our Trade is to be curtailed in its most profitable Branches, and Burdens beyond all possible Bearing, laid upon that which is suffered to remain, we shall be so far from being able to take off the manufactures of Great Brittain, that it will be scarce possible for us to earn our Bread.
>
> But what still heightens our apprehensions is, that these unexpected Proceedings may be preparatory to new Taxations upon us: For if our Trade may be taxed why not our Lands? Why not the Produce of our Lands & everything we possess or make use of?
>
> This we apprehend annihilates our Charter Right to govern and tax ourselves—It strikes at our British Privileges, which as we have never forfeited them, we hold in common with our Fellow Subjects who are Natives of Brittain: If Taxes are laid upon us in any shape without our having a legal Representation where they are laid, are we not reduced from the Character of free Subjects to the miserable State of tributary Slaves?[47]

And as James Otis, Jr. put it bluntly: "Taxation without representation is tyranny."[48]

The colonial response was immediate. Colonists held mass town meetings to pass resolutions condemning the Sugar Act. Radical pamphlets and newspapers heightened political tensions, while merchants organized boycotts of British goods. Wearing homespun cloth instead of imported textiles became a political statement. An early form of economic nationalism grew as the slogan "Buy American" gained popularity.

Instead of backing off, Parliament went further by passing the Stamp Act, which taxed the colonies even more directly. Americans were now required to purchase special stamped paper for all legal documents, newspapers, pamphlets, licenses, almanacs, dice, and playing cards. Even more revenue collectors would be appointed to enforce compliance.

Two months later, Parliament added yet more fuel to the fire by passing the Quartering Act. The law required colonial legislatures to provide housing, food, bedding, cooking utensils, firewood, candles, salt, vinegar, and either beer or cider for British troops garrisoned in their localities. The financial burden fell on colonial taxpayers, most of whom saw the British troops as occupiers rather than defenders.

Unsurprisingly, the colonists fought back even harder. They organized boycotts, destroyed commercial property, burned tax and government offices, and tarred and feathered pro-Parliament Tories and officials.*

In 1766, Benjamin Franklin went to London to testify before Parliament on behalf of his countrymen. He argued that the Crown was treating the Americans, not as valued and equal parts of the Empire, but as economic subordinates to be exploited. As a result, the mood of the colonists had been transformed:

> Q. What was the temper of America towards Great Britain before the year 1763?
>
> A. The best in the world. They submitted willingly to the government of the Crown, and paid, in all their courts, obedience to acts of Parliament. Numerous as the people are in the several old provinces, they cost you nothing in forts, citadels, garrisons or armies, to keep them in subjection. They were governed by this country at the expense only of a little pen, ink, and paper; they were led by a thread. They had not only a respect, but an affection for Great Britain; for its laws, its customs and manners, and even a fondness for its fashions, that greatly increased the commerce. Natives of Britain were always treated with particular regard; to be an *Old-England man* was of itself a character of some respect, and gave a kind of rank among us.
>
> Q. And what is their temper now?
>
> A. Oh, very much altered![49]

---

* Though it may sound humorous, tarring and feathering was a serious form of extrajudicial punishment used in colonial America and the early United States to intimidate and humiliate political opponents, tax collectors, and suspected loyalists. A crowd would strip or partially undress a person, coat their skin with hot tar and feathers, and parade them publicly, sometimes suspended from a pole. It could cause burns, infection, and lasting injury, and it was often accompanied by beatings and threats.

Given the logistical obstacles, ensuring genuine representation from 3,000 miles away would be difficult, even if Parliament relented. Nonetheless, Franklin still hoped that a total rupture could be avoided.

British merchants also asked Parliament to reconsider, since trade with the colonies had collapsed. One year later, Parliament repealed the Stamp Act. Americans celebrated with bonfires, parades, and toasts to King George III. But on the same day, Parliament enacted the Declaratory Act, asserting its right to legislate for the colonies "in all cases whatsoever."

It had become a matter of principle for Parliament as well. The demand for representation in the American colonies was extremely dangerous. There were now millions of British subjects around the world, and very few of them had any political say or representation in Parliament. Ireland—Britain's original colony—was paying particularly close attention. As Carl Van Doren wrote in his biography of Benjamin Franklin:

> The Irish were watching America. They, too, had long endured the repressive regulation of their trade by England. They too claimed the right to make their own laws and lay their own taxes. If Americans held out, Ireland would be encouraged and benefited. If the Americans lost, Ireland would lose with them.[50]

In 1767, Parliament again attempted to raise colonial revenues through a series of laws known as the Townshend Acts. These imposed duties on imported goods that the colonies could not produce themselves: glass, lead, paint, paper, and tea.

Unlike the direct internal taxes of the Stamp Act, these were external duties on imports, with even more enforcement mechanisms. Customs commissioners were given broad powers to issue search warrants authorizing entry into homes, warehouses, and ships to search for smuggled goods.

The Townshend Acts also suspended the New York Assembly for its refusal to comply with the Quartering Act, thereby threatening the very existence of representative government in America.

The colonists had felt their collective strength in the fight against the Stamp Act. Emboldened by their success, they rejected these new and even more blatant infringements on their privacy and property rights. The feeling of "us versus them" intensified.

Soldiers quartered in the cities were more than a political affront. They competed with locals for jobs—and women—leading to resentment, jeering, and fist fights in taverns and on the streets. On March 5, 1770, a crowd of rowdy Bostonians threw snowballs and chunks of ice at British soldiers. Five people were killed when the overstressed troops fired into the crowd, including Crispus Attucks, a dockworker and sailor of African and Indigenous descent.

For the colonists, this was proof positive that Parliament was willing to deprive them, not only of their rights, property, and dignity, but also of their very lives. Paul Revere's famous engraving, titled "The Bloody Massacre," inflamed anti-British sentiment in the colonies by portraying the soldiers' actions as premeditated murder. Sam Adams concurred, calling it "the bloody butchery."

With little revenue gained and much goodwill lost, Parliament repealed nearly all of its taxes in 1770, with the exception of tea, a symbolic assertion of Parliament's right to tax its subjects. They were determined to teach the American colonists a lesson—lest any of their other colonies think they had gotten soft.

Divergent class interests converge

Based on these experiences, the consciousness of the masses was transformed, as the molecular process of revolution slowly but surely percolated throughout American society.

In response to these repeated attacks, a broad alliance of "patriotic" colonists came together to defend their common interests. Urban merchants, artisans, craftsmen, mechanics, laborers, and shopkeepers, as well as rural farmers and western frontiersmen, agreed that Parliament had pushed things too far. Known as "Whigs," they confronted the "Tories" who remained loyal to the Crown.*

* The American "Whigs" of the First Revolution identified themselves with the English Whigs' class base in the mercantile and capitalist interests as opposed

Even Southern plantation owners were notably bold in their agitation against the British. While the danger of a slave rebellion was always present, their immediate concern was debt. By 1765, Virginia planters alone owed British merchants about £2 million. On the eve of the Revolution, Thomas Jefferson owed British creditors about £4,000—a small fortune at the time. More taxes meant more debt; more debt meant more subservience. On the eve of the war, on March 23, 1775, without a trace of irony, the slave-owning Virginia planter Patrick Henry expressed his opposition in this way:

> Is life so dear, or peace so sweet, as to be purchased at the price of chains and slavery? Forbid it, Almighty God! I know not what course others may take; but as for me, give me liberty or give me death![51]

As for the merchants, those with British family ties or government contracts remained loyal to the Crown. After all, they were richly rewarded with land and power for governing the colonies on its behalf. They feared trade disruptions and social chaos. Many others, however, could see that there was much to be gained from greater autonomy or outright independence. An America that could trade freely with all nations, develop a manufacturing base, control its own courts and currency, and fully exploit western lands would be a goldmine for the bold.

The Stamp Act crisis gave expression to the pent-up frustrations that had long simmered beneath the surface of colonial society. Confronted with parliamentary overreach, the interests of the rich and the poor appeared to coincide, albeit for different reasons. By appealing to abstract ideals of freedom and liberty, the wealthy mobilized the masses against the British. The top colonial military commander, General Thomas Gage, could see this:

> The Plan of the People of Property has been to raise the lower Class to prevent the Execution of the Law.[52]

---

to the conservative, landlord and pro-monarchy and Anglican Church "Tories." The 1833-52 Whigs had a different political center, being organized around opposition to Jackson and the slavocracy.

However, given the irreconcilable antagonism between the exploiters and the exploited, all cross-class alliances are temporary. By loosening the bonds of the status quo, the events of 1765 only exacerbated class divisions already embedded in American society. The historian Arthur M. Schlesinger, Sr., summed up the contradictory dynamic:

> [I]t became apparent that their agitation for commercial redress was unloosing social forces more destructive to business interests than the misguided acts of Parliament.[53]

Fearful of what they had unleashed, many of the wealthiest opponents of Parliament's taxes got cold feet. Compared to "mob rule," being forced to pay a bit more to the Crown was clearly the lesser evil. However, dialing down the heat was easier said than done.

In many ways, 1765 served as the "dress rehearsal" for 1775. As in Russia in 1905,* the liberals had flirted with mobilizing the masses against the autocracy, only to recoil. For America's men of property, harnessing the energy and aspirations of the masses—while not losing control of them—would be one of the revolution's most persistent dilemmas.

Gouverneur Morris, a conservative aristocrat and one of the main architects of the Constitution, was deeply alarmed by the masses that stood behind Adams:

> I stood in the balcony, and on my right hand were ranged all the people of property, with some few poor dependants, and on the other all the tradesmen, etc., who thought it worth their while to leave daily labor for the good of the country. The spirit of the English Constitution has yet a little influence left, and but a little. The remains of it, however, will give the wealthy people a superiority this time, but would they secure it, they must banish all schoolmasters, and confine all knowledge to themselves. This cannot be.

* The 1905 Revolution in Russia began with a typesetters' strike, which escalated into an all-out general strike. The high point was an attempted insurrection in Moscow, which was crushed in blood. Lenin stated that the October Revolution of 1917 could never have taken place without the previous experience of the Revolution of 1905.

> The mob begin to think and to reason. Poor reptiles! It is with them a vernal morning, they are struggling to cast off their winter's slough, they bask in the sunshine, and ere noon they will bite, depend upon it. The gentry begin to fear this. Their committee will be appointed, they will deceive the people, and again forfeit a share of their confidence. And if these instances of what with one side is policy, with the other perfidy, shall continue to increase, and become more frequent, farewell aristocracy. I see, and I see it with fear and trembling, that if the disputes with Britain continue, we shall be under the worst of all possible dominions. We shall be under the domination of a riotous mob.[54]

The masses get organized

As in all revolutionary processes, the colonists' consciousness was molded and remolded by the march of events. It was around this time that the first serious expression of American populism emerged, a recurring pattern in which the masses mobilize in the name of the amorphous "people" against a distant, corrupt status quo serving wealthy insiders.

Faced with Parliament's growing resistance and repression, ordinary Americans' desire for real and lasting change intensified. As the political programs and representatives thrown up by the movement were tested in practice, the stakes of the struggle became clearer. Inexorably, the masses moved from reform of the current system into open revolt. As Trotsky explained:

> The masses go into a revolution not with a prepared plan of social reconstruction, but with a sharp feeling that they cannot endure the old régime. Only the guiding layers of a class have a political program, and even this still requires the test of events and the approval of the masses. The fundamental political process of the revolution thus consists in the gradual comprehension by a class of the problems arising from the social crisis—the active orientation of the masses by the method of successive approximations.[55]

As the historian J. Franklin Jameson explained in *The American Revolution Considered as a Social Movement:*

> Allowance has to be made for one important fact in the natural history of revolutions, and that is that, as they progress, they tend to fall into the hands of men holding more and more advanced or extreme views, less and less restrained by traditional attachment to the old order of things.[56]

In the years leading to the Revolution, New England taverns and coffeehouses became hotbeds of revolutionary agitation. Daniel Webster would later call Boston's Green Dragon Tavern "the headquarters of the Revolution."

Although only 1,500 citizens of Boston were entitled by property qualifications to attend and vote at Town Hall meetings, the radicals had a gallery installed, and hundreds more crowded in to hear Sam Adams and other radical orators. There were clear elements of dual power* in these and similar meetings throughout the colonies, as the masses expressed themselves directly and took decisions in open defiance of the British-installed governors and legislatures.

The radical Whigs employed a highly nuanced range of tactics, including peer and religious pressure, mass boycotts and demonstrations, destruction of tax stamps and revenue offices, the tarring and feathering of colonial officials, street theater, and more. Contrary to the British propaganda, the intimidation and violence were by no means mindless and random. As historian T.H. Breen has noted:

> Colonists who refused to give up imported English tea for the common good faced increasing pressure from neighbors. This was a significant development, since what sustained colonial resistance in the face of intimidation from Parliament was the readiness of ordinary men and women to enforce the public will within their communities.[57]

During the Stamp Act movement, a crowd of 5,000 gathered in Boston—a third of the city's population. They hanged an effigy of stamp distributor Andrew Oliver from a giant elm designated

* A situation in which the old state apparatus has not yet been overthrown, but a new, embryonic state, typically representing another class, exists alongside it. This situation is tenuous and cannot last indefinitely; eventually, one must win over the other.

the "Liberty Tree." They then proceeded to destroy his office and vandalize his home. They then proceeded to behead the effigy, chanting, "liberty, property, and no stamps!" Oliver resigned the following day, and just like that, enforcement of the Stamp Act in Boston was a dead letter.

The Sons of Liberty were formed in 1765 as a direct response to the Stamp Act. Their name was inspired by the Irish MP, Isaac Barré, who had defended the American colonists as "sons of liberty" oppressed by British tyranny.

Linked through the colonies' already vibrant newspaper and pamphleteering network, they were not a single organization but a loose confederation of local groups that coordinated their activities through energetic correspondence.

Small merchants, artisans, and skilled workers dominated its ranks—these were the "middling sorts" of colonial society, as the emergent petty bourgeois were called. Like the Stamp Act movement generally, the Sons of Liberty formed a cross-class alliance, brought together by immediate circumstances to fight against a common enemy. Wealthy merchants like James Otis, Jr. and John Hancock in Boston lent their money and prestige, but according to historian Alfred F. Young:

> From 1765 to 1776, in the major seaboard cities the entry of mechanics into the public arena changed the character of politics. Mechanics and the laboring classes as a whole came alive politically for reasons they shared with other classes as well as for reasons of their own . . .
>
> Mechanics took part in committees, electoral politics, and formal associations and, in New England, in town meetings and county conventions.[58]

Sam Adams and the Committees of Correspondence

Boston's Samuel Adams gave the organization its revolutionary verve and backbone. Far from being afraid of the masses in the early days of the revolution, he embraced them—and they embraced him.

He referred to the ordinary Americans who gave the revolution its backbone as:

> The two venerable orders of men styled Mechanicks [craftsmen and artisans] and Husbandmen [farmers], the strength of every community.[59]

Adams also understood both the significance and limitations of the individual in history, and lent his strategic and propagandistic genius to the movement. He also understood the impact of events on mass consciousness. As he explained in a remarkable letter to Samuel Cooper dated April 30, 1776:

> I was very sollicitous the last Fall to have Governments set up by the people in every Colony. It appears to me to be necessary for many reasons. When this is done, and I am inclind to think it will be soon, the Colonies will feel their Independence—the Way will be prepared for a Confederation, and one Government may be formd with the Consent of the whole—a distinct State composd of all the Colonies with a common Legislature for great and General Purposes.
>
> This I was in hopes would have been the Work of the last Winter. I am disappointed but I bear it tollerably well. I am disposd to believe that every thing is orderd for the best, and if I do not find my self chargeable with Neglect I am not greatly chagrind when things do not go on exactly according to my mind. Indeed I have the Happiness of believing that what I most earnestly wish for will in due time be effected.
>
> *We cannot make Events. Our Business is wisely to improve them. There has been much to do to confirm doubting Friends & fortify the Timid. It requires time to bring honest Men to think & determine alike even in important Matters. Mankind are governed more by their feelings than by reason. Events which excite those feelings will produce wonderful Effects.*
>
> The Boston Port bill suddenly wrought a Union of the Colonies which could not be brot about by the Industry of years in reasoning on the necessity of it for the Common Safety. Since the memorable 19th of April [Lexington and Concord] one Event has brot another on, till Boston sees her Deliverance from those more than savage Troops upon which

> the execrable Tyrant so much relyed for the Completion of his horrid Conspiracys and America has furnishd herself with more than seventy Battalions for her Defence.
>
> The burning of Norfolk and the Hostilities committed in North Carolina have kindled the resentment of our Southern Brethren who once thought their Eastern Friends hot headed and rash; now indeed the Tone is alterd and it is said that the Coolness and Moderation of the one is necessary to allay the heat of the other. There is a reason that would induce one even to wish for the speedy arrival of the British Troops that are expected at the Southward. I think our friends are well prepared for them, and one Battle would do more towards a Declaration of Independency than a long chain of conclusive Arguments in a provincial Convention or the Continental Congress (our emphasis).[60]

Adams was deeply pious, a failed brewer, and had been disastrous as a tax collector. As described by historian William H. Burnside:

> Adams was of average height and muscular build. He carried himself straight in spite of an involuntary palsied movement of his hands and had light blue eyes and a serious, dignified manner. He was very fond of sacred music and sang in the choir of New South Church. Personable, he maintained a close relationship with his neighbors and was constantly chatting with those he met along the street. He had a gift for smoothing over disputes among his friends and acquaintances and was often asked to mediate a disagreement. Adams was a hard worker, and through the years his candle burned late at night as he kept up his extensive correspondence, much of which does not survive today. His second cousin, John Adams, likened him to John Calvin, partly because of his deep piety but also because of his personality: He was "cool . . . polished, and refined," somewhat inflexible, but consistent, a man of "steadfast integrity, exquisite humanity, genteel erudition, obliging, engaging manners, real as well as professed piety, and a universal good character."[61]

He was also an energetic political activist and a consistent revolutionary democrat who had been preparing for such a moment his entire adult life. He formed the Sons of Liberty and, later, the

Committees of Correspondence. It was Sam Adams who coordinated the mass boycott of British goods and of American merchants who sold them, led the Boston Tea Party, and called for the convening of the Continental Congress.

Thomas Jefferson was effusive in his praise, writing in an 1819 letter to Sam Adams's grandson:

> I can say that he was truly a great man, wise in council, fertile in resources, immovable in his purposes, and had, I think, a greater share than any other member, in advising and directing our measures, in the northern war especially. As a speaker, he could not be compared with his living colleague and namesake [John Adams], whose deep conceptions, nervous style, and undaunted firmness made him truly our bulwark in debate. But Mr. Samuel Adams, although not of fluent elocution, was so rigorously logical, so clear in his views, abundant in good sense, and master always of his subject, that he commanded the most profound attention whenever he rose in an assembly.[62]

The governor of Massachusetts had a different opinion. An American merchant and longtime British collaborator, Thomas Hutchinson despised Adams and everything he represented. In his view:

> [There wasn't a] greater incendiary in the King's dominion or a man of greater malignity of heart who has less scruples any measure however criminal to accomplish his purposes.[63]

As Alexander Winston wrote in *American Heritage* magazine:

> Everything Sam did for a decade smacked of sedition. As early as 1768, Hutchinson had secretly sent depositions to England to see if there might be grounds for his arrest. Parliament dusted off a neglected statute of Henry VIII that would bring all treasonable cases to London for trial. Tories were sure that Sam would now end on the gibbet, where he belonged. They gloated that he "shuddered at the sight of hemp."
>
> A Londoner wrote jubilantly to Hutchinson: "The talk is strong of bringing them over and trying them by impeachment. Do you write me word of their being seized, and I will send you an account of their

> being hanged." But the British solicitor general took a long look at the evidence and decided that it was not sufficient—yet.[64]

It's no accident that Sam Adams, rather than Washington or Jefferson, is often called "the Father of the American Revolution." And it's no wonder that by 1775, he was the most hated man in Tory America. In fact, the fighting at Lexington and Concord was sparked, not only because the redcoats aimed to seize critical stores of powder and ammunition, but because they hoped to arrest Sam Adams and John Hancock for treason. The Americans escaped only after being warned by Paul Revere and William Dawes in their famous midnight ride.

After Parliament retreated from the Townshend Acts in 1770, the mass fervor also died down. As we've seen, many big merchants who had toyed with the revolution lost their nerve and passed to the side of reaction and accommodation—never mind that they would be the main beneficiaries once British rule was overthrown.

However, Sam Adams and his extensive network of collaborators were far from satisfied with the results achieved, and were determined to keep the flame of revolt alive. To this end, in 1772, he formed the Committees of Correspondence in Massachusetts and proposed they be replicated throughout the colonies. Thomas Jefferson, who was serving as a member of the Virginia House of Burgesses at the time, concurred:

> We were all sensible that the most urgent of all measures was coming to an understanding with the other colonies to produce a unity of action, and for this purpose that a committee of correspondence in each colony would be the best instrument for intercommunication.[65]

Within months, the colonists had organized a systematic network to quickly and efficiently share information about British actions and to coordinate responses. Operating at multiple levels—town, county, and colonial—the Committees of Correspondence established both horizontal and vertical lines of communication. Local committees met regularly to discuss ideas, pass resolutions, and directly elect delegates to higher bodies. These bodies then enforced boycotts, organized militias, collected intelligence on British troop positions, and in some cases, administered justice.

In *Samuel Adams: The Life of an American Revolutionary*, John K. Alexander offers more insight into the elements of dual power represented by the Committees of Correspondence:

> Massachusetts's committees of correspondence proved especially vital since Governor Hutchinson, like the governor of every royal colony, could simply refuse to call the legislature into session or could dismiss it at any time. The committee-of-correspondence system allowed Whigs to establish a form of shadow government that constituted a way station on the road to installing extralegal governments in Massachusetts. As Samuel later said in appraising the Massachusetts committee system for a leading Pennsylvania Whig, "by this Means we have been able to circulate the most early Intelligence of Importance to our Friends in the Country, & to establish an Union which is formidable to our Adversaries.[66]

Another extremely interesting example of how these committees functioned is provided by historian George Elliott Howard:

> November 20, [1772], the committee of correspondence submitted to a town-meeting in Faneuil Hall its report, which comprised a "State of the Rights of the Colonists," drafted by Samuel Adams; a "List of the Infringements and Violations of Those Rights," prepared by Joseph Warren; and a "Letter of Correspondence" with the other towns of the province, written by Benjamin Church. Together these papers constituted the most radical and comprehensive statement of the case of the colonists which had yet appeared. The towns began at once to appoint similar committees; and during the early months of 1773 their replies were sent in. The substructure of a future national organization was thus laid. "The whole frame of it," says [Massachusetts Governor] Hutchinson, "was calculated to strike the colonists with a sense of their just claim to independence, and to stimulate them to assert it."

According to Daniel Leonard, "this is the foulest, subtlest, and most venomous serpent ever issued from the egg of sedition.[67]

And as historian T.H. Breen explains, commenting on the breadth of the committees:

The committees served to politicize daily life throughout the colonies. They functioned as schools for revolution. They shaped public opinion and discouraged dissent. To be sure, committees may have claimed that their members were "respectable" gentlemen, but in fact they were opening the gates to almost anyone prepared actively to participate in resistance to Great Britain. If the insurgency had involved only scattered cells—small groups of individuals willing to employ violence against the empire—it would never have succeeded. By openly recruiting and identifying so many supporters, however, the movement gained strength.[68]

In short, the Committees of Correspondence were as close to a revolutionary vanguard or party that we can find in this epoch of revolution. In that sense, Sam Adams was perhaps the nearest thing to an American Lenin or Trotsky.

Given the different class dynamics of his time, we should be wary of anachronistic analogies. Nonetheless, in his 18th-century way, Sam Adams understood that a revolutionary spark can light the bonfire of revolution. He intuited the need for a bold, farsighted leadership, a revolutionary program, propaganda, and agitation, as well as discipline and organization. He understood better than anyone the art of connecting revolutionary ideas with the living movement of the masses, and he was sublimely skilled at it.

Just as the most farsighted tsarist police spies recognized the embryonic potential of the Bolsheviks, Massachusetts Loyalist Daniel Leonard is alleged to have said the following about Sam Adams's committees:

I saw the small seed when it was planted; it was a grain of mustard. I have watched the plant until it has become a great tree.[69]

The revolutionary press

The publication and circulation of radical newspapers, pamphlets, broadsheets, and other printed matter exploded in conjunction with the masses' thirst for ideas and action. The Americans of the 1760s and '70s were a highly literate population, and they actively engaged in political discussion and debate—a classic hallmark of a prerevolutionary situation. As John Adams observed in 1765:

> A native of America who cannot read and write is as rare an appearance as a Jacobite or a Roman Catholic, i.e., as rare as a comet or an earthquake. It has been observed, that we are all of us lawyers, divines, politicians, and philosophers. And I have good authorities to say that all candid foreigners who have passed through this country, and conversed freely with all sorts of people here, will allow, that they have never seen so much knowledge and civility among the common people in any part of the world.[70]

Despite some efforts at censorship, there was far more scope for circulating the printed word in the thirteen colonies, as the authors and printing presses were thousands of miles from the authorities in London. Nevertheless, printers often operated in secret, and publications were almost always circulated hand to hand, making them difficult to suppress.

The committees and their press ensured that every British outrage, piece of legislation, or other infringement on colonial liberties was documented and disseminated throughout the population. It was similar to how today's alternative media circumvents the corporate legacy outlets. Popular articles, leaflets, and books were regularly read aloud in taverns, coffeehouses, and public squares. A single newspaper or handbill might thereby reach dozens of people. According to Dylan Jordan of the Historic New Orleans collection:

> While printed images stirred passions, colonists also had access to more intellectual appeals for independence. Pamphlets, cheap and easy to print, brought political theory into the hands of everyday people.

> They discussed these ideas in taverns, important gathering places for exchanging information. Many taverns had reading rooms stocked with newspapers and political tracts, and speakers would often read the latest news aloud for illiterate members of the public. Rum toasts denouncing British tyranny might be followed by a reading from Thomas Paine's *Common Sense* . . .[71]

Richard L. Bushman elaborated on the role of the press in *King and People in Provincial Massachusetts*:

> [T]he Whigs . . . turned to the public at large, through newspapers, pamphlets, and town meetings. They adopted the methods of the English opposition and mobilized a party press to inform and animate the people. For the first time in the history of the Bay colony, popular party leaders became public figures . . . [T]he leaders of the Revolutionary generation left a body of writings—tracts, newspaper essays, letters, and political treatises. The much broader public to which the Whigs appealed required communication through public media.[72]

And as Alexis de Tocqueville wrote in *Democracy in America*:

> Only a newspaper can deposit the same thought in a thousand minds at once.[73]

The effectiveness of the colonial distribution network explains Ben Franklin's enthusiasm for the free press and the need for a national postal service:

> Printers are educated in the Belief, that when Men differ in Opinion, both Sides ought equally to have the Advantage of being heard by the Publick; and that when Truth and Error have fair Play, the former is always an overmatch for the latter . . .[74]

In a preview of Lenin's conception of the revolutionary press, newspapers also served as collective organizers. They published meeting times and locations, announced boycotts and outed merchants who violated them, and called for other specific actions by patriots. In this way, radical ideas and organizational forms were spread, and dispersed localities were woven together into a coherent, continental movement. As Lenin would write more than a century later:

> The role of a newspaper, however, is not limited solely to the dissemination of ideas, to political education, and to the enlistment of political allies. A newspaper is not only a collective propagandist and a collective agitator, it is also a collective organizer . . .
>
> In this last respect, it may be likened to the scaffolding round a building under construction, which marks the contours of the structure and facilitates communication between the builders . . .
>
> With the aid of the newspaper, and through it, a permanent organization will naturally take shape.[75]

Popular newspapers of the time included the *Pennsylvania Journal, New-York Journal,* the *Massachusetts Spy,* and *Virginia Gazette.* However, the *Boston Gazette,* edited by Benjamin Edes and John Gill, was the *de facto* organ of the Sons of Liberty. Derided by colonial authorities, it churned out a stream of inflammatory articles that kept the revolutionary ember alive in New England and beyond.

Samuel Adams was a frequent contributor, writing under various pseudonyms. Equally skilled at both vitriol and humor, Adams not only matched but raised the mood of the masses by exposing the enemy's actions and intentions. He kept the authorities on the back foot with a steady barrage of invective, often blending religious imagery with the fiery rhetoric of the English Revolution. As tensions escalated toward war, the *Gazette* became increasingly explicit in its calls for military preparation.

In addition to advising its readers on how "Minutemen" militias should be drilled and organized, it offered ideas for procuring arms and ammunition.

British officials recognized the danger. Though it backfired badly, one of the Stamp Act's aims had been to clamp down on newspapers and pamphlets by imposing special taxes on these items. General Gage considered shutting the *Boston Gazette* down but feared the colonists' reaction. Later, during the occupation of cities like Boston, New York, and Philadelphia, British forces shut down patriot papers and destroyed their printing presses—just as the tsarist police would do to the Bolsheviks in the lead-up to October 1917.

However, newspapers weren't the only popular format for spreading ideas. The greater space pamphlets offered for expressing grievances and proposing solutions made them even more influential.

James Otis Jr.'s 1764 tract, *The Rights of the British Colonies Asserted and Proved*, was among the first to systematically argue that Parliament had no right to tax the colonies without their consent.[76]

In *Letters from a Farmer in Pennsylvania*, written from 1767–68, John Dickinson argued forcefully against the Townshend Acts.[77]

In 1774, Thomas Jefferson's instructions for Virginia's delegates to the Continental Congress were published as *A Summary View of the Rights of British America*. In it, he unequivocally rejected Parliament's authority over the colonies.[78]

However, nothing could compare to Thomas Paine's masterpiece, *Common Sense*. Published in January 1776, after the shooting war had already begun, it crystallized public sentiment and prepared the ideological ground for the Declaration of Independence. One might even argue that it was the American equivalent of *The Communist Manifesto*.

It sold an astounding 500,000 copies in a population of just 2.5 million—which included roughly 500,000 slaves. This would be the equivalent of selling 65 million copies of a booklet today.

Written in clear, ringing language that ordinary people could understand, it mocked the monarchy, made the case for independence, and universalized the cause of American freedom:

> The cause of America is, in a great measure, the cause of all mankind. Many circumstances hath, and will arise, which are not local, but universal, and through which the principles of all Lovers of Mankind are affected, and in the Event of which, their Affections are interested. . . .

> The sun never shined on a cause of greater worth. 'Tis not the affair of a city, a country, a province, or a kingdom, but of a continent—of at least one eighth part of the habitable globe. 'Tis not the concern of a day, a year, or an age; posterity are virtually involved in the contest, and will be more or less affected, even to the end of time, by the proceedings now . . .
>
> But Britain is the parent country, say some. Then the more shame upon her conduct. Even brutes do not devour their young, nor savages make war upon their families . . .
>
> Europe, and not England, is the parent country of America. This new world hath been the asylum for the persecuted lovers of civil and religious liberty from every part of Europe . . .
>
> Everything that is right or natural pleads for separation. The blood of the slain, the weeping voice of nature cries, 'tis time to part. Even the distance at which the Almighty hath placed England and America, is a strong and natural proof, that the authority of the one, over the other, was never the design of Heaven . . .
>
> To be always running three or four thousand miles with a tale or a petition, waiting four or five months for an answer, which when obtained requires five or six more to explain it in, will in a few years be looked upon as folly and childishness—There was a time when it was proper, and there is a proper time for it to cease . . .
>
> We have it in our power to begin the world over again. A situation, similar to the present, hath not happened since the days of Noah until now. The birthday of a new world is at hand.[79]

Enough said.

The Boston Tea Party

The United States was officially born on July 4, 1776. However, the revolutionary water broke with the Boston Tea Party on December 16, 1773.

It was not by accident that Boston became the nerve center of the revolution. In the final analysis, it was the development of the productive forces in the colonies, especially in New England and the

Mid-Atlantic, that made the revolution not only objectively possible but dialectically necessary.

As just one example, mass boycotts of British goods would have been impossible without the ability to produce many of the necessities of life domestically. The same was true when it came to waging war. As Engels explained in *Anti-Dühring*:

> The triumph of force is based on the production of arms, and this in turn on production in general—therefore, on "economic power", on the "economic situation", on the *material* means which force has at its disposal.[80]

Out of the developing economic base rose the human forces that would throw off the colonial yoke. The powder keg was set—and Sam Adams held the match.

In May 1773, Parliament took yet another swipe at the colonists with the Tea Act. Aimed, in part, at saving the struggling British East India Company, it granted the consortium a monopoly on tea sales in the colonies. London tried to sweeten the deal by lowering the overall price of tea by allowing the company to bypass the profit-taking middlemen in Britain. However, this undercut colonial merchants, who had built a lucrative business importing tea themselves, both above and below board.

More fundamentally, however, it reasserted Parliament's right to tax the colonies, as these imports would still carry the three-pence Townshend duty. Everyone could see through the clumsy attempt to trick Americans into accepting taxation without representation. The colonists rightfully feared that if they gave an inch, Parliament would take a mile. Accepting taxed tea at any price would acknowledge London's authority to tax the colonies, opening the way to unlimited taxation and subordination.

On November 5, 1773, Sam Adams denounced the maneuver in his Resolutions of the Town of Boston:

> Whereas it appears by an Act of the British Parliament passed in the last Sessions, that the East India Company are by the said Act allowed

to export their Teas into America, in such Quantities as the Lord of the Treasury shall Judge proper: And some People with an evil intent to amuse the People, and others thro' inattention to the true design of the Act, have so construed the same, as that the Tribute of three Pence on every Pound of Tea is not to be enacted by the detestable Task Masters there—Upon the due consideration thereof, *Resolved*, That the Sense of the Town cannot be better expressed on this Occasion, than in the words of certain Judicious Resolves lately entered into by our worthy Brethren the Citizens of Philadelphia—wherefore

Resolved, that the disposal of their own property is the Inherent Right of Freemen; that there can be no property in that which another can of right take from us without our consent; that the Claim of Parliament to tax America, is in other words a claim of Right to buy Contributions on us at pleasure—

2nd That the Duty imposed by Parliament upon Tea landed in America, is a tax on the Americans, or levying Contributions on them without their consent—

3rd That the express purpose for which the Tax is levied on the Americans, namely for the support of Government, the Administration of Justice, and the defence of His Majestys Dominions in America, has a direct tendency to render Assemblies useless, and to introduce Arbitrary Government and Slavery—

4th That a virtuous and steady opposition to the Ministerial Plan of governing America, is absolutely necessary to preserve even the shadow of Liberty, and is a duty which every Freeman in America owes to his Country to himself and to his Posterity—

5th That the Resolutions lately come by the East India Company, to send out their Teas to America Subject to the payment of Duties on its being landed here, is an open attempt to enforce the Ministerial Plan, and a violent attack upon the Liberties of America—

6th That it is the Duty of every American to oppose this attempt—

7th That whoever shall directly or indirectly countenance this attempt, or in any wise aid or abet in unloading receiving or vending the Tea sent or to be sent out by the East India Company while it remains subject to the payment of a duty here is an Enemy to America—

8th That a Committee be immediately chosen to wait on those Gentlemen, who it is reported are appointed by the East India Company to receive and sell said Tea, and to request them from a regard to their own characters and the peace and good order of this Town and Province immediately to resign their appointment.[81]

When the East India Company's ship *London* arrived in Charleston, South Carolina, that November, the local Sons of Liberty forced the tea to remain onboard. After 20 days, customs officials seized it for nonpayment of duties. The tea was unloaded and stored in damp warehouse cellars, where much of it rotted. After independence was declared, some that remained was sold to raise funds for the revolutionary cause.

When the ship *Polly* arrived at Chester, Pennsylvania, that December, a "welcome" committee of patriots "escorted" its captain to Philadelphia. There, he was confronted by a mass meeting of 8,000 people, the largest political gathering in colonial history until that time. They let him know in no uncertain terms that if he tried to unload his cargo, both it and his ship would be destroyed—and he likely wouldn't fare so well, either. The *Polly* headed back to England the next day, still fully loaded.

Things would turn out quite differently when the *Dartmouth*, *Eleanor*, and *Beaver* arrived in Boston Harbor in late November, laden with 342 chests of tea. Mass democratic assemblies were held as residents of Boston and the surrounding towns engaged in heated, tumultuous arguments over what to do with the cargo. Plenty of merchants and others participated on both sides of the debate, but the tone was set by Sam Adams and his rambunctious supporters.

On December 16, some 5,000 people gathered at the Old South Meeting House. Adams was adamant that the tea be sent back to England without paying the duty. Adams's longtime nemesis, Governor Hutchinson—who stood to profit if the tea were unloaded—refused to clear the ships for departure. At that point,

Adams is alleged to have told the crowd: "This meeting can do nothing more to save the country."

The time for talk was over, and the Rubicon was about to be crossed. What followed was far from a spontaneous outburst. A group of Sons of Liberty—some disguised as Mohawk Indians in a symbolic rejection of British civilization—marched to the wharf. Over the next three hours, in full public view, they systematically dumped 46 tons of tea into the water. Nothing else was damaged or stolen.

Historian Alfred F. Young highlighted the calculated character of this carefully calibrated violation of private property. It is worth quoting at length:

> At the Tea Party on the night of December 16, 1773, Hewes the citizen "volunteered" and became the kind of leader for whom most historians have never found a place. The Tea Party, unlike the Massacre, was organized by the radical Whig leaders of Boston. They mapped the strategy, organized the public meetings, appointed the companies to guard the tea ships at Griffin's Wharf, and planned the official boarding parties. They converted the town meetings into meetings of "the whole body of the people," one of which [Thomas] Hutchinson found "consisted principally of the Lower ranks of the People and even Journeymen Tradesmen were brought in to increase the number and the Rabble were not excluded yet there were divers Gentlemen of Good Fortunes among them . . ."
>
> The recollection of Joshua Wyeth, a journeyman blacksmith, verified Hewe's story in explicit detail: "It was proposed that young men, not much known in town and not liable to be easily recognized should lead in the business." Wyeth believed that "most of the persons selected for the occasion were apprentices and journeymen, as was the case with myself, living with Tory masters." Wyeth "had but a few hours warning of what was intended to be done." Those in the officially designated parties, about thirty men better known, appeared in well-prepared Indian disguises. As nobodies, the volunteers—anywhere from fifty to one hundred men—could get away with hastily improvised disguises. Hewes said he got himself up as an Indian and daubed his

"face and hands with coal dust in the shop of [a] blacksmith." In the streets "I fell in with many who were dressed, equipped, and painted as I was, and who fell in with me and marched in order to the place of our destination."

At Griffin's Wharf the volunteers were orderly, self-disciplined, and ready to accept leadership. [Hewes recalled:] "When we arrived at the wharf, there were three of our number who assumed an authority to direct our operations, to which we readily submitted. They divided us into three parties, for the purpose of boarding the three ships which contained the tea at the same time. The name of him who commanded the division to which I was assigned was Leonard Pitt [Lendell Pitts]. The names of the other commanders I never knew. We were immediately ordered by the respective commanders to board all the ships at the same time, which we promptly obeyed."

But for Hewes there was something new: he was singled out of the rank and file and made an officer in the field. "The commander of the division to which I belonged, as soon as we were on board the ship, appointed me boatswain, and ordered me to go to the captain and demand of him the keys to the hatches and a dozen candles. I made the demand accordingly, and the captain promptly replied, and delivered the articles; but requested me at the same time do no damage to the ship or rigging. We then were ordered by our commander to open the hatches, and take out all the chests of tea and throw them overboard, and we immediately proceeded to execute his orders; first cutting and splitting the chests with our tomahawks, so as thoroughly to expose them to the effects of the water. In about three hours from the time we went on board, we had thus broken and thrown overboard every tea chest to be found in the ship; while those in the other ships were disposing of the tea in the same way, at the same time. We were surrounded by British armed ships, but no attempt was made to resist us. We then quietly retired to our several places of residence, without having any conversation with each other, or taking any measures to discover who were our associates . . ."

> As the Tea Party ended, Hewes was stirred to further action on his own initiative . . . While the crews were throwing the tea overboard, a few other men tried to smuggle off some of the tea scattered on the decks. "One Captain O'Connor whom I knew well," said Hewes, "came on board for that purpose, and when he supposed he was not noticed, filled his pockets, and also the lining of his coat. But I had detected him, and gave information to the captain of what he was doing. We were ordered to take him into custody, and just as he was stepping from the vessel, I seized him by the skirt of his coat, and in attempting to pull him back, I tore it off." They scuffled. O'Connor recognized him and "threatened to complain to the Governor." "You had better make your will first," quoth Hewes, doubling his fist expressively, and O'Connor escaped, running the gauntlet of the crowd on the wharf. "The next day we nailed the skirt of his coat, which I had pulled off, to the whipping post in Charlestown, the place of his residence, with a label upon it," to shame O"Connor by "popular indignation.[82]

For his part, John Adams immediately recognized the significance of the moment and wrote in his diary:

> This is the most magnificent movement of all. There is a dignity, a majesty, a sublimity, in this last effort of the Patriots, that I greatly admire . . . This destruction of the tea is so bold, so daring, so firm, intrepid and inflexible, and it must have so important consequences, and so lasting, that I can't but consider it as an epocha in history.[83]

Others were appalled by the destruction of private property, including Ben Franklin, who was still on a diplomatic mission to London. Worried about the political risks involved, he considered it "an act of violent injustice" and thought the ruined tea should be paid for. However, after a humiliating dressing down by the Privy Council over the incident, he changed his tune. He returned to America in May 1775, fully committed to independence.

The Boston Tea Party marked the point of no return. A line in the sand had been drawn, and neither side could back down.

The Intolerable Acts and the Continental Congress

Brimming with imperial arrogance, Parliament decreed that the Port of Boston be closed until the colonists paid restitution for the lost tea and demonstrated their willingness to obey.

This was collective punishment at its cruelest. With the exception of military vessels and those carrying essential supplies approved by the governor, no ships could enter or leave the harbor. Thousands of Bostonians lost their livelihoods and literally faced starvation. Once again, Sam Adams was at the forefront, whipping up popular resistance:

> [W]e have receiv'd.a Copy of an Act of the British Parliament—which is inclosed, wherein it appears that the Inhabitants of this Town have been Tryed condemn'd and are to be punished by shutting up the Harbour and otherways, without their having been called to Answer for, nay, for ought that appears without their having been accused of any crime committed by them, for no such crime is alleged in the Act—the town of Boston is now Suffering the stroke of Vengeance in the Common cause of America, I hope they will sustain the Blow with Becoming Fortitude, and that the Effect of this cruel act Intended to intimidate and subdue the Spirits of all America will by the joint efforts of all be frustrated.[84]

As so often happens, the whip of reaction only radicalized the masses further. Colonists from Maine to Georgia rallied to the city's aid, sending food, supplies, and money overland. Anticipating the quip attributed to Benjamin Franklin at the signing of the Declaration of Independence, the masses instinctively understood that "We must all hang together, or most assuredly we shall all hang separately."

Then came the Coercive or Intolerable Acts, starting with the Massachusetts Government Act, passed in May of 1774. In a direct blow against New England's democratic traditions, the colony's royal charter was revoked and its governor was granted unprecedented powers. Hutchinson could now appoint and remove all government officials, judges, and sheriffs without the colonial legislature's input.

That same month saw the Administration of Justice Act, better known to Bostonians as the "Murder Act." Crown officials accused of capital crimes could have their trials transferred back to Britain or to another colony. Ostensibly intended to ensure fair trials for all in the politically charged atmosphere, in practice, it opened the door to criminal impunity.

An expanded Quartering Act was next, in June. Royal governors could now compel colonists to house British troops in occupied or unoccupied buildings—including private homes—if suitable quarters were not provided by the colonial legislatures.

Finally, though not formally part of the Coercive Acts, came the Quebec Act, which tripled the size of the Canadian province, including modern-day Michigan, Illinois, Indiana, Wisconsin, Ohio, and part of Minnesota. While progressive in recognizing the region's French cultural and legal heritage, it was perceived as an imposition of Catholic rule on regions that had long been overwhelmingly Protestant.

More importantly, however, it meant an end to westward expansion. Land claims held by colonial speculators and settlers were invalidated, and the potential for representative government in those regions was also eliminated. Though rarely cited as a major spark for the revolution, this was, in fact, one of its most important proximate causes.

George Washington summed up the colonists' attitude in a letter to George William Fairfax dated June 10, 1774:

> [I]n short the Ministry may rely on it that Americans will never be tax'd without their own consent that the cause of Boston the despotick Measures in respect to it I mean now is and ever will be considerd as the cause of America (not that we approve their cond[uc]t in destroyg the Tea) & that we shall not suffer ourselves to be sacrificed by piecemeal though god only knows what is to become of us, threatned as we are with so many hoverg evils as hang over us at present.[85]

Suddenly, Ben Franklin's Albany Plan of Union from two decades earlier didn't seem so far-fetched. Following a call to action by the Committees of Correspondence, the First Continental Congress was convened in September. Fifty-six delegates from twelve colonies—Georgia did not initially send representatives—gathered at Carpenters' Hall in Philadelphia.

Their first major step was to establish the Continental Association, a coordinated boycott of British goods, with a built-in escalation ladder. It was agreed that, starting December 1, 1774, no new British goods would be imported into the colonies, and that no one would consume the British goods they already possessed. If Britain didn't meet colonists' demands by September 1775, they would stop exporting goods to Britain and its other colonies.

To enforce compliance, grassroots Committees of Observation and Inspection were formed in every colony, county, and town. Their task was to monitor merchants and consumers for infractions of the pact. Violators' names would be made public, and they would be denounced as "enemies of American liberty." The similarities with the Committees of Public Safety that would emerge during the Great French Revolution just a few years later are striking.

These and other committees were a crucial feature of the American Revolution. The role of individuals and the quality of leadership in this process was essential, to be sure. However, far from being decided from above by a handful of wealthy conspiracists, the revolution was simultaneously imposed from below.

Historian Gordon S. Wood has written extensively on the popular radicalism of this period and the role played by the committees:

> As royal authority collapsed in the colonies in 1774–75, new local authorities —committees and congresses —began putting together new popular structures of authority from the bottom up. Americans, as one Maryland official complained, were coming to believe that "they ought not to submit to any appointments but those made by themselves.[86]

Given the level of development of the means of production at the time, this was always going to be a bourgeois, not a socialist revolution. The committees of the First Revolution may have been expressions of dual power, but they never reached the level of the Russian *soviets* in the 1905 and 1917 revolutions.

Nonetheless, ordinary Americans put their class stamp on the process, with implications for the revolutionary struggle we are waging today.

The impact of the Continental Association's boycott was impressive as British imports plummeted. To fill the void, colonial handicrafts and manufacturing received a boost, further incentivizing economic independence. The experience also gave the colonies a taste of what self-rule might look like—though coordinating a boycott was a far simpler task than running an entire country. After Lexington and Concord, the Association's committees provided the organizational framework for military mobilization and civil government.

Let us not forget, however, that the Congress was initially conceived as a forum for coordinating economic resistance to the Intolerable Acts while petitioning the Crown for redress of grievances. Many blamed Parliament specifically for their woes and still had illusions in King George III. Their primary aim was to assert their rights as Englishmen.

However, independence was a slippery slope. With the colonies banding together to coordinate decisions parallel to the official government, an important step toward political separation had been taken. This was reinforced by Congress's endorsement of the Suffolk Resolves, authored in September 1774 by Joseph Warren, the Boston physician and future martyr of Bunker Hill.

The Resolves declared the Coercive Acts unconstitutional and called for economic sanctions against Britain and the withholding of tax payments until they were repealed. They also called for the creation of a Massachusetts government independent of royal authority and the formation of local militias in anticipation of possible armed conflict. Major General Thomas Gage—the new royal governor of Massachusetts Bay—received the message loud and clear and reported to London that the colonists were preparing for war.

He wasn't wrong. Across the colonies, local committees were none-too-subtly gearing up for armed confrontation. On January 17, 1775, the Fairfax County, Virginia Committee of Safety Proceedings declared:

> [T]hat a well regulated Militia, composed of gentlemen freeholders, and other freemen, is the natural strength and only stable security of a free Government, and that such Militia will relieve our mother country from any expense in our protection and defence, will obviate the pretence of a necessity for taxing us on that account, and render it unnecessary to keep Standing Armies among us—ever dangerous to liberty . . .[87]

By May 10, 1775, Britain had not even attempted to redress the colonists' grievances, and a Second Continental Congress was convened, this time including delegates from Georgia.

However, it wasn't Parliament's laws alone that tipped the colonies into open rebellion. Three weeks earlier, blood had been shed at Lexington and Concord, with 49 Americans and 73 redcoats killed. The British had again shown their willingness to kill "their own" people. The stakes were now sky high for both sides.

Although some delegates still hoped to patch things up with London, it was no longer a question of exerting economic and political pressure, but of forming an alternative government and preparing for all-out war.

In mid-June 1775, just days before the fighting at Bunker Hill, the Continental Congress moved to create a unified "Continental" army and place it under a single commander. It unanimously appointed George Washington—the colonies' most recognized veteran—as commander in chief.

Despite his mixed military record, he was wealthy, respected, and had natural charisma and a martial bearing. According to John Adams, it was because Washington was always "the tallest man in the room"—and because he was the only one at the Continental Congress who attended every session in full military uniform.[88]

As it turned out, Washington was calm and brave under enemy fire, an excellent horseman, and a competent executive manager able to build strong teams around him. He was also admired by many in the burgeoning republican movement in France. They regarded him as a self-made New World man—never mind that he had married into much of his wealth. Nonetheless, his celebrity would come in handy when it came to drawing the French into the war at a later stage. In the more than slightly over-the-top opinion of historian Peter Henriques:

> Countless contemporaries testified to his charisma. Washington, James Monroe said, possessed "a deportment so firm, so dignified, but yet so modest and composed I have never seen in any other person." Another acquaintance recollected, "There was in his whole appearance an unusual dignity and gracefulness, which at once secured him profound respect, and cordial esteem. He seemed born to command his fellow men."
>
> "No man could approach him but with respect," Gouverneur Morris wrote. "None was great in his presence." Henry Knox noted that an aide to British General William Howe appeared "awestruck" upon being presented to General Washington. Another man, who had been presented to the Kings of England and France, said neither monarch induced the feeling he experienced meeting Washington. French officer upon French officer spoke similarly after interchanges with the man they and many others called His Excellency. Benjamin Rush declared one "could distinguish him to be a general from among 10,000 people," adding that there was not a European ruler who, alongside Washington, would not look like a servant.[89]

The Continental Army's top commander was also able to retreat in good order—a skill that would serve him in good stead in the years to come.

Washington's near-impossible task was to transform the undisciplined and scattered colonial militias into a centralized, professional force capable of fighting British regulars head-on. At first, he had just 14,000 men and little powder at his disposal. But as news of the new army spread, volunteers from the backwoods started flowing in, many of them skilled marksmen bringing with them rifled, instead of smooth-bore muskets.

On June 22, 1775, Congress authorized the emission of $2 million in currency to fund the war effort. However, without the power to tax, the infamous Continental dollar suffered from chronic devaluation. By the end of the war, the colonial government had issued $241 million in such "Continentals," and by 1781, it had lost 99 per cent of its value.

Independence declared

By the spring of 1776, the balance had been tipped. After the publication of *Common Sense*, several colonies had instructed their Congressional delegates to vote for total separation from Britain.

North Carolina was the first, officially instructing its delegates to vote for independence with the Halifax Resolves, on April 12, 1776. On May 4, Rhode Island formally renounced its allegiance to King George III. Virginia's resolution for independence came on May 15. On June 7, 1776, Virginia's Richard Henry Lee formally introduced a Congressional resolution declaring:

> Resolved, That these United Colonies are, and of right ought to be, free and independent States, that they are absolved from all allegiance to the British Crown, and that all political connection between them and the State of Great Britain is, and ought to be, totally dissolved.
>
> That it is expedient forthwith to take the most effectual measures for forming foreign Alliances.
>
> That a plan of confederation be prepared and transmitted to the respective Colonies for their consideration and approbation.[90]

Yet another committee was formed, this time to draft a declaration to that effect, with the thirty-three-year-old Virginian, Thomas Jefferson, as the primary author. Drawing on the ideas of Aristotle, Cicero, Locke, and George Mason, Jefferson synthesized thousands of years of human striving for freedom in what would become one of the most important documents in history. After many revisions and intense debate, the Declaration of Independence was adopted on July 2, 1776, and formally proclaimed on July 4.

Opening with a poetic defense of the unalienable right to revolution, Jefferson then enumerated twenty-seven specific grievances against the Crown. These painted an inflammatory picture of tyranny that included: imposing taxes without colonial consent; dissolving representative assemblies; obstructing the administration of justice; maintaining standing armies in peacetime without legislative approval; quartering troops in private homes; cutting off colonial trade with other parts of the world; and depriving many colonists of trial by jury.

Jefferson accused King George III of waging war against his own people, burning towns, and inciting "domestic insurrections"—by which he meant slave rebellions. He also accused the royal sovereign of encouraging attacks by "merciless Indian savages."

The Declaration's 1,337 words reverberated around the world. It was printed in thousands of copies and read aloud in hundreds of localities, often accompanied by parades and the celebratory firing of guns. In town after town, the King's arms—a symbol of British rule—were taken down and burned. A statue of George III on New York City's Bowling Green was torn down and eventually melted down into 42,088 bullets for the revolution.

But detailing the colonists' grievances was the easy part. The hard part was formalizing the basis for cooperation between the states, not in lofty rhetoric, but in messy reality. After decades resisting centralized power, it was a tall ask to expect the newly independent states to give up even an iota of their sovereignty. They may have been largely united against the British Crown, but they had divergent economies, histories, cultures, and objectives, not to mention their own territorial disputes.

To give two examples, both New York and New Hampshire claimed the territory that would become Vermont. The dispute led to the formation of the independent Vermont Republic, which lasted from 1777 to 1791. Only then did Vermont join the Union as the 14th state. As for the boundary between North and South Carolina, it was only finalized in 1815, after multiple violent skirmishes and land surveys.

On November 15, 1777, after more than a year of tense deliberation, Congress finally adopted the Articles of Confederation. A "firm league of friendship" was to exist among the newly christened

"United States of America"—as wishy-washy a formulation as there ever was.

Out of necessity, the states agreed that Congress could wage war, conduct diplomacy, and settle disputes between states, but could not tax, regulate commerce, or even enforce its decisions. Every state had one vote, regardless of its population, economy, or congressional delegation.

In George Washington's considered opinion, the Articles of Confederation had produced:

> [A] half-starved, limping Government that appears to be always moving upon crutches and tottering at every step.[91]

As the war progressed, the limitations of this arrangement very nearly doomed the newborn country before it could take its first tentative steps.

Opening shots: The New England and Canadian campaigns

The course of the war was a protracted slog, filled with exhilarating ups and demoralizing downs for both sides before the final British surrender in 1783. Most British regulars and German mercenaries fought for money and glory. Most Americans fought for hearth and home. Even if they were in class conflict with the home-grown elites, they were even more opposed to foreign occupation.

As a result, "the balance of resolve" tipped in favor of the Americans; they were willing to fight just a bit harder and suffer a bit longer than their enemies. Military skill and materiel matter, but in all revolutions, economics, politics, and morale ultimately determine the outcome.

Nevertheless, war is the continuation of politics by other means. Before we examine various aspects of the class struggle during and after the Revolution, let's briefly review the major campaigns, battles, and turning points.

Several significant events took place before independence was formally declared. After the politically pregnant but militarily minor skirmishes at Lexington and Concord, came the protracted siege of British-occupied Boston.

The heaviest fighting took place on June 17, 1775, at Breed's Hill, though it came to be known as the Battle of Bunker Hill. The British succeeded in capturing colonial fortifications but suffered heavy losses and failed to break the encirclement. It was here that the famous line, "Don't fire until you see the whites of their eyes!" was uttered, as the American commanders encouraged their troops to conserve ammunition.

Lt. John Waller, one of the British Marines who stormed the Americans' position, described the carnage:

> I cannot pretend to describe the Horror of the Scene within the Redoubt, when we entered it, 'twas streaming with Blood and strew'd with dead and dying Men, the Soldiers stabbing some and dashing out the Brains of others was a sight too dreadful for me to dwell any longer on.[92]

The Americans also suffered heavy casualties. However, they demonstrated they could rival the redcoats in ferocity and resolve, if not discipline. The British were forced to accept that the conflict would not be resolved quickly and could escalate into a major, costly war.

To prevent British reinforcements from coming down from Canada, Ethan Allen and Benedict Arnold captured the strategic fort of Ticonderoga on the southern tip of Lake Champlain. Among the prizes were 59 cannons, some large mortars, other artillery pieces, and supplies.

Colonel Henry Knox—a 25-year-old Boston bookseller with no practical military experience—led the "noble train of artillery" that hauled the cannons across 300 wintry miles to Boston. Once Washington placed them on the Dorchester Heights overlooking Boston, the British were forced to evacuate, resulting in a strategic victory for the patriots.

That same winter, the Americans launched a bold yet ill-conceived invasion of Canada. Richard Montgomery and Benedict Arnold led the campaign. Their goal was to neutralize Canada as a military threat—and perhaps make it the 14th colony. The two-pronged attack was plagued by severe weather, disease, and misfortune. The adventure ended in disaster on New Year's Eve at the gates of Quebec City. Though unlikely to succeed, the Americans would have transformed both the map and historical course of North America if they had prevailed.

Down in Boston, 10,000 surrounded and outnumbered British troops evacuated the city along with 1,100 loyalists in March 1776. They regrouped in Halifax, Nova Scotia, leaving no British garrison in any of the 13 colonies.

Many Americans believed the war was over. However, the British were far from giving up on their lucrative colonies. They merely needed a more reliable foothold from which to subdue the rebels. Having retained control of Canada, they posed a continual threat to the Americans from the north throughout the war.

Washington loses New York City

Given the particular fervor of the New Englanders, General William Howe turned his attention to the Mid-Atlantic instead. New York City had a large loyalist population and an excellent harbor at the mouth of the Hudson River, making it an attractive base of operations. If the British could control this strategically and commercially important waterway, New England would be cut off from the rest of the colonies. In the summer of 1776, Howe moved his army south to take the city.

Anticipating his adversary's move, Washington had also assembled his forces in the area. His general orders to the Continental Army before the Battle of Long Island in August 1776 sought to inspire his as-yet untested soldiers:

> The time is now near at hand which must probably determine whether Americans are to be freemen or slaves; whether they are to have any property they can call their own . . .
>
> The fate of unborn millions will now depend, under God, on the courage and conduct of this army. Our cruel and unrelenting enemy leaves us

> only the choice of brave resistance, or the most abject submission. We have, therefore, to resolve to conquer or die . . .
>
> Let us therefore rely upon the goodness of the cause, and the aid of the Supreme Being, in whose hands victory is, to animate and encourage us to great and noble actions. The eyes of all our countrymen are now upon us, and we shall have their blessings and praises, if happily we are the instruments of saving them from the tyranny meditated against them. Let us therefore animate and encourage each other, and show the whole world that a Freeman, contending for liberty on his own ground, is superior to any slavish mercenary on earth.[93]

Unfortunately, his military skills didn't match his political rhetoric. He was apparently convinced that the British landing at Gravesend Bay near present-day Bay Ridge was a diversion. So he divided his army—something only a talented few military commanders have ever gotten away with.

The largest battle of the war was fought in Brooklyn on August 27, 1776, and it nearly led to the annihilation of Washington's forces. However, British overconfidence, foggy weather, and energetic patriot boatmen allowed Washington to execute a daring nighttime retreat across the East River into Manhattan.

In the weeks that followed, the British pressed their advantage. In October and November, they fought the Battles of Kip's Bay, White Plains, Fort Washington, and Fort Lee, pushing Washington out of New York and into New Jersey, inflicting heavy losses. The British would occupy New York City for the remainder of the war.

As Washington's army retreated, they joined Nathanial Greene's forces at Fort Lee and continued to withdraw through Hackensack, Newark, New Brunswick, and Princeton, with British General Charles Cornwallis in hot pursuit. By December 7–8, the Americans had crossed the Delaware River into Pennsylvania. Morale plummeted as enlistments expired and desertions rose. The revolution appeared to be dead and buried.

While Washington was being pushed across New Jersey, another pivotal confrontation unfolded in the north. The Battle of Lake

Champlain, also known as the Battle of Valcour Island, took place on October 11, 1776, as American forces under Benedict Arnold faced the British fleet led by Sir Guy Carleton. Despite being defeated, Arnold again demonstrated great courage and tactical skill.

The late-season fighting forced the British to halt operations and go into winter quarters, which delayed their invasion along the Lake Champlain–Hudson corridor until 1777. As a result, the Americans had time to regroup, contributing to their decisive victory at Saratoga.

Back in the Mid-Atlantic, Washington's men shivered and starved, while Howe and his officers settled in for a cozy winter of New York City society balls. The Continental Army had dwindled from over 20,000 men to fewer than 3,000 effectives, many of whom were without shoes, winter clothing, weapons, or ammunition.

The British could hardly hide their disdain for the colonial riff-raff. As John Chester Miller wrote in *Origins of the American Revolution*:

> Englishmen made the mistake of belittling Americans' courage and strength to such a degree that it was difficult to regard colonial resistance seriously. An American, it was said in many quarters, was an unmitigated coward—"the lowest of Mankind, and almost of a different Species from the English of Britain . . ."
>
> Instead of hardy pioneers, braving the perils of ocean and wilderness, Americans were pictured as cowards whose ancestors had fled the mother country rather than fight for liberty in England. They had brought with them, however, the germs of Levelism and democracy which, sprouting in the soil of the New World, now promised to prostrate that small part of the American army which was not already rendered powerless by faintheartedness.[94]

And as Theodore Draper relates:

> In February 1775, Col. James Grant rose in the Commons to say that he had served in America and "knew the Americans very well, was certain

> they would not fight; they would never dare to face an English army, and that they did not possess any of the qualifications necessary to make a good soldier."
>
> In March 1775, the earl of Sandwich, first lord of the Admiralty, gave assurances that the British forces faced "raw, undisciplined, cowardly men . . . Believe me, my Lords, the very sound of a cannon would carry them off . . . as fast as their feet could carry them.[95]

If ever there was an underdog, it was George Washington's Continental Army.

"The times that try men's souls"

At this darkest hour, Thomas Paine again lent his pen to the patriot cause in his *American Crisis* papers. Unlike the philosophical logic of *Common Sense*, this was an emotional appeal and a call to arms:

> These are the times that try men's souls. The summer soldier and the sunshine patriot will, in this crisis, shrink from the service of their country; but he that stands by it *now*, deserves the love and thanks of man and woman. Tyranny, like hell, is not easily conquered; yet we have this consolation with us, that the harder the conflict, the more glorious the triumph.[96]

This was a critical moment; thousands of Patriot enlistments were set to expire on December 31, 1776. If Washington didn't act immediately, he would be left without an army altogether. Recognizing the gravity of the situation, on December 23, 1776, Paine's words were read aloud to Washington's demoralized troops, huddled on the banks of the Delaware.

On Christmas night, Washington led his troops in the now-immortalized river crossing, followed by a surprise attack on the Hessian troops* encamped at Trenton. Though only a minor engagement militarily, the defeat and capture of nearly 1,000

---

* German mercenary soldiers hired as auxiliaries to the British Army. Referred to as such by the Americans because many hailed from the German states of Hesse-Cassel and Hesse-Hanau.

fearsome Germans was a morale-boosting game-changer. As the American General James Wilkinson wrote in his memoirs:

> The joy diffused throughout the union by the successful attack against Trenton reanimated the timid friends of the revolution and invigorated the confidence of the resolute. Perils and sufferings still in prospect were considered the price of independence, and every faithful citizen was willing to make the sacrifice. Success had triumphed over despondency, and the heedless, headlong enthusiasm, which led the colonists to arms, had settled down into a sober sense of their condition, and a deliberate resolution to maintain the contest at every hazard, and under every privation.[97]

After Trenton, Washington launched another bold strike. During the "Ten Crucial Days," December 25 to January 3, he personally led troops into battle at Princeton. When the Americans faltered, he rode to the front, rallied his men, and led a successful charge that broke the British defenses. A fervent believer that Providence was on his side, this was neither the first nor the last time he would recklessly put his life on the line. With another modest but politically important victory under his belt, he settled into winter quarters at Morristown, New Jersey.

His urgent task was to rebuild and resupply his vastly diminished army. Resentful of British occupation, New Jersey militiamen were the first to rally to his banner. Civil war raged in the countryside as farms were pillaged and women were raped. Patriots forced fence-sitting Americans to join them or be hanged. They waged guerrilla warfare against British foraging parties, killing more British and Hessian troops in hit-and-run attacks than in set battles. For good reason, New Jersey is known as the "Crossroads of the Revolution."

By mid-May, Washington had assembled 12,000 men. His new army was harder and drawn more heavily from society's most marginal and desperate layers than the first. Debtors, felons, indentured servants, British deserters, apprentices, and other landless poor joined to fight for a free country, free land, and free rum. Many were German and Irish immigrants who didn't speak English.

Free and enslaved Black people, some standing in for their masters, also joined. Some enlisted for up to three years and a $10 bonus. Others signed on for the war's duration, $20, and 100 acres of Western land.

The fighting resumed in late summer 1777. That August, in Central New York, the Americans fended off the British and Haudenosaunee forces besieging Fort Stanwix, thus preventing British control of the Hudson-Mohawk corridor. That same month, they defeated a combined British-Hessian force at Bennington, Vermont.

However, the bulk of the American forces were concentrated farther south to prevent the British from taking the country's de facto capital, Philadelphia. At the Battle of Brandywine, fought on September 11, Washington was again beaten by Howe, opening the road to the City of Brotherly Love. In an attempt to redeem himself, Washington launched an overly complex and ultimately failed attack on Germantown. Nonetheless, his tenacity impressed potential European allies, including the French.

Then came the Battles of Saratoga. American forces under Horatio Gates and Benedict Arnold confronted British General John Burgoyne in New York's Hudson Valley. The first engagement, at Freeman's Farm on September 19, was indecisive. The second, at Bemis Heights on October 7, was a total American victory. Burgoyne's army imploded and was forced to surrender nearly 6,000 troops. Saratoga marked a key turning point in the war. Upon receiving the news, Washington wrote his brother:

> I most devoutly congratulate you, my Country, and every well-wisher to the Cause on this Signal Stroke of Providence.[98]

On November 1, 1777, the Continental Congress proclaimed the First National Day of Thanksgiving. The resounding result played a crucial role in convincing the French to team up with the Americans to strike blows at their cross-channel rivals. The course of the war had been decisively altered. However, many more years of suffering would be necessary before it could be brought to a decisive conclusion at Yorktown.

Building yet another army

Washington and his men spent the bitter winter of 1777–78 at Valley Forge, just 20 miles from Philadelphia. 2,000 of his 12,000 troops died from starvation, disease, malnutrition, and exposure, and countless others deserted. 1,000 died in February alone. Washington paid tribute to those who stuck it out:

> Naked and starving as they are, we cannot enough admire the incomparable patience and fidelity of the soldiery.[99]

Meanwhile, Washington made his headquarters in a handsome stone house rented from a local mill owner. He lived there with his wife, Martha, as well as the Marquis de Lafayette, several aides, and eight servants, including slaves.

Nathaniel Greene, Washington's most trusted general, was a fellow natural leader and organizer. Appointed as quartermaster, Greene understood that armies ultimately run on logistics. Once he turned his skilled attention to this task, things began to turn around: food, tools, hardware, clothing, muskets, and bayonets began to flow into the camp, and log cabins replaced canvas tents.

On February 6, 1778, the Franco-American Treaty of Alliance and Treaty of Amity and Commerce transformed the conflict into a global war. As a result, France began providing the Americans with crucial naval power, troops, financial support, and supplies. Things were looking up, and a steady stream of patriots joined or rejoined Washington's encampment.

A few weeks later, the eccentric Prussian military officer Friedrich Wilhelm von Steuben arrived at Valley Forge and began systematically training the Continental Army in European military drill and discipline. Although a fervent fan of the American cause, he was at first dismayed by the American people. Yet, as historian Paul Lockhart relates:

> "The genius of this nation," Steuben wrote to an old comrade in Prussia after the war, "is not to be compared . . . with that of the Prussians,

> Austrians, or French. You say to your soldier, 'Do this,' and he does it; but I am obliged to say, 'This is the reason why you ought to do that,' and then he does it."[100]

Within weeks, the disheveled Continental Army was starting to look like a professional fighting force. By late Spring, Valley Forge was the fourth-largest city in the country, home to 20,000 men, women, and children from all thirteen colonies, who spoke dozens of European, African, and Indigenous languages. Against these odds, Washington once again pulled a rabbit out of a hat, rebuilding an army from almost nothing.

In the summer of 1778, the new army resumed campaigning in the stifling New Jersey heat, fighting a brutal draw at the Battle of Monmouth. Nonetheless, the British could no longer hold Philadelphia, and Von Steuben's training was clearly giving results.

Britain's "Southern Strategy" and the road to Yorktown

After looting Philadelphia on their way out, the British shifted gears yet again, temporarily giving up on almost the entirety of the North. In doing so, they hoped to find more Loyalist support among the slaveocrats. However, they alienated many Southerners by promising freedom to escaped slaves who joined their army, and by destroying plantations and farms. The Hessians, in particular, had a reputation for thorough looting.

The British captured Savannah, Georgia, on December 29, 1778, and successfully defended it against a combined American-French siege in the fall of 1779.

In 1779, the Americans kept busy with a series of genocidal campaigns against the Indians, as we'll discuss further down.

1780 opened with a series of British wins as the fighting in the South descended into partisan savagery. In May of that year, British forces captured Charleston, South Carolina, along with roughly 5,000 Continental troops—one of the worst American defeats of the war. That September, the strategic Hudson River stronghold of West Point was nearly lost when a disgruntled Benedict Arnold plotted to hand it over to the British in exchange for a high command in the British Army.

At the Battle of Waxhaws on May 29, British cavalry under Banastre Tarleton defeated Colonel Abraham Buford's force. Patriot accounts alleged that Tarleton's men cut down Americans who were attempting to surrender in cold blood—thereafter known as "Tarleton's Quarter."

In August, British forces under Cornwallis routed Horatio Gates's army at Camden, South Carolina, in what many consider the most humiliating patriot loss of the Revolution. After Camden, Congress replaced Gates with the exceptional Nathanael Greene, who formally took command of the Southern Department in December 1780.

On October 7, 1780, the southern tide began to turn in the patriots' favor with the Battle of Kings Mountain in South Carolina. Scots-Irish militiamen—known as "overmountain men"—succeeded in killing or capturing a 1,000-strong loyalist force.

Then, on January 17, 1781, Daniel Morgan used a double envelopment maneuver to destroy the British cavalry at the Battle of Cowpens. In one of the most brilliant tactical victories in American military history, he avenged the Americans who had been massacred by Banastre Tarleton. Battles at Guilford Courthouse in March and Eutaw Springs in September rounded out the fighting in the Carolinas with a pair of Pyrrhic British victories.

Finally, after a three-week siege, the British were trapped on the Virginia peninsula near Yorktown by American and French troops, supported by the French Navy. Although sporadic fighting would continue for another year, Cornwallis's loss and subsequent surrender of 8,000 troops on October 19, 1781 was the conflict's last major engagement.

Cornwallis was conspicuously absent from the surrender ceremony, and his sword was handed to the Americans by a subordinate. James Thacher, who served as a medical doctor in the American army, wrote the following in his memoirs:

> We are not to be surprised that the pride of the British officers is humbled on this occasion, as they have always entertained an exalted opinion of their own military prowess, and affected to view the Americans as a contemptible, undisciplined rabble. But there is no display of magnanimity when a great commander shrinks from the inevitable misfortunes of war, and when it is considered that Lord Cornwallis has frequently appeared in splendid triumph at the head of his army by which he is almost adored, we conceive it incumbent on him cheerfully to participate in their misfortunes and degradations, however humiliating; but it is said he gives himself up entirely to vexation and despair.[101]

On September 3, 1783, the Treaty of Paris officially ended the war, and American independence was formally recognized.

This begs the crucial question: how did a largely improvised army and fledgling government manage to defeat the world's mightiest Empire, especially in light of the many setbacks and strategic shifts outlined above?

The answer lies partly in the British predicament. Despite their formidable navy, army, and thousands of mercenaries, they were an expeditionary force fighting far from home. They faced a hostile population, could not destroy the Continental Army, and failed to control much territory beyond a few major cities. While they won many battles, they struggled to win the ones that truly shaped public opinion.

It is also worth emphasizing the role of the French. The Americans certainly acquitted themselves with courage in many battles and endured inhuman conditions in between. But without France's economic and military support, they likely could not have held out as long as they did. By threatening British imperial interests elsewhere in the world, the French forced Britain to spread its forces thin. In one of history's many rich ironies, however, France's financial assistance to the Americans contributed to the fiscal crisis that bankrupted the *ancien régime*, setting the stage for its own revolutionary overthrow just a few years later.

Whatever one might think about the vain, aristocratic Washington and the rest of the so-called Founding Fathers, it took no small amount of calculated courage to rebel on that scale. By aiming for total separation, they faced execution for treason if they had failed.

As for Washington's less-than-spectacular military prowess, he at least understood the asymmetries of what was ultimately a war of attrition. Like the consuls of the early Roman Republic,* he doggedly rebuilt his army's discipline and morale, time and again, no matter how many times he was beaten. With the population and resources of an enormous continent to draw on, he was able to hold out longer than his opponents. In this, he followed in the footsteps of the Roman general, Quintus Fabius Maximus, whose patient "Fabian" strategy—avoiding major battles while preserving his army—helped wear down Hannibal and buy Rome the time it needed to win the Second Punic War.

In short, the Continental Army didn't need to defeat the redcoats outright; it just needed to survive and make British victory impossible. As Henry Kissinger would later observe about Vietnam:

> The conventional army loses if it does not win. The guerrilla wins if he does not lose.[102]

The revolutionary masses

There is more than a grain of truth in the idea that white men of property stood on both sides of the conflict. After all, it was ultimately white men of property who reaped the greatest rewards.

However, a general without an army is not likely to win many battles, let alone a revolutionary war. Behind the emergent American bourgeoisie stood hundreds of thousands of ordinary men and women. Many were willing to fight, suffer, and die for liberty. Just as there are "two Americas" today, there were, broadly speaking, two kinds of patriots: those with plenty of wealth, and those without.

* Highest elected office of the Roman Republic. Two consuls were elected every year, each with the power of veto over the other. Outside of the city of Rome, the consuls served as commanders in chief of the Roman legions with unlimited powers during military campaigns.

For decades, the common wisdom was that roughly one-third of colonists backed independence, another third sided with the King, and the final third were neutral. Some, such as Quakers and Mennonites, opposed the war for religious reasons. Others barely knew what was happening because they were more concerned with basic survival on the far western frontier.

However, more modern research suggests a balance of 40–45 per cent committed patriots, 15–20 per cent actively supporting the Crown, with the rest somewhere in between. Regardless of the exact figures, most colonists just wanted peace, prosperity, and stability. When the colonial relationship could no longer ensure these conditions, independence became inevitable. Although plenty of Americans were inspired to fight after reading the fiery political tracts of the day, most were probably motivated by personal and practical concerns rather than sweeping ideological goals.

Waging the war over eight long years took a heroic collective effort, and ordinary Americans contributed far more than soldiers. They provisioned and supplied the armies, manufactured muskets, cannons, and ammunition, and bought bonds from the Continental Congress with their meager savings to fund the resistance. They also offered food, medical assistance, and refuge to the wounded and those hunted by the British, putting themselves at enormous risk.

Women played an unsung but crucial role. During the anti–Stamp Act and Townshend Act movement, many participated in the loosely organized Daughters of Liberty. They helped enforce boycotts and produced homespun cloth to increase the self-sufficiency of the colonies. During the war, they organized "spinning bees" to provide garments for the troops. Many managed farms, taverns, and other businesses when their fathers, brothers, or husbands were absent or deceased. Others acted as spies and informants, passing crucial information about British troop movements to the rebels. Camp followers, usually the wives, widows, or daughters of enlisted men—not officers—performed hard physical labor under difficult conditions for little or no compensation.

Also, although America lacked a navy, its smugglers ran the British lines to import supplies. Privateers—state-sanctioned pirates—disrupted British shipping, capturing 600 British vessels worth $18 million.

In short, revolutionary victory required more than lofty ideas and military hardware, as important as these were. It depended on the collective efforts of a plurality of ordinary Americans.

The people in arms

As Marxists, we recognize that in the final analysis, fundamental social change can only come through the use of force. As Engels succinctly put it in *Anti-Dühring*:

> [F]orce . . . plays yet another role in history, a revolutionary role; that, in the words of Marx, it is the midwife of every old society pregnant with a new one, that it is the instrument with the aid of which social movement forces its way through and shatters the dead, fossilised political forms.[103]

As we've seen, the British authorities were not about to back down in the face of mere protests and petitions. In their view, the Declaration of Independence was merely a laughable statement of intent. If the colonies wanted their freedom, they would have to win it by force. But who would do the fighting?

These days, the word "militiaman" conjures up images of right-wing, neofascist gun nuts patrolling the US-Mexico border for undocumented immigrants. However, in the American Revolution, the colonial and state militiamen were a vibrant expression of the armed people. Also known as Minutemen, they were the volunteer army of ordinary Americans, ready to grab their muskets at a moment's notice.

The origins of the militias date back to the earliest colonial settlements. At that time, every able-bodied man was typically required to serve for the common defense. Militia units often elected their own officers. This reflected the relatively egalitarian structure of colonial society, at least among white men.

After the first ambush-style skirmishes between redcoats and Minutemen at Lexington and Concord, as many as 20,000 armed men from as far away as Vermont and New Hampshire surged into the Boston area. A circle of campfires ten miles long surrounded the city, which was practically an island at the time, connected to the mainland only by the narrow "Boston Neck." These were yeoman farmers, ordinary workingmen, small-scale artisans, the poor, whites, Blacks, and Stockbridge Indians from Western Massachusetts. This was an elemental, mass-armed uprising in open defiance of the state, an anticipation of the early armies of the French Republic.

In the disdainful view of the British general, John Burgoyne, they were "a rabble in arms, flushed with insolence."[104] And yet, it was these part-time soldiers who drove the British out of Boston.

All told, an estimated 350,000 Americans fought for the patriots during the eight-year war. This sounds impressive—and it was. Still, it needs to be qualified. Never were there more than 90,000 under arms at any given time, and sometimes as few as 12,000. Even at its peak, the Continental Army proper never exceeded 35,000 soldiers. State militias always supplemented the regular army, often serving for weeks or months. The vast majority of those who fought were men, but some women also served, including a small number who fought in combat, sometimes disguised as men. After 1778, France contributed about 12,000 troops and significant naval power to the American cause.

For their part, the British fielded about 50,000 regulars, plus around 30,000 German mercenaries—mainly from Hesse-Kassel. Up to 50,000 Americans also fought for the British.

It is also important to highlight the participation of slaves and free Blacks on both sides. The British organized several such units, including the Black Dragoons, Black Pioneers, and Lord Dunmore's infamous "Ethiopian Regiment." About 3,000–5,000 served in combat. Many other escaped slaves served as laborers, servants, guides, and spies.

On the patriot side, between 5,000 and 9,000 Black soldiers and sailors served during the war. Despite their relatively small numbers, they played an outsized role. Though most units were segregated, others were integrated, something that wouldn't be seen again until after World War II. Not all served voluntarily; some were compelled to do so as substitutes for their masters. And while some fought for freedom from Britain, others fought because they had been promised emancipation.

Unsurprisingly, New England was ahead of the historical curve on this particular question. Coming from a state where 40 per cent of the population were slaves, Washington had been shocked to see Black men under arms when he arrived to take command of his army in Massachusetts, where just 2 per cent of the population was enslaved.

In a preview of the 54th Massachusetts Regiment, which would see distinguished service during the Civil War, the 1st Rhode Island Regiment is widely regarded as the first predominantly Black regiment in US military history. On February 14, 1778, the Rhode Island General Assembly passed the "Slave Enlistment Act." The statute authorized the enlistment of "every able-bodied Negro, Mulatto, or Indian Man Slave" in the newly formed regiment. The law further resolved:

> [T]hat every Slave, so enlisting, shall, upon his passing Muster . . . be immediately discharged from the Service of his Master or Mistress; and be absolutely *free*, as though he had never been encumbered with any Kind of Servitude or Slavery. And in Case such Slave shall, by Sickness or otherwise, be rendered unable to maintain himself, he shall not be chargeable to his Master or Mistress, but shall be supported at the Expense of the State.[105]

The "Black Regiment's" heroism was highlighted in an article by Farrell Evans:

> Led by all-white officers, the Black regiment saw its first combat experience at the Battle of Rhode Island. On August 29, 1778, the regiment was on assignment at Aquidneck Island in Narragansett Bay

> near Newport, where they had been tasked with guarding a defensive position anchoring the Continental Army's right wing.
>
> Over the course of the battle, the regiment drove back three Hessian (German) regiments of the British army. "It was in driving back these furious attacks that our Black regiment distinguished itself with deeds of great valor," remembered a regiment member. "Yes, this was a regiment of Negroes, fighting for our liberty and independence."
>
> Major General John Sullivan spoke for Washington's satisfaction at the regiment's performance when he said, "by the best information the commander-in-chief thinks that the regiment will be entitled to a proper share of the honors of the day.[106]

As compared to the British regulars and Hessians, these were truly the "people in arms."

The Continental Army and guerrilla warfare

As in all revolutionary civil wars, everything from the chain of command to logistics to basic sanitation often got quite messy. It was precisely to introduce a modicum of discipline that Congress approved the formation of the Continental Army. In addition, such a force could be deployed more flexibly and strategically anywhere in the country, unlike militias, which were limited to their state boundaries.

In this, there are some noteworthy similarities to the formation of the Red Army in 1918 under Trotsky, created to defend the young Soviet Republic in Russia. Just as the Continental Army evolved from the colonial militias, the Red Army emerged from the chaotic workers' militias and Red Guards. To defeat the centralized imperialist firepower that sought to crush them, both revolutions had to transform enthusiastic but undisciplined volunteers into a professional fighting force.

Both the Continental Army and Red Army accomplished this, at least in part, with the aid of trained military professionals who threw in their lot with the revolution. Despite their efforts to maximize military efficiency, however, both armies were compelled to fight alongside partisan detachments and local militias that continued to operate semi-independently.

However, there is one crucial difference. Though most of the Continental Army was composed of men of little or no property, it was ultimately an instrument of the nascent American bourgeoisie. The Red Army, at least in its revolutionary period under Lenin and Trotsky, was an instrument of the workers' state—and it was fully conscious of that role. As Trotsky wrote in "The Red Soldier's Manual":

> Without discipline there can be no organization, no industry, no government, no coordinated action, no victory. In military affairs discipline is even more important, more necessary than anywhere else. Discipline in the Red Army means submission to the laws of the workers' and peasants' government, observance of the rules of the army, exemplary fulfillment of military duties and of the orders of the commanders and commissars.
>
> In capitalist armies discipline is based on class divisions; the privates have to submit to the aristocratic and bourgeois officers. In the Red Army the commanding staff is being recruited from among the peasants and workers. The discipline of the Red Army is based not on submission, but upon the necessity for an adequate division of labor, adequate leadership and responsibility.[107]

In short, Washington and Trotsky both led expressions of "the armed people," but each represented different classes with different historical missions.

Washington took command of the Continental Army at Cambridge, Massachusetts, on July 3, 1775. Unlike the militias, the Continental soldiers signed up for longer enlistments, first one year, and later three or until the war's end. Modeled on European forces of the period, it featured a hierarchical command structure with officers appointed from above, not by democratic election.

However, desiring discipline and structure is not the same as achieving it. The Continental Army faced chronic shortages of munitions and equipment, and was wracked by disease and desertion. Under the Articles of Confederation, there was no central power to enforce financial requisitions, and the states bickered over whether or not everyone was pulling their weight. As a result, soldiers often went months without being paid, while their families at home risked starvation. In January 1781, Pennsylvania and New Jersey soldiers mutinied over unpaid wages, lack of supplies, and expired enlistments. At times, simply keeping the army intact was itself a victory.

Some estimates suggest that as many as 25 per cent of Continental Army soldiers deserted at some point during the war, especially during winter, planting season, after major defeats, or when the fighting was close to their own homes, which they were desperate to personally defend. In addition, it must be said that both Continental Army soldiers and militia engaged in the occasional plundering of American property, which only undermined support for the Revolution.

Major battles typically involved both Continental regulars and militia units called up to defend their home areas. These brought with them invaluable knowledge of local geography and conditions. However, Washington and other Continental officers often expressed frustration with the militia's unreliability, and militiamen often resented the regular army's hierarchy and harsh discipline. In the words of historian Richard M. Ketchum:

> This was a society unlike any in the world, in which people placed great value on their status as independent individuals, beholden to no man. They were suspicious of standing armies and impatient of discipline, and while they realized the need to resist the enemy, they preferred to do so on their own terms at a time and place of their own choosing. It did not make for the kind of army on which generals could pin great hopes.[108]

The Continental Army was eventually able to conduct prolonged campaigns and to fight set-piece battles against British regulars. But the militias excelled at sabotage, harassing enemy supply lines, and guerrilla warfare. After all, they knew the terrain like the back of their hand and had the support of the local population.

While popular imagination often focuses on big battles like Bunker Hill, Saratoga, and Yorktown, much of the Revolutionary War was fought as an irregular, guerrilla insurgency, relying on stealthy hit-and-run tactics. The British complained that the Americans, and especially the militia, didn't "fight like gentlemen." Instead, they picked off officers from afar and hid behind trees, "like Indians." At times, they even engaged in scorched-earth tactics to deny supplies to the British. Today, they would be considered not merely rebels, but terrorists.

British and German troops were better trained, had better artillery, more ammunition, and more reliable supply lines. Why should the patriots always fight them head-on? As in Vietnam, Iraq, and Afghanistan, the ability for insurgents to blend in with the locals made it virtually impossible to target them without resorting to atrocities against civilians—something that also happened during the Revolution.

As it happens, lessons from the American experience would be studied by later anticolonial movements around the world, from Asia to Africa and Latin America. The tactics used by Ethan Allen and his Vermont "Green Mountain Boys," as well as Thomas Sumter, Andrew Pickens, and the "Swamp Fox" Francis Marion in the Carolina backcountry swamps were strikingly similar to those later used by Mao Zedong, Ho Chi Minh, and Che Guevara.

The creation of the Continental Army marked a crucial step toward the formation of an American national identity and bourgeois state apparatus. But the militias remained the heart and soul of the revolt—ordinary citizens taking up arms to defend their homes and liberties. As we'll see, after the revolution, the legacy of these relatively egalitarian "bodies of armed men" would have to be stamped out to ensure a monopoly of violence in the hands of the American bourgeois state.

Revolutionary civil war

The fratricidal nature of the conflict made it particularly brutal as neighbors were pitted against neighbors and families were torn apart. Fathers disowned sons, brothers fired shots at each other, and women were forced to choose between their husbands and their fathers. As happened during and after the Civil War, the events of the revolution led to generations of bitterness. Benjamin Franklin's own son, William, who served as the royal governor of New Jersey, remained a loyalist to the end and was never reconciled with his father, even after the revolution.

Especially in the South, the guerrilla nature of much of the fighting devolved into savage raids, ambushes, rapes, and revenge killings between neighbors. Land disputes, family feuds, grudges, and economic rivalries blended with political loyalties. Farms were torched, livestock stolen or killed, wells poisoned, and mills, bridges, ferries, and roads were destroyed. Dead bodies were mutilated and prisoners tortured, scalped, shot, or hanged. In the Carolina backcountry, the conflict erupted into chaos that neither Congress nor the British authorities could control, as the line between soldiers and civilians was blurred beyond recognition.

Neutrality was all but impossible in many areas as both sides demanded oaths of allegiance, requisitioned supplies, and punished those who wouldn't go all in on their side. Patriots often treated loyalists even more harshly than British soldiers, as they considered them traitors. Loyalists were beaten, imprisoned without trial, tarred and feathered, and their property was expropriated or destroyed.

In response, loyalists formed military units of their own, including the notorious Queen's Rangers. Originally formed in 1776, they provided a model of military efficiency and ruthless unconventional tactics under the leadership of Robert Rogers and, later, more infamously, under Lieutenant Colonel John Graves Simcoe.

Both sides committed acts that would be considered war crimes by modern standards. Some patriots captured by the British were summarily hanged for treason. After the Battle of Kings Mountain, the victorious patriots hanged nine loyalist prisoners in retaliation for previous loyalist executions.

In 1778, British-allied Indians and loyalists massacred hundreds of patriot civilians in Cherry Valley, New York, and in the Wyoming Valley of Pennsylvania. Men, women, and children were slaughtered, houses were burned, and survivors were left homeless as winter approached.

Even the Haudenosaunee Confederacy turned on itself during the Revolution. While Mohawk, Seneca, Cayuga, and Onondaga warriors fought with the British, Oneida and Tuscarora warriors sided with the Americans in the defense of Fort Stanwix. This led to the collapse of the Great Law of Peace that had united the Six Nations for centuries, a function of the impossible pressures faced by Indigenous peoples when confronted with relentless American expansionism.

These days, conservatives, liberals, and reformists alike decry the "Red Terror"* and the formation of the *cheka*† under the leadership of Felix Dzerzhinsky during the Russian Revolution. They have probably never even heard of the Committee for Detecting and Defeating Conspiracies, a New York–based surveillance and counterintelligence unit that specialized in rooting out loyalists.

It was headed by John Jay, the future Federalist and first Chief Justice of the United States. The committee used informants, intercepted correspondence, and held inquisitorial proceedings. Suspects' right to due process was limited, and the committee could arrest or imprison people merely out of suspicion. Refusal to swear oaths of loyalty to the patriot cause was itself considered evidence of disloyalty, even when it was refused on religious grounds. The committee could restrict the movement of suspects and their families.

* The so-called Red Terror refers to measures taken by the Bolsheviks in response to the assassination of prominent Bolshevik leaders and the attempted murder of Lenin by terrorists. These measures were a defensive response to the White Terror of the counterrevolutionaries, who wished to drown the revolution in blood.

† Revolutionary intelligence service created by the Bolsheviks during the Russian Civil War to root out counterrevolutionaries.

Jay's committee also had the power to recommend the confiscation of property for reasons of "national security"—and to generate revenue for the cash-strapped revolutionary government. It could also order that suspected loyalists be sent behind British lines or exiled to other colonies. In all of this, there was no appeals process, independent review, or accountability.

The hypocrisy of today's capitalist apologists is evident. In defense of bourgeois private property, any methods and means are allowed. But if similar measures are taken to defend a workers' state, they are condemned as terrorism and barbarism. That being said, we should not confuse the repression and restriction of basic rights by the capitalists today, during their system's period of senile decay, with the defensive measure demanded by their progressive revolutionary struggle for power. In the words of Herbert Aptheker:

> [O]ne must not depict the nature of the sturdy ancestor in terms of the foul offspring.[109]

By definition, revolutions and civil wars are divisive and polarizing. Whether we like it or not, they tend to be bloody and brutal affairs. However, there is a simple way to avoid the kinds of excesses seen in the past. Under modern conditions, the sheer numbers and economic leverage of the working class could bring capitalist society to its knees with virtually no bloodshed. However, this will only be possible if the full power of the proletariat is mobilized by a farsighted Marxist leadership committed to the total overthrow of capitalism.

Economic dislocation, death, and disease

The First Revolution saw hundreds of military clashes across a vast theater of war. These engagements ranged from major battles involving thousands to small skirmishes between pickets or patrols. In between battles, armies established camps and scoured the land for provisions, not always gently, as we have seen. Virtually no corner of the colonies went untouched.

As usual during epoch-making crises, some people profited handsomely from the chaos, while others lost everything they had.

For the majority, life got very hard for a very long time. The scale of suffering the first generation of Americans had to endure to win their freedom is unfathomable to those living in the United States today.

Trade collapsed virtually overnight as Parliament tried to squeeze the colonies into submission. Exports fell from £3 million in 1774 to almost nothing by 1776, leading to dire shortages. With thousands of men under arms at any given time, labor was also in short supply, disrupting both farming and manufacturing.

Between 1775 and 1781, prices increased by as much as 10,000 per cent in some localities. A pound of butter that cost $0.10 in 1777 cost $12 by 1779. The Continental dollar was so devalued that, as George Washington ruefully observed, "A wagon-load of money will scarcely purchase a wagon-load of provisions."[110]

Boston saw bread riots in 1777, and women in Poughkeepsie, New York, seized tea from merchants they accused of hoarding supplies. The economic privations and political tensions were so severe that the population of some major cities simply collapsed. Philadelphia's fell from 40,000 to 20,000, and New York's fell from 25,000 to just 5,000 early in the war, before British occupation brought the loyalist crowds back. Tens of thousands on both sides of the divide found themselves as internally displaced refugees.

Wartime deaths for the patriots are estimated at about 25,000. The British and Germans suffered around 24,000 and 8,000 deaths, respectively. However, these numbers are somewhat deceiving. Patriot combat deaths numbered around 6,800, while the British lost between 7,000 and 8,000 in battle. Another 3,000–4,000 American loyalists are estimated to have died on the battlefield or from their wounds.

The real killer was disease. Nearly 75 per cent of soldiers who died during the war succumbed to microbial or viral infections, including as many as 11,000 American prisoners of war who died on British penal ships. Malnutrition weakened immune systems, and primitive knowledge of sanitation and medicine often meant the cure was worse than the malady.

Typhus, carried by lice, spread quickly. Dysentery came from contaminated water. Malaria, scurvy, and pneumonia also stalked the land. But the most feared disease, by far, was smallpox. The illness killed 30 per cent of those infected. Survivors were often left permanently scarred.

The role of disease in shaping world history, and wars in particular, is not generally appreciated. For example, a crippling smallpox epidemic swept through the Continental Army during the 1775–76 campaign against Canada. It cut the army's combat effectiveness in half and changed the course of the conflict. As John Adams wrote the aftermath:

> Our Misfortunes in Canada, are enough to melt an Heart of Stone. The Small Pox is ten times more terrible than Britons, Canadians and Indians together. This was the Cause of our precipitate Retreat from Quebec, this the Cause of our Disgraces at the Cedars. — I dont mean that this was all. There has been Want, approaching to Famine, as well as Pestilence. And these Discouragements seem to have so disheartened our Officers, that none of them seem to Act with Prudence and Firmness.[111]

In another example, George Washington's 1777 decision to inoculate his soldiers with smallpox to induce immunity is considered one of his most important achievements. As he wrote to Patrick Henry:

> [Smallpox] is more destructive to an Army in the Natural way than the Enemy's Sword.[112]

Such was the state of affairs at the end of the war. The colonists would soon learn that, as hard as leaving the British Empire had been, the first few years living without it would be even harder.

A continental war for and against empire

Most people associate the Revolution with battles fought in New England, the Hudson Valley, the Mid-Atlantic states, Virginia, and perhaps, the Carolinas. But the fighting ranged well beyond that core, from Canada to the Caribbean, from Florida to Indiana. It even extended into the Atlantic Ocean and off the British coast, with the exploits of the Scottish-born American captain John Paul Jones at the Battle of Flamborough Head.

Like the Seven Years' War, the Revolution was part of a broader international struggle between the great powers for colonial domination. As we've seen, France, Spain, and Russia all had designs on parts of North America. Controlling the New World's colossal wealth and denying it to their rivals would greatly affect their fortunes in the Old World.

The American merchant capitalists and slave lords saw themselves as potential players in this early version of the "Great Game" as well. They, too, were determined to conquer and expand. It was not by accident that they styled themselves the *Continental* Congress, or that they built a *Continental* Army.

Already at this stage, the seeds of American imperialism were being sown. In many ways, the revolution had always been about land. The prospect of owning your own plot and being beholden to no one but yourself was the original version of the "American Dream."

The Americans were, therefore, "colonists" in a double sense. Not only were they residents of the British colonies in rebellion, but they also had every intention of colonizing the continent once they were freed from royal restrictions. Even while engaged in a life-and-death fight against the British Empire, they worked to carve out an even bigger American empire of their own. Only the recalcitrant Indigenous population stood in their way. Previewing the actions of modern-day Israel, the American settlers took advantage of the wartime disorder to accelerate their expansionist aims.

The Battle of Oriskany, fought near Fort Stanwix on August 6, 1777, was one of the bloodiest battles of the entire war. An American relief column of about 800 militia, accompanied by Oneida warriors, was ambushed by British-allied Mohawks. With heavy casualties on both sides, it further fractured the already reeling Haudenosaunee Confederacy. The Treaty of Fort Stanwix, signed in 1784, forced massive land cessions on the Six Nations, treating them as conquered peoples even though many of them had remained neutral or supported the Americans.

In 1778–79, George Rogers Clark led a campaign against British frontier posts and their Indigenous allies in the Illinois Country, west of the Appalachian Mountains. After a grueling winter march, Clark forced the surrender of Fort Sackville at Vincennes on February 25, 1779, establishing an American foothold in present-day Indiana that strengthened US claims and supported further westward expansion.

In the summer of 1779, Washington sent troops under John Sullivan and James Clinton on a punitive expedition into the Finger Lakes region of New York, partly to avenge the Cherry and Wyoming Valley massacres, partly to scout the region for future colonial settlement. In a letter dated May 31, 1779, Washington sent Sullivan detailed instructions:

> The expedition you are appointed to command is to be directed against the hostile tribes of the six nations of Indians, with their associates and adherents. The immediate objects are the total destruction and devastation of their settlements and the capture of as many prisoners of every age and sex as possible . . .
>
> I would recommend that some post in the center of the Indian Country should be occupied with all expedition, with a sufficient quantity of provision; whence parties should be detached to lay waste all the settlements around, with instructions to do it in the most effectual manner; that the country may not be merely overrun but destroyed.[113]

It doesn't get any more explicit than that. Washington may have risen to the pinnacle of Virginia society, but he was an indebted and addicted land speculator. Over his lifetime, he bought and sold tens of thousands of acres belonging to the Indians. From an early age, he understood that the future lay in the West, and consolidating the continent under American control was his all-consuming vision.

Sullivan's military excursion was just a small step toward making that vision a reality. What followed was a scorched-earth campaign that can only be described as genocidal. 160,000 bushels of corn and hundreds of acres of beans, squash, fruit orchards, and other vital foodstuffs were destroyed. With the onset of winter, thousands faced starvation.

After 40 Haudenosaunee villages in New York and Pennsylvania were burned to the ground, George Washington became known among the Indians as "the town destroyer." These were well-ordered villages with vibrant local economies, laid-out streets, and log cabins. Some even had glass windows. Men, women, and children were slaughtered in cold blood. The scale of the atrocities was unthinkable, with some soldiers skinning their victims' legs to make riding boots.

Then, in 1782, American militiamen massacred 96 Delaware (Lenape) Indians—mostly women and children—at the Moravian mission village of Gnadenhutten in Ohio. As the Delawares sang Christian hymns in a church, the Pennsylvania militiamen entered the village and voted on whether or not they should kill them. A majority were in favor, so they systematically murdered them with mallets and then scalped them. This, despite a 1778 alliance negotiated between the United States and the Delawares at the Treaty of Fort Pitt.

To add insult to injury, the Treaty of Paris made no mention of Indigenous peoples. The Revolutionary War may have been over, but a further century of wars, massacres, treaty violations, deliberate humiliation, and reservations awaited the continent's original inhabitants.

As for Thomas Jefferson, his vision was to build an "Empire of Liberty," starting with the continental United States. In 1803, he used his executive authority as president to purchase 828,000 square miles of land from France—lands still occupied by dozens of Indian nations. In a February 27, 1803 letter to William Henry Harrison, then serving as the territorial governor of Indiana, he outlined his views on dealing with the Indigenous population:

> [T]his letter being unofficial, and private, I may with safety give you a more extensive view of our policy respecting the Indians, that you may the better comprehend the parts dealt out to you in detail through the

official channel, and observing the system of which they make a part, conduct yourself in unison with it in cases where you are obliged to act without instruction. Our system is to live in perpetual peace with the Indians, to cultivate an affectionate attachment from them, by every thing just and liberal which we can do for them within the bounds of reason, and by giving them effectual protection against wrongs from our own people.

The decrease of game rendering their subsistence by hunting insufficient, we wish to draw them to agriculture, to spinning and weaving. The latter branches they take up with great readiness, because they fall to the women, who gain by quitting the labors of the field for those which are exercised within doors. When they withdraw themselves to the culture of a small piece of land, they will perceive how useless to them are their extensive forests, and will be willing to pare them off from time to time in exchange for necessaries for their farms and families . . . In this way our settlements will gradually circumscribe and approach the Indians, and they will in time either incorporate with us as citizens of the US or remove beyond the Mississippi. The former is certainly the termination of their history most happy for themselves. But in the whole course of this, it is essential to cultivate their love. As to their fear, we presume that our strength and their weakness is now so visible that they must see we have only to shut our hand to crush them, and that all our liberalities to them proceed from motives of pure humanity only. Should any tribe be foolhardy enough to take up the hatchet at any time, the seizing of the whole country of that tribe and driving them across the Mississippi, as the only condition of peace, would be an example to others, and a furtherance of our final consolidation.[114]

And as Jefferson expressed in a letter to Alexander von Humboldt in 1813:

You know, my friend, the benevolent plan we were pursuing here for the happiness of the aboriginal inhabitants in our vicinities. We spared nothing to keep them at peace with one another. To teach them agriculture and the rudiments of the most necessary arts, and to encourage industry

> by establishing among them separate property. In this way they would have been enabled to subsist and multiply on a moderate scale of landed possession. They would have mixed their blood with ours, and been amalgamated and identified with us within no distant period of time. On the commencement of our present war [the War of 1812], we pressed on them the observance of peace and neutrality, but the interested and unprincipled policy of England has defeated all our labors for the salvation of these unfortunate people. They have seduced the greater part of the tribes within our neighborhood, to take up the hatchet against us, and the cruel massacres they have committed on the women and children of our frontiers taken by surprise, will oblige us now to pursue them to extermination, or drive them to new seats beyond our reach.[115]

Indigenous Americans wouldn't be recognized as citizens until 1924, long after most of their lands had been expropriated. To this day, they are treated like second-class inhabitants of their native continent—that is, when they aren't marginalized and ignored altogether.

The world turned upside down

On October 19, 1781, over 7,000 British and Hessian troops marched out of Yorktown to lay down their arms before George Washington and the Marquis de Lafayette. According to contemporary accounts, the British band played a tune called "The World Turn'd Upside Down."[116] An old song from the years of the English Revolution, it had been made popular by the anti-monarchist Levellers and Diggers, with lyrics about absurd inversions of the natural order:

> If buttercups buzz'd after the bee,
>
> If boats were on land, churches on sea,
>
> If ponies rode men and if grass ate the cows,
>
> And cats should be chased into holes by the mouse,
>
> If the mamas sold their babies to the gypsies for half a crown;
>
> If summer were spring and the other way round,
>
> Then all the world would be upside down . . .

To see a man walking with his heels in the air,
And his head and his nose turning down;
To see a man pulling his horse by the tail
Is enough to amaze the whole town.
But now the world is turn'd upside down.[117]

If the surrendering band truly played this tune, it was a fitting choice, indeed.

The British continued to occupy New York and a handful of other positions until the Treaty of Paris was officially signed in September 1783. However, the Empire's will to continue fighting had been broken. When the Prime Minister, Lord North, received news of Cornwallis's surrender, he is reported to have exclaimed, in a fit of apoplexy, "Oh God! It is all over!"

To be sure, the British Empire would continue to dominate much of the globe for another century. But the seeds of its eventual fall from global preeminence were already present in the loss of its American colonies. Over the next few decades, the thirteen disparate states expanded rapidly and began to coalesce into a formidable power, eventually outshining their former overlord. All of this, and more, flowed from the achievement of American independence.

Let's not forget that this was the first successful war of colonial independence in the modern era. The repercussions and long-term social transformations that resulted can hardly be overstated.

Thomas Pownall, a Member of Parliament and former governor of Massachusetts, wrote the following in a 1780 work urging Europe to recognize the new country:

> On the other hand, *this new system* of power, united in and moving round its own proper center, "*had dissolved the effect of all artificial* repulsions which force would create, and hath *formed those natural connections by and under* which its actual interest exists." Founded in Nature, it is growing, by accelerated motions, and accumulated accretion of parts into an independent, organized being, a great and powerful empire. *It has taken its equal station with the nations of the earth.*

> *Video solem orientem in occidente* [I see the sun rising in the West].
>
> North America is become a new primary planet in the system of the world, which while it takes its own course, in its own orbit, must have effect on the orbit of every other planet, and shift the common center of gravity of the whole system of the European world.
>
> North America is *de facto* an independent power *which has taken its equal station with other powers*, and must be so *de jure.*[118]

And as the British statesman Edmund Burke expressed it:

> A great revolution has happened—a revolution made, not by chopping and changing of power in any one of the existing states, but by the appearance of a new state, of a new species, in a new part of the globe.[119]

Although the *fundamental* class basis of the ruling elite remained essentially the same as before independence, this was nonetheless an earth-shaking political and social revolution. In the words of Gordon S. Wood:

> A new democratic society was developing, becoming both a cause and a consequence of the Revolution . . . The older hierarchical and homogeneous society of the eighteenth century . . . now finally fell apart, to be replaced over the subsequent decades with new social relationships and ideas and attitudes, including a radical blurring of the distinction between gentlemen and the rest of society . . .
>
> The "people" were now told repeatedly that they rightfully had a place in politics, and lest they should forget, there were thousands of new rising popular tribunes, men who lacked the traditional attributes of gentlemanly leaders, to remind them, cajole them, even frighten them into political and social consciousness. Under such pressures, the old eighteenth-century world was transformed within a generation or so after independence.[120]

The awakening of the masses to political life was certainly one of the most significant elements of the revolutionary process. Another was the question of expropriations. Relative to the size of the economy and population, the Revolution and its aftermath saw private property expropriated on a scale rarely seen in world history. Already in 1779, Pennsylvania's Divestment Act had confiscated the Penn family's proprietary lands and manorial rights and turned them into public property to be sold or otherwise redistributed.

The Treaty of Paris stipulated that Congress would "recommend" that loyalist property be restored and that no further confiscations occur. However, the Americans simply ignored the recommendation. Every state in the new Union passed laws enabling the confiscation of loyalist property. An estimated £10 million worth of such property was seized, without compensation or legal recourse.

In New York, all lands and rents of the Crown were expropriated, as well as 2.5 million acres of manorial estates. This included the Van Rensselaer manor—which was two-thirds the size of Rhode Island—and the Phillipse estate, which stretched over 300 square miles. The DeLancey family, which had one of the largest fortunes in America, lost property valued at over £100,000.

In North Carolina, the estate of Lord Granville, comprising one-third of the entire colony, was also expropriated. The situation was similar in Virginia, where the Fairfax estate of six million acres was taken over, even though Lord Fairfax hadn't sided with the Tories.

Many of the estates were broken up into smaller parcels—an important land reform and a cornerstone of the national-democratic revolution. The aim was to create a large class of small, independent farmers. However, market pressures would inevitably erode these measures as larger landowners gobbled up smaller ones. Thus was the Jeffersonian dream of a yeomen's republic negated in practice by the impersonal laws of capitalist accumulation.

Another legacy of feudal land tenure imported into the colonies were quit-rents, annual payments made by landholders to a proprietor or the Crown to acknowledge ongoing ownership rights. The collection of these payments had collapsed during the Revolution, and were phased out altogether in the years that followed.

What remained of inheritance laws such as entail and primogeniture were also abolished in the years and decades after the

Revolution, though the timing varied by state. Individual property rights, not hereditary privilege, now reigned supreme. This allowed property to be divided more equally among heirs and made land more freely transferable in general. However, after a generation or two of partible inheritance, many plots became too small to be viable, further fueling the frenzy for land in the West.

The official churches that existed in some colonies were also cut off from government funding as legal separation of church and state eventually became the norm throughout the new country.

As for slavery, it was outlawed or put on a path toward abolition in several Northern states both during and after the Revolution, a tremendous step forward for human freedom. However, the practice received a new lease on life in the South after the invention of the cotton gin in 1793. The international slave trade was banned, effective in 1808, but illegal smuggling and the domestic slave trade continued for decades. By the eve of the Civil War, there were more slaves in the country than there had been people at the end of the Revolution.

A *nouveau riche* sprang up almost overnight, as lawyers, skilled craftsmen, merchants, and bankers rose up to fill the vacuum left by the fleeing Tories and British colonial officials. As many as 100,000 loyalists fled the country, mainly to Canada, though some ended up in Britain, the Bahamas, and the Caribbean. This was among the largest political and economic emigrations in modern history—10 times as many per capita as fled the French Revolution between 1789 and 1792.

Many of these emigrants were among New England's and New York's wealthiest and most educated. As for those loyalists who remained in the new country, some were forced into the ranks of ordinary workers after their property was expropriated. Many former loyalists faced discrimination or social ostracism for decades. In some states, laws barred them from voting, holding office, or practicing certain professions, including law and medicine. Others enacted bills of attainder, targeting specific loyalists for punishment without trial. Still others were required to swear loyalty oaths to the new government, and refusal could result in the loss of citizenship rights.

Women whose husbands had fought for the losing side were publicly humiliated and their children harassed. The children of dead or exiled loyalists were often left destitute or placed with patriot families, who treated them like servants.

Benjamin Franklin's estranged son, William, was imprisoned for two years, and his property was confiscated. The Anglican minister, Samuel Seabury, was arrested multiple times, and his church closed. Eventually, he was forced to flee to England.

In a letter to a British cabinet official, Lord Hardwicke, a New York loyalist, described the predicament faced by those still loyal to the crown during the six-month British evacuation of New York City:

> The Rebels breathe the most rancorous and malignant Spirit everywhere. Committees and Associations are formed in every Colony, and Resolves passed that no Refugees shall return nor have their Estates [land property] restored. The Congress and Assemblies look on tamely and want [lack] either the Will or the Power to check [stop] those Proceedings. In short, the Mob now reigns as fully and uncontrolled as in the Beginning of our Troubles, and America is as hostile to Great Britain at this Hour as she was at any Period during the War.[121]

*Vae victis!**

Aspirations betrayed

Most participants in great events are unaware of the underlying factors that motivate their actions. Economic and political interests are ideologically refracted and expressed in terms of "freedom versus tyranny," "democracy versus monarchy," "mob rule versus order," and so on.

Very often, the masses are more clear about what they *don't* want than what they *do* want. Nonetheless, necessity finds a way to

---

* Latin for *Woe to the vanquished!*

express itself, and when conditions are ripe, events can take on a life of their own.

By now, it should be clear that different classes had conflicting aspirations for the revolution. Different social layers fought for and against opposing conceptions of property, freedom, and democracy. As Alan Taylor wrote in *American Revolutions*:

> Historians debate how revolutionary the revolution was in its consequences. Some find little substantive change and focus on continuities from the colonial era. Other scholars emphasize expanding economic opportunities and increased political participation by common white men as radical consequences of the revolution. Both views convey only part of the story. The revolution intensified trends already underway, including political assertion by common men, territorial expansion at native expense, and the westward spread of slavery. Acceleration and intensification combined continuity with change.
>
> The greatest transformation came in the terms of political debate. Rather than generate clear resolutions, the revolution created powerful new contradictions.[122]

For the majority, freedom meant having neither masters nor bosses. For the rich merchants, it meant the freedom to accumulate land and capital and to exploit wage labor. For the slavocracy, it meant the right to own, buy, and sell both land and humans.

As for democracy, most people probably conceive of it as majority-rule decision-making by the people. For the propertied minority, however, it means maintaining their power and privilege while giving the *illusion* of majority rule. It was the *masses* who imposed the ideal of democracy on the country's mythology. Unfortunately, wanting something isn't the same as achieving it in practice.

In the final analysis, it always comes down to power and property, whether in land, capital, slaves, etc. The only democracy the Founders favored was democracy for the bourgeoisie and the slave owners, though reconciling those divergent forms of exploitation would prove impossible in the medium term.

Though we can't conduct a retroactive survey, it's fair to assume most ordinary patriots were motivated by the same things that motivate ordinary workers today: the desire for peace, stability, and a better life for their children. In the context of colonial America, we must also add land to the motivating factors. Those with little or none of it had done most of the fighting and dying. When the war ended, it was only natural that they expected to be rewarded.

To survive wartime conditions, many small producers had been forced to devote more energy to producing goods for sale on the market, instead of for their own consumption. Consequently, stronger market pressures came to bear on rural areas that had previously been subsistence-oriented natural economies.

No longer able to produce all the necessities of life through the combined efforts of the household, they were compelled to buy a wider range of goods from local merchants with ties to the commercial centers on the coast. When there wasn't enough money to cover what was needed, merchants extended credit. This initiated a cycle of indebtedness, further tying small producers to the market as they focused on producing even more commodities for the market.

These processes intensified after the war, particularly in the Northeast. As a result, the burden of debt grew even more onerous, as governments raised taxes on land to keep themselves afloat—at a time when there was very little hard currency in circulation.

In 1787, the Northwest Territory was created. This established the precedent that western lands would be federal property rather than the property of individual states. However, instead of being given to landless veterans, most of these lands were sold to well-heeled speculators. As a result, some managed to acquire new land in the West, but many others had to live off the parcels they already occupied. Furthermore, Article 6 of the Northwest Ordinance explicitly stated:

> There shall be neither slavery nor involuntary servitude in the said territory, otherwise than in the punishment of crimes whereof the party shall have been duly convicted.[123]

This was an important precedent that appeared to put slavery on a path to extinction. We will see in Part Two of this book how this played out.

In the immediate aftermath of the Revolution, the countryside was a pressure cooker of accumulating class rage. Unable to pay their taxes or debts—let alone make a dignified living—many of those who had fought and sacrificed for independence now found themselves driven to financial ruin, foreclosure, and debtors' prison. As we will see further down, this pushed some into open rebellion against the new government.

In the decades that followed, countless small merchants and craftsmen were pushed into the ranks of the urban poor and proletariat, unable to keep up with the growing power of capital. The class struggles between the big merchants and independent household producers in the 1780s and 1790s transformed the rural economy in the North. Over time, this would unleash the agricultural and industrial revolutions of the 19th century, setting the stage for the Civil War and the rise of organized labor.

As an aside, it's worth noting that early attempts by artisans and workers to collectively organize to defend their interests were prosecuted as "illegal combinations in restraint of trade"—i.e., racketeering. Trade unions would be treated as criminal conspiracies well into the early 19th century.

As for women, despite their sacrifices and contributions to the Patriot cause, they were also largely excluded from the revolution's gains. Women's political rights and full citizenship were not recognized by the Constitution. As a result, they couldn't own property in their own names, sign contracts, or control their own wages. They didn't even have the right to custody over their own children. Under the legal doctrine of "coverture," married women had no independent legal identity—their legal existence was "covered" by their husbands.

Women would remain barred from voting and holding office for well over a century. They only won the vote in 1920, in the aftermath of the Russian Revolution, which granted women the right to vote in 1917.

A famous exchange of letters between Abigail Adams and her husband, John, written when he was serving at the Continental Congress, exposes the hypocrisy:

> Abigail: "I long to hear that you have declared an independency—and by the way in the new Code of Laws which I suppose it will be necessary for you to make I desire you would Remember the Ladies, and be more generous and favourable to them than your ancestors. Do not put such unlimited power into the hands of the Husbands. Remember all Men would be tyrants if they could. If perticuliar care and attention is not paid to the Laidies we are determined to foment a Rebelion, and will not hold ourselves bound by any Laws in which we have no voice, or Representation.
>
> That your Sex are Naturally Tyrannical is a Truth so thoroughly established as to admit of no dispute, but such of you as wish to be happy willingly give up the harsh title of Master for the more tender and endearing one of Friend. Why then, not put it out of the power of the vicious and the Lawless to use us with cruelty and indignity with impunity. Men of Sense in all Ages abhor those customs which treat us only as the vassals of your Sex. Regard us then as Beings placed by providence under your protection and in immitation of the Supreem Being make use of that power only for our happiness."[124]
>
> John: "As to your extraordinary Code of Laws, I cannot but laugh. We have been told that our struggle has loosened the bands of Government everywhere. That children and apprentices were disobedient—that schools and colleges were grown turbulent—that Indians slighted their guardians and Negroes grew insolent to their masters.
>
> But your letter was the first intimation that another tribe more numerous and powerful than all the rest were grown discontented.—This is rather too coarse a compliment, but you are so saucy, I won't blot it out."[125]
>
> Abigail: "I can not say that I think you very generous to the Ladies, for whilst you are proclaiming peace and good will to Men, Emancipating all Nations, you insist upon retaining an absolute power over Wives. But you must remember that Arbitary power is like most other things

> which are very hard, very liable to be broken—and notwithstanding all your wise Laws and Maxims we have it in our power not only to free ourselves but to subdue our Masters, and without voilence throw both your natural and legal authority at our feet."[126]

The longstanding American tradition of kicking rank-and-file military veterans to the curb was also inaugurated in the 1780s. Even when they were compensated for their service, payment was often delayed or paid in Continental dollars or other promissory notes rendered nearly worthless by depreciation and inflation. Many veterans returned to devastated farms and families, condemned to poverty with little in the way of public assistance. It wasn't until 1818—long after the war—that Congress passed the first nationwide pension law for Revolutionary War veterans.

Little wonder that a group of officers at Washington's postwar headquarters in Newburgh, New York, floated the idea of a coup. Their idea was to march on Congress to pressure it to cough up their back pay and pensions—or else. Many of them were deeply suspicious of the masses and favored installing a "strong man," perhaps even a monarchy—though "King George I" of the United States wouldn't have gone over too well.

In the famous "Newburgh Address," Washington appealed to his officers' honor, underscoring his sacrifices to the cause of liberty during the war, including his failing eyesight. Given his stature, he was able to defuse the crisis. As he later put it, the army "is a dangerous instrument to play with." Most Americans have no idea how close the new country came to descending into military dictatorship and an even more terrible civil war, even before the republic was fully founded.

In short, for most ordinary Americans, the outcome fell well short of their expectations. For many others, the result wasn't merely disappointing, but downright reactionary.

Sold down the river

Unsurprisingly, the chaos of the revolution wobbled the slave system. With thousands of men away fighting, discipline on the plantations was undermined. The British—longtime masters of "divide and rule"—saw an opportunity. On November 7, 1775, Virginia's Royal Governor, Lord Dunmore, offered freedom to slaves who escaped their rebel masters and fought for the British. Within months, between 800 and 1,000 had joined his "Ethiopian Regiment."

Sir Henry Clinton's Philipsburg Proclamation of 1779 promised freedom to *any* slave who escaped, not just those who joined the British army. By the war's end, up to 100,000 slaves self-emancipated and fled to British lines.

After the American victory, between 20,000 and 30,000 Black loyalists and escaped slaves were evacuated by the British. Most ended up in Britain, the Bahamas, Jamaica, and Florida. However, around 3,000 were resettled to the harsh climate of Nova Scotia. Not only did they face extreme racism, but they were denied the land grants they had been promised. In 1792, approximately 1,200 of them left Canada for Sierra Leone in West Africa, and established Freetown.

Some British officers sold individuals who had been promised their freedom back into slavery or kept them as personal servants. The majority, however, were simply left behind. Most of these were later recaptured by their former masters. George Washington—who owned 317 men, women, and children over his lifetime—personally reclaimed several who had fled his estate at Mount Vernon. Many slaves who fought for the patriots were also re-enslaved after the war despite promises of freedom—a classic American bait-and-switch.

In the North, where slavery was less economically ingrained, slow-drip emancipation began during the revolution. Vermont banned slavery altogether in 1777. However, emancipation was so gradual that in some cases, individuals remained enslaved for decades. In the case of New York, slavery only ended on July 4, 1827—more than 50 years after the Declaration of Independence. And despite their nominal "freedom," free Blacks faced restrictions on voting, movement, and economic opportunity.

Rather than disappearing, as some founders hoped, the institution of slavery intensified and expanded into new territories. As the slave population increased, so did profits, and Southern states passed stricter laws to control the enslaved and complicate manumission.

The case of Thomas Jefferson graphically illustrates the impossibility of squaring the circle of genuine human liberty with private property of any kind. In his *Notes on the State of Virginia*, he recognized the moral rot slavery introduced into human relations:

> The whole commerce between master and slave is a perpetual exercise of the most boisterous passions, the most unremitting despotism on the one part, and degrading submissions on the other . . .
>
> There must doubtless be an unhappy influence on the manners of our people produced by the existence of slavery among us.[127]

He also understood that the practice simply couldn't go on forever:

> Nothing is more certainly written in the book of fate than that these people are to be free.[128]

And yet, the same person who wrote that "all men are created equal" owned more than 600 slaves over his lifetime. He even had six children with one of his slaves, Sally Hemings, all of whom inherited their mother's status as chattel property. Though he eventually freed the four children who survived infancy, Hemings was never formally emancipated, and their two youngest were only freed after Jefferson's death in 1826.

The moral bankruptcy didn't go unnoticed. As the English literary critic Samuel Johnson asked:

> How is it that we hear the loudest yelps for liberty among the drivers of Negroes?[129]

And as Abigail Adams had written to her husband in September 1774:

> It allways appeard a most iniquitious Scheme to me-fight ourselfs for what we are daily robbing and plundering from those who have as good a right to freedom as we have. You know my mind upon this Subject.[130]

Though it neither excuses nor justifies their actions, men of property like Jefferson were products of their time. The nauseating hypocrisy wasn't merely an individual failing. Rather, it expressed the limits and contradictions of capitalist emergence in a society deeply enmeshed with slave property. Capital's preference may be to exploit wage labor directly, but in its period of primitive accumulation, it will add to its corpulent mass by any means necessary.

Given these contradictions, the origins of the abolitionist movement can also be found in this epoch. James Forten was a free Black war veteran and sailmaker from Philadelphia. He used the fortune he made from his business to support the abolitionist cause. As historian Julie Winch has demonstrated, Forten eloquently exposed the absurdity of slavery in a country made "free" through revolution:

> Forten set the Revolutionary generation against their heirs and found the latter sadly wanting. He praised "Those patriotick citizens, who, after resting from the toils of an arduous war, which achieved our Independence," framed a state constitution that declared: "All men are born equally free and independent, and have certain inherent and indefensible rights, among which are those of enjoying life and liberty."
>
> This was the body of laws under which people of color and whites had been privileged to live. Now it seemed that lawmakers were denying the basic humanity of Black people. "[W]hy are we not to be considered as men? Has the *god* who made the white man and the Black, left any record declaring us a separate species?" . . .
>
> Many of our ancestors were brought here more than one hundred years ago; many of our fathers, many of ourselves, have fought and bled for the Independence of our country . . . [L]et the motto of our Legislature be: "The Law knows no distinction."[131]

Benjamin Rush, a renowned physician and signer of the Declaration of Independence, helped establish the Pennsylvania Society for Promoting the Abolition of Slavery in 1775. Considered the "Father of American Psychiatry," he advocated for free public schools, the compassionate treatment of the mentally ill, and the education of women—a radical departure from the norms of the time.

Speaking to the need to radically transform American morality, religion, education, criminal justice, and slavery, Rush famously wrote:

> There is nothing more common than to confound the terms of *the American Revolution* with those of *the late American war*. The American *war* is over, but this is far from being the case with the American *Revolution*. On the contrary, nothing but the first act of the great drama is closed. It remains yet to establish and perfect our new forms of government; and to prepare the principles, morals, and manners of our citizens for these forms of government after they are established and brought to perfection.[132]

In his truly enlightened view, slavery was a "national crime." He warned that the institution would corrupt the American experiment in freedom:

> The plant of Liberty is of so tender a nature that it cannot thrive long in the neighbourhood of slavery.[133]

Decades later, in a speech delivered on July 5, 1852, Frederick Douglass powerfully summed up the meaning of American Independence from the slaves' perspective:

> I am not included within the pale of this glorious anniversary! Your high independence only reveals the immeasurable distance between us. The blessings in which you, this day, rejoice, are not enjoyed in common. The rich inheritance of justice, liberty, prosperity, and independence, bequeathed by your fathers, is shared by you, not by me. The sunlight that brought light and healing to you has brought stripes and death to me. This Fourth of July is yours, not mine. You may rejoice, I must

> mourn. To drag a man in fetters into the grand illuminated temple of liberty, and call upon him to join you in joyous anthems, were inhuman mockery and sacrilegious irony . . .
>
> What, to the American slave, is your Fourth of July? I answer; a day that reveals to him, more than all other days in the year, the gross injustice and cruelty to which he is the constant victim. To him, your celebration is a sham; your boasted liberty, an unholy license; your national greatness, swelling vanity; your sounds of rejoicing are empty and heartless; your denunciation of tyrants, brass fronted impudence; your shouts of liberty and equality, hollow mockery; your prayers and hymns, your sermons and thanksgivings, with all your religious parade and solemnity, are, to him, mere bombast, fraud, deception, impiety, and hypocrisy—a thin veil to cover up crimes which would disgrace a nation of savages. There is not a nation on the earth guilty of practices more shocking and bloody than are the people of the United States, at this very hour.[134]

The masses fight back

Needless to say, the masses didn't accept all of this passively. They had been mobilizing and struggling in their own interests since at least 1765, and could see everything they had fought for slipping away.

In the 1760s, the Regulator movement had spread in one form or another through all thirteen colonies. Small farmers took direct action against governmental institutions, seeking to "regulate" the application of the law to make it fairer for the poor.

Their immediate grievances were the crushing debt, lack of hard currency, and tax burden imposed by the states' merchant-dominated legislatures. Creditors demanded immediate payment in hard currency, not payment in kind or over time. After court orders led to land seizures and foreclosures, the masses took things into their own hands. Mass meetings were held, threats were made against judges, sheriffs, lawyers, and creditors, and armed crowds prevented county courts from sitting, thus blocking debt proceedings and foreclosures.

After the war, the extrajudicial democratic action of the rural poor came roaring back on an even higher level. In 1782, a radical

Presbyterian minister, Samuel Cullick Ely, led an uprising in western Massachusetts. Ely posed things sharply in class terms, denouncing the "gentlemen" and "great men" who dominated the state's political and economic life, enriching themselves at the expense of the masses.

The militia was called in to repress the movement, and Ely was arrested and imprisoned. After an armed crowd stormed the jail and freed him, he fled to the then-independent republic of Vermont, whose authorities refused to extradite him back to Massachusetts.

As the postwar economic depression deepened, thousands more were threatened with the humiliation of debtor's prison. In 1786, an even larger revolt broke out. Daniel Shays—a Revolutionary War captain who had received an ornamental sword from the Marquis de Lafayette—became the best-known leader of a mass uprising of indebted Massachusetts farmers and veterans.

As Howard Zinn and Anthony Arnove detailed in *Voices of A People's History of the United States*:

> Massachusetts farmer Plough Jogger, speaking about his grievances to one of the illegal conventions where opposition to the legislature was organized, said:
>
> "I've labored hard all my days and fared hard. I have been greatly abused, have been obliged to do more than my part in the war; been loaded with class rates, town rates, province rates, Continental rates, and all rates . . . been pulled and hauled by sheriffs, constables and collectors, and had my cattle sold for less than they were worth. I have been obliged to pay and nobody will pay me. I have lost a great deaf by this man and that man and t'other man, and the great men are going to get all we have, and I think it is time for us to rise and put a stop to it, and have no more courts, nor sheriffs, nor collectors, nor lawyers, and I know that we are the biggest party, let them say what they will . . . We've come to relieve the distresses of the people. There will be no court until they have redress of their grievances."[135]

Local militias sent to suppress the revolt fraternized with the rebels. Haunted by memories of Bacon's Rebellion, which saw Virginia's capital burned to the ground, wealthy Massachusetts merchants paid for a new contingent of troops without ties to the area in rebellion. Due to a combination of uncertain leadership, unclear aims, bad luck, and bad weather, the rebellion fizzled out after a few months. Nonetheless, it had a profound impact on subsequent American history.

Writing from his ambassadorship in prerevolutionary Paris, the ever-contradictory Thomas Jefferson was surprisingly sympathetic. It was in a letter about the Shaysites, written to William Stephens Smith on November 13, 1787, that he wrote the famous lines:

> The tree of liberty must be refreshed from time to time with the blood of patriots and tyrants. It is its natural manure.[136]

And in a letter to James Madison dated January 30, 1787, he maintained that opinion:

> I hold it that a little rebellion now and then is a good thing, and as necessary in the political world as storms in the physical. Unsuccessful rebellions, indeed, generally establish the encroachments on the rights of the people which have produced them. An observation of this truth should render honest republican governors so mild in their punishment of rebellions as not to discourage them too much. It is a medicine necessary for the sound health of government.[137]

However, most men of property were horrified. In a letter to Henry Knox, George Washington summed up their fears:

> [I]f three years ago any person had told me that at this day, I should see such a formidable rebellion against the laws and constitutions of our own making as now appears I should have thought him a bedlamite—a fit subject for a mad house . . . [If the government]shrinks, or is unable to enforce its laws . . . anarchy and confusion must prevail.[138]

In a letter to James Madison, Washington went into even more detail on the conundrum the American ruling class found itself in. In it, he quotes from an extremely interesting letter he himself had received from Henry Knox:

No morn ever dawned more favourably than ours did; and no day was ever more clouded than the present! Wisdom, and good examples are necessary at this time to rescue the political machine from the impending storm. Virginia has now an opportunity to set the latter, and has enough of the former, I hope, to take the lead in promoting this great and arduous work. Without some alteration in our political creed, the superstructure we have been seven years raising at the expence of so much blood and treasure, must fall. We are fast verging to anarchy and confusion!

A letter which I have just received from Genl Knox, who had just returned from Massachusetts (whither he had been sent by Congress consequent of the commotion in that State) is replete with melancholy information of the temper, and designs of a considerable part of that people. Among other things he says:

"There creed is, that the property of the United States, has been protected from confiscation of Britain by the joint exertions of *all*, and therefore ought to be the *common property* of all. And he that attempts opposition to this creed is an enemy to equity and justice, and ought to be swept from off the face of the Earth."

Again:

"They are determined to anihillate all debts public and private, and have Agrarian Laws, which are easily effected by the means of unfunded paper money which shall be a tender in all cases whatever."

He adds:

"The numbers of these people amount in Massachusetts to about one fifth part of several populous Counties, and to them may be collected, people of similar sentiments from the States of Rhode Island, Connecticut, and New Hampshire, so as to constitute a body of twelve or fifteen thousand desperate, and unprincipled men. They are chiefly of the young and active part of the Community."

How melancholy is the reflection, that in so short a space, we should have made such large strides towards fulfilling the prediction of our transatlantic foe! "Leave them to themselves, and their government will

> soon dissolve." Will not the wise and good strive hard to avert this evil? Or will their supineness suffer ignorance, and the arts of self-interested designing disaffected and desperate characters, to involve this rising empire in wretchedness and contempt? What stronger evidence can be given of the want of energy in our governments than these disorders? If there exists not a power to check them, what security has a man for life, liberty, or property? To you, I am sure I need not add aught on this subject, the consequences of a lax, or inefficient government, are too obvious to be dwelt on. Thirteen Sovereignties pulling against each other, and all tugging at the foederal head will soon bring ruin on the whole; whereas a liberal, and energetic Constitution, well guarded and closely watched, to prevent incroachments, might restore us to that degree of respectability and consequence, to which we had a fair claim, and the brightest prospect of attaining. With sentiments of the sincerest esteem etc.[139]

The contradictory Abigail Adams, writing this time to her husband's rival, Thomas Jefferson, was less equally disgusted by the "deplorables" of her day:

> Ignorant, restless desperadoes, without conscience or principles, have led a deluded multitude to follow their standard, under pretense of grievances which have no existence but in their imaginations.[140]

Echoing the Levellers of the English Revolution, with their demands for greater social equality, these armed expressions of popular discontent scared the daylights out of the ruling class leaders of the still deeply disunited states, directly influencing the adoption of a Constitution with a stronger Executive than had existed in the original Articles of Confederation.

Between 1791 and 1794, a few years after the Constitution was adopted, Western Pennsylvania farmers, many of them war veterans, rose up to resist Alexander Hamilton's excise tax on whiskey. Accompanied by Hamilton, President Washington personally led an army of 13,000 to crush the rebellion—larger than most forces he had commanded during the Revolution itself.

The message was clear: the new government would use military force against its own citizens to protect the interests of the bankers, big merchants, and plantation overlords. Now that they were in power, the American ruling class wasn't quite so keen on revolution.

As someone called "Freeman" wrote ironically in the *Worcester Magazine* at the time of Shays's Rebellion:

> When we had other *Rulers*, Committees and Conventions of the people were lawful—they were then necessary, but since I *myself* became a ruler, they cease to be lawful—he people have no right to examine my conduct.[141]

Adopting the Constitution

In the sweltering summer of 1787, 55 delegates from the thirteen states met again in Philadelphia's Independence Hall to decide the fate of the continent. Nearly half of the attendees were slaveowners, and 30 of them were veterans of the war. Their task was to draft a new Constitution.

The Articles of Confederation had outlived their usefulness. Without a strong central state, the American ruling class would be unable to deal with its enemies, both foreign and domestic. As James Madison expressed it at Virginia's Constitutional ratification convention:

> If we take experience for our guide, we shall find still more instructive direction on this subject. The weakness of the existing articles of the Union, shewed itself during the war. It has manifested itself since the peace, to such a degree as admits of no doubt to a rational, intelligent, and unbiassed mind, of the necessity of an alteration: Nay, this necessity is obvious to all America—It has forced itself on the minds of the people . . .
>
> Its debility was perceived almost as soon as it was put in operation—A recapitulation of the proofs which have been experienced of its inefficacy, is unnecessary.—It is most notorious, that feebleness universally marked its character—Shall we be safe in another war in the same situation?

> That instrument required the voluntary contributions of the States, and thereby sacrificed some of our best privileges.—The most intolerable and unwarrantable oppressions were committed on the people during the late war. The gross enormity of those oppressions might have produced the most serious consequences, were it not for the spirit of liberty, which preponderated against every consideration.[142]

Despite these pressures, the proceedings of the Constitutional Convention nearly collapsed on several occasions. The contradictions to be smoothed over were many, as free states and slave states, large states and small states presented competing visions of federal structure and power. With the specter of the Shaysites haunting them, however, they hung together and focused on their work. Only through grudging unity had they succeeded in wresting power from the British, and the same would be required to keep power from falling into the hands of a dictator, the masses—or each other.

The safety valve of the Western frontier allowed for many compromises, and the internal class struggles necessitated them. Most of these were overt concessions to the slavocracy. As Herbert Aptheker explained:

> The Constitution of the United States, as originally drafted, was a bourgeois-democratic document for the governing of a slaveholder-capitalist republic. It did not represent a renunciation of the American Revolution, but rather a consolidation of that Revolution by the classes which had led it.[143]

Engels also highlighted the contradiction embedded in the very foundation of the American republic:

> [I]t is significant of the specifically bourgeois character of these human rights that the American constitution, the first to recognize the rights of man, in the same breath confirms the slavery of the colored races existing in America: class privileges are proscribed, race privileges sanctified.[144]

In other words, slavery's inclusion in the Constitution was a feature, not a bug. The final document was scrupulously careful not to mention the word "slavery." Instead, it used euphemisms such as "other persons" and "persons held to service or labor." The Three-Fifths Compromise, the Fugitive Slave Clause, and allowing the slave trade to continue until 1808 effectively nationalized the institution.

In yet another compromise, the federal system divided sovereignty between states and the national government. The blurry line between the two remains a source of friction to this day, and was, of course, one of the issues that precipitated the Civil War.

Then there was the "Great Compromise," also known as the "Connecticut Compromise,"which created a bicameral legislature. To balance the needs of small and large states, seats in the House of Representatives would be based on population to accommodate large states, but all states would be eligible for two Senators, regardless of population. This gave outsized political clout to the more rural, and thereby typically more conservative states.

After much horse-trading and rancor, the draft was finalized on September 17, 1787. As it proclaimed to the world:

> We the People of the United States, in Order to form a more perfect Union, establish Justice, insure domestic Tranquility, provide for the common defense, promote the general Welfare, and secure the Blessings of Liberty to ourselves and our Posterity, do ordain and establish this Constitution for the United States of America.[145]

However, "We the People" consisted of just 39 signatories. Of the 16 other delegates, some had left early, while others refused to sign because they disagreed with the final product. So much for the myth that this "divinely inspired" piece of paper represented the broad-based consensus of the population.

In fact, estimates suggest that only around 160,000 people voted to elect delegates to the state ratification conventions, out of a total population of roughly four million. There was never a popular referendum. In other words, just 4 per cent of the total population,—around 25 per cent of white adult males—participated. Of the elected delegates, only a slight majority voted in favor of adopting the new statutes. In Massachusetts, the vote was 187 to 168. In New York, it was 30 to 27. In New Hampshire, 57 to 47. In Virginia, 89 to 79.

However, by mutual agreement, just nine states had to ratify for the Constitution to take effect. New Hampshire became the ninth state on June 21, 1788, putting the Constitution into effect for the ratifying states even before the major states of Virginia and New York had held their conventions.

For its part, Rhode Island rejected the project by a vote of 2,708 to 237 in a March 1788 referendum. The state only acceded to join the Union after the federal government threatened to treat it as a foreign country and impose tariffs on its goods. On May 29, 1790, its new ratifying convention approved the Constitution by a mere whisker, 34 to 32. This was nearly three years after the Constitutional Convention and more than a year into Washington's presidency.

The reticence expressed by significant minorities in all states wasn't mere obstinacy. It reflected widespread popular opposition to the Constitution among small farmers, artisans, and others who could see that the new system was designed to protect the interests of big merchants, creditors, and large property holders—at their expense.

Federalists and Anti-Federalists

Now that the Tory-loyalist faction of American politics had been submitted and expelled, the different factions of the patriot propertied classes fought over how best to nurture capitalist development while preserving chattel slavery.

To push back against the centralizing tendencies of the "Federalists," the "Anti-Federalists" pressed for a bill of rights and other amendments to safeguard the rights of individuals and the states vis-à-vis the federal government. Despite claims by some modern-day libertarians, however, the conflict was not a simple contest between populist democracy and bourgeois-aristocratic centralism.

The Anti-Federalists played to the interests of yeoman farmers, petty merchants, and others dependent on small-scale production, who feared being swallowed up and subordinated to bigger players.

They also appealed to land speculators and other minor powerbrokers who didn't want their local authority and autonomy undermined.

The Anti-Federalists also included Southern planters who saw federal authority as a potential threat to their chattels, despite the Constitution's explicit protections. They could see the danger posed by the embryo of commercial-industrial capital to their peculiar mode of exploitation, and didn't trust Northerners to commit fully to suppressing slave uprisings.

In short, the Anti-Federalists' Jeffersonian vision of a country made up of "independent" producers—to include everyone from agrarian households to plantation slaveowners—was backward-looking idealist utopianism.

The Federalists, by contrast, represented the emerging forces of American capitalism, which required greater centralization. They were the political representatives of the big commercial and financial interests that stood to gain the most from integrated national markets, a stable currency and system of public credit, contract enforcement, bankruptcy laws, corporate charters, and state-supported economic development to facilitate the circulation of commodities and capital.

While all private property of the means of production was to be respected, the most important property of all was big property and big capital, which would be protected through the federal courts and constitutional limitations on state legislatures. Furthermore, the Federalists supported subsidies for domestic manufacturing, internal improvements, and, as needed, protectionist tariffs.

And that's a dirty little secret of the US ruling class. Despite all the lip service paid to the inviolability of *laissez-faire* economic policies,* American capitalism has benefited from state intervention and handouts intended to spur capitalist development and concentrate wealth in a few hands *from the very beginning*. It's a bourgeois state, after all, and the idea that it stands impartially above the classes is a fairy tale.

---

* French for "let it happen"; in economics, the idea that the government should not interfere with competition on the "free" market.

As Marx and Engels explained:

> The executive of the modern state is but a committee for managing the common affairs of the whole bourgeoisie.[146]

From Alexander Hamilton to the early railroad barons, Andrew Carnegie, John D. Rockefeller, Big Auto, Big Finance, and Big Tech, none of them could have achieved what they did without favorable laws, subsidies, bailouts, and other forms of direct and indirect support from the state. For all the talk of economic liberalism, it has *always* been socialism in reverse: handouts to the ultrarich, paid for by the working majority through taxes and austerity.

To back all of this up, the Federalists advocated what we might call a variant of "peace through strength." They argued that the federal government needed the resources and military capacity to deter European powers, suppress internal rebellions, and intensify the dispossession of Indigenous peoples.

To allay the concerns of the Anti-Federalists and the mistrustful masses standing behind them, a bill of rights was ratified on December 15, 1791, nearly four years after the Constitution itself. Many states had ratified the foundational document only on condition that such protections be added. The Bill of Rights consisted of the first ten amendments to the Constitution. It provided for explicit protections of individual and collective liberties, as well as defending the states against federal overreach.

Insofar as these basic democratic rights can be used to facilitate the struggle for socialism, Marxists defend them against encroachment by the bourgeois state. However, we have no illusions that in and of themselves they guarantee genuine freedom. Remember: bourgeois equality is equality *on paper*, not equality *in life*.

In the words of the sharp-tongued satirist, Anatole France:

> At this task they must labor in the face of the majestic equality of the laws, which forbid rich and poor alike to sleep under the bridges, to beg in the streets, and to steal their bread.[147]

And as Lenin elaborated in a 1914 polemic against a liberal professor:

> In the United States of America, as in other advanced countries, there are no medieval privileges. All citizens are equal in political rights. But are they equal as regards their *position in social production*?
>
> No, Mr. Tugan, they are not. Some own land, factories, and capital and live on the unpaid labor of the workers; these form an insignificant minority. Others, namely, the vast mass of the population, own no means of production and live only by selling their labor-power; these are proletarians.
>
> In the United States of America, there is no aristocracy, and the bourgeoisie and the proletariat enjoy *equal* political rights. But they are *not* equal in *class* status: one class, the capitalists, owns the means of production and lives on the unpaid labor of the workers. The other class, the wage-workers, the proletariat, own no means of production and live by selling their labor-power in the market.[148]

In short, this was the chaotic road to the adoption of the Constitution, which, as amended 27 times, regulates American political and economic life to this day. It was the product of intense intra- and interclass struggles, as the revolutionary victors moved might and main to consolidate their control of the spoils. As Marx and Engels explained in the *German Ideology*:

> [A]ll struggles within the State, the struggle between democracy, aristocracy, and monarchy, the struggle for the franchise, etc., etc., are merely the illusory forms…in which the real struggles of the different classes are fought out among one another . . .[149]

And as Trotsky explained in his unfinished 1940 classic, "The Class, the Party and the Leadership":

> [A] people is comprised of hostile classes, and the classes themselves are comprised of different and in part antagonistic layers which fall under different leadership; furthermore every people falls under the influence of other peoples who are likewise comprised of classes. Governments do

> not express the systematically growing "maturity" of a "people" but are the product of the struggle between different classes and the different layers within one and the same class, and, finally, the action of external forces—alliances, conflicts, wars and so on.[150]

George Washington, who generally aligned with the Federalists, was unanimously elected by the Electoral College in 1788–89 as the country's first president. There was no other plausible choice. John Adams, another leading Federalist, finished second and became vice president under the Constitution's original electoral rules. Washington was inaugurated on April 30, 1789, in New York City, the first capital of the US under the new Constitution.

The Constitution was both revolutionary and counterrevolutionary. It was progressive insofar as capitalism still had many decades of productive life left to develop the productive forces. It was reactionary insofar as it stemmed the flood tide of revolution, curbed the "unrealistic" aspirations of the masses, and codified property rights that condemned the majority to exploitation and oppression.

There can be no doubt, however, that the revolutionary reshuffling of the decks brought about profound changes to American society. In the words of the Marxist historian George Novack:

> The first American revolution and its war for independence was a genuine people's movement. Such movements destroy much that has become rotten and is ready for burial. But, above all, they are socially creative, bringing to birth institutions that provide the ways and means for the next surge forward.[151]

The young American bourgeoisie now held political and economic power, and it proceeded to establish structures, laws, and institutions to line its pockets and defend its interests. It used state power to root out any unneeded vestiges of the old set up and to lay solid foundations for its eventual rise to world preeminence. The new boss was the same as the old boss—only different.

Capitalism sinks deeper roots

Though uneven and incomplete, the basic elements of the national-democratic revolution had been carried out. These established the conditions for the flourishing of capitalism on the American continent.

All of these changes would pay incalculable dividends in the long run. In the short term, however, it wasn't all milk and honey for the new rulers. The Shaysite uprising was just one of many intractable headaches.

Most foreign nations—governed as they were by kings and nobles—viewed the United States with contempt and refused to negotiate favorable treaties with it. Spain, which controlled the vital port of New Orleans, closed the Mississippi to American shipping. Britain refused to evacuate military posts in the Northwest Territory, as promised in the Treaty of Paris. Barbary pirates seized American ships in the Mediterranean, and Congress couldn't raise the money to build a navy or pay tribute for their release.

Peace brought economic depression, not immediate prosperity, as wartime profiteering, speculation, and smuggling came to an end. The loss of preferred credit and trading status within Britain's commercial empire made it harder to access foreign banks and markets. Despite earlier efforts to build a home industry, British goods flooded the vacuum left by the dislocation of the postwar period, undercutting many American manufacturers. Farmers faced foreclosure as they couldn't repay debts in hard currency, since the official dollar "wasn't worth a Continental."

State governments issued their own paper money to relieve the debts of their constituents, but this introduced even greater dysfunction to interstate commerce. Different states had different currencies, different trade policies, and even erected tariff barriers against each other. During the war, Congress had borrowed over $11 million and printed $241 million in paper money, with the states issuing another $209 million. But there was little of substance to back it all up. The inflationary debt crisis that resulted contributed to the economic nightmare of the "Critical Period," lasting roughly until the adoption of the Constitution.

The task of reorganizing the American economy and putting it on a viable footing fell to Alexander Hamilton, an ambitious West Indian immigrant who had attached himself to Washington. He was the brilliant yet amoral piledriver of American capitalist property relations. He would have almost certainly been a contender for the presidency at a certain stage, but was explicitly excluded by the constitutional prohibition against the foreign-born. Some have speculated that the prohibition was aimed at Hamilton specifically.

Making him the country's first Secretary of the Treasury was like putting the fox in charge of the henhouse. Until his untimely death in a duel with Aaron Burr in 1804, he relentlessly laid the foundations for the system we still live under today. His economic program was a blueprint for transforming the country from an agricultural exporter of raw materials into a commercial, manufacturing power that would eventually outcompete Britain.

Already in 1781, Hamilton had given Robert Morris a sneak preview of his main plan:

> A national debt if it is not excessive will be to us a national blessing.[152]

His goal was to bind the propertied classes to the federal government by giving them a material stake in the success of the American state. He would achieve this through federal assumption of state war debts, a national bank, protective tariffs, subsidies for manufacturing, and more. In this way, he harnessed the power of both the private and public sectors to accelerate capital accumulation.

To kick things off, he presided over one of the most audacious insider-trading swindles in American history. In his 1790 "Report on Public Credit," he proposed that the federal government assume the states' debts and redeem securities issued during the war at full value:

> To justify and preserve their confidence; to promote the increasing respectability of the American name; to answer the calls of justice; to restore landed property to its due value; to furnish new resources both

> to agriculture and commerce; to cement more closely the union of the States; to add to their security against foreign attack; to establish public order on the basis of an upright and liberal policy—these are the great and invaluable ends to be secured by a proper and adequate provision, at the present period, for the support of public credit.[153]

However, the decision to proceed with his proposal was only made public after Hamilton's speculator pals had sent agents across the country to buy up thousands of bonds from cash-strapped veterans and farmers for pennies on the dollar. Incalculable fortunes were made when Congress eventually funded them at par.

Through this colossal transfer of wealth from the poor to the rich, Hamilton created American finance capitalism, virtually overnight. A handful of ultra-wealthy creditors now had a direct interest in the federal government's longevity and centralization. When James Madison proposed that the original bondholders receive at least some compensation, Hamilton and his cronies squashed the initiative. The all-American pastime of living well beyond one's means had started with a bang.

Also in 1790, Hamilton called for the creation of a Bank of the United States, modeled on the Bank of England, to centralize financial power and provide capital for commercial development. Again, as far back as 1781, Hamilton was crystal clear as to his aims:

> The tendency of a national bank is to increase public and private credit . . . Industry is increased, commodities are multiplied, agriculture and manufacturers flourish, and herein consists the true wealth and prosperity of a state.[154]

Anti-Federalists such as Jefferson and Madison argued that Congress had no constitutional authority to do this. Hamilton's argument in favor was that the bank was "necessary and proper" so as to execute Congress's fiscal powers. Washington sided with Hamilton's "broad construction" of implied Constitutional powers, setting a precedent for expansive federal government.

The Bank of the United States was to be a private corporation with an initial seed of $10 million in capital; $8 million from private investors and $2 million from the federal government. I.e., even more public money would be poured into expanding private capital.

With the power to issue paper money, hold government deposits, and make loans, the Bank of the United States became the largest financial institution in the country. It concentrated capital in the hands of wealthy merchants and speculators, providing them with credit for commercial ventures while making it difficult for small farmers and merchants to secure credit for themselves.

Then, in 1791, Hamilton issued his "Report on Manufactures" and his "Report on a Mint." The former advocated for protective tariffs, subsidies for manufacturers, and federal support for industrial development. The latter established a national currency backed by gold and silver to grease the wheels of commercial transactions and speculation. To top off his program, he encouraged the importation of skilled workers and capital from Europe, as well as strong patent laws to encourage profitable innovation.

That same year, Hamilton established the Society for Establishing Useful Manufactures, a private corporation chartered to build an industrial city on the site of modern-day Paterson, New Jersey. Under Hamilton's influence, the New Jersey legislature exempted the project from taxes, allowed it to hold unlimited property, and even allowed it to control water rights and build canals to facilitate its activities. When the whole scheme collapsed in 1792 due to speculation and bankruptcy, it set off America's first financial crisis.

Far from *laissez-faire* capitalism, this was an ambitiously American variant of state capitalism—i.e., using government power and economies of scale to promote private accumulation, a practice that remains alive and well to this day. Every single company now considered "too big to fail" has benefited in one way or another from public dollars. And virtually every major institution of American capitalism—Wall Street, the Federal Reserve, industrial policy, the national debt—can be traced back to Alexander Hamilton.

For his part, the "Anti-Federalist" Thomas Jefferson had no qualms leveraging the forces of the market to accelerate the expropriation of Indian lands. In his 1803 letter to William Henry Harrison, he outlined his plan for using trading posts to drive Indians into debt, thus forcing them to relinquish their lands as payment:

> [T]o promote this disposition to exchange lands which they have to spare and we want, for necessaries, which we have to spare and they want, we shall push our trading houses, and be glad to see the good and influential individuals among them run in debt, because we observe that when these debts get beyond what the individuals can pay, they become willing to lop th[em off] by a cession of lands.[155]

To paraphrase Gore Vidal, from the beginning, the United States has always had only "one party, the Property Party . . . and it has two right wings."

The class character of the US Constitution

Most of the Founding Fathers looked to the Roman Republic for inspiration. They saw themselves as Enlightenment patricians, wisely ruling over ordinary plebeians. Never mind that Rome ended with power concentrated in a few hands, the rise of Caesarism,* and eventual overthrow by "barbarians" who, in many ways, had become better Romans than the Romans themselves. As Gore Vidal stated in an interview:

> Democracy is something America has never really practiced. Because the Founding Fathers hated two things: monarchy and democracy. They wanted a republic, a replica of the Roman or Venetian republics. They didn't even like the etymology of the word "democracy."[156]

* After periods of intense class struggle, both forces can become exhausted and reach a deadlock. In this situation, the state can rise above the classes and gain a certain degree of independence, often in the form of a dictatorship centered around an individual. This phenomenon in the ancient world was referred to as Caesarism, in modern times, as Bonapartism.

Given the material conditions of the time, many of the ideals expressed by the radicals who spurred the masses to fight for independence were objectively unattainable. The revolution's potential was necessarily constrained and conditioned by the stage of development of the productive forces and classes in society at that time; it could not have been anything other than a bourgeois revolution.

In the final analysis, the revolution was always about defending and expanding private property in land, capital, and slaves. And once independence was achieved, the only real question was how best to continue this process on an even higher level.

The Constitution's protections for private property are woven throughout its handful of pages: From the Contract Clause, which prevents states from impairing contracts, to the prohibition on bills of attainder, to the Fifth Amendment's requirement that property not be taken without "due process of law" and "just compensation."

Alexander Hamilton was refreshingly honest about the class nature of his program.

> All communities divide themselves into the few and the many. The first are the rich and well-born, the other the mass of the people . . . The people are turbulent and changing; they seldom judge or determine right. Give therefore to the first class a distinct, permanent share in the government . . .[157]

> Inequality will exist as long as liberty exists. It unavoidably results from that very liberty itself.[158]

Speaking at the Constitutional Convention, Gouverneur Morris was equally candid. As James Madison observed in his notes on the debate:

> He thought property ought to be taken into the estimate as well as the number of inhabitants. Life and liberty were generally said to be of more value than property. An accurate view of the matter would, nevertheless, prove that property was the main object of society. The savage state was more favorable to liberty than the civilized; and sufficiently so to life. It was preferred by all men who had not acquired a taste for property;

> it was only renounced for the sake of property which could only be secured by the restraints of regular government. These ideas might appear to some new, but they were nevertheless just. If property, then, was the main object of government, certainly it ought to be one measure of the influence due to those who were to be affected by the government.[159]

Despite standing on the opposite side of that era's political divide, James Madison was in total agreement. As he wrote in the Federalist Papers Number 10:

> The latent causes of faction are thus sown in the nature of man; and we see them everywhere brought into different degrees of activity, according to the different circumstances of civil society. A zeal for different opinions concerning religion, concerning government, and many other points, as well of speculation as of practice; an attachment to different leaders ambitiously contending for pre-eminence and power; or to persons of other descriptions whose fortunes have been interesting to the human passions, have, in turn, divided mankind into parties, inflamed them with mutual animosity, and rendered them much more disposed to vex and oppress each other than to co-operate for their common good. So strong is this propensity of mankind to fall into mutual animosities, that where no substantial occasion presents itself, the most frivolous and fanciful distinctions have been sufficient to kindle their unfriendly passions and excite their most violent conflicts. But the most common and durable source of factions has been the various and unequal distribution of property. Those who hold and those who are without property have ever formed distinct interests in society. Those who are creditors, and those who are debtors, fall under a like discrimination. A landed interest, a manufacturing interest, a mercantile interest, a moneyed interest, with many lesser interests, grow up of necessity in civilized nations, and divide them into different classes, actuated by different sentiments and views. The regulation of these various and interfering interests forms the principal task of modern legislation, and involves the spirit of party and faction in the necessary and ordinary operations of the government.[160]

John Adams also sided clearly with the "gentlemen" of property versus the "simplemen" who had none:

> The people, in all nations, are naturally divided into two sorts, the gentlemen and the simplemen, a word which is here chosen to signify the common people. By gentlemen are not meant the rich or the poor, the high-born or the low-born, the industrious or the idle; but all those who have received a liberal education, an ordinary degree of erudition in liberal arts and sciences, whether by birth they be descended from magistrates and officers of government, or from husbandmen, merchants, mechanics, or laborers; or whether they be rich or poor. We must, nevertheless, remember, that *generally* those who are rich, and descended from families in public life, will have the best education in arts and sciences, and therefore the gentlemen will ordinarily, notwithstanding some exceptions to the rule, be the richer, and born of more noted families. By the common people we mean laborers, husbandmen, mechanics, and merchants in general, who pursue their occupations and industry without any knowledge in liberal arts or sciences, or in any thing but their own trades or pursuits; though there may be exceptions to this rule, and individuals may be found in each of these classes who may really be gentlemen.
>
> Now it seems to be clear, that the gentlemen in every country are, and ever must be, few in number, in comparison of the simplemen. If you please, then, by the democratical portion of society we will understand the common people, as before explained; by the aristocratical part of the community we will understand the gentlemen. The distinctions which have been introduced among the gentlemen, into nobility greater or lesser, are perfectly immaterial to our present purpose; knights, barons, earls, viscounts, marquises, dukes, and even princes and kings, are still but gentlemen, and the word noble signifies no more than knowable, or conspicuous. But the gentlemen are more intelligent and skilful, as well as generally richer and better connected, and therefore have more influence and power than an equal number of the common people. There is a constant energy and effort in the minds of the former to increase the

advantages they possess over the latter, and to augment their wealth and influence at their expense.

This effort produces resentments and jealousies, contempt, hatred, and fear, between the one sort and the other. Individuals among the common people endeavor to make friends, patrons, and protectors among the gentlemen. This produces parties, divisions, tumults, and war. But as the former have most address and capacity, they gain more and more continually, until they become exorbitantly rich, and the others miserably poor. In this progress, the common people are continually looking up for a protector among the gentlemen, and he who is most able and willing to protect them acquires their confidence. They unite together by their feelings, more than their reflections, in augmenting his power, because the more power he has, and the less the gentlemen have, the safer they are. This is a short sketch of the history of that progress of passions and feelings which has produced every simple monarchy in the world; and, if nature and its feelings have their course without reflection, they will produce a simple monarchy forever. It has been the common people, then, and not the gentlemen, who have established simple monarchies all over the world. The common people, against the gentlemen, established a simple monarchy in Caesar at Rome, in the Medici at Florence, etc., and are now in danger of doing the same thing in Holland; and if the British constitution should have its euthanasia in simple monarchy, according to the prophecy of Mr. Hume, it will be effected by the common people, to avoid the increasing oppressions of the gentlemen.[161]

And again:

The great question will forever remain, *who shall work?* Our species cannot all be idle. Leisure for study must ever be the portion of a few. The number employed in government must forever be very small. Food, raiment, and habitations, the indispensable wants of all, are not to be obtained without the continual toil of ninety-nine in a hundred of mankind. As rest is rapture to the weary man, those who labor little will always be envied by those who labor much, though the latter in

> reality be probably the most enviable. With all the encouragements, public and private, which can ever be given to general education, and it is scarcely possible they should be too many or too great, the laboring part of the people can never be learned. The controversy between the rich and the poor, the laborious and the idle, the learned and the ignorant, distinctions as old as the creation, and as extensive as the globe, distinctions which no art or policy, no degree of virtue or philosophy can ever wholly destroy, will continue, and rivalries will spring out of them. These parties will be represented in the legislature, and must be balanced, or one will oppress the other. There will never probably be found any other mode of establishing such an equilibrium, than by constituting the representation of each an independent branch of the legislature, and an independent executive authority, such as that in our government, to be a third branch and a mediator or an arbitrator between them. Property must be secured, or liberty cannot exist.
>
> But if unlimited or unbalanced power of disposing property, be put into the hands of those who have no property, France will find, as we have found, the lamb committed to the custody of the wolf. In such a case, all the pathetic exhortations and addresses of the national assembly to the people, to respect property, will be regarded no more than the warbles of the songsters of the forest. The great art of law-giving consists in balancing the poor against the rich in the legislature, and in constituting the legislative a perfect balance against the executive power, at the same time that no individual or party can become its rival. The essence of a free government consists in an effectual control of rivalries. The executive and the legislative powers are natural rivals; and if each has not an effectual control over the other, the weaker will ever be the lamb in the paws of the wolf. The nation which will not adopt an equilibrium of power must adopt a despotism. There is no other alternative.[162]

In the final analysis, despite their obfuscating appeals to popular democracy and liberty in the abstract, both the Federalists and Anti-Federalists represented the interests of property. Whereas Hamilton represented commercial and financial capital, Jefferson's Democratic-Republicans represented agrarian interests and the slaveocracy, which generally preferred a less expensive and less intrusive central government. This first iteration of the American two-party system was known as the First Party System, lasting roughly from 1792 to 1824.

Although the pressure of the masses clearly played a role, the struggle over the nuts and bolts of the Constitution was ultimately an intra-class conflict among the rulers, not an interclass conflict between the rulers and ruled. Neither side in the Constitutional debates represented the interests of those who labor for a living. Both defended capitalist property relations; they merely disagreed over how those relations should be encouraged to develop, and how much slavery should figure in the equation. It is telling that once Jefferson was in the presidency, he kept key "Hamiltonian" structures, including the federal fiscal system and public credit.

Both the Federalists and the Anti-Federalists made their mark on American history, but it is clear which faction prevailed in the long run. It's ironic that the most romanticized aspects of the Revolution and Constitution belong to the backward-looking Anti-Federalists, while the Federalists can claim credit for the unapologetically capitalist, yet at-the-time historically progressive elements.

In short, the Federalists won out because they were on the right side of history. Capitalism thrives on larger markets, complex financial systems, greater commercial integration, and stronger state capacity to facilitate accumulation and suppress popular discontent.

A revolution unfinished

Political democracy was only partially achieved by the First Revolution. Women, Indians, free Blacks, and the propertyless poor remained without the vote. Slaves—who counted as three-fifths of a person when it came to calculating a state's population—obviously didn't get a vote either. Subsequent class struggles forced the ruling class to grant a broadly expanded franchise. But millions remain excluded to this day, either over technicalities or due to objective limitations on their ability to participate.

Crucially, the Founders' model of a democratic republic rather than a direct democracy ensured that "representatives" would filter the popular will. As James Madison wrote in the Federalist Number 51:

> If men were angels, no government would be necessary. If angels were to govern men, neither external nor internal controls on government would be necessary. In framing a government which is to be administered by men over men, the great difficulty lies in this: you must first enable the government to control the governed; and in the next place oblige it to control itself.[163]

As we've seen, Gouvernor Morris of New York feared the "mob rule" of popular democracy. But he also recognized capital's organic tendency to concentrate wealth and power. As James Madison's notes on the debates over the Constitution indicate, Morris's advocacy for a bicameral legislature was intended to balance these two dangers:

> The Rich will strive to establish their dominion and enslave the rest. They always did. They always will. The proper security against them is to form them into a separate interest. The two forces will then controul each other. Let the rich mix with the poor and in a Commercial Country, they will establish an oligarchy. Take away commerce, and the democracy will triumph. Thus it has been all the world over. So it will be among us. Reason tells us we are but men: and we are not to expect any particular interference of Heaven in our favor. By thus combining & setting apart, the aristocratic interest, the popular interest will be combined against. it. There will be a mutual check and mutual security.[164]

However, while the system's intricate checks and balances are partly intended to prevent an individual or branch of government from attaining tyrannical power, the main thing to be checked is *the will of the laboring majority.* The whole point is to prevent even the whiff of fundamental change that could threaten the regime of private property.

The institution of the Electoral College is a glaring example. In practice, it means that the highest office in the national government is not directly elected by the people—and never has been.

As of 2026, a mere 538 electors actually vote for the president, with a simple majority of 270 or more deciding the issue. Thousands of other officials are appointed directly by the president or by Congress, making them effectively unaccountable to the electorate.

As for Congress, the Senate is a kind of "House of Lords," with more political power per capita allocated to less populated states. Until 1913, Senators weren't even elected by popular vote, but were appointed by the state legislatures. Furthermore, only one-third of the Senate is up for election every two years. Even if the masses were to go wild at the polls and elect an entire cohort of revolutionaries, there would still be a two-thirds supermajority of the old guard in place to keep a lid on things. Other patently undemocratic rules, like the Senate filibuster, further blow up the myth that Congress somehow expresses the popular will.

Meanwhile, seats in the House of Representatives are allocated based on population, making it "more democratic." But really speaking, a system is either genuinely democratic or it isn't really democratic at all.

During the "Federalist era" of Washington's two-term presidency, big strides were made toward cementing the country into a united whole. However, many contradictions had not been resolved. The states may have coalesced into a semi-centralized political union, but tremendous sectional differences and other disagreements remained. Powerful centrifugal forces tugged implacably at the country's ostensible unity, as the North, South, East, and West developed at different rhythms and in different directions.

One perennial fault line was the question of the Western lands. The Constitution provided a basic framework for territorial expansion but didn't specify how new territories would be incorporated into the union, whether their residents would have the rights of citizens, or whether slavery could be extended into them.

Which brings us to the most glaring contradiction of all. Although the First Revolution was bourgeois in essence, it allowed a precapitalist mode of exploitation to remain dominant across vast swathes of the country, cutting across the agrarian reform and political democracy components of the revolution.

Although plenty of Northern Federalists harbored antislavery sentiments, they felt they could coexist with the practice as long as it didn't interfere with their core interests. In the early days of the republic, there was room enough on the continent for an array of productive and exploitative forms.

In the decades that followed, *extensive* development of the productive forces continued as the colonists moved ever westward. Eventually, however, enough of the population was concentrated on the Eastern seaboard that *intensive* development grabbed a gear. The drive to revolutionize the means of production under competitive pressures was unleashed. A home market for American-made capital and consumer goods emerged, further impelling the Industrial Revolution.

Slave-produced cotton would become central to the meteoric rise of American industrial and finance capitalism. However, by not laying the basis for the transformation of Southern agriculture along capitalist lines, as had been done in the North, the can was merely kicked down the road. In the decades after the Revolution, a series of additional compromises were cobbled together in a doomed effort to hold things together before the whole thing unraveled. Cohabitation in a single nation-state simply couldn't last forever.

Slavery was America's original sin. From its inception, it was the dynamite in its foundations. In just a few decades, that dynamite would explode in a second, even bloodier revolution and civil war.

"The representatives of the bourgeoisie understand that for the sake of overthrowing Negro slavery, of overthrowing the rule of the slaveowners, it was worth letting the country go through long years of civil war, through the abysmal ruin, destruction and terror that accompany every war. But now, when we are confronted with the vastly greater task of overthrowing capitalist wage-slavery, of overthrowing the rule of the bourgeoisie—now, the representatives and defenders of the bourgeoisie, and also the reformist socialists who have been frightened by the bourgeoisie and are shunning the revolution, cannot and do not want to understand that civil war is necessary and legitimate.

The American workers will not follow the bourgeoisie. They will be with us, for civil war against the bourgeoisie. The whole history of the world and of the American labor movement strengthens my conviction that this is so."

— Vladimir Lenin, "Letter to American Workers"
August 20, 1918

Part Two: The US Civil War

The US Civil War saw four years of the most brutal warfare the world had ever seen. Picking up where the First Revolution left off, it was the foundry that forged the American nation-state.

Untangling the complexities of this period is vital if we are to understand the country as it exists today. In the words of William Faulkner, the great novelist of the American South: "The past is never dead. It's not even past."[1] And as Marx explained:

> Men make their own history, but they do not make it as they please; they do not make it under self-selected circumstances, but under circumstances existing already, given and transmitted from the past. The tradition of all dead generations weighs like a nightmare on the brains of the living.[2]

Marx and Engels recognized the revolutionary significance of the war and attentively followed its many economic, political, military, and diplomatic twists and turns. They produced dozens of extremely insightful articles and letters about these events, all of which are highly recommended.

Marx even wrote a letter to Abraham Lincoln on behalf of the First International,* congratulating him on his reelection in 1864. It is worth quoting in full:

> Sir: We congratulate the American people upon your reelection by a large majority. If resistance to the Slave Power was the reserved watchword of your first election, the triumphant war cry of your reelection is Death to Slavery.
>
> From the commencement of the titanic American strife, the workingmen of Europe felt instinctively that the star-spangled banner carried the destiny of their class. The contest for the territories which opened the *dire épopée*,† was it not to decide whether the virgin soil of immense tracts should be wedded to the labor of the emigrant or prostituted by the tramp of the slave driver?
>
> When an oligarchy of 300,000 slaveholders dared to inscribe, for the first time in the annals of the world, "slavery" on the banner of Armed Revolt, when on the very spots where hardly a century ago the idea of one great Democratic Republic had first sprung up, whence the first Declaration of the Rights of Man was issued, and the first impulse given to the European revolution of the eighteenth century; when on those very spots counterrevolution, with systematic thoroughness, gloried in rescinding "the ideas entertained at the time of the formation of the old constitution," and maintained slavery to be "a beneficent institution," indeed, the old solution of the great problem of "the relation of capital to labor," and cynically proclaimed property in man "the cornerstone of the new edifice"—then the working classes of Europe understood at once, even before the fanatic partisanship of the upper classes for the Confederate gentry had given its dismal warning, that the slaveholders' rebellion was to sound the tocsin for a general holy crusade of property

---

* The International Working Men's Association, later known as the First International, was founded in September 1864, six weeks before Lincoln's reelection, with Marx and Engels's close involvement. The first-ever international proletarian organization, it paved the way for the growth of working-class organization and the spread of Marxist ideas.

† French for "telling of an epic"

> against labor, and that for the men of labor, with their hopes for the future, even their past conquests were at stake in that tremendous conflict on the other side of the Atlantic.
>
> Everywhere they bore therefore patiently the hardships imposed upon them by the cotton crisis, opposed enthusiastically the proslavery intervention of their betters—and, from most parts of Europe, contributed their quota of blood to the good cause.
>
> While the workingmen, the true political powers of the North, allowed slavery to defile their own republic, while before the Negro, mastered and sold without his concurrence, they boasted it the highest prerogative of the white-skinned laborer to sell himself and choose his own master, they were unable to attain the true freedom of labor, or to support their European brethren in their struggle for emancipation; but this barrier to progress has been swept off by the red sea of civil war.
>
> The workingmen of Europe feel sure that, as the American War of Independence initiated a new era of ascendancy for the middle class, so the American Antislavery War will do for the working classes. They consider it an earnest of the epoch to come that it fell to the lot of Abraham Lincoln, the single-minded son of the working class, to lead his country through the matchless struggle for the rescue of an enchained race and the reconstruction of a social world.[3]

In the final analysis, the origins of the Civil War ultimately trace back to the country's founding and the incomplete nature of the First Revolution. As we have seen, the fight for independence was won, but many of the historical tasks associated with the national-democratic revolution remained incomplete. Another colossal revolutionary upheaval and restructuring of the country was needed to facilitate the untrammeled development of American capitalism.

Just as the First Revolution was about far more than breaking away from Britain, the Civil War was not a simple matter of "good" Northerners versus "bad" Southerners. It was not a monolithic struggle of slavery-hating capitalists, antiracist workers, and independent yeomen versus a united bloc of slavery-loving plantation owners and racist dirt farmers. As we will see, the reality was far more complex.

However, in broad strokes, it was a titanic confrontation between the historically progressive agricultural-industrial capitalism of the North and the counterrevolution of the South's plantation-slave owners. As Marx succinctly summarized the conflict:

> The present struggle between the South and North is . . . Nothing but a struggle between two social systems, the system of slavery and the system of free labor. The struggle has broken out because the two systems can no longer live peacefully side by side on the North American continent. It can only be ended by the victory of one system or the other.[4]

In just a few lines, Marx grasped the essence of the struggle far more profoundly than most textbooks. As dialectical materialists, we must always base ourselves on the fundamentals. We should never approach clashes between revolution and counterrevolution in a mechanical, one-sided manner. Nor should we try to make sense of such events on the basis of ahistorical morality. Our historical "true North" lies in the ever-evolving class and property relations of any given society.

What made the Civil War a genuine revolution is that it was not merely driven from above. Though the role of leadership played an essential role, there was also massive participation by ordinary Northern workers and small farmers fighting to defend the country's political unity and, ultimately, to smash slavery. They did so under the banner of the Union and freedom, some driven by religious righteousness, others by the spirit of 1776.

Many were political émigrés who had fled Europe after failed revolutions of 1848.* Two hundred thousand German immigrants

---

* Beginning in France, a wave of revolutions swept across Europe in 1848. The working class was at the forefront of the struggle against the old feudal order, raising its own independent class demands for the first time in history. Terrified by the potential power of the workers, the bourgeoisie betrayed the revolution. Many European revolutionaries came to the US in the wake of the counterrevolution and later participated in the American Civil War.

served in the Union army, among them many revolutionary veterans. Tens of thousands of class fighters from Ireland and other countries also fought for the Union. After 1863, nearly 200,000 self-emancipated slaves served arms-in-hand in Union uniforms. The civilian population also contributed greatly to the cause.

In short, if the First Revolution was a civil war, then the Civil War was an even more thoroughgoing revolution. And while the events of the late 18th century are replete with heroic examples of mass struggle and sacrifice, when it comes to the sheer drama of American history, nothing quite compares to the Civil War.

It's not for nothing that Marx called it "the greatest event of the age."[5] Engels referred to it as "the first grand war of contemporaneous history.[6] And Lenin, in his inimitable style, wrote that only a "pedant" and an "idiot" could deny "the immense, world-historic, progressive, and revolutionary significance of the American Civil War of 1863–65."[7]

Class struggle rising

In the decades before Sumter, capitalism continued to tighten its grip on the American economy, and the unresolved contradictions of the First Revolution metastasized. There were deep class contradictions on either side of the sharpening sectional divide, and the tensions between rich and poor, slaveowners and slaves regularly erupted to the surface.

The number of propertyless wage earners expanded as artisans and other small producers were driven out of business and off their lands. The old craft model of apprentices becoming journeymen and then independent masters was being snuffed out as printers, tailors, cobblers, carpenters, shipwrights, machinists, and others were transformed into permanently dependent wage laborers with no hope of ever rising into property.

Accelerating technological innovation and a rising stream of impoverished immigrants put downward pressure on wages. Between 1820 and 1860, some five million Europeans landed on American shores. The Germans and Irish arrived in huge numbers, fleeing local conflicts, famine, revolutions, and economic crises. As market competition and capital's power over wage labor intensified, the bosses pushed for harsher discipline, speedups, longer hours, and lower labor costs.

Working from "sunup to sundown" was the norm in many trades, and laborers naturally resisted working 11- to 14-hour days, depending on the season. The struggle over the surplus value produced by the workers was continuous, exacerbated by periodic economic panics and slumps. The downturns of 1837 and 1857 hit especially hard. In response to all of this, there were many strikes or "turn-outs" by urban artisans and immigrant laborers, usually over wages and the ten-hour day.

In 1834 and 1836, women workers in Lowell, Massachusetts, stopped production over wage cuts and speedups. In 1835, a citywide general strike for the ten-hour day paralyzed Philadelphia. In 1836, tailors and other journeymen struck in New York City over wages and the working day. In 1850, it was the turn of New York City's printers, who struck over wages and for more control of their workshops.

In 1851, railroad workers on the Erie line struck, a preview of the momentous events of 1877. In the 1850s, New England was swept by a wave of walkouts and other job actions by shoemakers and leather workers. Already in this period, identity politics was used by the bosses to divide and conquer the workers along racial, ethnic, and religious lines.

There were also tenant uprisings in upstate New York, including the famous "Anti-Rent War," which began in the late 1830s, peaked in the mid-1840s, and flared up again in 1849–51. This was a mass rural insurgency in the Hudson Valley and Catskills against the manorial "patroon" system, a survival of the Dutch colonial era. Disguised as "Calico Indians," tenant farmers resisted sheriffs and rent collectors and sometimes attacked landlords and their agents, echoing both the Boston Tea Party and the Shaysites.

In the spirit of the First Revolution, mass meetings, strike committees, newspapers, pamphlets, and even attempts at independent political organization were part of the general ferment in both urban and rural areas. These were met with injunctions, police violence, militia deployments, and prosecutions for "conspiracy" or rioting. In a preview of the Red Scare, many laborers were blacklisted as employers coordinated with each other and the state. Such was life for the early working class in the "free labor" North.

Insoluble contradictions

The country's question of questions, however, remained that of chattel slavery. Slavery was the root cause of most political crises in the early years of the republic, and was the *casus belli** for open war in 1861. Aside from property in land, property in humans was the single biggest asset in the American economy, worth nearly $4 billion in 1860.

In 1820, Thomas Jefferson described the ruling class's dangerous conundrum as follows:

> [W]e have the wolf by the ears, and we can neither hold him, nor safely let him go. Justice is in one scale, and self-preservation in the other.[8]

Deep-seated racism had settled into every part of the country, even among some abolitionists. Although they would end up fighting against slavery objectively, a majority of Northern whites were suspicious of Black people, and especially freed slaves, who were seen as competitors for jobs and land. And of course, the incessant conflicts with Indigenous nations over land also raged in the antebellum period† and during the Civil War itself.

As discussed in Part One through Colin Woodard's *American Nations* framework, there were significant economic and cultural differences within both the North and the South. The combined and uneven patterns of development from the colonial period only intensified as the country moved from infancy into adolescence.

---

* Latin for "occasion of war"; an act or an event that either provokes or is used to justify a war.

† Latin for "before the war"; the period from the end of the War of 1812 to the beginning of the American Civil War.

For example, the economies and interests of the Upper South differed from those of the Deep South. In Delaware, Maryland, Virginia, Kentucky, and parts of North Carolina and Tennessee, agriculture was generally more diversified, and the enslaved population was less concentrated than in the Cotton Belt. Delaware's economy was far more closely tied to the Mid-Atlantic commercial world, and Baltimore was both a major port and an important manufacturing center by the antebellum period. In many cases, enslaved people born in the Upper South were sold "down the river" through the domestic slave trade into the harsher conditions of the Deep South.

In the South Carolina lowcountry—Georgia, Alabama, Mississippi, Louisiana, and Texas—extensive cotton, sugar, and rice plantations meant far larger concentrations of slaves. Property in slaves, combined with enormous tracts of land, wasn't merely part of the social order; it was the essence of the region's financial system. Like other forms of property, slaves could be mortgaged, pledged as collateral, and insured. Policies sometimes covered loss of life, injury, and the risks associated with being hired out or transported. When claims for damages were paid, the proceeds went to slaveholders or to creditors with a legal interest in the "property," not to the slave's family.

By contrast, large parts of the South, including much of Appalachia, the pine barrens, and parts of the Ozarks, were unsuited for plantation agriculture and were heavily populated by small farmers, tenants, and landless whites of Scots-Irish descent who did not profit directly from slavery.

As an example of Northern diversity, consider the differences between New England states like Massachusetts and Connecticut and frontier states like Minnesota and Wisconsin. The rapidly industrializing Northeast had little in common with "free soil, free labor" homesteaders on the Northwest frontier, most of whom were more focused on dispossessing Indigenous peoples and securing land than on the plight of Southern slaves. And while those closer to the coast were already caught in capital's web, those deeper in the interior did everything they could to escape it.

All of these contradictory tendencies were expected to live in peace and harmony in the same nation-state—an untenable proposition unless serious adjustments were made.

Political economy in the antebellum North

As we saw in Part One, after winning independence, the young republic lost its favored status within the British Empire. It also lost its privileged access to markets and credit. War debts, an unstable currency, trade disruptions, and the end of wartime privateering pushed the economy into a deep depression. These challenges led to rising taxes and a spiral of debt, sparking the populist "Regulator" movements. After these uprisings were defeated, greater centralization of the federal state was reflected in the Constitution. Hamilton's program strengthened capitalism's grip on the economy, especially in the Northeast.

However, in the Northwest—the Ohio Valley and the Great Plains—it was still possible to survive as a subsistence farmer. So long as would-be yeomen could access enough land to sustain a family in a "natural economy," they faced little compulsion to revolutionize production or to accumulate land, labor, and capital.

As the decades passed, however, these regions also became saturated, and independent producers began to feel the squeeze of the moneyed economy. They were increasingly compelled to specialize and produce for sale on the market. However, specialized output requires improved methods and increasingly expensive tools. To pay for all of this, farmers had to borrow money for capital improvements and to buy items they had previously produced themselves. As their debts accumulated, their focus shifted even further toward marketable cash crops rather than diversified production for direct consumption.

The country's expanding network of canals and railroads reflected the need to transport the rising volume of commodities. This, in turn, fed back into the growing vortex of the market. As markets expanded, ever-larger commercial farms and manufacturers produced commodities explicitly for exchange.

Merchant-landlords who specialized in aggregating and selling both cash agricultural products and consumer goods came to dominate local areas. This led to greater social stratification, as some producers accumulated more land and capital and could hire more laborers than others.

Rising debts and taxes forced many small holders to sell their property. Deprived of their own means of production, they had no option but to become tenant farmers or itinerant wage laborers. All of this accelerated the social division of labor and laid the basis for the rise of industrial and finance capital. Such is the ruthless logic of capitalism.

By the 1840s, a tipping point had been reached, and petty-commodity agricultural production for the market was dominant across the North. A majority of the region's independent farmers, artisans, and small-scale manufacturers had been transformed into petty-commodity–producing tenant farmers, wage laborers, petty capitalists, and in some cases, industrialists and bankers.

Political economy in the antebellum South

The future Confederate States of America was no monolith, either. It, too, had plenty of yeomen, tenant farmers, and landless wage laborers. By the 1850s, the South also had some manufacturing, accounting for around 10 per cent of the nation's total. On the eve of the Civil War, as many as 10 per cent of slaves worked in urban centers including Richmond and Charleston, in industries including mining, iron smelting, tanning, cotton spinning, and weaving. In fact, slaves accounted for roughly 20 per cent of the population in most Southern cities. In Charleston, South Carolina, slaves and free Blacks outnumbered whites.

According to historian Alan D. Watson, urban slaves worked, "as stevedores on the docks, pilots along the rivers, and cooks, stewards, and sailors on ships."[9]

And as explained by Troy L. Kickler for the North Carolina History Project:

> It also was not uncommon to find urban slaves working in factories. During the Civil War, Tredegar Iron Works in Richmond, Va., for one, used skilled slave labor. During the war, Tredegar, along with its associated plants, employed approximately 1,200 slaves and free Blacks. (By May 1863, 343 slaves comprised 59 per cent of the work force among Tredegar's affiliates in Georgia.)
>
> Even though their skills were in high demand, slaves, of course, did not have the opportunities to negotiate wages like their free Black counterparts, who increased their compensation during the war. By the war's end, writes one historian, Tredegar produced much of the South's firepower—1,600 cannons and 90 per cent of shot and cannonballs.[10]

Nonetheless, large plantations with 20 or more slaves producing cotton, tobacco, and sugar for the domestic and world markets were predominant, even though they accounted for just 12 per cent of slaveholders.

However, the political economy of American chattel slavery contained an intractable contradiction. On the one hand, slave plantations produced oceans of cash crops for exchange on the world capitalist market. On the other hand, they were relatively self-sufficient, producing use-values for immediate consumption.

Although the usually indebted slave lords imported luxuries for their ostentatious displays of wealth, their plantations could produce nearly everything else, often sharing a limited division of labor with other plantations in the area. For example, while some plantations focused on producing foodstuffs in addition to cotton or tobacco, others specialized in the production of bricks for use in urban construction and on the plantations themselves. Gangs of slaves—including children as young as six years old—dug, molded, and sun-baked clay before firing it in kilns and loading the finished products onto carts or boats for transportation to worksites.

Unlike capitalists, slave owners could not lay off their workforce whenever they wanted. Agriculture is cyclical, so the so-called "planters"—who did none of the planting themselves—had to keep their "tools with a voice" occupied year-round. This was necessary not only to maximize returns on their investment but also to make it harder for slaves to organize mass resistance. As the saying goes, "idle hands are the devil's workshop."

Periodic slave uprisings were the ultimate expression of the class struggle in the antebellum South. But the day-to-day class struggle was largely over how much time slaves had to work for their masters versus working for themselves.

When they weren't laboring in their masters' fields or homes, slaves grew a variety of crops for their own use, as well as raising animals, fishing, and hunting to supplement their diets. They made their own clothes and manufactured simple tools and other basic goods on-site. Some skilled slaves—such as blacksmiths, carpenters, coopers, musicians, painters, cabinetmakers, cobblers, tailors, and skilled domestic workers—were loaned out to other masters on a part-time basis, earning tips and sometimes wages, which could be used to buy their own freedom. In an effort to diversify their income streams, some planters even used their chattels to grow food crops for sale at local markets.

Cotton, however, was king. In 1860, that crop alone accounted for 60 per cent of the South's agricultural output by value and over 50 per cent of total US exports. With his characteristically penetrating insight, Marx summed things up as follows:

> [N]egro labor in the Southern States of the American Union preserved something of a patriarchal character, so long as production was chiefly directed to immediate local consumption. But in proportion, as the export of cotton became of vital interest to these states, the overworking of the Negro and sometimes the using up of his life in seven years of labor became a factor in a calculated and calculating system. It was no longer a question of obtaining from him a certain quantity of useful products. It was now a question of production of surplus labor itself.[11]

As far as capital was concerned, therefore, the so-called "peculiar institution" contained a fatal flaw. The system's structural constraints were a brake on revolutionizing the region's agriculture through capital-intensive mechanization and the hiring of wage labor. Although social inertia played a certain role, this was largely because so much of the plantation owners' capital was tied up in "means of production in human form." Although there were some innovations and changes introduced over the years, broadly speaking, the Southern economy remained much the same in the 1850s as it had been in the 1820s.

This limited the free development of internal markets and the ever-wider circulation of commodities throughout the country, which was precisely what Northern capitalism required to keep growing. So while Southern plantation slavery accelerated the development of capitalism in Britain and the North, its internal contradictions cut across the development of capitalism in its home region. The two broad sections of the country were on a collision course with history—and with each other.

Everything turns into its opposite

The Industrial Revolution in Britain and the rise of textile mills created an insatiable demand for cotton. Eli Whitney's invention of the cotton gin in 1793 revolutionized the technology used to process the plants' finicky fibers. It also fueled the need for more slaves to cultivate the labor-intensive crop.

As a result, between 1790 and 1860, the slave population more than quadrupled to nearly four million, 90 per cent of which was concentrated on rural plantations. It was this explosion in demand for slave labor—long after the formal end of the Transatlantic slave trade in 1808—that eventually burst the limits of the federal Union so painstakingly crafted by the country's founders.

As we've seen, forming the Union was possible only through a series of concessions to the slavocracy. For decades, Southern slaveholders exerted outsized influence in the federal government, despite the region's smaller population. A majority of early US presidents were Southern-born, and Southerners were frequently prominent on the Supreme Court. In 1790, a bargain linking Hamilton's plan for federal assumption of state Revolutionary War debts with the permanent location of the national capital produced the Residence Act and the Funding Act. Under that deal, the federal government remained in Philadelphia temporarily and then moved to the malarial swamplands of Washington, DC in 1800.

For over half a century, the two sections had maintained a symbiotic, if at times, strained relationship. As we have seen, their interests had coincided in the struggle against the British, various Indigenous nations, the Shaysites, and other internal rebellions in the years after the first revolution.

Furthermore, the exploitation of slave labor played a crucial role in the primitive accumulation of American capital. Building on Hegel, Marx emphasized that it was not merely *from* slavery that this original accumulation emerged, but *through* it.

Enormous fortunes were made on this trade, and not only in the slave states. Despite the moral objections of many New Englanders and Quakers, slavery was not only tolerated, but was actively encouraged for the simple reason that it was profitable.

In fact, historians estimate that in the two decades preceding the war, New York City derived between one-third and one-half of its wealth from the nexus of slavery and cotton. Despite never growing a single boll of cotton, the future capital of capitalism served as a commercial liaison between the North and the South. It controlled an estimated 40 per cent of the South's cotton exports. The city pocketed about $80 million per year in commissions, shipping, insurance, and warehousing fees. This is why many New York merchants and bankers initially opposed both war and abolition.

NYC's Mayor, Fernando Wood, at one point proposed secession from New York state and the Union. Wood was at the heart of the infamous Tammany Hall. He was keen to keep the revenues from the slave and cotton trade flowing, as these greased the wheels of the city's Democratic Party political patronage machine. As a "free city," the city of "Tri-Insula" could maintain and even deepen its connections with "our aggrieved brethren of the Slave States, [with whom] we have friendly relations and a common sympathy."[12] Though his proposal went nowhere, this highlights the close connection between early American capitalism and slavery.

On the above basis, the two sections were able to negotiate the joint sharing of power within the same state for several decades. But all good things come to an end. Eventually, this mutually beneficial relationship hit its limits and was transformed into its opposite.

Politics is concentrated economics, and the rise and fall of parties and politicians ultimately reflect deeper class interests and contradictions. Since a state and its apparatus must ultimately express the material interests of one class or another, something had to give.

Maintaining sectional parity in Congress became a nonnegotiable imperative for both sides. However, the North's population grew significantly faster, driven by immigration and higher birth rates. The Southern economy served to discourage immigration, as free white laborers were unwilling to compete with slaves. Furthermore, the planters had no interest in attracting potential abolitionists or free-soilers.

Between 1800 and 1860, the US population grew from just over five million to more than 31 million. By 1860, the states that remained in the Union held about 22 million people, while those that seceded held about nine million, nearly four million of whom were enslaved. This disparity gave the North a decisive advantage in available military manpower and industrial workers, and threatened to give it insurmountable control over federal politics.

Then, of course, there was the question of Western lands. By the 1850s, the only way the big planters could meet the worldwide demand for cotton was to expand the territories under cultivation by slaves. Soil depletion by the nutrient-greedy crop increased the pressure. Growing international competition also threatened their dominance. They needed more land on which to grow cotton, or other useful ways to put their slaves to work, for example, in ranching or mining operations out West.

Geographic expansion became essential to their survival as a class. It was a question of systemic life or death. This is why they dreamed of building a hemispheric slave empire through the conquest of Cuba, Central America, and Mexico.

However, *containing* slavery was equally life-or-death for the Northern capitalists. They could survive only if capitalist relations continued to spread. Capital is animated by an unquenchable thirst to expand markets and convert as many humans as possible into juridically free wage laborers, which is the source of its lifeblood—surplus value.

Put simply, the capitalists needed wage laborers to exploit and consumers with the means to purchase the goods they manufactured. Chattel slavery had played an important role in the past, but was ultimately an inefficient utilization of finite land and labor. Furthermore, the plantation economy could never evolve a robust consumer market. Under pain of extinction, the North was compelled to impose its own economic forms on the nation-state as a whole, including in the West.

Needless to say, the North and South had incompatible visions for the future.

After the US stole half of Mexico in 1848, the debate over what mode of exploitation would dominate the newly acquired territories intensified. For the slave owners, "free soil and free labor" in the West was the equivalent of abolition and the loss of their enormous privileges and power, whether immediately or in the not-too-distant future.

In an attempt to square the circle, John C. Calhoun, a South Carolina Senator and former vice president, came up with the concept of "nullification." This was the legal theory that individual states had the authority to invalidate federal laws deemed unconstitutional within their own borders. He saw the exclusion of slavery from the West—and in particular, California's admission as a free state—as equivalent to destroying the South. In the Spring of 1850, just days before his death, Calhoun issued a dark warning from the Senate floor:

The North is making the most strenuous efforts to appropriate [the territory acquired by the United States in the Mexican-American War] to herself, by excluding the South from every foot of it . . . The United States, since they declared their independence, have acquired 2,373,046 square miles of territory, from which the North will have excluded the South, if she should succeed in monopolizing the newly-acquired Territories, about three-fourths of the whole, leaving to the South but about one-fourth . . .[13]

There is a question of vital importance to the Southern section, in reference to which the views and feelings of the two sections are as opposite and hostile as they can possibly be.

I refer to the relation between the two races in the Southern section, which constitutes a vital portion of her social organization. Every portion of the North entertains views and feelings more or less hostile to it. Those most opposed and hostile regard it as a sin, and consider themselves under the most sacred obligation to use every effort to destroy it. Indeed, to the extent that they conceive that they have power, they regard themselves as implicated in the sin, and responsible for not suppressing it by the use of all and every means. Those less opposed and hostile regard it as a crime—an offense against humanity, as they call it and, altho not so fanatical, feel themselves bound to use all efforts to effect the same object; while those who are least opposed and hostile regard it as a blot and a stain on the character of what they call the Nation, and feel themselves accordingly bound to give it no countenance or support . . .[14]

If the agitation goes on, the same force, acting with increased intensity, as has been shown, will finally snap every cord, when nothing will be left to hold the States together except force . . .

How can the Union be saved? To this I answer, there is but one way by which it can be, and that is by adopting such measures as will satisfy the States belonging to the Southern section that they can remain in the Union consistently with their honor and their safety . . . The question, then, is this—By what can this be done?[15]

There is but one way by which it can with any certainty; and that is by a full and final settlement, on the principle of justice, of all the questions at issue between the two sections. The South asks for justice, simple justice, and less she ought not to take . . .

But can this be done? Yes, easily; not by the weaker party, for it can of itself do nothing—not even protect itself—but by the stronger. The North has only to will it to accomplish it—to do justice by conceding to the South an equal right in the acquired territory, and to do her duty by causing the stipulations relative to fugitive slaves to be faithfully fulfilled—to cease the agitation of the slave question, and to provide for the insertion of a provision in the Constitution, by an amendment, which will restore to the South in substance the power she possessed of protecting herself before the equilibrium between the sections was destroyed by the action of this Government. There will be no difficulty in devising such a provision—one that will protect the South, and which at the same time will improve and strengthen the Government instead of impairing and weakening it.

But will the North agree to this? It is for her to answer the question. But, I will say, she can not refuse, if she has half the love of the Union which she professes to have, or without justly exposing herself to the charge that her love of power and aggrandizement is far greater than her love of the Union. At all events, the responsibility of saving the Union rests on the North, and not on the South . . .

It is time, Senators, that there should be an open and manly avowal on all sides, as to what is intended to be done. If the question is not now settled, it is uncertain whether it ever can hereafter be; and we, as the representatives of the States of this Union, regarded as Governments, should come to a distinct understanding as to our respective views, in order to ascertain whether the great questions at issue can be settled or not. If you, who represent the stronger portion, can not agree to settle them on the broad principle of justice and duty, say so; and let the States we both represent agree to separate and part in peace.

> If you are unwilling we should part in peace, tell us so; and we shall know what to do when you reduce the question to submission or resistance. If you remain silent, you will compel us to infer by your acts what you intend.[16]

Like a couple in an unhappy marriage, two very different socio-economic entities and distinct national identities were forced to coexist within the same legal framework. An almighty political crisis was inevitable. The framework of the original US Constitution and Bill of Rights had reached its limits and was about to burst in violent and dramatic fashion.

It was in this tense atmosphere that Lincoln gave his famous "House Divided" speech in 1858:

> In *my* opinion, it *will* not cease, until a *crisis* shall have been reached, and passed.
>
> "A house divided against itself cannot stand."
>
> I believe this government cannot endure, permanently half *slave* and half *free.*
>
> I do not expect the Union to be *dissolved*—I do not expect the house to *fall*—but I *do* expect it will cease to be divided.
>
> It will become *all* one thing, or *all* the other.
>
> Either the *opponents* of slavery, will arrest the further spread of it, and place it where the public mind shall rest in the belief that it is in course of ultimate extinction; or its *advocates* will push it forward, till it shall become alike lawful in all the States, *old* as well as *new—North* as well as *South.*[17]

The theft of Indian lands intensifies

In the decades after the Revolution, American colonists continued to systematically dispossess the Indigenous peoples of the continent. Coming from a world without private property, the Indians were at a disadvantage when it came to dealing with the unhinged greed of a people motivated by the relentless pursuit of the same. As the leader of the Shawnee nation, Tecumseh, lamented in 1810:

> *Sell a country! Why not sell the air, the great sea, as well as the earth?* Did not the Great Spirit make them all for the use of his children?[18]

And in the words of the Sauk chief, Black Hawk:

> My reason teaches me that land cannot be sold. The Great Spirit gave it to his children to live upon, and cultivate, as far as is necessary for their subsistence; and so long as they occupy and cultivate it, they have the right to the soil — but if they voluntarily leave it, then any other people have a right to settle upon it. Nothing can be sold, but such things as can be carried away.[19]
>
> I was told that, according to the treaty, we had no *right* to remain upon the lands *sold*, and that the government would *force* us to leave them. There was but a small portion, however, that *had been sold*; the balance remaining in the hands of the government, we claimed the right (if we had no other) to "live and hunt upon, as long as it remained the property of the government," by a stipulation in the same treaty that required us to evacuate it *after* it had been sold. This was the land that we wished to inhabit, and thought we had the best right to occupy.[20]

The pattern of encroachment was as underhanded as it was repetitive. Hundreds of treaties were signed with the federal government, often under economic or physical duress, or by individuals with no authority to do so. Often before the ink was even dry, settlers claimed lands and resources unquestionably belonging to the Native nations, using threats or violence to back up their claims. When the Indians dared to complain or strike back, militiamen or federal troops would carry out "punitive expeditions" in the name of "Western civilization." Following the Indians' all-but-inevitable defeat, the noose was squeezed tighter, and their lands and resources shrank even further.

Washington's Secretary of War, Henry Knox, was forthcoming about the cynicism involved in these rarely consensual exchanges:

> The Indians being the prior occupants, possess the right of the soil. It cannot be taken from them unless by their free consent, or by the right of conquest in case of a just war.[21]

To give official cover to this murderous expropriation, a variety of legal doctrines were conjured up. In order that land could be bought, sold, or otherwise subjected to market forces, it first had to be transformed into alienable property.

In the extraordinary case of *Johnson v. M'Intosh*, which came before the Supreme Court in 1823, Chief Justice John Marshall came up with a brazenly racist justification for the colonization of the continent. In his view, European "discovery" of the Americas gave the discovering power "ultimate dominion":

> Discovery gave an exclusive right to extinguish the Indian title of occupancy, either by purchase or by conquest.[22]

In other words, Europeans had an overriding claim to the continent *long before they "discovered" the Western Hemisphere.* Never mind the millions of people already living there—they were merely "occupants." Since Indigenous peoples lacked capitalist private property and markets, they had no legal claim to the land in the first place.

Another workaround was to consider Indigenous peoples "nations" when it came to negotiating treaties, but to deny them nationhood when such sovereignty got in the way of stealing their land. In the case of *Cherokee Nation v. Georgia*, Marshall ruled:

> [T]he Indians are acknowledged to have an unquestionable, and heretofore an unquestioned, right to the lands they occupy until that right shall be extinguished by a voluntary cession to our government. It may well be doubted whether those tribes which reside within the acknowledged boundaries of the United States can, with strict accuracy, be denominated foreign nations. They may more correctly, perhaps, be denominated domestic dependent nations. They occupy a territory to which we assert a title independent of their will, which must take effect in point of possession when their right of possession ceases; meanwhile,

> they are in a state of pupilage. Their relations to the United States resemble that of a ward to his guardian. They look to our government for protection, rely upon its kindness and its power, appeal to it for relief to their wants, and address the President as their great father . . .
>
> The Court has bestowed its best attention on this question, and, after mature deliberation, the majority is of opinion that an Indian tribe or nation within the United States is not a foreign state in the sense of the constitution, and cannot maintain an action in the Courts of the United States . . .[23]

And when purchase or outright conquest wasn't possible, or the process of swindling them through treaties moved too slowly, the state authorized the forced relocation of entire peoples. In a preview of modern times, the government at times used the hypocritical cover of "humanitarianism," arguing that moving Indians further west was the only way to protect them from settler violence.

Andrew Jackson was a particularly vicious agent of westward expansion. A rough-and-tumble early American populist, Jackson built an aggressive cross-class coalition by mobilizing poor, land-hungry whites while ultimately serving the slavocracy and land speculators. In his Second Annual Message, in 1830, he explained what his policy would mean:

> The consequences of a speedy removal will be important to the United States, to individual States, and to the Indians themselves. The pecuniary advantages which it promises to the Government are the least of its recommendations. It puts an end to all possible danger of collision between the authorities of the General and State Governments on account of the Indians. It will place a dense and civilized population in large tracts of country now occupied by a few savage hunters.
>
> By opening the whole territory between Tennessee on the north and Louisiana on the south to the settlement of the whites it will incalculably strengthen the SW frontier and render the adjacent States strong enough to repel future invasions without remote aid. It will relieve the whole State of Mississippi and the western part of Alabama of Indian occupancy, and

> enable those States to advance rapidly in population, wealth, and power. It will separate the Indians from immediate contact with settlements of whites; free them from the power of the States; enable them to pursue happiness in their own way and under their own rude institutions; will retard the progress of decay, which is lessening their numbers, and perhaps cause them gradually, under the protection of the Government and through the influence of good counsels, to cast off their savage habits and become an interesting, civilized, and Christian community.[24]

His fifth annual message, delivered in 1833, was a variation on the same racist theme:

> My original convictions upon this subject have been confirmed by the course of events for several years, and experience is every day adding to their strength. That those tribes can not exist surrounded by our settlements and in continual contact with our citizens is certain. They have neither the intelligence, the industry, the moral habits, nor the desire of improvement which are essential to any favorable change in their condition. Established in the midst of another and a superior race, and without appreciating the causes of their inferiority or seeking to control them, they must necessarily yield to the force of circumstances and ere long disappear.[25]

In other words, instead of curbing the settlers, Jackson cleared the way for them, all to prepare a massive expansion of slave plantations. With the Indian Removal Act of 1830, Congress authorized the president to exchange Indigenous lands in the East for lands in the West and to fund removal. Put bluntly, it gave him the power and financial resources needed to carry out mass deportations under inhuman conditions. What followed was one of the blackest episodes in American history—and that's saying something.

In the late 1830s, thousands of Cherokee, Choctaw, Creek, Chickasaw, and Seminole were forcibly removed from Georgia, Alabama, Mississippi, Tennessee, Florida, and parts of North Carolina. They were walked overland in a horrific death march to the newly created "Indian Territory" in present-day Oklahoma.

At least 4,000 and as many as 15,000 are believed to have perished on the infamous "Trail of Tears."

Army officer John G. Burnett, who participated in the events of May 1838, later described some of the scenes he had witnessed:

> Men working in the fields were arrested and driven to the stockades. Women were dragged from their homes by soldiers whose language they could not understand. Children were often separated from their parents and driven into the stockades with the sky for a blanket and the earth for a pillow. And often the old and infirm were prodded with bayonets to hasten them to the stockades.
>
> In one home death had come during the night. A little sad-faced child had died and was lying on a bear skin couch and some women were preparing the little body for burial. All were arrested and driven out leaving the child in the cabin. I don't know who buried the body.
>
> In another home was a frail Mother, apparently a widow and three small children, one just a baby. When told that she must go, the Mother gathered the children at her feet, prayed a humble prayer in her native tongue, patted the old family dog on the head, told the faithful creature goodbye, with a baby strapped on her back and leading a child with each hand started on her exile. But the task was too great for that frail Mother. A stroke of heart failure relieved her sufferings. She sunk and died with her baby on her back, and her other two children clinging to her hands.
>
> Chief Junaluska who had saved President Jackson's life at the battle of Horse Shoe witnessed this scene, the tears gushing down his cheeks and lifting his cap he turned his face toward the heavens and said, "Oh my God, if I had known at the battle of the Horse Shoe what I know now, American history would have been differently written."
>
> At this time, 1890, we are too near the removal of the Cherokees for our young people to fully understand the enormity of the crime that was committed against a helpless race. Truth is, the facts are being concealed from the young people of today. School children of today do not know that we are living on lands that were taken from a helpless race at the bayonet point to satisfy the white man's greed.[26]

The parallels between all of this and modern-day Zionist "ethnic cleansing" of the Levant are truly breathtaking.

All compromises lead to Sumter

According to historian Shelby Foote—a none-too-thinly-veiled Confederate sympathizer—the Civil War resulted from a failure "to do the thing [Americans] really have a genius for, which is compromise."[27]

From a Marxist perspective, there can be no permanent compromise on fundamental class questions. In the final analysis, one class or another must exercise power. One class or another must dominate political, economic, and cultural life. All great issues are ultimately decided through open class struggle: in the workplace, on the streets, and, when push comes to shove, on the battlefield. They are not decided at the ballot box, in Congress, or in the judiciary.

Nonetheless, the generations that followed the Founding Fathers did their utmost to avoid the unavoidable crisis for as long as possible. As historian Bruce Levine explained:

> Many political leaders cheered both the 1820 and 1850 compromises as resolutions of the slavery conflict. Each did, for a time, formally decide the specific questions then in contention. But neither testified to the existence of an overriding, nationwide spirit of conciliation among the population, and neither resolved the fundamental, underlying dispute over slavery, its merits, and its future in the United States.
>
> In both 1820 and 1850, compromise advocates had found it impossible to pass the measures they offered in a single bill. Too many Northern congressmen objected to the concessions being made to the South (such as admitting Missouri as a slave state or strengthening the fugitive slave bill), and too many Southern congressmen felt the same way about concessions offered to the North (such as outlawing slavery in much of the Louisiana Purchase or admitting California effectively as a free state). Therefore, single "omnibus" compromise bills were broken up into separate measures so that each could be voted upon and passed by distinct, shifting majorities.

> In both the North and the South, many who disliked all or part of the compromise packages agreed to abide by them for the sake of maintaining national peace. But the opposing sentiments that made both the 1820 and 1850 compromises so difficult to enact ultimately undermined each of them.[28]

As we've seen, the status of the western territories had been a burning issue since before the Revolution. The intensity of the debate was amplified after Thomas Jefferson purchased Louisiana from Napoleon in 1803, quadrupling the country's landmass.

As a temporary stopgap, the Missouri Compromise of 1820 allowed Missouri to enter the Union as a slave state in exchange for Maine's separation from Massachusetts and admission as a free state. This ensured that the delicate balance of congressional power was maintained. Furthermore, with the exception of Missouri, the compromise barred slavery north of latitude 36°30' in the remaining Louisiana Purchase territory. Tensions had been relieved momentarily, but the arrangement set a precedent for the further expansion of slavery.

As the years passed, thwe economy and population continued to grow, and the interests of the two sections drifted even further apart. Concrete questions about the role of government flowed from this divergence. For example, should the federal government raise revenue to invest in major infrastructure projects like roads, canals, ports, and, later, railroads? Should it impose protective tariffs to nurture American manufacturing and create a stable home market? Should it establish and sustain a strong national bank to stabilize currency and credit while restraining lending by state banks? Should modest plots of western land be made available on favorable terms to encourage free-labor settlement and market expansion?

Broadly speaking, this was the program of the Whig Party* and Henry Clay's "American System." Emerging in late 1833

* The Whig Party was founded by Henry Clay and Daniel Webster in 1833. Its name was borrowed from the British Whigs, a name in turn inspired by the 1648 Scottish "Whiggamore" rebellion against King Charles I. Andrew Jackson's rule was cast as a monarchy, and the new party as defenders of republican ideals.

and formally organized in 1834, the new Whig coalition brought together National Republicans, Anti-Masons, and anti-Jackson Democrats. The name "Whig" deliberately echoed the American Revolutionary-era opponents of monarchical power and was used to cast Andrew Jackson as "King Andrew." The party drew support from merchants, manufacturers, professionals, and sections of the commercializing farmers.

Or should the federal government be more hands-off, keep expenditures low and leave economic development mainly to the states and private enterprise, with preferential access to western lands for slave plantations? Broadly speaking, these were key themes of Jacksonian Democracy—especially its Southern wing—and later of Southern Democrats. They tended to oppose federally funded internal improvements, which they saw as channeling national resources toward Northern and Western commercial development while asking Southerners to help foot the bill. The South also tended to favor lower tariffs and freer trade, which supported its export-oriented economy and reduced the cost of imported manufactured goods.

Lasting from roughly 1828 to 1854, these were the opposing political forces that dominated the country's Second Party System.

Tensions flared again with the Tariff of 1828, a tax on imported goods passed to defend the Northern industrialists who were finding it hard to compete with cheap manufactured goods from Britain. Denounced by Southerners as the "Tariff of Abominations," they saw it as a form of "tribute" to be paid to the North. Things spiraled quickly into the Nullification Crisis of 1832–33[†], with South Carolina already raising the specter of secession.

† A political crisis over the Tariffs of 1828 and 1832, passed by the federal government to protect Northern industry from foreign competition. The burden of tariffs fell disproportionately on the agrarian South, which imported more European manufactured goods than the North. South Carolina passed an Ordinance of Nullification in 1832, declaring the tariffs to be unconstitutional and, therefore, illegal within its borders. When South Carolina began military preparations to combat federal enforcement of the tariffs, Congress authorized President Andrew Jackson to use force against the state. The Compromise

Since there was little manufacturing to protect in their region, and since tariffs generally raised prices, Southern politicians such as John C. Calhoun argued that states could nullify federal tariffs within their borders. According to his reading of the US Constitution:

> Their great and leading principle is that the general Government emanated from the people of the several States, forming distinct political communities, and acting in their separate and sovereign capacity, and not from all of the people forming one aggregate political community; that the Constitution of the United States is, in fact, a compact, to which each state is a party, in the character already described; and that the several States, or parties, have a right to judge of its infractions; and in case of a deliberate, palpable, and dangerous exercise of power not delegated, they have the right, in the last resort, to use the language of the Virginia resolutions, "*to interpose for arresting the progress of the evil, and for maintaining, within their respective limits, the authorities, rights, and liberties appertaining to them.*"
>
> This right of interposition, thus solemnly asserted by the State of Virginia, be it called what it may, State right, veto, nullification, or by any other name, I conceive to be the fundamental principle of our system, resting on facts historically as certain as our Revolution itself, and deductions as simple and demonstrative as that of any political or moral truth whatever; and I firmly believe that on its recognition depend the stability and safety of our political institutions . . .
>
> I solemnly believe it to be the only solid foundation of our system, and of the Union itself; and that the opposite doctrine, which denies to the States the right of protecting their reserved powers, and which would vest in the General Government (it matters not through what Department) the right of determining, exclusively and finally, the powers delegated to it, is incompatible with the sovereignty of the States, and of the Constitution itself, considered as the basis of a federal Union.[29]

Tariff of 1833 ended the crisis, but didn't resolve any of the underlying tensions between free and slave states.

Calhoun's deeper worry was that the measure would set a dangerous precedent when it came to the South's core interest: slavery. After all, if the federal government could impose taxes or tariffs on unwilling states—just as the British had done to its colonists—it might one day restrict or destroy slavery. In late 1832, South Carolina formally adopted an Ordinance of Nullification, declaring the tariffs unconstitutional and threatening secession if the federal government used force to enforce them.

Though broadly sympathetic to the slaveocracy, Andrew Jackson was an even stronger advocate of a centralized state apparatus, at least in this case, and especially when it was under his control. Previewing Lincoln's arguments against secession, he had a very different interpretation of the Constitution. In no uncertain terms, he condemned South Carolina's actions as rebellious and threatened to send in federal bayonets. He feared a different precedent. If the states could selectively apply or ignore federal laws, then the Union was a dead letter.

> The laws of the United States must be executed. I have no discretionary power on the subject—my duty is emphatically pronounced in the Constitution. Those who told you that you might peaceably prevent their execution, deceived you—they could not have been deceived themselves. They know that a forcible opposition could alone prevent the execution of the laws, and they know that such opposition must be repelled. Their object is disunion, but be not deceived by names: disunion, by armed force, is *treason*. If you are, on the head of the instigators of the act be the dreadful consequences—on their heads be the dishonor, but on yours may fall the punishment—on your unhappy State will inevitably fall all the evils of the conflict you force upon the government of your country. It cannot accede to the mad project of disunion, of which you would be the first victims—its first magistrate cannot, if he would, avoid the performance of his duty—the consequence must be fearful for you, distressing to your fellow-citizens here, and to the friends of good government throughout the world . . .[30]

> The Constitution of the United States, then, forms a *government*, not a league; and whether it be formed by compact between the States, or in any other manner, its character is the same. It is a government in which all the people are represented, which operates directly on the people individually, not upon the States—they retained all the power they did not grant. But each State having expressly parted with so many powers as to constitute jointly with the other States a single nation, cannot from that period possess any right to secede, because such secession does not break a league, but destroys the unity of a nation, and any injury to that unity is not only a breach which would result from the contravention of a compact, but it is an offense against the whole Union. To say that any State may at pleasure secede from the Union, is to say that the United States are not a nation . . .[31]

In 1833, Congress passed the Force Bill, authorizing military enforcement of tariff collection. Had Henry Clay not brokered a Compromise Tariff that gradually lowered rates, the Civil War might have broken out nearly 30 years earlier. South Carolina eventually backed down, but not before performatively "nullifying" the Force Bill to save face.

All of this took place shortly after Nat Turner's 1831 Rebellion in Virginia, in which over 60 white people were killed. This was the nightmare that had haunted every slave society since the Haitian Revolution. Fear and anxiety were sky high.

The slave owners unleashed a wave of terror as columns of militia and armed posses scoured the countryside. Turner was eventually captured and subjected to a deliberately theatrical execution: he was hanged, drawn and quartered, beheaded, and then buried in an unmarked grave. As many as 200 other slaves, most of whom had nothing to do with the uprising, were massacred to set an example. This was terror as policy: the ruling class reserved the right to kill at will. The message was clear: any hint of resistance to the status quo would be answered, not with "justice," but with indiscriminate slaughter.

The Turner revolt amped up the South's siege mentality and hardened its political reflexes—tightening slave codes further, expanding surveillance and patrols, and stoking the paranoid conviction that any outside criticism of slavery was tantamount to incitement of servile rebellion.

A "Wicked" War with Mexico

After a long and bloody revolutionary war of its own, Mexico won independence from Spain in 1821. In an attempt to bring some order to the anarchy on its Northern border, it opened its sprawling province of Tejas to American settlement—on condition that the colonists learn Spanish and respect the country's laws. Unsurprisingly, few of them learned the local language or respected the law, and many brought their chattel slaves with them.

By 1829, the Mexicans had realized that this concentration of Americans within its borders was a threat. It closed the province to further immigration, banned slavery, reinstated property taxes, and increased tariffs on American goods. In response, President Jackson offered to buy the territory for $5 million, but the Mexicans flatly refused.

Given the economic and political turmoil it was undergoing, the Mexican government was too weak to enforce its laws. By 1835, 30,000 Americans lived in Tejas, outnumbering residents of Spanish descent by a ratio of six to one. After a convenient pretext was found to blame the Mexicans for starting a fight, the so-called "Texas Revolution" had started. In reality, it was a slaveowners' rebellion, a preview of both Confederate secession and US imperialist predation.

Impelled by the racist mythology of Manifest Destiny, the Americans embarked on one of the biggest land grabs in human history. Not only the Indians, but the Mexicans would be forced to submit to the rising American colossus.

Jingoist* American papers like the *New York Herald* whipped up support for immediate US intervention and annexation, decrying the "rapacious and bloody Spaniard":

> The Anglo-Saxon race is intended by an overruling Providence to carry the principles of liberty, the refinements of civilization, and the advantages of the mechanic arts through every land, even those now barbarous. The prostrate savage and the benighted heathen shall yet be imbued with Anglo-Saxon intelligence and culture, and be blessed with the institutions, both civil and religious, which are now our inheritance. Mexico, too, must submit to the o'erpowering influence of the Anglo-Saxon.[32]

After a series of skirmishes, battles, and sieges, Texas proclaimed its independence from Mexico on March 2, 1836. It existed as an independent republic for just under a decade before being annexed into the Union as a slave state in 1845. However, Mexico refused to recognize either Texan independence or its annexation by the US.

A dispute over the Texas–Mexico boundary led President James K. Polk to order US troops into the contested Nueces Strip between the Nueces and Rio Grande rivers. Conveniently, yet another pretext for war was found—the "Thornton Affair," in which American dragoons were ambushed by Mexican cavalry on Mexican territory—and fighting began in April 1846.

In his May 11 message to Congress, Polk played to American patriotism while deliberately fudging the facts on the ground:

> The cup of forbearance had been exhausted even before the recent information from the frontier of the Del Norte. But now, after reiterated menaces, Mexico has passed the boundary of the United States, has invaded our territory and shed American blood upon the American soil. She has proclaimed that hostilities have commenced, and that the two nations are now at war.

* Extreme chauvinism or nationalism marked especially by aggressive foreign policy.

> As war exists, and, notwithstanding all our efforts to avoid it, exists by the act of Mexico herself, we are called upon by every consideration of duty and patriotism to vindicate with decision the honor, the rights, and the interests of our country.[33]

Congress officially declared war on May 13, 1846. Lasting from 1846 to 1848, the conflict saw the Americans invade on multiple fronts, including Zachary Taylor's northern campaign, which captured Monterrey in September 1846; Winfield Scott's amphibious landing and siege of Vera Cruz in March 1847; and Scott's subsequent overland march, culminating in the occupation of Mexico City in September 1847.

The war served as a training ground for West Point's "Class of 1846," many of whom would confront each other as enemies during the Civil War. From U.S. Grant, William T. Sherman, and George Meade on the Union side to Robert E. Lee, James Longstreet, and Thomas "Stonewall" Jackson for the Confederates, Mexico was a rite of passage and an opportunity to hone the art of war.

On February 2, 1848, the fighting ended with the Treaty of Guadalupe Hidalgo. Under its terms, Mexico was forced to recognize the US annexation of Texas, with its border at the Rio Grande. It was also forced to cede around half its territory, including the modern-day US states of California, Nevada, Utah, Arizona, New Mexico, Colorado, and Wyoming, as well as parts of Kansas, Oklahoma, and Texas. In total, around half a million square miles were added to the country's already considerable bulk.

However, not everyone had been keen on transforming the American republic into a de facto empire through predatory war. Abraham Lincoln was a vocal critic, and his fledgling congressional career was derailed as a result. Future Civil War hero and president, Ulysses S. Grant, considered it, not only "wicked,"[34] but:

> . . . one of the most unjust [wars] ever waged by a stronger against a weaker nation. It was an instance of a republic following the bad example of European monarchies, in not considering justice in their desire to acquire additional territory.[35]

And as Ralph Waldo Emerson prophetically warned:

> The US will conquer Mexico, but it will be as the man swallows the arsenic, which brings him down in turn. Mexico will poison us.[36]

Compromise hits its limit

As with previous territorial expansions, differences over how the lands conquered from Mexico should be administered added to the already frenzied national debate over slavery. In 1846, Pennsylvania congressman David Wilmot had proposed a ban on slavery in any territory the US might gain as a result of the war. The motion's failure left open the possibility that the vast new lands bordering the Deep South would see an extension of the slave power.

In 1848, Senator Lewis Cass attempted to bridge the gap with his proposal for "popular sovereignty," later championed by Stephen A. Douglas. The idea was that settlers in each US territory should simply vote on whether or not to allow slavery. Although this approach appeared "democratic" on the surface, anti-slavery forces feared it could be manipulated to allow the institution to creep north of the 36°30⊠ barrier agreed upon during the Missouri Compromise.

In 1850, another major crisis led to yet another slew of compromises, a package of five separate laws that included the Fugitive Slave Act. The proximal cause was the growing success of the Underground Railroad. This was a clandestine web of Black and white abolitionists and financiers who helped runaway slaves evade their masters. With vigilance committees established to provide security, its "conductors" guided tens of thousands of "passengers" through a complex network of "stations" to eventual safety in the North and Canada. Similar, less formalized routes helped several thousand slaves from the Deep South and Texas escape into Mexico. The slavocracy was up in arms and wanted Northerners to honor their constitutional commitment to defend their property rights.

The Old Whig, Henry Clay, wasn't called "The Great Compromiser" for nothing. He was determined to win approval of the Compromise of 1850 to keep the republic within the fraying limits of its governing statutes:

> Let me, Mr. President, in conclusion, say that the most disastrous consequences would occur, in my opinion, were we to go home, doing nothing to satisfy and tranquillize the country upon these great questions. What will be the judgment of mankind, what the judgment of that portion of mankind who are looking upon the progress of this scheme of self-government as being that which holds the highest hopes and expectations of ameliorating the condition of mankind—what will their judgment be? Will not all the monarchs of the Old World pronounce our glorious republic a disgraceful failure? Will you go home and leave all in disorder and confusion—all unsettled—all open? The contentions and agitations of the past will be increased and augmented by the agitations resulting from our neglect to decide them.
>
> Sir, we shall stand condemned by all human judgment below; and of that above it is not for me to speak. We shall stand condemned in our own consciences, by our own constituents, and by our own country. The measure may be defeated. I have been aware that its passage for many days was not absolutely certain . . . But, if defeated, it will be a triumph of ultraism and impracticability—a triumph of a most extraordinary conjunction of extremes; a victory won by abolitionism; a victory achieved by free-soilism; a victory of discord and agitation over peace and tranquillity; and I pray to Almighty God that it may not, in consequence of the inauspicious result, lead to the most unhappy and disastrous consequences to our beloved country.[37]

Building on the provisions already in the Constitution, the Fugitive Slave Act decreed that all slaves were to be returned to their owners regardless of the state in which they were caught. Special commissioners were appointed with the power to issue warrants and certificates for the return of alleged escaped slaves. They were to be paid $10 if they ruled in favor of the slaveholder, but only $5 if they freed the accused—a clear financial incentive to side with the slave catchers. Accused fugitives were denied the right to a jury trial and were not permitted to testify on their own behalf. The testimony of the slaveholder or his agent, along with an affidavit, was typically sufficient to prove ownership.

Furthermore, federal marshals were required to enforce the law, and ordinary citizens could be impressed to assist in capturing fugitives. Failure to comply could result in fines of up to $1,000 and imprisonment. Anyone who aided a fugitive slave—including by providing food or shelter—could be fined $1,000 and imprisoned for up to six months.

These measures were intended to compensate for California's admission as a free state. The urgency to incorporate the territory stemmed from the discovery of gold in 1849. Laws, order, and infrastructure had to be established on the Pacific coast to facilitate the extraction and shipment of mineral wealth back East.

On the surface, the Fugitive Slave Act appeared to be a clear win for the slavocracy. However, just as the South had resented the passage of protective tariffs in 1828, Northerners were outraged by the new legislation, which effectively deputized slave catchers in every part of the country. In a speech given to the Senate by the future Secretary of the Treasury and eventual Chief Justice of the Supreme Court, Salmon P. Chase:

> [O]ur responsibilities are limited by our powers; and however clear it may be that we are bound by allegiance to democratic principle to condemn, to mitigate, to abolish slavery wherever we can constitutionally do so, it is equally clear that we are not bound, and that we have no right to interfere with slavery by legislation beyond the sphere of our constitutional powers.
>
> We have no power to legislate on the subject of slavery in the States. We have power to prevent its extension, and to prohibit its existence within the sphere of the exclusive jurisdiction of the General Government. Our duty, therefore, is to abstain from interference with it in the States. It is also our duty to prohibit its extension into national territories, and its continuance where we are constitutionally responsible for its existence.[38]

Ralph Waldo Emerson was equally incensed:

> This filthy enactment was made in the nineteenth century, by people who could read and write. I will not obey it, by God.[39]

In 1854, the abolitionist newspaperman, William Lloyd Garrison, railed against the law in an impassioned speech:

> The abolitionism which I advocate is as absolute as the law of God, and as unyielding as his throne. It admits of no compromise. Every slave is a stolen man; every slaveholder is a man stealer. By no precedent, no example, no law, no compact, no purchase, no bequest, no inheritance, no combination of circumstances, is slaveholding right or justifiable. While a slave remains in his fetters, the land must have no rest. Whatever sanctions his doom must be pronounced accursed. The law that makes him a chattel is to be trampled underfoot; the compact that is formed at his expense, and cemented with his blood, is null and void; the church that consents to his enslavement is horribly atheistical; the religion that receives to its communion the enslaver is the embodiment of all criminality. Such, at least, is the verdict of my own soul, on the supposition that I am to be the slave; that my wife is to be sold from me for the vilest purposes; that my children are to be torn from my arms, and disposed of to the highest bidder, like sheep in the market. And who am I but a man? What right have I to be free, that another man cannot prove himself to possess by nature? Who or what are my wife and children that they should not be herded with four-footed beasts, as well as others thus sacredly related?[40]

As for Frederick Douglass, he considered it "the most cruel, unconstitutional and scandalous outrage of modern times."[41]

In a pair of speeches given in the summer of 1852, he added:

> In glaring violation of justice, in shameless disregard of the forms of administering law, in cunning arrangement to entrap the defenceless, and in diabolical intent, this Fugitive Slave Law stands alone in the annals of tyrannical legislation. I doubt if there be another nation on

> the globe, having the brass and the baseness to put such a law on the statute-book.[42]

> Human government is for the protection of rights; and when human government destroys human rights, it ceases to be a government, and becomes a foul and blasting conspiracy; and is entitled to no respect whatever.[43]

The rise of the Republican Party

In 1852, Harriet Beecher Stowe's *Uncle Tom's Cabin* was published. It detailed the corrupting and anti-Christian horrors of slavery, further galvanizing abolitionist sentiment in the North and infuriating the South. Though likely apocryphal, legend has it that Lincoln greeted Stowe at the White House with the words: "So you're the little woman who wrote the book that started this great war."

In 1854, the Kansas-Nebraska Act created two new territories: Kansas and Nebraska. It opened both to popular sovereignty, in part to clear the way for a transcontinental railroad. However, the sticky contradictions of this approach quickly surfaced.

Pro- and antislavery forces flooded into Kansas Territory, held competing elections, formed rival governments in rival capitals, and fought a vicious slow-burning guerrilla conflict that came to be called "Bleeding Kansas." As historian Nicole Etcheson succinctly put it in a review of *The Border Between Them* by Jeremy Neely:

> Missourians pioneered a slave frontier. They expected Kansas to be part of this dynamic economy, but free soil migrants resisted.[44]

This ultimately proved too much for the Second Party System: the Whigs imploded, and the Democrats split along sectional lines. As economic and social forces transform—often imperceptibly—new parties emerge, and old ones collapse or reinvent themselves. Such periods are typically marked by heightened instability and by a search for ideas, leaders, and forms of political expression that can break the impasse and point the way forward.

It was in this context that a wild and wonderful parade of parties and movements emerged in the 1850s, from the anti-immigrant, anti-Catholic "Order of the Star-Spangled Banner"—the secret core of the "Know-Nothing Party"—to the American Party and the Free Soil Party.

Out of the chaos, the Republican Party emerged as an overwhelmingly sectional party. They mainly represented Northern industrialists, small shopkeepers, farmers, abolitionists, and settlers. A fusion of antislavery forces, the party included "Conscience Whigs,"* free labor and Free Soil supporters who opposed slavery's expansion, radical abolitionists, and some Northern Democrats who rejected popular sovereignty.

Their platform was built on the old Whig Party program, favoring federal investment in infrastructure, tariffs to encourage "the development of the industrial interests of the whole country," and "liberal wages" for the working man.[45] Most Republican politicians were not motivated by love for Black people or for workers. Rather, they understood, consciously or unconsciously, that slave labor and its spread into new lands was an impediment to the consolidation and expansion of capitalism and wage labor.

In 1856, the new party nominated the famous explorer John C. Frémont as its first presidential candidate. The South denounced him as a radical abolitionist. The Republican campaign slogan—"Free Soil, Free Men, Frémont"—captured the party's demographic appeal. He lost to the Democratic candidate, James Buchanan, but the party's strong showing proved it was no flash in the pan.

Also in 1856, Massachusetts Senator Charles Sumner was brutally beaten in the Senate chamber by Representative Preston Brooks of South Carolina after Sumner gave a speech against slavery. In it, he denounced proslavery violence in Kansas and personally mocked

* A New England–based, Massachusetts-centered faction of the Whig Party. In contrast to the proslavery "Cotton Whigs," the "Conscience Whigs" were morally opposed to slavery and against the annexation of Texas and the Mexican War.

Senator Andrew Butler of South Carolina. According to the official website of the US Senate:

> In his "Crime Against Kansas" speech, Sumner identified two Democratic senators as the principal culprits in this crime—Stephen Douglas of Illinois and Andrew Butler of South Carolina. He characterized Douglas to his face as a "noise-some, squat, and nameless animal . . . not a proper model for an American senator." Andrew Butler, who was not present, received more elaborate treatment. Mocking the South Carolina senator's stance as a man of chivalry, the Massachusetts senator charged him with taking "a mistress . . . who, though ugly to others, is always lovely to him; though polluted in the sight of the world, is chaste in his sight—I mean," added Sumner, "the harlot, Slavery."[46]

Brooks, a relative of Butler's, walked up to Sumner at his desk three days later and struck him repeatedly with a cane, leaving his victim severely injured and out of the Senate for years. He presented the assault as a defense of Southern "honor." Many white Southerners celebrated Brooks as a hero and sent him replacement canes. In the North, Sumner was seen as a martyr to the abolitionist cause.

Then, in 1857, the infamous Dred Scott case came before the Supreme Court. Chief Justice Roger Taney ruled as follows:

> A free Negro of the African race, whose ancestors were brought to this country and sold as slaves, is not a "citizen" within the meaning of the Constitution of the United States.
>
> When the Constitution was adopted, they were not regarded in any of the States as members of the community which constituted the State, and were not numbered among its "people or citizen[s]." Consequently, the special rights and immunities guarantied to citizens do not apply to them. And not being "citizens" within the meaning of the Constitution, they are not entitled to sue in that character in a court of the United States, and the Circuit Court has not jurisdiction in such a suit.
>
> The only two clauses in the Constitution which point to this race, treat them as persons whom it was *morally* lawful to deal in as articles of property and to hold as slaves.

> Since the adoption of the Constitution of the United States, no state can by any subsequent law make a foreigner or any other description of persons citizens of the United States, nor entitle them to the rights and privileges secured to citizens by that instrument.
>
> A State, by its laws passed since the adoption of the Constitution, may put a foreigner or any other description of persons upon a footing with its own citizens, as to all the rights and privileges enjoyed by them within its dominion, and by its laws. But that will not make him a citizen of the United States, nor entitle him to sue in its courts, nor to any of the privileges and immunities of a citizen in another State.
>
> The change in public opinion and feeling in relation to the African race, which has taken place since the adoption of the Constitution, cannot change its construction and meaning, and it must be construct[ed] and administered now according to its true meaning and intention when it was formed and adopted.[47]

In other words, since Black people were not US citizens, they were not entitled to any of the rights of citizenship. Therefore, slaves brought by their owners to free states remained slaves, even if slavery was banned in that state. Furthermore, Congress lacked the power to ban slavery in the territories. This effectively made slavery legal nationwide, enraging its opponents even further.

Over the course of the 1850s, one crisis was layered on another, and the march toward a general conflagration accelerated. The political pressure cooker was compounded by the Panic of 1857, a classic crisis of capitalist overproduction that triggered a crippling contraction in credit.

Many historians consider this to be the first truly nationwide crisis of American capitalism. It hit Northern industry and Western farmers hardest. In these regions, the Republican program of state-supported economic development gained a wider audience, and the slaveholders' grip on federal politics became even more intolerable.

But what tipped the balance once and for all was the "meteor of the war,"[48] as Herman Melville christened the indomitable abolitionist, John Brown.

The abolitionists

Abolitionism had been around since the First Revolution, but it was a minority political movement prior to the Civil War. Antislavery sentiment was particularly fervent among Mennonites and Quakers in New England and in parts of Pennsylvania and New York. As the years passed, however, it gained traction in parts of the West, and some abolitionists even emerged in the South. Many were zealously passionate about their cause, some to the point of messianism. Their ranks included religious leaders such as Henry Ward Beecher and newspaper editors such as William Lloyd Garrison. Elijah P. Lovejoy was an early martyr of the movement, murdered by a proslavery mob in Alton, Illinois in 1837.

Most abolitionists simply wanted to reform slavery out of existence, not ban it overnight. Although they opposed slavery on moral or economic grounds, many didn't believe there could be genuine equality between Black people and whites. Some argued that freed slaves should be resettled somewhere in Africa or South America.

As for what the slaves themselves thought about abolition, historian Ira Berlin offers an interesting perspective:

> Enslaved men and women hated their confinement and sought every opportunity to break the shackles that bound them, but opposition to their own enslavement—or even the enslavement of others—did not automatically make them abolitionists. For much of their history—indeed, for much of human history—the notion of a world purged of slavery was simply unimaginable. Abolition, like any other social movement, was rooted in history and confined in time and space. Prior to the American Revolution and its ideology of universal equality, there were few movements to contemplate, let alone to join.[49]

Despite the initial weakness of the movement, however, abolitionism struck fear into the hearts of Southern slave owners. Almost as much as they feared slave uprisings, they feared losing control of the federal government to those with even mild antislavery sentiments.

Some abolitionists were activists on the Underground Railroad, like Harriet Tubman. Born into slavery on Maryland's Eastern Shore, she escaped in 1849 and returned again and again, using a network of free Black communities, Quakers, coded messages, and meticulous operational discipline to evade slave catchers and informants.

According to the National Park Service, Tubman personally rescued about 70 people from chattel slavery—including family and friends—during roughly 13 trips back to Maryland. As a scout and guide for the Union Army, she helped lead the Combahee Ferry Raid of 1863, which freed more than 700 slaves in coastal South Carolina.

Other abolitionists were consistent revolutionary democrats, like the incomparable orator and former slave, Frederick Douglass. After escaping from Maryland at the age of 20 in 1838, he rose to prominence as an abolitionist lecturer, author, and newspaper publisher. Though not a Marxist, he had a sophisticated understanding of history, the class struggle, politics, and economics.

In his view, slavery was not merely a moral stain on the republic but a political and economic system upheld by law and violence—with the complicity of Northern capital. As opposed to those abolitionists who denounced the Constitution as inherently proslavery, he argued that it could be interpreted and used as an antislavery instrument in the struggle for equal rights and citizenship.

During the war, Douglass agitated relentlessly in favor of transforming the legalistic war for the Union into a revolutionary war against slavery. He demanded immediate emancipation, equal pay and treatment for Black soldiers, and the right of Black people to fight as citizens for the liberation of all slaves. His writing was muscular and poetic, and his ability to condense powerful ideas into combative prose remains an inspiration to this day. Take, for example, this excerpt from a speech on "West India Emancipation," delivered August 4, 1857:

> Let me give you a word of the philosophy of reform. The whole history of the progress of human liberty shows that all concessions yet made to

> her august claims have been born of earnest struggle. The conflict has been exciting, agitating, all-absorbing, and for the time being, putting all other tumults to silence. It must do this or it does nothing. If there is no struggle there is no progress. Those who profess to favor freedom and yet deprecate agitation are men who want crops without plowing up the ground; they want rain without thunder and lightning. They want the ocean without the awful roar of its many waters.
>
> This struggle may be a moral one, or it may be a physical one, and it may be both moral and physical, but it must be a struggle. Power concedes nothing without a demand. It never did and it never will. Find out just what any people will quietly submit to and you have found out the exact measure of injustice and wrong which will be imposed upon them, and these will continue till they are resisted with either words or blows, or with both. The limits of tyrants are prescribed by the endurance of those whom they oppress. In the light of these ideas, Negroes will be hunted at the North and held and flogged at the South so long as they submit to those devilish outrages and make no resistance, either moral or physical. Men may not get all they pay for in this world, but they must certainly pay for all they get. If we ever get free from the oppressions and wrongs heaped upon us, we must pay for their removal. We must do this by labor, by suffering, by sacrifice, and if needs be, by our lives and the lives of others.[50]

And then there was John Brown, an unparalleled revolutionary abolitionist who believed that "what is needed is action—action!"

Born in Connecticut and raised in Ohio, Brown was a pious, austere Calvinist who believed fervently in the equality of Black and white people. Impoverished for much of his life, he failed at a wide range of petty commercial and agricultural ventures, including land surveying. He fathered 20 children, some of whom eventually fought and died at his side.

Brown had no illusions in the political process or reform of any kind. He understood to his very marrow that the slave-owning aristocracy would not give up its property without a fight. He played a prominent role in Bleeding Kansas, leading the Pottawatomie

Creek massacre, in which five proslavery settlers were taken from their cabins and hacked to death with swords.

In May 1858, he convened a meeting of supporters in Chatham, Ontario, to raise money and support for his next endeavor. He planned an audacious series of raids into Appalachia to free and arm hundreds of slaves. His aim was to establish a mountain stronghold of liberated bondsmen that would spread panic across the South and make the continuation of slavery economically unviable. He even had 1,000 steel-tipped pikes manufactured with which to equip his army.

His preparations culminated in his ill-fated October 16, 1859, raid on the US federal arsenal at Harpers Ferry in modern-day West Virginia. In one of those twists of history in which the Civil War is so rich, it was Robert E. Lee, at that time a lieutenant colonel, who led the detachment of Marines that captured Brown and his comrades. The future Confederate cavalry officer J.E.B. Stuart was also present.

Defiant and honest to the very end, he understood that he could be most useful to his lifelong cause if he were martyred. As he wrote to his wife:

> I have been whipped, as the saying is, but I am sure I can recover all the lost capital occasioned by that disaster; by only hanging a few moments by the neck; and I feel quite determined to make the utmost possible out of a defeat.[51]

In his testimony and speech to the court during his trial, he maintained his dignity and defended his action on behalf of the enslaved:

> I want you to understand that I respect the rights of the poorest and weakest of colored people, oppressed by the slave system, just as much as I do those of the most wealthy and powerful . . . The cry of distress of the oppressed is my reason, and the only thing that prompted me to come here . . .
>
> I wish to say, furthermore, that you had better— all you people at the South—prepare yourselves for a settlement of that question, that must

> come up for settlement sooner than you are prepared for it. The sooner you are prepared, the better. You may dispose of me very easily,—I am nearly disposed of now, but this question is still to be settled,—this Negro question, I mean; the end of that is not yet . . .[52]
>
> [H]ad I so interfered in behalf of the rich, the powerful, the intelligent, the so-called great, or in behalf of any of their friends, either father, mother, brother, sister, wife, or children, or any of that class, and suffered and sacrificed what I have in this interference, it would have been all right, and every man in this Court would have deemed it an act worthy of reward rather than punishment.
>
> I believe that to have interfered as I have done, as I have always freely admitted I have done, in behalf of His despised poor, was not wrong, but right. Now, if it is deemed necessary that I should forfeit my life for the furtherance of the ends of justice, and mingle my blood further with the blood of my children, and with the blood of millions in this slave country whose rights are disregarded by wicked, cruel, and unjust enactments, I submit: so let it be done![53]

On his way to the gallows, he slipped a note to his jailer:

> I, John Brown, am now quite certain that the crimes of this guilty land can never be purged away but with blood. I had, as I now think, vainly flattered myself that without very much bloodshed, it might be done.[54]

And as he rode his own coffin to the place where he would be hanged, he is reputed to have remarked: "This is a beautiful country. I did not have the chance to see it before."[55]

Among those who witnessed his execution on December 2, 1859, in Charles Town, Virginia (now West Virginia), was John Wilkes Booth.

John Brown's actions and state-sanctioned murder sent shockwaves around the country. His words and deeds captured the imagination of the masses throughout the North. From the outset of the war, troops sang "John Brown's Body" around the campfire and at public reviews. When the poet and abolitionist, Julia Ward Howe, heard this revolutionary anthem, she wrote the "Battle Hymn of the Republic" to the same tune. Many other, even more explicitly revolutionary versions were also penned, offering an insight into the fervor that took hold at all levels of Northern society during the war.

Henry David Thoreau, who had met Brown on at least two occasions, wrote an extraordinary and impassioned speech titled "A Plea for Captain John Brown," which he delivered to the citizens of Concord, Massachusetts, on October 30, 1859. It is well worth reading in full, but below are a few excerpts:

> A man of rare common-sense and directness of speech, as of action; a transcendentalist above all, a man of ideas and principles—that was what distinguished him. Not yielding to a whim or transient impulse, but carrying out the purpose of a life. I noticed that he did not overstate anything, but spoke within bounds. I remember, particularly, how, in his speech here, he referred to what his family had suffered in Kansas, without ever giving the least vent to his pent-up fire. It was a volcano with an ordinary chimney flue.
>
> Also referring to the deeds of certain Border Ruffians, he said, rapidly paring away his speech, like an experienced soldier, keeping a reserve of force and meaning, "They had a perfect right to be hung." He was not in the least a rhetorician, was not talking to Buncombe or his constituents anywhere, had no need to invent anything but to tell the simple truth, and communicate his own resolution; therefore, he appeared incomparably strong, and eloquence in Congress and elsewhere seemed to me at a discount. It was like the speeches of Cromwell compared with those of an ordinary king . . .[56]
>
> When I expressed surprise that he could live in Kansas at all, with a price set upon his head, and so large a number, including the authorities, exasperated against him, he accounted for it by saying, "It is perfectly well understood that I will not be taken."
>
> Much of the time for some years, he has had to skulk in swamps, suffering from poverty and from sickness, which was the consequence of exposure, befriended only by Indians and a few whites. But though it might be known that he was lurking in a particular swamp, his foes

> commonly did not care to go in after him. He could even come out into a town where there were more Border Ruffians than Free State men, and transact some business, without delaying long, and yet not be molested; for, said he, "No little handful of men were willing to undertake it, and a large body could not be got together in season."
>
> I am here to plead his cause with you. I plead not for his life, but for his character—his immortal life; and so it becomes your cause wholly, and is not his in the least. Some eighteen hundred years ago Christ was crucified; this morning, perchance, Captain Brown was hung. These are the two ends of a chain which is not without its links. He is not Old Brown any longer; he is an angel of light.
>
> I see now that it was necessary that the bravest and humanest man in all the country should be hung. Perhaps he saw it himself. I *almost fear* that I may yet hear of his deliverance, doubting if a prolonged life, if *any* life, can do as much good as his death . . .
>
> I foresee the time when the painter will paint that scene, no longer going to Rome for a subject; the poet will sing it; the historian record it; and, with the Landing of the Pilgrims and the Declaration of Independence, it will be the ornament of some future national gallery, when at least the present form of slavery shall be no more here. We shall then be at liberty to weep for Captain Brown. Then, and not till then, we will take our revenge.[57]

Frederick Douglass was even more poetic when describing Brown's world-historical significance:

> His zeal in the cause of my race was far greater than mine—it was as the burning sun to my taper light—mine was bounded by time, his stretched away to the boundless shores of eternity. I could live for the slave, but he could die for him. The crown of martyrdom is high, far beyond the reach of ordinary mortals, and yet happily no special greatness or superior moral excellence is necessary to discern and in some measure appreciate a truly great soul. Cold, calculating and unspiritual as most of us are, we are not wholly insensible to real greatness; and when we are brought in contact with a man of commanding mold, towering high and alone

above the millions, free from all conventional fetters, true to his own moral convictions, a "law unto himself," ready to suffer misconstruction, ignoring torture and death for what he believes to be right, we are compelled to do him homage.

[W]e yet stand too near the days of slavery, and the life and times of John Brown, to see clearly the true martyr and hero that he was and rightly to estimate the value of the man and his works. Like the great and good of all ages-the men born in advance of their times, the men whose bleeding footprints attest the immense cost of reform, and show us the long and dreary spaces, between the luminous points in the progress of mankind-this our noblest American hero must wait the polishing wheels of after-coming centuries to make his glory more manifest, and his worth more generally acknowledged . . . That which time has done for other great men of his class, that will time certainly do for John Brown. The brightest gems shine at first with subdued light, and the strongest characters are subject to the same limitations . . .

But the question is, Did John Brown fail? He certainly did fail to get out of Harper's Ferry before being beaten down by United States soldiers; he did fail to save his own life, and to lead a liberating army into the mountains of Virginia. But he did not go to Harper's Ferry to save his life. The true question is, Did John Brown draw his sword against slavery and thereby lose his life in vain? and to this I answer ten thousand times, No! No man fails, or can fail who so grandly gives himself and all he has to a righteous cause. No man, who in his hour of extremest need, when on his way to meet an ignominious death, could so forget himself as to stop and kiss a little child, one of the hated race for whom he was about to die, could by any possibility fail.

Did John Brown fail? Ask Henry A. Wise in whose house less than two years after, a school for the emancipated slaves was taught. Did John Brown fail? Ask James M. Mason, the author of the inhuman fugitive slave bill, who was cooped up in Fort Warren, as a traitor less than two years from the time that he stood over the prostrate body of John Brown. Did John Brown fail? Ask Clement C. Vallandingham, one other of the

> inquisitorial party; for he too went down in the tremendous whirlpool created by the powerful hand of this bold invader.
>
> If John Brown did not end the war that ended slavery, he did at least begin the war that ended slavery. If we look over the dates, places and men, for which this honor is claimed, we shall find that not Carolina, but Virginia-not Fort Sumter, but Harper's Ferry and the arsenal-not Col. Anderson, but John Brown, began the war that ended American slavery and made this a free Republic. Until this blow was struck, the prospect for freedom was dim, shadowy and uncertain. The irrepressible conflict was one of words, votes and compromises. When John Brown stretched forth his arm the sky was cleared. The time for compromises was gone—the armed hosts of freedom stood face to face over the chasm of a broken Union-and the clash of arms was at hand. The South staked all upon getting possession of the Federal Government, and failing to do that, drew the sword of rebellion and thus made her own, and not Brown's, the lost cause of the century.[58]

And when Malcolm X was asked if white people could join his Organization of Afro-American Unity, he replied: "If John Brown were still alive, we might accept him.[59]

As for the South, it went completely ballistic. Edmund Ruffin, a rabid secessionist often credited with firing the first shot at Fort Sumter, had this to say:

> The murderer and robber and fire-raiser so notorious for these crimes in his Kansas career and now the attempter of the thousand-fold horrors in Virginia, is, for these reasons, the present idol of the North.[60]

Many Southerners had been openly contemplating secession for years. Some believed that if they left the Union, they could build a slave empire called the "Golden Circle" by conquering Mexico, the Caribbean, and perhaps even South America. After all, Cuba already had 400,000 slaves, plenty of undeveloped land, and the plantation owners there looked to the US for support in their struggle against Spanish colonialism.

John Brown's raid on Harpers Ferry overflowed the secessionist cup. As Marx wrote to Engels on January 11, 1860, in the wake of Brown's martyrdom:

> In my view, the most momentous thing happening in the world today is the slave movement—on the one hand, in America, started by the death of Brown, and in Russia, on the other. You will have read that the aristocracy in Russia literally threw themselves into constitutional agitation and that two or three members of leading families have already found their way to Siberia. At the same time, Alexander has displeased the peasants, for the recent manifesto declares outright that, with emancipation, "the Communistic principle" must be abandoned. Thus, a "social" movement has been started both in the West and in the East. Together with the impending downbreak in Central Europe, this promises great things.
>
> I have just seen in the *Tribune* that there's been another slave revolt in Missouri which was put down, needless to say. But the signal has now been given. Should the affair grow serious by and by, what will become of Manchester [and its cotton mills]?[61]

As far as most Southerners were concerned, Brown's actions were proof positive that white Northerners were conspiring to spark a mass slave uprising, expropriate the South's property, and destroy their civilization. Across the slave states, plans were made, arms purchased, and militias drilled in preparation for a decisive showdown.

In a November, 1859 letter to North Carolina Governor John W. Ellis, a constituent wrote:

> The Harpers Ferry insurrection is of considerable benefit to this section of the State, all persons seem very anxious now to have a well organized militia and I am endeavoring to second their wish. We have been admonished by the *Father* of our Country, to prepare for War, in time of peace and wish to profit by his advice.[62]

And as Governor Ellis wrote to the US Secretary of War, John Floyd:

> The Sense of insecurity prevailing among the people of this State, renders it necessary that I should apply to you for arms to place in the hands of the militia . . . I wish to procure from the Government, two thousand long range rifles with bayonets attached, for the use of the State of North Carolina.[63]

A war for slavery

After the Civil War, "Lost Cause" apologists attempted to prettify the antebellum South. They called the conflict the "War of Northern Aggression" and insisted it was about defending states' rights and the Constitution.

Insofar as the Southern states fought for their right to exploit slave labor, they had a point. The Constitution did, in fact, allow and protect slavery. As the Founders had written in Article IV, Section 2, better known as the "Fugitive Slave Clause":

> No person held to service or labor in one state, under the laws thereof, escaping into another, shall, in consequence of any law or regulation therein, be discharged from such service or labor, but shall be delivered up on claim of the party to whom such service or labor may be due.[64]

In this sense, the Southern cause was effectively an attempt to forcibly keep the country at an earlier stage of its development, for the benefit of a reactionary class of fewer than 400,000 slaveholders.

Of these, just 12 per cent owned more than 20 slaves, around 46,000 individuals. 3 per cent—roughly 11,000 individuals—owned 50 or more slaves. Less than 1 per cent—approximately 1,800 families—owned 100 or more slaves. A mere 13 plantations had between 500 and 1,000 slaves, and only a single plantation, in South Carolina, had more than 1,000 slaves. The concentration of wealth, and by extension, political power, was staggering. These were the class interests that led to the declaration of the Confederacy.

It is clear, therefore, that in terms of direct ownership, slavery didn't affect most people in the South. And yet, most nonslaveholding white Southerners identified with and defended the institution anyway. Though they may have resented the wealth, power, and aristocratic arrogance of the large slaveholders, many aspired to own slaves themselves and to join the ranks of society's elite.

After centuries of racist scaremongering, the prospect of four million freed slaves terrified them. At root, they saw them as competition for increasingly scarce land and jobs. Slavery gave many poor whites with little or no land someone they could feel superior to. They may have been poor, but at least they weren't slaves, nor were they Black.

More immediately, many Southerners defend their home states and region from the Yankees. Shelby Foote gave voice to this sentiment in Ken Burns's famous documentary on the Civil War. As he relates, when a captured Confederate private was asked why he had taken up arms, he answered simply: "I'm fighting because you're down here."[65]

However, it is an inconvenient fact for those who tried to muddy the waters after the war that on the eve of secession, hundreds of Southern officials admitted openly that it was, in fact, all about slavery. They repeatedly and explicitly denounced the threat posed to slavery by the rising industrial and political power of the North.

As an example, South Carolina's ordinance of secession complained that the federal government was not upholding laws passed to guarantee the sanctity of slave property, and decried:

> [A]n increasing hostility on the part of the non-slaveholding States to the institution of slavery, has led to a disregard of their obligations, and the laws of the General Government have ceased to effect the objects of the Constitution.[66]

Mississippi's declaration of secession was even more explicit:

> Our position is thoroughly identified with the institution of slavery—the greatest material interest of the world. Its labor supplies the product which constitutes by far the largest and most important portions of commerce of the earth. These products are peculiar to the climate verging on the tropical regions, and by an imperious law of nature, none but the black race can bear exposure to the tropical sun. These products

> have become necessities of the world, and a blow at slavery is a blow at commerce and civilization. That blow has been long aimed at the institution, and was at the point of reaching its consummation. There was no choice left us but submission to the mandates of abolition, or a dissolution of the Union, whose principles had been subverted to work out our ruin.[67]

In fact, the only real difference between the US and the Confederate constitutions was that explicit language was added in several articles and sections, making it clear that no "law denying or impairing the right of property in Negro slaves shall be passed."

In his "Cornerstone" speech, Alexander Stephens, the Confederate vice president, laid out the real reasons for secession while explaining the new statutes:

> The new constitution has put at rest, forever, all the agitating questions relating to our peculiar institution, African slavery, as it exists amongst us, the proper status of the Negro in our form of civilization. This was the immediate cause of the late rupture and present revolution. Jefferson, in his forecast, had anticipated this as the "rock upon which the old Union would split." He was right. What was conjecture with him is now a realized fact. But whether he fully comprehended the great truth upon which that rock stood, and stands, may be doubted.
>
> The prevailing ideas entertained by him and most of the leading statesmen at the time of the formation of the old constitution, were that the enslavement of the African was in violation of the laws of nature; that it was wrong in principle, socially, morally, and politically. It was an evil they knew not well how to deal with, but the general opinion of the men of that day was that, somehow or other, in the order of Providence, the institution would be evanescent and pass away.
>
> This idea, though not incorporated in the constitution, was the prevailing idea at that time. The constitution, it is true, secured every essential guarantee to the institution while it should last, and hence no argument can be justly urged against the constitutional guarantees thus secured, because of the common sentiment of the day. Those ideas, however, were

fundamentally wrong. They rested upon the assumption of the equality of races. This was an error. It was a sandy foundation, and the government built upon it fell when the "storm came, and the wind blew."

Our new government is founded upon exactly the opposite idea; its foundations are laid, its cornerstone rests, upon the great truth that the Negro is not equal to the white man; that slavery, subordination to the superior race, is his natural and normal condition. This, our new government, is the first in the history of the world based upon this great physical, philosophical, and moral truth. This truth has been slow in the process of its development, like all other truths in the various departments of science. It has been so even amongst us.

Many who hear me, perhaps, can recollect well that this truth was not generally admitted, even within their day. The errors of the past generation still clung to many as late as twenty years ago. Those at the North, who still cling to these errors, with a zeal above knowledge, we justly denominate fanatics. All fanaticism springs from an aberration of the mind, from a defect in reasoning. It is a species of insanity. One of the most striking characteristics of insanity, in many instances, is forming correct conclusions from fancied or erroneous premises; so with the anti-slavery fanatics.

Their conclusions are right if their premises were. They assume that the Negro is equal, and hence conclude that he is entitled to equal privileges and rights with the white man. If their premises were correct, their conclusions would be logical and just, but their premise being wrong, their whole argument fails.

I recollect once of having heard a gentleman from one of the northern states, of great power and ability, announce in the House of Representatives, with imposing effect, that we of the South would be compelled, ultimately, to yield upon this subject of slavery, that it was as impossible to war successfully against a principle in politics, as it was in physics or mechanics. That the principle would ultimately prevail. That we, in maintaining slavery as it exists with us, were warring against a principle, a principle founded in nature, the principle of the equality of men.

> The reply I made to him was that, upon his own grounds, we should, ultimately, succeed, and that he and his associates, in this crusade against our institutions, would ultimately fail. The truth announced that it was as impossible to war successfully against a principle in politics as it was in physics and mechanics, I admitted, but told him that it was he, and those acting with him, who were warring against a principle. They were attempting to make things equal, which the Creator had made unequal.[68]

As Marx commented at the time:

> The question of the principle of the American Civil War is answered by the battle slogan with which the South broke the peace. Stephens . . . declared in the Secession Congress, that what essentially distinguished the Constitution hatched at Montgomery from the Constitution of the Washingtons and Jeffersons was that now for the first time, slavery was recognized as an institution good in itself, and as the foundation of the whole state edifice, whereas the revolutionary fathers, men steeped in the prejudices of the eighteenth century, had treated slavery as an evil imported from England and to be eliminated in the course of time.[69]

The irony, of course, is that far from being about states' rights in the abstract, the slave states wanted the federal government to protect the institution *on their behalf.* And for decades, it did. When this was no longer 100 per cent guaranteed for all eternity, they wanted out of the Union.

To provide moral cover for the abominable practice, the big plantation owners presented slavery as a benign institution, a blessing bestowed upon inferior subhumans by their racial superiors. They attacked the hypocrisy of the Northern speculators and investors who pocketed vast sums through the slave trade, though they owned no slaves themselves. George Fitzhugh, a prominent proslavery "intellectual" from Virginia, was among the most vocal critics of Northern capitalism. In his 1857 book, *Cannibals All! or, Slaves Without Masters*, he argued:

> The Negro slaves of the South are the happiest, and in some sense, the freest people in the world. The children and the aged and infirm work

> not at all, and yet have all the comforts and necessaries of life provided for them. They enjoy liberty because they are oppressed neither by care nor labor. The women do little hard work, and are protected from the despotism of their husbands by their masters.
>
> The Negro men and stout boys work, on the average, in good weather, no more than nine hours a day. The balance of their time is spent in perfect abandon. Besides, they have their Sabbaths and holidays. White men, with so much of license and liberty, would die of ennui; but Negroes luxuriate in corporeal and mental repose. With their faces upturned to the sun, they can sleep at any hour . . .[70]
>
> Capital commands labor, as the master does the slave. Neither pays for labor, but the master permits the slave to retain a larger share of the results of his own labor than do the capitalists the free laborer . . . Free laborers have not a thousandth part of the rights and liberties of Negro slaves. Indeed, they have not a single liberty, unless it be the right or liberty to die.[71]

James Henry Hammond, a South Carolina senator and plantation owner, echoed Fitzhugh in his infamous "Mudsill Speech," delivered to the US Senate in 1858:

> In all social systems, there must be a class to do the menial duties, to perform the drudgery of life. That is, a class requiring but a low order of intellect and but little skill. Its requisites are vigor, docility, and fidelity. Such a class you must have, or you would not have that other class which leads progress, civilization, and refinement . . .
>
> Fortunately for the South, she found a race adapted to that purpose to her hand. A race inferior to her own, but eminently qualified in temper, in vigor, in docility, to stand the climate, to do her work. We use them for our purpose, and call them slaves . . .
>
> The difference between us is that our slaves are hired for life and well compensated; there is no starvation, no begging, no want of employment among our people, and not too much employment either. Yours are hired by the day, not cared for, and scantily compensated, which may be proved in the most painful manner, at any hour in any street in any of

> your large towns. Why, you meet more beggars in one day, in any single street of the city of New York, than you would meet in a lifetime in the whole South.
>
> We do not think that whites should be slaves either by law or necessity. Our slaves are black, of another and inferior race. The status in which we have placed them is an elevation. They are elevated from the condition in which God first created them, by being made our slaves. None of that race on the whole face of the globe can be compared with the slaves of the South. They are happy, content, unaspiring, and utterly incapable, from intellectual weakness, ever to give us any trouble by their aspirations. Yours are white, of your own race; you are brothers of one blood. They are your equals in natural endowment of intellect, and they feel galled by their degradation.
>
> Our slaves do not vote. We give them no political power. Yours do vote, and, being the majority, they are the depositories of all your political power. If they knew the tremendous secret, that the ballot-box is stronger than "an army with banners," and could combine, where would you be? Your society would be reconstructed, your government overthrown, your property divided, not as they have mistakenly attempted to initiate such proceedings by meeting in parks, with arms in their hands, but by the quiet process of the ballot-box. You have been making war upon us to our very hearthstones. How would you like for us to send lecturers and agitators North, to teach these people this, to aid in combining, and to lead them?[72]

On the eve of the war, slaves were the number one asset in the country, accounting for roughly 16 per cent of all household wealth.

Cotton was king, and the textile mills in England and in the North had a voracious appetite for its fibers. 80 per cent of the world's cotton, and 77 per cent of the 800 million pounds of cotton transformed into cloth in the great factories in Great Britain, was produced by slaves in the American South.

As a result, the Confederates thought they held some pretty strong cards when they decided to strike out on their own. They purposely withheld exports and even burned 2.5 million bales of cotton at the start of the war to drive up prices and ramp up the economic pressure. While they were successful in creating shortages, however, they failed miserably in their effort to compel Britain to enter the war on their side, or, at the very least, to grant them formal recognition.

In short, the four million humans who generated the vast majority of Southern wealth and a good proportion of Northern wealth were not slaves for the sake of it, or due to racism in the abstract. They were slaves *to make profits for capital*, which will happily rake in value from any and all forms of exploitation. Slavery was big money, and the racist poison that accompanied it was intended to justify that economic reality.

The politics of crisis

The 1860 election was an unholy mess. Though he didn't even appear on the ballot in ten Southern states, Abraham Lincoln was declared the winner in a four-way race with 39.8 per cent of the popular vote and 180 electoral delegates.

Stephen A. Douglas, the "Little Giant," won 29.5 per cent and 12 electoral votes for the Northern Democrats.

John C. Breckinridge, the sitting vice president, represented the Southern wing of the Democratic Party and won 18.1 per cent and 72 electoral votes.

Finally, John Bell won 12.6 per cent of the vote and 39 electoral votes for the Constitutional Union Party. This was a last-ditch effort by conservative Unionists, primarily in the border states, who sought to evade the slavery question altogether.

Just six years after the Republican Party's founding, it was sending a president to the White House. If John Brown's actions had overflowed the cup of secession and war, Lincoln's election shattered it into a million pieces. Upon his victory, Massachusetts abolitionist Charles Francis Adams proclaimed:

> The great revolution has actually taken place. The country has once and for all thrown off the domination of the slaveholders.[73]

However, it would be several months before Lincoln took the oath of office. The sitting president, James Buchanan, was a "dough face"—a Northerner who sympathized with the South. He was completely paralyzed by the crisis. In his view, it was illegal for the South to secede, but it was equally illegal for the federal government to stop secession by force. What to do?

On December 3, 1860, just weeks before secession was declared, Buchanan delivered his Fourth Annual Message to Congress. In it, he tried to appease the Southern states while simultaneously dissuading them from leaving the Union:

> The fact is that our Union rests upon public opinion, and can never be cemented by the blood of its citizens shed in civil war. If it cannot live in the affections of the people, it must one day perish. Congress possesses many means of preserving it by conciliation, but the sword was not placed in their hand to preserve it by force . . .
>
> In order to justify secession as a constitutional remedy, it must be on the principle that the Federal Government is a mere voluntary association of states, to be dissolved at pleasure by any one of the contracting parties. If this be so, the Confederacy [of the United States] is a rope of sand, to be penetrated and dissolved by the first adverse wave of public opinion in any of the states.
>
> In this manner, our thirty-three states may resolve themselves into as many petty, jarring, and hostile republics, each one retiring from the Union without responsibility whenever any sudden excitement might impel them to such a course. By this process, a Union might be entirely broken into fragments in a few weeks, which cost our forefathers many years of toil, privation, and blood to establish.
>
> The question fairly stated is: Has the Constitution delegated to Congress the power to coerce into submission a state which is attempting to withdraw or has actually withdrawn from the Confederacy? If answered in the affirmative, it must be on the principle that the power has been conferred upon Congress to declare and to make war against a State. After much serious reflection, I have arrived at the conclusion that no

> such power has been delegated to Congress or to any other department of the Federal Government.[74]

Though he personally despised slavery, Lincoln was really a "moderate" in that he sought only to limit slavery's spread into the territories, as he recognized it was protected elsewhere by the Constitution.

As he had expressed in 1854, shortly after the Kansas-Nebraska Act:

> This *declared* indifference, but as I must think, covert *real* zeal for the spread of slavery, I cannot but hate. I hate it because of the monstrous injustice of slavery itself. I hate it because it deprives our republican example of its just influence in the world—enables the enemies of free institutions, with plausibility, to taunt us as hypocrites—causes the real friends of freedom to doubt our sincerity, and especially because it forces so many really good men amongst ourselves into an open war with the very fundamental principles of civil liberty—criticizing the Declaration of Independence, and insisting that there is no right principle of action but *self-interest*.[75]

In a speech given in Chicago on July 10, 1858, he elaborated further:

> I am not, in the first place, unaware that this government has endured eighty-two years, half slave and half free. I know that. I am tolerably well acquainted with the history of the country, and I know that it has endured eighty-two years, half slave and half free. I *believe*—and that is what I meant to allude to there—I *believe* it has endured because, during all that time, until the introduction of the Nebraska Bill, the public mind did rest, all the time, in the belief that slavery was in course of ultimate extinction. ["Good!" "Good!" and applause.]
>
> That was what gave us the rest that we had through that period of eighty-two years; at least, so I believe. I have always hated slavery, I think as much as any Abolitionist. [Applause.] I have been an Old Line Whig. I have always hated it, but I have always been quiet about it until this new era of the introduction of the Nebraska Bill began. I always believed that everybody was against it, and that it was in the course

> of ultimate extinction. (Pointing to Mr. Browning, who stood nearby.) Browning thought so; the great mass of the nation has rested in the belief that slavery was in the course of ultimate extinction. They had reason to believe.
>
> The adoption of the Constitution and its attendant history led the people to believe so, and that such was the belief of the framers of the Constitution itself. Why did those old men, about the time of the adoption of the Constitution, decree that slavery should not go into the new territory, where it had not already gone? Why declare that within twenty years the African Slave Trade, by which slaves are supplied, might be cut off by Congress? Why were all these acts? I might enumerate more of these acts—but enough.
>
> What were they but a clear indication that the framers of the Constitution intended and expected the ultimate extinction of that institution. [Cheers.] And now, when I say, as I said in my speech that Judge Douglas has quoted from, when I say that I think the opponents of slavery will resist the farther spread of it, and place it where the public mind shall rest with the belief that it is in course of ultimate extinction, I only mean to say, that they will place it where the founders of this Government originally placed it.[76]

However, everyone knew that an end to expansion would inevitably lead to the institution's demise. As Marx wrote at the time:

> A strict confinement of slavery within its old terrain, therefore, was bound according to economic law to lead to its gradual extinction, in the political sphere to annihilate the hegemony that the slave states exercised through the Senate, and finally to expose the slaveholding oligarchy within its own states to threatening perils from the "poor whites."
>
> In accordance with the principle that any further extension of slave Territories was to be prohibited by law, the Republicans therefore attacked the rule of the slaveholders at its root. The Republican election victory was accordingly bound to lead to open struggle between North and South.[77]

The country's political temperature was at a boiling point. Even so, with the possible exception of fire-eating secessionists* like William Lowndes Yancey, militant abolitionists like John Brown, and the commanding general of the US Army at the time, Winfield Scott, very few people in the antebellum period foresaw the full scale of the cataclysm that loomed. And whatever they expected, none could have anticipated the profound social and economic changes the war would unleash.

Secession

Many in the South welcomed Lincoln's election, viewing it as a convenient excuse for secession. They believed they were revolutionaries, following the founding generation, and defending themselves and the Constitution against tyrannical attempts to despoil citizens of their rightful property. It wouldn't be the first time in history that revolution was conflated with counterrevolution.

Some argued the North had *de facto* seceded from the Union, which clearly sanctioned slavery, and that the government in Washington had been usurped by radical lunatics. Others saw the US Constitution as a failed experiment and wanted to replace it with an explicitly proslavery constitution, as we have seen.

Nonetheless, until the last moment, many on both sides hoped an agreement could be reached. Maybe, even at this late hour, further protections for slavery could be guaranteed within the Union. Failing that, an amicable separation could perhaps be negotiated, including a gentleman's agreement on federal property within the seceding states.

But the hard-core secessionists wanted to present the incoming Lincoln administration with a *fait accompli*.† This would limit his room for maneuver and pressure other slave states to join their cause.

---

* Named for their fiery rhetoric, fire-eaters were a loose grouping of extreme proslavery Democrats who vociferously advocated for secession.

† French for "accomplished fact"; something that has already happened or been done and cannot be changed.

To this end, on December 20, 1860, South Carolina announced it was leaving the Union. The state's Declaration of Secession complained that the Northern states had "denounced as sinful the institution of slavery" and had "encouraged and assisted thousands of our slaves to leave their homes." It asserted that Lincoln's election by a "sectional party" committed to restricting slavery made it impossible for them to remain in the Union.[78]

South Carolina was followed in relatively quick succession by the Cotton Belt states of Mississippi, Florida, Alabama, Georgia, Louisiana, and Texas. Four more states eventually seceded, bringing the total to 11 out of a total of 33 states in the Union at that time.

In response, Lincoln took a pragmatic, measured, and diplomatic approach, in large part to avoid provoking key states like Virginia, Kentucky, Missouri, and Maryland, which had not yet seceded. His hope was that pro-Union sentiment in the South would eventually assert itself and force a quick reunion.

According to Lincoln lore, when a well-wisher assured Lincoln that God was on his side in the conflict, the president retorted: "I hope to have God on my side, but I must have Kentucky." This neatly sums up the political, economic, and strategic importance of the border states.

In his first inaugural speech, Lincoln did his best to be all things to all people, offering an olive branch to the South, while refusing to accept that any states had left the Union, no matter what they declared:

> I have no purpose, directly or indirectly, to interfere with the institution of slavery in the States where it exists. I believe I have no lawful right to do so, and I have no inclination to do so . . .[79]
>
> In *your* hands, my dissatisfied fellow-countrymen, and not in *mine*, is the momentous issue of civil war. The government will not assail *you*. You can have no conflict without being yourselves the aggressors . . .
>
> We are not enemies, but friends. We must not be enemies. Though passion may have strained, it must not break our bonds of affection. The mystic chords of memory, stretching from every battlefield and patriot

> grave to every living heart and hearthstone all over this broad land, will yet swell the chorus of the Union, when again touched, as surely they will be, by the better angels of our nature.[80]

> [N]o State, upon its own mere motion, can lawfully get out of the Union,—that *resolves* and *ordinances* to that effect are legally void; and that acts of violence, within any State or States against the authority of the United States, are insurrectionary or revolutionary, according to circumstances.[81]

> The power confided to me, will be used to hold, occupy, and possess the property and places belonging to the government, and to collect the duties and imposts; but beyond what may be necessary for these objects, there will be no invasion—no using of force against, or among the people anywhere.[82]

In short, secession represented the tyranny of the minority over the majority. The Union had been entered into by collective agreement and the individual states could not unilaterally dissolve it. He put the onus for secession and violence on the Southern states themselves, and firmly declared that he would defend property belonging to the nation as a whole.

This was a clear reference to Fort Sumter, a federal installation occupied by US troops that guarded access to Charleston's harbor. Though not of decisive strategic importance, Sumter had come to symbolize all federal laws, property, and the Union as a whole.

However, not even the most carefully chosen words by the most eloquent of all American presidents could shut the Pandora's box that had been opened. Several weeks earlier, on February 18, Jefferson Davis had been inaugurated as president of the Confederate States of America. As historian Bruce Catton put it, Jefferson and Lincoln were "the rival leaders of two nations in a land that could hold only one."[83]

Even at this late stage, many refused to believe disunion was possible. Most people in the North assumed it was merely a case of political brinkmanship taken too far, a hardline negotiating tactic to extract concessions. At most, they thought they were faced with a fairly minor regional rebellion. They believed that, without expending too much blood or treasure, they could reestablish the Union on more or less the old lines.

As for the South, many sincerely believed they could simply walk away from the United States and continue their regional system as they had for centuries, minus Yankee interference.

Not everyone in the South was for secession, and not everyone in the North favored the South's forcible reincorporation. Some wanted Lincoln to simply let the Southern states go. However, as often occurs in such situations, events moved quickly, a critical mass was reached, and the time came when only muskets, cannons, horses, ironclads, and railroads could decide the issue.

After months of mounting tensions, Fort Sumter was fired upon by Confederate forces on April 12, 1861. Major Robert Anderson, commander of the US Army troops holding the harbor island, held out for 34 hours before lowering the US flag. The attack was met with jubilation and celebration throughout the South. Contemporary accounts describe a carnival-like atmosphere as crowds gathered to witness the bombardment.

Mary Boykin Chesnut, a prominent diarist from South Carolina, captured the fervor in Charleston:

> Anderson will not capitulate.
>
> Yesterday's was the merriest, maddest dinner we have had yet. Men were audaciously wise and witty. We had an unspoken foreboding that it was to be our last pleasant meeting. . .
>
> I do not pretend to go to sleep. How can I? If Anderson does not accept terms at four, the orders are, he shall be fired upon.
>
> I count four, St. Michael's bells chime out and I begin to hope. At half-past four the heavy booming of a cannon. I sprang out of bed, and on my knees prostrate I prayed as I never prayed before . . . Certainly fire had begun. The regular roar of the cannon, there it was. And who could tell what each volley accomplished of death and destruction?

> The women were wild there on the housetop. Prayers came from the women and imprecations from the men. And then a shell would light up the scene. Tonight, they say, the forces are to attempt to land . . .
>
> We watched up there, and everybody wondered why Fort Sumter did not fire a shot . . .
>
> Do you know, after all that noise and our tears and prayers, nobody has been hurt. Sound and fury signifying nothing! A delusion and a snare . . .
>
> Not by one word or look can we detect any change in the demeanor of these Negro servants. Lawrence sits at our door, sleepy and respectful, and profoundly indifferent. So are they all. They carry it too far. You could not tell that they even heard the awful roar going on in the bay, though it has been dinning in their ears night and day. People talk before them as if they were chairs and tables, and they make no sign. Are they stolidly stupid, or wiser than we are, silent and strong, biding their time?[84]

William L. Yancey, known as the "Orator of Secession," declared at a rally in Montgomery, Alabama:

> The man and the hour have met. We may now hope that prosperity, honor, and victory await [Jefferson Davis's] administration.[85]

On the following day, *The Charleston Mercury* proclaimed:

> The tea has been thrown overboard. The revolution of 1860 has been initiated.[86]

The Rubicon had been crossed, the die had been cast, and only open war could decide the question. On April 15, Lincoln called for 75,000 militia volunteers to serve for 90 days to suppress the rebellion. Although Kentucky, Missouri, Maryland, and Delaware remained tenuously in the union, the call for troops to "coerce" the South pushed Virginia, Arkansas, North Carolina, and Tennessee into the Confederacy.

Virginia's decision to leave the Union was particularly decisive. This all but guaranteed a long and bloody war as it had the largest economy and population of all the slave states. Reflecting the contradictory nature of the Southern states, the western part of Virginia seceded from the state and rejoined the Union in 1863 as West Virginia.

Abraham Lincoln and the role of the individual in history

It is ABC for Marxists that revolutions give expression to profound social and economic contradictions. But the precise outcome of these processes flows from a struggle of living forces, including countless accidental elements that cannot be predicted in advance. Although the role of the individual in expressing historical necessity can be decisive at certain nodal points of development, the main course of events is not decided by the subjective will of individual participants.

In *War and Peace*, Leo Tolstoy challenged the "great man" theory of history exemplified by the worship of individuals like Napoleon or Washington. Tolstoy argued that such historical figures were not the makers of history, but rather its instruments, carried along by forces beyond their control:

> A king is history's slave.
>
> History, that is, the unconscious, general, hive life of mankind, uses every moment of the life of kings as a tool for its own purposes.
>
> Though Napoleon at that time, in 1812, was more convinced than ever that it depended on him *verser (ou ne pas verser) le sang de ses peuples* . . .* he had never been so much in the grip of inevitable laws, which compelled him, while thinking that he was acting on his own volition, to perform for the hive life—that is to say, for history—whatever had to be performed.[87]

Though he didn't live to see the publication of Tolstoy's epic novel, Abraham Lincoln appears to have drawn the same conclusion. As he put it:

> I claim not to have controlled events, but confess plainly that events have controlled me.[88]

---

* French for "to shed (or not to shed) the blood of his peoples"

Lincoln's ideas and actions evolved dramatically over the course of the conflict, offering an illuminating example of reformism passing over into revolution. Initially, he adopted a largely legalistic approach, seeking merely to put down a regional rebellion while maintaining the status quo, including slavery. He was only a hardliner on the question of its extension into the territories.

However, events, events, events that compelled him to pursue a revolutionary war of destruction and expropriation of slave property, which was the root cause and support for the revolt. Had he limited himself to reestablishing the old order, he would have almost certainly failed. However, once he recognized the changed conditions and let himself be swept along by the tide, he left his mark on the process and helped transform it into a truly revolutionary struggle, which, in turn, took on a life of its own.

As Marx recognized in 1862:

> President Lincoln never ventures a step forward before the tide of circumstances, and the general call of public opinion forbid[s] further delay. But once "Old Abe" realizes that such a turning point has been reached, he surprises friend and foe alike by a sudden operation executed as noiselessly as possible.[89]

Marx's writings reveal both his puzzlement and admiration for Lincoln's pragmatism and uniquely American temperament. As commander in chief, Lincoln had to handle his family, friends, rivals, cabinet, generals, media, and public opinion with a Machiavellian touch, in the very best and original sense of that word. His masterful, step-by-step balancing act between the different pressures and players—most of whom thought they were smarter and better qualified to be president than a backwoods country lawyer—is truly unparalleled in the whole of American history.

Historian Doris Kearns Goodwin wrote an entire book on the subject. In *Team of Rivals: The Political Genius of Abraham Lincoln*, she explains:

> Lincoln's political genius [was] revealed through his extraordinary array of personal qualities that enabled him to form friendships with men who had previously opposed him; to repair injured feelings that, left untended, might have escalated into permanent hostility; to assume responsibility for the failures of subordinates; to share credit with ease; and to learn from mistakes. He possessed an acute understanding of the sources of power inherent in the presidency, an unparalleled ability to keep his governing coalition intact, a tough-minded appreciation of the need to protect his presidential prerogatives, and a masterful sense of timing. His success in dealing with the strong egos of the men in his cabinet suggests that in the hands of a truly great politician the qualities we generally associate with decency and morality—kindness, sensitivity, compassion, honesty, and empathy—can also be impressive political resources.[90]

Lincoln understood full well that war is the continuation of politics by other means and cannot always be avoided:

> In a choice of evils, war may not always be the worst. Still I would do all in my power to avert it, except to neglect a constitutional duty. As to slavery, it must be content with what it has. The voice of the civilized world is against it; it is opposed to its growth or extension. Freedom is the natural condition of the human race in which the Almighty intended men to live. Those who fight the purposes of the Almighty will not succeed. They always have been, they always will be, beaten.[91]

After decades of compromise with the centrifugal forces of states' rights particularism, the inheritors of Alexander Hamilton's Federalists finally won the day, in the person of Abraham Lincoln. The need to finance and mobilize the human and material resources required for victory led to unprecedented centralization—through tariffs, taxes, a military draft, the first national paper currency, and even partial nationalization of the railroads and telegraphs.

"The coming fury"

Washington, DC, is surrounded by the then–slave states of Virginia and Maryland. The threat posed to the capital, to Lincoln, and his government was extremely high in the first few weeks of the war. The only way to get loyal troops to defend the city ran through Baltimore, where pro-Confederate sentiment ran high. On April 19, 1861, a secessionist mob attacked Massachusetts troops bound for Washington. Four soldiers and 12 civilian rioters died in the melee.

Although Lincoln was trained as a lawyer and was meticulously attentive to the letter of the law, he wasn't about to let mere pieces of paper lead to the dissolution of the Union. He waged war by any means necessary to ensure the survival of his government and country.

To keep states like Maryland and Missouri in the Union, and to defend the Constitution as a whole, Lincoln was more than willing to bend certain aspects of that document beyond recognition.

This included the suspension of *habeas corpus** in parts of the country, the creation of a secret service, the imposition of an internal passport system for citizens, and the arrest and imprisonment of pro-Confederate dissenters. These included the mayors of Baltimore and Washington, DC, Congressman Henry May, former Kentucky governor Charles Morehead, and many Northern newspaper editors. While it is not clear exactly how many people the government arrested for antiwar protests during the war, estimates range as high as 38,000.

On the surface, this would appear to be a clear-cut condemnation of Lincoln, who seemed to be acting like a tyrant. However, as Trotsky explained:

> Lincoln's significance lies in his not hesitating before the most severe means once they were found to be necessary in achieving a great historic aim posed by the development of a young nation. The question lies not

* Latin for "you have the body"; a legal procedure allowing anyone detained or imprisoned by the authorities to challenge their detention before a judge.

> even in which of the warring camps caused or itself suffered the greatest number of victims. History has different yardsticks for the cruelty of the Northerners and the cruelty of the Southerners in the Civil War. A slave-owner who through cunning and violence shackles a slave in chains, and a slave who through cunning or violence breaks the chains—let not the contemptible eunuchs tell us that they are equals before a court of morality![92]

In the case of Lincoln, a revolutionary war to uproot slavery was, indeed, a historically justified end. Or, to paraphrase the Radical Republican* Thaddeus Stevens,† the laws of war supersede the laws of the Constitution.

The North's initial strategy for subduing the South was the Anaconda Plan, devised by the Union's general-in-chief, Winfield Scott. The plan called for the coordinated strangulation of the South through the combined action of Union land and naval forces. A blockade of the Confederate coastline and a push down the Mississippi River would split the Confederacy in half militarily and economically. Scott described his plan in a May 3, 1861 letter to General George McClellan:

> We rely greatly on the sure operation of a complete blockade of the Atlantic and Gulf ports soon to commence. In connection with such blockade we propose a powerful movement down the Mississippi to the ocean, with a cordon of posts at proper points, and the capture of Forts Jackson and Saint Philip; the object being to clear out and keep open this great line of communication in connection with the strict blockade of the sea-board, so as to envelop the insurgent States and bring them to terms with less bloodshed than by any other plan. I suppose there

* Faction within the Republican Party emerging in the mid-1850s. Radical Republicans advocated for the immediate abolition of slavery, political and social equality for Black Americans, and harsher policies for the South during Reconstruction.

† House Representative from Pennsylvania from 1859 until his death in 1868. A leading Radical Republican, Stevens was an ardent abolitionist and advocate for the rights of freedpeople and Black Americans. He favored expropriating Southern plantations and dividing up the land among the freedpeople.

> will be needed from twelve to twenty steam gun-boats, and a sufficient number of steam transports (say forty) to carry all the personnel (say 60,000 men) and material of the expedition; most of the gun-boats to be in advance to open the way, and the remainder to follow and protect the rear of the expedition, etc. This army, in which it is not improbable you may be invited to take an important part, should be composed of our best regulars for the advance and of three-years' volunteers, all well officered, and with four months and a half of instruction in camps prior to (say) November 10. In the progress down the river all the enemy's batteries on its banks we of course would turn and capture, leaving a sufficient number of posts with complete garrisons to keep the river open behind the expedition. Finally, it will be necessary that New Orleans should be strongly occupied and securely held until the present difficulties are composed.[93]

The plan was widely ridiculed in the press by both sides, and the aging Scott was forced into retirement. Though it would take far more time, blood, and treasure than Scott had imagined, a far more aggressive version of his plan, combined with the occupation of Tennessee and the march across Georgia are what eventually led to military victory, at least in its broad strokes; this, and the eventual transformation of the war into one of revolutionary liberation, with the participation of thousands of former slaves.

At the beginning of the war, the Union army was just 16,000 strong, and most of them were stationed on the western frontier. To complicate matters for the Union, a healthy chunk of the West Point–trained officer corps—though by no means all of the best military cadres—went over to the Confederacy.

So while the South got people like Robert E. Lee, Stonewall Jackson, James Longstreet, and J.E.B. Stewart, the North got Ulysses S. Grant, William Tecumseh Sherman, Philip Sheridan, and, despite his many faults, the master organizer, George McClellan. In addition, both sides had their fair share of military dilettantes and incompetent "political generals," who had received their commissions merely because they had the wealth and wherewithal to raise and equip their own units.

Many in the Confederacy were convinced that Northerners would be pushovers. They saw them as soft and effete, unlike the fiery and martial people of the South. However, as George Ticknor wrote from Boston shortly after the bombardment of Fort Sumter:

> [There was] much enthusiasm [in the North], much deep earnestness. Men and money are profusely offered; the best blood among us volunteering and going, and money untold following them . . .
>
> We have been slow to kindle, but we have made a Nebuchadnezzar's furnace of it at last, and the heat will remain, and the embers will smolder, long after the flames that now light up everything shall cease to be seen or felt.[94]

And as William T. Sherman presciently told a Southern friend in Louisiana in the days after South Carolina announced it was leaving the Union:

> You, you people of the South, believe there can be such a thing as peaceable secession. You don't know what you are doing . . . This country will be drenched in blood. God only knows how it will end . . .
>
> It is all folly, madness, a crime against civilization! . . .
>
> You people speak so lightly of war; you don't know what you're talking about. War is a terrible thing! . . .
>
> You mistake, too, the people of the North. They are a peaceable people but an earnest people, and they will fight too, and they are not going to let this country be destroyed without a mighty effort to save it.
>
> Besides, where are your men and appliances of war to contend against them? The Northern people not only greatly outnumber the whites at the South, but they are a mechanical people with manufactures of every kind; while you are only agriculturists—a sparse population covering a large extent of territory, and in all history no nation of mere agriculturists ever made successful war against a nation of mechanics . . .

> The North can make a steam engine, locomotive, or railway car; hardly a yard of cloth or pair of shoes can you make. You are rushing into war with one of the most powerful, ingeniously mechanical, and determined people on earth—right at your doors. You are bound to fail. Only in your spirit and determination are you prepared for war. In all else, you are totally unprepared, with a bad cause to start with.
>
> At first, you will make headway, but as your limited resources begin to fail, shut out from the markets of Europe by blockade, as you will be, your cause will begin to wane . . . if your people will but stop and think, they must see in the end that you will surely fail.[95]

As for why white Northerners sacrificed so much in the war, Eric Foner offers the following insights in his review of Gary W. Gallagher's *The Union War*:

> The Civil War, Gallagher announces at the outset, was "a war for Union that also killed slavery." Emancipation was an outcome (an "astounding" outcome, Lincoln remarked in his second Inaugural Address) but, Gallagher insists, it always "took a back seat" to the paramount goal of saving the Union. Most Northerners, he says, remained indifferent to the plight of the slaves. They embraced emancipation only when they concluded it had become necessary to win the war. They fought because they regarded the United States as a unique experiment in democracy that guaranteed political liberty and economic opportunity in a world overrun by tyranny. Saving the Union, in the words of Secretary of State William H. Seward, meant "the saving of popular government for the world." . . .
>
> Before the war, slavery powerfully affected the concept of self-government. Large numbers of Americans identified democratic citizenship as a privilege of whites alone—a position embraced by the Supreme Court in the Dred Scott decision of 1857. Which is why the transformation wrought by the Civil War was so remarkable. As George William Curtis, the editor of Harper's Weekly, observed in 1865, the war transformed a government "for white men" into one "for mankind." That was something worth fighting for.[96]

After Fort Sumter, Lincoln had called for 75,000 three-month volunteers. But he was eventually forced to muster 42,000 more, followed by another 500,000, and to extend the term of enlistment to three years. To meet these needs, he was compelled to institute a national draft. By the end of the war, more than 2.1 million people had served in the Union army, which became the largest, best-trained, and best-equipped military force on the planet. Significantly, roughly 180,000 of these were Black troops, most of them former slaves.

As for the South, tens of thousands rushed to volunteer in 1861, and the Confederate armies rapidly grew into the hundreds of thousands. It was a colossal and enthusiastic mobilization on both sides.

However, the war would be neither short nor easy. Even in the early battles, casualties were alarmingly high by the standards of earlier American wars.

On July 21, 1861, at the First Battle of Bull Run, the Union army was humiliated after enjoying initial success. Known to the Confederates as First Manassas, it shattered everyone's hopes for a quick war. Picnic-goers from nearby Washington, DC—who had gathered to witness the end of the rebellion—were caught up in the panic, leaving a trail of broken carriages alongside abandoned cannons on the road back to the capital.

At the Battle of Fort Donelson, fought from February 11–16, 1862, in western Tennessee, the recently reenlisted Ulysses S. Grant captured a Confederate fort and approximately 15,000 prisoners.

At Pea Ridge in Arkansas, in March of 1862, the Union secured Missouri for the North and ended major Confederate operations in the state.

At the Battle of Hampton Roads, also fought in early March 1862, the heavily armored "ironclads"—the USS *Monitor* and CSS *Virginia* (formerly the *Merrimack*)—met off the coast of Virginia, revolutionizing naval warfare.

And in late March 1862, at the Battle of Glorieta Pass in New Mexico Territory, the Union ended Confederate ambitions in the Southwest in what would later be called the "Gettysburg of the West."

As significant as these encounters were, however, none of them could compare with the truly unimaginable death and destruction that would follow.

A new kind of war

Everything changed on April 6 and 7, 1862, near a small country church in southwestern Tennessee called "Shiloh," meaning "place of peace" in ancient Hebrew. In just two days, over 13,000 Union soldiers and 10,000 Confederates were killed or wounded—more than in all earlier American wars combined. For comparison, there had been about 4,750 total casualties at the first Battle of Bull Run.

As Ulysses S. Grant would later write in his extraordinary memoirs:

> I saw an open field, in our possession on the second day, over which the Confederates had made repeated charges the day before, so covered with dead that it would have been possible to walk across the clearing, in any direction, stepping on dead bodies, without a foot touching the ground . . .
>
> Up to the battle of Shiloh, I, as well as thousands of other citizens, believed that the rebellion against the government would collapse suddenly and soon [if] a decisive victory could be gained over any of its armies. [But after Shiloh,] I gave up all idea of saving the Union except by complete conquest.[97]

The country was shocked by the carnage. Though distraught at the mounting cost in blood and treasure, and under pressure to remove Grant, Lincoln stood by him. As he put it, "*I can't spare this man, he fights.*"[98]

On another occasion, when was accused of drinking while on duty, Lincoln is reported to have asked:

> But can you tell me where he gets his whiskey?
>
> We cannot, Mr. President. But why do you desire to know?
>
> Because if I can only find out, I will send a barrel of this wonderful whiskey to every general in the Army.[99]

These small anecdotes offer wonderful insight into Lincoln as a leader. He was a student of people and knew how to make the best of their talents and abilities despite their weaknesses, often using humor to make a deeper point. As we've seen, he knew how to build a team from contradictory personalities and interests, and he had no problem sharing credit with others, as long as the job was done right.

However, if the truth be told, a substantial layer of the Union high command was politically conservative and fought for reunion first and foremost—not for a decisive social revolution. Many hoped that a show of force would bring the seceded states back with slavery and the old ruling class largely intact. Commanders like George B. McClellan repeatedly overestimated the enemy and handled their armies with paralyzing caution. Others, such as Ambrose Burnside and Joseph Hooker, proved unequal to the demands of top command—whether through caution, misjudgment, or simple incompetence—and the result was delay, squandered opportunities, and staggering losses.

As an example, after Bull Run, McClellan proceeded to build up a highly trained, well-drilled, and expensive force, the Army of the Potomac. But he kept finding excuses not to use it. He was broadly sympathetic with the South and hoped the seceded states and their slaves would return to the Union after a blusterous show of force. Deeply contemptuous of Lincoln, he privately referred to his commander in chief as the "original gorilla,"[100] "an idiot," and a "well meaning baboon":[101]

> I can never regard him with other feelings than those of thorough contempt—for his mind, his heart, and his morality.[102]

McClellan's lack of initiative led an exasperated Lincoln to exclaim in the Spring of 1862:

> If General McClellan does not want to use the army for some days, I should like to borrow it and see if it cannot be made to do something.[103]

Marx was even sharper in his criticism, describing McClellan's generalship as "itself sufficient to secure the downfall of the strongest and best disciplined army."[104] The weakness of the Northern generals had a political and class basis:

> McClellan and most of the officers of the regular army who got their training at West Point are more or less bound to their old comrades in the enemy camp by the ties of *esprit de corps*. They are inspired by the same jealousy of the *parvenus* among the "civilian soldiers."
>
> In their view, the war must be waged in a strictly businesslike fashion, with constant regard to the restoration of the Union on its *old* basis, and therefore must above all be kept free from revolutionary tendencies and tendencies affecting matters of principle. A fine conception of a war that is essentially a war of principles! The first generals of the English Parliament fell into the same error.* "But," says Cromwell, "how changed everything was as soon as men took the lead who professed a principle of godliness and *religion*!"[105]

For the first two years, the fighting went quite badly for the Union in the Eastern theater, due largely to political vacillation and infighting among the generals. This led to extreme swings in Northern morale and confidence. However, despite the hardships, the mass of the population, including the soldiery, remained resolutely behind the war and wanted it carried through to the end.

Meanwhile, in the Western theater, significant gains were being made. Ulysses S. Grant's strategic and operational genius, coolness and tenacity under fire, and personal familiarity with the enemy commanders he faced led to one hard-fought Union victory after another. Almost like dominoes, he took Forts Henry and Donelson in Tennessee in February 1862, giving the Union control of crucial river routes into the heart of the Confederacy. After the bloody but decisive win at Shiloh in April, Grant turned his attention to the key

* The parallel with the first stages of the English Revolution is particularly apt. The struggle against the monarchy was originally led by Parliament, whose members wasted time vacillating and seeking common ground with the royalist camp. Once Oliver Cromwell and the more radical elements took over leadership of the revolution, however, things accelerated quickly, galvanizing mass support for Cromwell's Model Army across the country.

Mississippi stronghold of Vicksburg. According to Lincoln, "The war can never be brought to a close until that key is in our pocket."[106]

As for General Grant, Lincoln had high hopes and expectations:

> He doesn't worry and bother me . . . He isn't shrieking for reinforcements all the time. He takes what troops we can safely give him . . . and does the best he can with what he has got. And if Grant only does this thing down there . . . why, Grant is my man and I am his the rest of the war.[107]

The border states and the civil war within the Civil War

Throughout most of the South, the outbreak of war had cut across Unionist sentiment and pushed the majority of the population behind the Confederacy. There were, of course, continued class contradictions, political dissenters, desertions, and even a few mutinies in the Confederacy. But on both sides of the divide, the initial mood was one of mass enthusiasm for the war. In some cases it was popular enthusiasm that drove the politicians and even shaped military policy.

Several decades later, Trotsky described the disposition of the Viennese masses at the outbreak of World War I. Infected as they were with patriotism and nationalism, they had no inkling of the nightmare that lay ahead:

> The people whose lives, day in and day out, pass in a monotony of hopelessness are many; they are the mainstay of modern society. The alarm of [war] mobilization breaks into their lives like a promise; the familiar and long-hated is overthrown, and the new and unusual reigns in its place. Changes still more incredible are in store for them in the future. For better or worse? For the better, of course, what can seem worse to [an ordinary person] than "normal" conditions?[108]

This was the general mood on both sides of the American conflict as hundreds of thousands mobilized to participate in what they assumed would be a short and glorious little adventure.

However, the situation was far more complicated in the border states—slave states that did not secede from the Union—as well as in parts of seceded states where Unionist sentiment remained strong. Securing or maintaining the allegiance of as many of these contested regions as possible was critical to both sides, both economically and strategically. As Lincoln wrote to a supporter in September of 1861:

> I think to lose Kentucky is nearly the same as to lose the whole game. Kentucky gone, we can not hold Missouri, nor, as I think, Maryland. These all against us, and the job on our hands is too large for us. We would as well consent to separation at once, including the surrender of this capital.[109]

Though deeply divided, Lincoln's birth state ended up staying in the Union, providing key logistics support and supplies, including horses and mules. Maryland, Delaware, and Missouri also remained, though just barely. And as we've seen, Western Virginia seceded from Virginia outright and formed a new state.

In other areas, localized civil wars raged within the larger conflict, as was seen during the First Revolution. The idea that the Civil War was a "war between brothers" was literally true in many areas. At Gettysburg, for example, Confederate and Union soldiers from Maryland confronted each other on Culp's Hill, calling out greetings and insults to former friends and neighbors while attempting to kill each other.

The conflict in the border states often took on a particularly savage character, with punitive raids, sabotage, and violence tearing apart rural communities. As historian Michael Fellman explains in *Inside War*:

> Guerrilla struggle, perhaps the prevalent form of war in history, is also the most devastating challenge to any notion of civility or virtue in war. In this sense, guerrilla war approaches total war, the war of all against all . . . [G]uerrilla war was quite widespread along the border between the South and the North during the American Civil War. From the hills of western Virginia, North Carolina, and Georgia, through the mountain

> hollows of East Tennessee and Kentucky to the wooded, hilly farmlands of Missouri, bands of guerrillas wandered the countryside striking terror in all those around them.[110]

Guerrilla fighting was also widespread in parts of the Confederacy occupied by Union troops. In his review of *A Savage Conflict: The Decisive Role of Guerrillas in the American Civil War*, historian Jeremy Neely explains the breadth and depth of Civil War guerrillaism:

> With only a portion of southern guerrillas entering the government's service as partisan rangers, a great many others prowled the countryside of their own accord, sowing terror and confusion among foes, civilian and Federal, and threatening to unleash a popular conflagration that might rage beyond the authorities' control. Sutherland does a masterful job of sorting through the sprawling and tangled guerrilla ranks; his careful explication of historical labels is particularly good.
>
> *Guerrilla*, he writes, generally indicated those who participated in irregular combat, including self-styled *scouts*, *rangers*, and *raiders*. Many southern guerrillas identified themselves as *partisans*, especially near the start of the war, but after 1862 the term largely came to indicate those who rode in the service of the Confederate government. *Bushwhacker* often referred to lone gunmen but carried connotations of cowardice or extraordinary meanness and thus came to apply to many deserters, ruffians, and outlaws. Sutherland notes that many Union soldiers referred to all guerrillas as bushwhackers. Unionist guerrillas, on the other hand, included *Red Legs*, *buffaloes*, and *jayhawkers*.
>
> Confederate expectations about the possibilities and perils of irregular combat soon proved correct. Guerrillas did indeed become principal antagonists of the Union army throughout much of the West and South. Irregular activity brought Federal soldiers any number of intractable headaches during the military occupation of border states like Missouri and Kentucky. Protecting river and rail traffic and maintaining relative order were the troops' primary responsibilities, but they generally struggled to engage and defeat local guerrillas. Union leaders responded by adopting an increasingly forceful approach that targeted not only

> guerrillas but also the civilian population that sheltered and supported them. Perhaps the most famous and far-reaching example of this strategy was Order Number 11, which called for the depopulation of several western Missouri counties following the massacre of more than 150 men and boys in Lawrence, Kansas, in August 1863.[111]

John S. Mosby led Confederate partisan rangers in northern Virginia, using hit-and-run raids on Union supply lines with official Confederate authorization. William C. Quantrill and his gang were notorious for their brutality on the Missouri–Kansas border, where the line between soldiers, civilians, and outlaws was far from clear. But as intense as all of this was, it wasn't the only form of civil strife in the midst of the broader war.

Class struggle during the Civil War

The class struggle is a constant feature of all societies divided into classes. Sometimes, war dampens the open expression of these tensions. At others, it is the catalyst for an all-out revolution. We've seen some ways in which civil war raged within the sectional war. But both regions also experienced internal class conflicts that shaped the course of events.

At the start of the war, the Union Army's ranks were brimming with enthusiastic volunteers. As the battle fronts bogged down, however, the patriotic fervor subsided, and Lincoln was compelled to turn to conscription.

The Enrollment Act of March 3, 1863, introduced the first federal military draft in US history—though the Confederacy had passed a similar law nearly a year earlier. It made all male citizens and immigrant men who had filed for citizenship between the ages of 20 and 45 liable for military service.

Most controversially, the act allowed wealthy men to avoid service by paying a $300 commutation fee or by hiring a substitute to serve in their place. As in other American wars, the burden of military service fell disproportionately on the working poor and immigrants, particularly the Irish, who already faced economic hardship and discrimination. At a time when ordinary laborers earned just $1 per day, the exemption effectively meant that it was "a rich man's war but a poor man's fight."

The Enrollment Act also granted sweeping powers to federal provost marshals to enforce conscription, including the authority to arrest draft dodgers and deserters. This expansion of federal power into communities across the North was unprecedented and deeply resented by many who saw it as a tyrannical overreach—of the very kind earlier generations had rebelled against.

The law's implementation was chaotic and often blatantly corrupt. Local draft boards wielded enormous discretionary power, and fraud was rampant. The substitution system led to coercion and yet another market in human bodies, with brokers and bounty agents profiting by matching draftees with available substitutes.

Tensions over these iniquities boiled over in July 1863, culminating in the New York City Draft Riots. The chaos lasted four days and resulted in the deaths of over 100 people. Understandably, the rioters attacked draft offices and the homes of the wealthy.

However, since the class struggle in the US is so often interlaced with reactionary thread, they also targeted Black New Yorkers. Some blamed them for the war; others simply saw them as economic competitors and convenient scapegoats. Black men were lynched, the Colored Orphan Asylum was burned to the ground, and Black people's homes and businesses were destroyed. Order was only restored when federal troops, fresh from the fields of Gettysburg, were deployed to suppress the rioters.

On a far more positive note, the embryonic workers' movement of the prewar period continued to evolve and take shape during the war. While some union shops suspended their operations altogether for the duration of the fighting—because most or all of the workers had joined the military—others became more organized and militant.

The Northern economy boomed during the war. Profiteering and corruption soared off the charts. Nonetheless, there was unprecedented demand for manufactured goods—uniforms, weapons, ammunition, shoes, and countless other supplies. Due to labor shortages in many industries as men left for military service, workers who remained had increased leverage against their employers.

As a result, union membership grew substantially during the war, particularly among skilled craftsmen, who used their privileged positions to demand better wages and conditions. Typographers, molders, machinists, locomotive engineers, and shoemakers were among the most active in forming unions. The National Typographical Union, founded in 1852, grew significantly during the war, as did the Iron Molders' International Union, formed in 1859.

Despite the pressure not to disrupt the war effort, workers continued to strike for better conditions as wages lagged behind inflation. Railroad workers occasionally downed tools but were usually aggressively suppressed, given the rails' strategic importance. Ironworkers, foundry workers, and longshoremen in port cities like Boston and New York also withheld their labor to win concessions from their employers. There were important strikes by machinists in Philadelphia and shoemakers in Lynn, Massachusetts. Pennsylvania coal miners struck for higher wages and better safety conditions. Shortly after the war, miners in Michigan's Upper Peninsula also went on strike. Workers also began to coordinate across different trades, forming central labor councils in major cities.

Unsurprisingly, employers and newspapers denounced strikes and unions as unpatriotic and even treasonous, arguing that they gave aid and comfort to the Confederacy. Workers countered that profiteering contractors were the real traitors to the Union cause, pointing to warehouses full of hoarded supplies while troops on the frontline did without.

Some labor leaders, particularly German-Americans coming from a socialist background, understood that slavery degraded all labor and supported abolition on a class basis. They recognized that as long as millions of laborers were forced to work without wages, the bargaining power of all workers vis-à-vis the bosses would be undermined.

Other workers, particularly Irish immigrants, feared that emancipation would flood the labor market with freedmen willing to work for lower wages. Employers sometimes used Black workers to break strikes, deliberately inflaming racial tensions to cut across working-class solidarity. Proslavery Democrats cynically exploited these fears, warning white workers that abolition would destroy their livelihoods.

In the South, of course, the most fundamental expression of the class struggle was between the slaves and their masters, as we'll discuss further down. But there were other important manifestations as well.

The Confederacy may have been built on a foundation of slavery, but that didn't mean white Southern society was homogeneous. As we've seen, only around 46,000 people made up the slavocracy proper.

Similar to the Union version it predated, the Confederate conscription law of 1862 led to cries of "rich man's war, poor man's fight." The legislation allowed wealthy planters to avoid military service by hiring substitutes or claiming exemption if they owned 20 or more slaves.

Denounced as the "Twenty Negro Law," this created deep resentment among poor whites who had no such offramp. Many yeoman farmers and landless rural laborers came to see the war as a conflict to defend the property interests of the planter aristocracy at their expense. This would have important repercussions during Reconstruction.

As the war dragged on, and economic and military conditions worsened, desertion spread through the Confederate armies. Entire regions, particularly in the Appalachian backwoods of North Carolina, Georgia, and East Tennessee, saw the rise of pro-Union sentiment and even armed resistance to Confederate authority. In some areas, Confederate troops had to be diverted from the front lines to suppress internal dissent and guerrillas. In Jones County, Mississippi, Confederate army deserters and Unionists led by Newton Knight established a quasi-independent community known as the "Free State of Jones" that resisted until after the end of the war.

Perhaps the most dramatic example of class struggle not involving slaves was the Richmond Bread Riot of April 1863. Hundreds of women marched through the Confederate capital, breaking into shops and warehouses, taking food and other goods. Jefferson Davis himself came out to confront the rioters, threatening to order troops to fire on them if they did not disperse. Similar scenes played out in other Southern cities.

After the war, these contradictory tendencies would coalesce as Northern workers organized to defend their interests against the industrial robber barons of the Gilded Age, and many Southern freedmen and poor whites came together to push back against the old masters in a new guise.

Marx's perspectives on the war

Marx and Engels took great interest in the war, writing in detail about the politics, economics, and military campaigns. They wrote articles for the *New York Tribune* and other newspapers. Engels, who had military experience and was a keen student of military history, often provided detailed strategic and tactical assessments of major battles. Sometimes, he even ghostwrote articles for his friend, who was busy drafting the first volume of *Capital.*

Their correspondence and published articles provide a remarkable running commentary on the progress of the war and many wonderful insights into their thinking and method. That being said, they observed from a distance and had limited personal knowledge of the ins and outs of American politics and society. Their personal letters were never intended for publication and they sometimes included off-the-cuff remarks they might not publish in a more polished theoretical or analytical work.

Engels had an amateur's passion for military science that led him to a careful study of the United States's geography, waterways, rail lines, mountains, and other strategic features. In March 1862, he and Marx outlined their remarkable grasp of the strategic situation in *Die Presse*:

> Cast a glance at the geographical shape of the secessionists' territory, with its long stretch of coast on the Atlantic Ocean and its long stretch of coast on the Gulf of Mexico. So long as the Confederates hold

> Kentucky and Tennessee, the whole formed a great compact mass. The loss of both these states drives an enormous wedge into their territory, separating the states on the North Atlantic Ocean from the States on the Gulf of Mexico.
>
> The direct route from Virginia and the two Carolinas to Texas, Louisiana, Mississippi and even, in part, to Alabama leads through Tennessee, which is now occupied by the Unionists. The sole route that, after the complete conquest of Tennessee by the Union, connects the two sections of the slave states goes through Georgia. *This proves that Georgia is the key to the secessionists' territory.* With the loss of Georgia, the Confederacy would be cut in two sections, which would have lost all connections with one another . . .
>
> From the foregoing considerations, it follows:
>
> The Potomac is not the most important position in the war theater. The seizure of Richmond and the advance of the Potomac army further South—difficult on account of the many rivers that cut across the line of march—could produce a tremendous moral effect. From a purely military standpoint, they would decide nothing.[112]

Though initially elated by the war's revolutionary potential, however, by the middle of 1862, Engels had grown quite pessimistic about the Union's military prospects. Writing to Marx on July 30, he gave vent to his frustration and expressed serious doubts about the North's prospects for victory:

> Things are going awry in America and, in fact, Mr. Stanton is after all chiefly to blame in that, after the conquest of Tennessee, sheer boastfulness led him to stop recruiting, so that the army was doomed to grow constantly weaker at the very time when it particularly needed reinforcing with a view to a rapid and decisive offensive. With a steady influx of recruits, the war had hitherto not, perhaps, been decided, but there could be no doubt about its successful outcome. Moreover, the run of victories had ensured a brisk supply of recruits.
>
> This measure was all the more inane in that, at that very time, the South was calling up all men aged between 18 and 35, i.e., staking everything

on one throw. It is these men, who have meanwhile become seasoned troops, that have since enabled the Confederates to gain the upper hand everywhere and assured them the initiative. They pinned down Halleck, drove Curtis out of Arkansas, beat McClellan, and, in the Shenandoah Valley, under Jackson, gave the signal for guerrilla bands, which are now already penetrating as far as the Ohio. Stanton could not have acted more stupidly had he tried.

Again, when Stanton saw that he would be unable to oust McClellan from the command of the Potomac Army, he perpetrated the stupidity of reducing McClellan's strength by detaching special commands to Frémont, Banks, and McDowell, and *dispersing the forces with a view to displacing McClellan.* Not only was McClellan defeated as a result, but public opinion is laying the blame for that defeat, not on McClellan, but on Stanton. Serves Mr. Stanton right.

None of this would have signified, and it might even have been all to the good inasmuch as the war might at last have been conducted along revolutionary lines. But there's the rub. Defeats don't spur these Yankees on; they just make them flabby. If things have come to such a pass that, to get recruits at all, they say they are prepared to take them on for *only 9 months,* then this is tantamount to admitting: "We're in the shit and all we want is a make-believe army to do some saber-rattling during the peace negotiations." Those 300,000 volunteers were the criterion, and in refusing to muster them, the North is declaring that it doesn't, *au fond,* give a damn about the whole thing. And then, what cowardice on the part of the government and Congress!

They shrink from conscription, from resolute fiscal measures, from attacking slavery, from everything that is urgently necessary; everything's left to amble along at will, and, if some factitious measure finally gets through Congress, the honorable Lincoln hedges it about with so many clauses that it's reduced to nothing at all. It is this flabbiness, this wilting like a pricked balloon under the pressure of defeats, which has destroyed an army, the strongest and the best, and left Washington virtually undefended; it is this complete absence of any resilience among the people at large which proves to me that it is all up. The occasional mass

> meeting, etc., means nothing at all, and doesn't even rival the excitement of a presidential election.
>
> Add to that a complete want of talent. One general more stupid than the other. Not one who would be capable of the slightest initiative or of an independent decision. For three months, the initiative has again rested wholly with the enemy. Then, the fiscal measures, each one crazier than the last. Fecklessness and cowardice everywhere except among the common soldiers. The same applies to the politicians—just as absurd, just as much at a loss. And the *populus* is more feckless than if it had idled away 3,000 years under the Austrian scepter.
>
> For the South, on the other hand, it's no use shutting one's eyes to the fact—the affair is a matter of life and death. Our not getting any cotton is one proof of this. The guerrillas in the border states are another. But, in my view, what clinches the matter is the ability of an agrarian population, after such complete isolation from the rest of the world, to endure such a war and, having suffered severe defeats and the loss of resources, men, and territory, nevertheless to emerge victorious and threaten to carry their offensive into the North. On top of that, they are really fighting quite splendidly, and what remained of union feeling, save in the mountain districts, will now, with the reoccupation of Kentucky and Tennessee, undoubtedly evaporate."
>
> If they get Missouri, they will also get the territories, and then the North might as well pack up and go home. As I have already said, unless the North instantly adopts a revolutionary stance, it will get the terrible thrashing it deserves—and that's what seems to be happening.[113]

Marx, however, had a more optimistic outlook. In his view, Engels—affectionally called "the General" by the Marx family—was in danger of missing the forest for the trees. In one of the extremely rare cases in which the two disagreed about anything, Marx gently reminded his lifelong collaborator to always stay grounded in the class and economic fundamentals. Engels was absolutely correct that the crisis facing the Union was in large part a question of leadership. However, as Marx explained, a change in leadership could transform the same military machine into an unstoppable juggernaut. On August 7, 1862, he sent a profoundly prescient reply:

> I don't quite share your views on the American Civil War. I do not believe that all is up. From the outset, the Northerners have been dominated by the representatives of the border slave states, who were also responsible for pushing McClellan, that old partisan of Breckinridge, to the top.
>
> The South, on the other hand, acted as a single whole right from the very start. The North itself turned slavery into a pro- instead of an anti-Southern military force. The South leaves productive labor to the slaves and could thus take the field undisturbed with its fighting force intact. It had a unified military leadership; the North did not. That there was no strategic plan is evident if only from the maneuverings of the Kentucky Army after the capture of Tennessee.
>
> In my view, all this is going to take another turn. The North will, at last, wage the war in earnest, have recourse to revolutionary methods, and overthrow the supremacy of the border slave statesmen. One single Negro regiment would have a remarkable effect on Southern nerves.
>
> The difficulty of raising 300,000 men is, I should say, purely political. The Northwest and New England wish to and will compel the government to abandon the diplomatic warfare they have waged hitherto, and are now making terms on which the 300,000 men shall come forth. If Lincoln doesn't give way—which he will, however—there'll be a revolution.
>
> As regards the lack of military talent, the choice of generals, hitherto dependent purely on diplomatic and party chicanery, has hardly been calculated to bring it to the fore. However, I should say that General Pope was a man of energy.
>
> As for financial measures, they are clumsy as, indeed, they are bound to be in a country where in fact taxation has hitherto been non-existent—so far as the country as a whole is concerned—but not nearly as silly as the measures taken by Pitt and co. I should say that the present depreciation of money is attributable not to economic, but to purely political grounds, namely distrust. It will therefore change when policy changes.

> The long and the short of it is, I think, that wars of this kind ought to be conducted along revolutionary lines, and the Yankees have so far been trying to conduct it along constitutional ones.[114]

He hammered the same points in an August 9 article in *Die Presse*:

> [Lincoln] errs only if he imagines that the "loyal" slaveholders are to be moved by benevolent speeches and rational arguments. They will yield only to force.
>
> So far, we have only witnessed the first act of the Civil War—the *constitutional* waging of war. The second act, the *revolutionary* waging of war, is at hand . . . No matter how the dice may fall in the fortunes of war, even now it can safely be said that Negro slavery will not long outlive the Civil War.[115]

And in another letter to Engels, dated September 10, he elaborated even further:

> As regards the Yankees, I am assuredly still of my previous opinion that the North will finally prevail; certainly the Civil War may go through all sorts of episodes, even armistices, perhaps, and be long drawn out.
>
> The South would and could only conclude peace on condition that it received the border slave states. In this event, California would also fall to it; the Northwest would follow, and the entire Federation, with perhaps the exception of the New England states, would form a single country once more, this time under the acknowledged supremacy of the slaveholders. It would be the reconstruction of the United States on the basis demanded by the South. This, however, is impossible and will not happen.
>
> The North can, for its part, only conclude peace if the Confederacy limits itself to the old slave states and those confined between the Mississippi River and the Atlantic. In this case, the Confederacy would soon come to its blessed end. Intervening armistices, etc., on the basis of a status quo, could at most entail pauses in the prosecution of the war.
>
> The manner in which the North wages war is only to be expected from a bourgeois republic, where fraud has so long reigned supreme. The South,

> an oligarchy, is better adapted thereto, particularly as it is an oligarchy where the whole of productive labor falls on the Negroes and the four millions of "white trash" are filibusterers by profession. All the same, I would wager my head that these boys come off second best, despite "Stonewall Jackson." To be sure, it is possible that it will come to a sort of revolution in the North itself first.
>
> It seems to me that you let yourself be swayed a little too much by the military aspects of things.[116]

Just one month later, Lincoln issued the preliminary Emancipation Proclamation. The historic declaration transformed the character of the war, exactly as Marx had foreseen.

The "friction and abrasion" of war

In Lincoln's legalistic view, nullification was nonsense, and the Confederate states had never actually left the Union. The Constitution and the Union had been adopted by mutual consent and could only be dissolved by the same.

An enemy of slavery at heart, he nonetheless felt that his hands were tied by its Constitutional sanction. Not only did he feel he lacked the legal or military prerogative to expropriate slave property, but he feared alienating the all-important slave border states that had not seceded. In his first annual address to Congress in December 1861, just a few months into the war, Lincoln had been very clear:

> In considering the policy to be adopted for suppressing the insurrection, I have been anxious and careful that the inevitable conflict for this purpose shall not degenerate into a violent and remorseless revolutionary struggle. I have, therefore, in every case, thought it proper to keep the integrity of the Union prominent as the primary object of the contest on our plan, leaving all questions which are not of vital military importance to the more deliberate action of the legislature.[117]

However, as Union forces crept deeper into the Confederacy, self-emancipating slaves forced the issue.

Early in the war, there had been no clear policy, and many fugitive slaves were actually returned to their Confederate owners when they crossed over to Union lines. They were, after all, "animate property," and the rights of property had to be respected.

Then, in May of 1861, three slaves being used to build Confederate defenses entered the Union camp at Fort Monroe in Hampton Roads, Virginia. Instead of returning them to slavery, General Benjamin Butler held them as "contraband of war," much like a shipment of guns or ammunition would be, if intercepted at sea.

Despite the lack of clarity, this apparently simple and limited war measure expressed a deeper historical necessity and took on a life of its own. It set a new precedent, and word spread fast throughout the Confederacy—among both slaves and slaveowners.

Slaves had resisted their masters for centuries in innumerable ways: they slowed down the pace of work, disabled machinery, feigned sickness, and destroyed crops. They argued and fought with their masters and overseers. Many stole livestock, food, or valuables. Some learned to read and write, which was legally forbidden. Others burned forests or buildings or killed their masters with improvised weapons or poison.

Countless thousands escaped to Northern states, Canada, and Mexico, or to the immense swamplands of the South, where they established independent maroon communities or joined Native American tribes, as was the case with the Black Seminoles. Others committed suicide or mutilated themselves to ruin their value as property. The dislocation of the war now offered a golden opportunity to resist and escape en masse.

In an attempt to address the status of escaped slaves, Congress passed the First Confiscation Act on August 6, 1861. It authorized the confiscation of any Confederate property, including slaves directly employed in military service, for example, building fortifications or transporting supplies. However, it did not go so far as to declare those individuals free. It merely "freed them from their owners' claims," a juridically ambiguous status.

Just a few weeks later, on August 30, John C. Frémont, now serving as commanding general of the Western Department in Missouri, issued a proclamation declaring martial law and freeing the slaves of Confederate supporters in his jurisdiction. Lincoln was alarmed at Frémont's audacity and ordered him to modify his proclamation to comply with the cautious limits of the First Confiscation Act. When Frémont refused, Lincoln countermanded the order. A few months later, Frémont was relieved of his command.

In April 1862, Lincoln signed a bill providing compensated emancipation in the District of Columbia, paying up to $300 per slave. Approximately 3,000 people were freed, and about $1 million was paid to former owners. Due to the intransigence of the slaveocracy, however, this was the only instance of compensated emancipation actually implemented.

On May 9, 1862, General David Hunter, commander of the Department of the South, issued a similar proclamation declaring all slaves in Georgia, Florida, and South Carolina "forever free." Once again, Lincoln overruled Hunter's order, emphasizing that only the president had the authority to take such an action.

Though they were stymied by Lincoln's cautious approach, these haphazard attempts at military emancipation helped shape public opinion in favor of the policy. The idea that the Confederates should be deprived of their labor force, which allowed them to field more soldiers, gained traction.

Many abolitionist Union officers were veterans of the failed 1848 revolutions in Europe, known as "'48ers." They brought with them revolutionary, republican, and democratic ideals, and in some cases, outright Marxism. Officers like August Willich, Carl Schurz, and Franz Sigel combined military experience with passionate anti-slavery convictions, forming a vocal abolitionist faction within the Union Army. Joseph Weydemeyer, a correspondent and close collaborator of Marx and Engels, served in the Union Army as a volunteer officer, ultimately earning the rank of colonel as an artillery commander.

All of this had an impact on Lincoln. On July 12, 1862, in a speech to congressional representatives of the border states, he made a final appeal for compensated emancipation:

> You prefer that the constitutional relation of the states to the nation shall be practically restored, without disturbance of the institution; and if this were done, my whole duty, in this respect, under the constitution, and my oath of office, would be performed. But it is not done, and we are trying to accomplish it by war. The incidents of the war can not be avoided. If the war continues long, as it must, if the object is not sooner attained, the institution in your states will be extinguished by mere friction and abrasion, by the mere incidents of the war. It will be gone, and you will have nothing valuable in lieu of it. Much of its value is gone already.
>
> How much better for you, and for your people, to take the step which, at once, shortens the war, and secures substantial compensation for that which is sure to be wholly lost in any other event. How much better to thus save the money which else we sink forever in the war. How much better to do it while we can, lest the war, ere long, render us pecuniarily unable to do it. How much better for you, as seller, and the nation as buyer, to sell out, and buy out, that without which the war could never have been, than to sink both the thing to be sold, and the price of it, in cutting one another's throats.[118]

His appeal fell on deaf ears. On July 17, Congress passed the Second Confiscation Act. Among other provisions, it declared that slaves held by those engaged in the rebellion, who escaped to Union lines or were found in areas occupied by Union forces, would be "forever free of their servitude."

The stage was nearly set for the Emancipation Proclamation. First, however, Lincoln had to prepare the broader public for the revolutionary measure.

Emancipation and the evolution of Abraham Lincoln

In August 1862, Lincoln wrote to the abolitionist newspaper editor, Horace Greeley:

> My paramount object in this struggle is to save the Union, and is *not* either to save or to destroy slavery. If I could save the Union without freeing *any* slave, I would do it, and if I could save it by freeing *all* the slaves, I would do it; and if I could save it by freeing some and leaving others alone, I would also do that.[119]

Although he appears to take a wishy-washy position, it seems evident that Lincoln had already decided that emancipation was the most powerful weapon in the Union's arsenal. He realized that the Union was not merely fighting the Confederate armies, but the majority of the Southern population, which saw it as a defensive war. Without slaves, the Confederate war effort and economy would quickly run into the ground.

In short, to bring the war to a quicker end, the social and economic foundations of the rebellion had to be undermined. Lincoln needed to find the right moment and the right way to unveil his proposal.

Just a few weeks later, on September 17, 1862, the Union and Confederate armies clashed in the fields of Antietam, Maryland. To this day, it remains the single bloodiest 24-hour period in American military history. Though not an overwhelming Union victory, McClellan succeeded in turning back Robert E. Lee's first Northern incursion.

On September 22, Lincoln used the momentum to announce his Emancipation Proclamation. He warned that if any state, or part of a state, was still in rebellion on January 1, 1863, then:

> All persons held as slaves within any State, or designated part of a State, the people whereof shall then be in rebellion against the United States, shall be then, thenceforward, and forever free.[120]

As a concession to the loyal border states, the proclamation left slavery intact in those states, at least for the time being. But because it applied to areas where seven-eighths of the slaves lived, the logic of the measure would also lead to freedom for the rest.

Writing that October, Marx commented on Lincoln's unassuming yet profoundly revolutionary action:

> Lincoln's proclamation is even more important than the Maryland campaign. Lincoln is a *sui generis* figure in the annals of history. He has no initiative, no idealistic impetus, no *cothurnus*, no historical trappings. He gives his most important actions always the most commonplace form . . .
>
> His latest proclamation, which is drafted in the same style, the manifesto abolishing slavery, is the most important document in American history since the establishment of the Union, tantamount to the tearing up of the old American Constitution.[121]

Not only did the proclamation free the slaves in areas of rebellion, but it also allowed them to be armed and brought into the Union Army. Ulysses S. Grant was enthusiastically in favor of this measure. As he put it:

> By arming the Negro we have added a powerful ally. They will make good soldiers and taking them from the enemy [will] weaken him in the same proportion they strengthen us. I am therefore most decidedly in favor of pushing this policy.[122]

The inexorable logic of revolution had asserted itself. As Lincoln predicted, the war's "friction and abrasion" undermined the material basis for the rebellion.

In an April 4, 1864, letter to Albert G. Hodges, the editor of the *Frankfort Commonwealth*, Lincoln explained the evolution of his thinking. It is worth quoting at length:

> I am naturally anti-slavery. If slavery is not wrong, nothing is wrong. I cannot remember when I did not so think and feel. And yet I have never understood that the Presidency conferred upon me an unrestricted right to act officially upon this judgment and feeling.
>
> It was in the oath I took that I would, to the best of my ability, preserve, protect, and defend the Constitution of the United States. I

could not take the office without taking the oath. Nor was it my view that I might take an oath to get power, and break the oath in using the power. I understood, too, that in ordinary civil administration, this oath even forbade me to practically indulge my primary abstract judgment on the moral question of slavery.

I had publicly declared this many times, and in many ways. And I aver that, to this day, I have done no official act in mere deference to my abstract judgment and feeling on slavery. I did understand, however, that my oath to preserve the constitution to the best of my ability imposed upon me the duty of preserving, by every indispensable means, that government—that nation—of which that constitution was the organic law. Was it possible to lose the nation, and yet preserve the constitution?

By general law, life and limb must be protected; yet often a limb must be amputated to save a life; but a life is never wisely given to save a limb. I felt that measures, otherwise unconstitutional, might become lawful by becoming indispensable to the preservation of the constitution through the preservation of the nation. Right or wrong, I assumed this ground, and now avow it . . .

When, early in the war, General Fremont attempted military emancipation, I forbade it because I did not then think it an indispensable necessity. When a little later, General Cameron, then Secretary of War, suggested the arming of the Blacks, I objected, because I did not yet think it an indispensable necessity. When, still later, General Hunter attempted military emancipation, I again forbade it, because I did not yet think the indispensable necessity had come.

When, in March, May, and July 1862, I made earnest and successive appeals to the border states to favor compensated emancipation, I believed the indispensable necessity for military emancipation, and arming the Blacks would come, unless averted by that measure. They declined the proposition, and I was, in my best judgment, driven to the alternative of either surrendering the Union, and with it, the Constitution, or of laying strong hand upon the colored element. I chose the latter.

> In choosing it, I hoped for greater gain than loss, but of this, I was not entirely confident. More than a year of trial now shows no loss by it in our foreign relations, none in our home popular sentiment, none in our white military force—no loss by it any how or any where. On the contrary, it shows a gain of quite a hundred and thirty thousand soldiers, seamen, and laborers. These are palpable facts, about which, as facts, there can be no caviling. We have the men, and we could not have had them without the measure.[123]

As Eric Foner writes in *The Fiery Trial*:

> While celebrating the proclamation, the *Christian Recorder* urged its Black readers to give thanks to Sumner, Stevens, Lovejoy, Chase, and other "apostles of liberty" for their role in changing public opinion and government policy. But popular sentiment does not exist independently of political leadership . . . In his own way, Lincoln helped to create the public sentiment that made emancipation possible.[124]

The evolution of Lincoln's thinking on this question undoubtedly played a role in the way emancipation played out. However, his epochal proclamation was really just the culmination of a century-long struggle to transform enslaved Africans from property to people, dating back to the First Revolution.

Presidential Reconstruction under Lincoln

Whether the Union armies, warships, officers, or soldiers intended it, the entire social structure of the South was being turned upside down, even before emancipation became official policy. As Union forces closed in on all sides, hundreds of thousands of slaves crossed over their lines. They helped the Union effort in countless ways, including, eventually, as uniformed soldiers.

As historian Steven Hahn has emphasized:

> However much Black struggles for literacy and against discrimination within the ranks helped transform their political consciousness and prospects in Civil War America, it was undoubtedly their efforts on the battlefield that proved most consequential. For it was in the face

> of military stalemate and of grave doubts about their potential military contributions that the federal government embarked on the mass recruitment of African-American men. And it was only military victory that could secure the freedom that many black soldiers and their families had tentatively attained.[125]

In many areas, a majority of white people abandoned their lands, leaving their chattels behind. Newly masterless slaves welcomed the advancing Union troops as liberators while at the same time occupying and working their former masters' abandoned lands themselves. This was the molecular process of revolution in action as military encampments became enmeshed with self-organizing slaves. These and other unintended consequences resulted from what had started as the suppression of a regional rebellion.

Although the Reconstruction era followed the end of the war, the process of reintegrating the seceded states began in regions held by the Union army while the fighting still raged elsewhere. This was mainly through executive orders issued by Lincoln in his capacity as commander in chief.

As more Confederate territory came under Union military occupation, one pressing task was to reassert federal control and reconstitute loyal state governments. By late 1863, momentum was building, and Union forces occupied most of Tennessee, along with significant parts of Arkansas, Mississippi, Louisiana, and Virginia."

On December 8, Lincoln issued a Proclamation of Amnesty and Reconstruction. Known as the "Ten Percent Plan," it offered full pardons to most Confederates who took an oath of allegiance to the Union and accepted emancipation. The proposal was remarkably lenient, excluding only high-ranking Confederate officials and military officers from automatic pardon. Once a mere 10 per cent of a state's 1860 voters took the oath, they could establish a new state government and send a delegation to Congress.

However, it left many questions about the future status of the former slaves. Though it required the rebellious states to abolish the institution, it regarded freedpeople as "a laboring, landless, homeless class," with no mention of civil or voting rights.

Lincoln's moderate approach sought to undermine Confederate morale by offering ordinary Southerners an easy path back to the Union. Some Republicans were satisfied, since no step backwards had been taken on emancipation. In the words of Charles Sumner:

> [Lincoln] makes emancipation the cornerstone of reconstruction and I am ready to accept any system which promises this result.[126]

However, the more Radical members of the caucus were outraged. In letter to General Benjamin Butler, Wendell Phillips argued that the easy amnesty program:

> [m]akes the Negro's freedom a mere sham . . . What McClellan was on the battlefield—"Do as little hurt as possible!"—Lincoln is in civil affairs—"Make as little change as possible!"[127]

Congressional Radicals responded with the Wade-Davis Bill, which would have imposed much harsher terms for readmission. 50 per cent of a seceded state's voters would have to take an "ironclad oath" swearing they had never supported the Confederacy, and would have to guarantee basic rights to freedmen.

However, Lincoln pocket-vetoed* the bill because he refused to be "inflexibly committed to any single plan of restoration."[128] This led to growing tensions between the executive and legislative branches over who should control reconstruction policy—a controversy that would only intensify once Lincoln was no longer on the scene.

Revolutionary war

The stakes were now unambiguous. Marx's "second act, the revolutionary waging of war," would be even more bitter and bloody than the first. An essential component in waging it to its conclusion was the arming of Black soldiers. As the fiery Radical Republican,

* An indirect, absolute veto when a US President receives a bill but is unable or unwilling to reject and return the bill to an adjourned Congress within the 10-day period.

Thaddeus Stevens, argued even before emancipation and the arming of freed slaves had been made official policy:

> The war will not end until the government shall more fully recognize the magnitude of the crisis; until they have discovered that this is an internecine war in which one party or the other must be reduced to hopeless feebleness and the power of further effort shall be utterly annihilated. It is a sad but true alternative.
>
> The South can never be reduced to that condition so long as the war is prosecuted on its present principles. The North, with all its millions of people and its countless wealth, can never conquer the South until a new mode of warfare is adopted. So long as these states are left the means of cultivating their fields through forced labor, you may expend the blood of thousands and billions of money, year by year, without being any nearer the end, unless you reach it by your own submission and the ruin of the nation.
>
> Slavery gives the South a great advantage in time of war. They need not and do not withdraw a single hand from the cultivation of the soil. Every able-bodied white man can be spared for the army. The Black man, without lifting a weapon, is the mainstay of the war . . .
>
> Give [the general] the sword in one hand and the book of freedom in the other, and he will soon sweep despotism and rebellion from every corner of this continent.[129]

In his speech, "Men of Color, To Arms," delivered in Rochester, New York, on March 2, 1863, Frederick Douglass made an impassioned appeal:

> When first the rebel cannon shattered the walls of Sumter and drove away its starving garrison, I predicted that the war then and there inaugurated would not be fought out entirely by white men. Every month's experience during these dreary years has confirmed that opinion. A war undertaken and brazenly carried on for the perpetual enslavement of colored men, calls logically and loudly for colored men to help suppress it.

> Only a moderate share of sagacity was needed to see that the arm of the slave was the best defense against the arm of the slaveholder. Hence with every reverse to the national arms, with every exulting shout of victory raised by the slaveholding rebels, I have implored the imperiled nation to unchain against her foes, her powerful black hand.
>
> Slowly and reluctantly that appeal is beginning to be heeded. Stop not now to complain that it was not heeded sooner. It may or it may not have been best that it should not. This is not the time to discuss that question. Leave it to the future. When the war is over, the country is saved, peace is established, and the black man's rights are secured, as they will be, history with an impartial hand will dispose of that and sundry other questions.
>
> Action! Action! not criticism, is the plain duty of this hour. Words are now useful only as they stimulate to blows. The office of speech now is only to point out when, where, and how to strike to the best advantage. There is no time to delay. The tide is at its flood that leads on to fortune. From East to West, from North to South, the sky is written all over, "Now or never."
>
> Liberty won by white men would lose half its luster. "Who would be free themselves must strike the blow." "Better even to die free, than to live slaves." This is the sentiment of every brave colored man amongst us . . .
>
> By every consideration which binds you to your enslaved fellow-countrymen, and the peace and welfare of your country; by every aspiration which you cherish for the freedom and equality of yourselves and your children; by all the ties of blood and identity which make us one with the brave Black men now fighting our battles in Louisiana and in South Carolina, I urge you to fly to arms, and smite with death the power that would bury the government and your liberty in the same hopeless grave.[130]

Although some Black infantry units had been formed in Louisiana, Kansas, and South Carolina after the Second Confiscation and Militia Act of July 1862, the first official all-Black unit formed in the aftermath of the Emancipation Proclamation was the 54th

Massachusetts. Mustered in early February 1863 by the abolitionist governor of that state, with help from Frederick Douglass, it was later immortalized in the film *Glory*. An image depicting the unit's heroic charge on Fort Wagner, South Carolina, is featured on the cover of this book.

In total, around 180,000 Black soldiers served in the Union army, roughly 10 per cent of the total. Around half were former "contrabands," a quarter were from loyal border states, and roughly 45,000 were free Blacks from the North.

Of the 40,000 Black soldiers who died during the war, 10,000 died in combat, while 30,000 died from infection or disease. When the Confederates fought or captured Black troops, they were especially targeted or massacred outright, as occurred at Fort Pillow and the Battle of the Crater during the siege of Petersburg.

Unsurprisingly, given the country's deeply racist roots, discrimination continued even in uniform, and Black soldiers were paid less than white ones until later in the war. As explained by historian Paul D. Escott:

> The Militia Act passed in 1862 had set the pay of white privates at $13 per month, with $3.50 added each month as a clothing allowance. In the expectation that African Americans would serve mainly as laborers, that law set their wages at $10 per month, from which $3 was deducted for the expense of clothing. To make matters worse, often this meager pay was late or long delayed in coming. Black troops protested against these inequities, both as a matter of principle and for practical reasons.[131]

Despite this much-needed boost of manpower, however, the war was far from over. Plenty of trials, tribulations, reversals, and close calls remained for the Union—not to mention hundreds of thousands more deaths.

The "high-water mark" of the rebellion

After federal troops and state militia were routed at Bull Run, Lincoln was confronted with the grim reality that the Union lacked a field army capable of defending Washington and taking the offensive.

After Fort Sumter, there was no shortage of volunteers, but the early regiments were enlisted for short terms, were poorly trained, and were scattered among separate departmental commanders.

As during the First Revolution, a genuine national fighting force had to be built from the disparate units sent to Washington by the Northern states. What was needed was a unified command and professional staff, standardized training and discipline, a logistical machine to transport and supply hundreds of thousands of men, and a plan to defend the capital while targeting the Confederate capital at Richmond.

Since neither Washington nor von Steuben were available, the task fell to George B. McClellan, a West Point graduate and former railroad executive who had shown promise in a handful of early engagements in western Virginia. On July 27, 1861, he was placed in command of the main Union forces around Washington. Despite his brashness and megalomania, "Little Mac" successfully built the Army of the Potomac into a formidable fighting force capable of confronting its main rival, the Army of Northern Virginia.

A brilliant administrator, McClellan built imposing fortifications around Washington, organized a modern supply and medical system, and drilled his troops into tip-top shape. His troops idolized him for it. As we've seen, "Little Napoleon" had as low an opinion of Lincoln as he had delusions of grandeur in himself. As he wrote in a letter to his wife:

> I find myself in a new and strange position here--Predt, Cabinet, Genl Scott & all deferring to me . . .[132]
>
> [I almost think] were I to win some small [military] success now, I could become Dictator or anything else that might please me.[133]

Unfortunately, having built it to perfection, McClellan was loath to use his bright, shiny army. Meanwhile, Northern newspapers clamored, "On to Richmond!", urging a march on the Confederate capital, just 100 miles from Washington. When McClellan finally set his lumbering army in motion with the Peninsula Campaign, he crept forward at a glacial pace.

Despite enjoying substantial numerical superiority, he insisted he needed still more troops. He repeatedly overestimated Confederate strength and froze up. The Confederates even deceived him with "Quaker guns"—painted logs set up to resemble artillery. His tepid attempt to take Richmond failed after Lee beat him back in the Seven Days' Battles.

After Antietam, McClellan's caution again set in. He declined to pursue the enemy aggressively, allowing Lee's army to withdraw back into Virginia. This, combined with his fractious relationship with civilian leadership, led Lincoln to remove him from command in early November 1862.

His replacement was General Ambrose Burnside, whose exuberant whiskers became known as "sideburns." Chosen largely because other senior options were unacceptable or unavailable, he had been reluctant to take the job. Like other Union commanders, Burnside was a perfectly capable general officer when assigned to more limited roles. Unfortunately, he proved unable to master the operational skills required for the scale of war imposed by the rapidly advancing technology and gargantuan armies of the period.

His first major engagement was the Battle of Fredericksburg, fought in northern Virginia in December 1862. The result was a catastrophic and senseless slaughter. For reasons known only to himself, Burnside sent wave after wave of troops in futile charges against Marye's Heights and its well-entrenched defenders.

With the Confederate artillery commanding the heights overlooking the town, it was like shooting fish in a barrel. Roughly 12,500 Union soldiers were killed, wounded, or missing, with the Confederates losing 5,000–6,000. It was after this pointless butchery that Robert E. Lee is alleged to have said:

> It is well that [war] is so terrible! We should grow too fond of it![134]

Burnside then attempted to cross the Rappahannock River to maneuver around the Confederates to strike at Richmond, but wet weather had turned the roads to glue. After the failure of the ignominious "mud march," Burnside was replaced by General Joseph Hooker in late January 1863. Confidence inside the Army of the Potomac was in free fall—but it still had a ways to go before hitting rock bottom.

"Fighting Joe" Hooker had a reputation as a tough, energetic organizer, though his massive ego and tense relationships with civilian leaders left plenty to be desired. His immediate priority was to repair morale, tighten up supply, and improve camp sanitation. In these respects, he largely succeeded. He also began building a stronger Union cavalry, an arm in which the Army of the Potomac had lagged since the start of the war.

That May, Hooker faced off against Robert E. Lee and his eccentric yet brilliant subordinate, Stonewall Jackson, at a small crossroads known as Chancellorsville, not far from Fredericksburg. This was Lee's masterpiece battle, as he riskily divided his forces—outnumbered roughly two to one—and sprang a bold and bloody surprise on the Union troops, inflicting 17,000 casualties on Hooker, while suffering just 12,000 himself.

A resounding tactical victory in the short run, the battle was devastating for the South in the long run. While the Union army could sustain such losses, the Confederates simply could not. More immediately, Stonewall Jackson was accidentally shot by his own troops on his way back from a reconnaissance sortie. He died a few days later, depriving Lee of his most trusted and tested commander.

Nonetheless, the victory emboldened Lee to attempt a second invasion of the North, this time into Pennsylvania. His aim was to strike a blow at Union morale and turn the Northern population against the war. In the best case, he might even outflank the Army of the Potomac and descend on Washington, DC. The move also allowed his armies to live off Northern lands, giving Virginia a moment to recover from the ravages of war.

Lee's expedition began in June 1863 and culminated over the first three days of July in the war's most famous battle. Almost serendipitously, roughly 170,000 soldiers converged on the small crossroads town of Gettysburg. Adding to the drama, the new commander of the Army of the Potomac, George G. Meade, had been in charge for only a few days when the fighting began. When a courier arrived to inform him of his promotion, Meade reportedly assumed he was about to be arrested—an indication of just how fraught politics and infighting were within the Union high command.

What followed was the war's largest and bloodiest battle. The idyllic town's rolling hills and fields witnessed both wanton carnage and acts of astonishing collective and individual heroism and sacrifice, inspiring countless books, articles, and films.

On July 1, Union cavalry under John Buford fought a delaying action on the ridges west of town to buy time for the main force of infantry to arrive. As Union I Corps came up, units including Wisconsin's "Iron Brigade" joined the fighting. As Confederate pressure mounted through the afternoon, Union lines were pushed back through Gettysburg to the strong high ground running from Culp's Hill down to Cemetery Ridge, setting the stage for the massive, three-day battle for control of the heights.

July 2 saw the frenzied slaughter in the Wheatfield, Peach Orchard, and Devil's Den. Confederate General Richard S. Ewell attacked the Union right at Culp's Hill and East Cemetery Hill, but failed to break the Union "fishhook" line despite enormous casualties. The 1st Minnesota charged down Cemetery Ridge to plug a gap at the last moment, and Joshua Chamberlain and the 20th Maine executed a textbook bayonet charge at Little Round Top, saving the Union flank from being rolled up.

On July 3, Lee made a final, desperate attempt to break the Union line by sending George Pickett's men on a glorious but doomed charge across open fields. Shouting "Remember Fredericksburg!", Union troops poured withering cannon and musket fire into their ranks. Nonetheless, Pickett's men reached the crest of the ridge before falling back.

The furthest point reached by Pickett's assault on Cemetery Ridge became known as the "High Water Mark of the Confederacy." Had they broken through, little could have stopped them from marching on Washington to force terms of surrender on Lincoln. Instead, the Army of Northern Virginia was nearly shattered, leading a tearful Lee to admit, "It is all my fault." He retreated back into Maryland, with Meade's forces too exhausted to pursue them.

A few months later, on November 19, 1863, Lincoln arrived in Gettysburg by train to dedicate the Soldiers' National Cemetery. In one of the shortest yet most compelling speeches in history, he placed Gettysburg in its broader historical context:

> Four score and seven years ago, our fathers brought forth on this continent, a new nation, conceived in Liberty, and dedicated to the proposition that all men are created equal.
>
> Now we are engaged in a great civil war, testing whether that nation, or any nation so conceived and so dedicated, can long endure. We are met on a great battlefield of that war. We have come to dedicate a portion of that field, as a final resting place for those who here gave their lives that that nation might live. It is altogether fitting and proper that we should do this.
>
> But, in a larger sense, we cannot dedicate—we cannot consecrate—we cannot hallow—this ground. The brave men, living and dead, who struggled here, have consecrated it, far above our poor power to add or detract. The world will little note, nor long remember what we say here, but it can never forget what they did here. It is for us the living, rather, to be dedicated here to the unfinished work which they who fought here have thus far so nobly advanced. It is rather for us to be here dedicated to the great task remaining before us—that from these honored dead we take increased devotion to that cause for which they gave the last full measure of devotion—that we here highly resolve that these dead shall not have died in vain—that this nation, under God, shall have a new birth of freedom—and that government of the people, by the people, for the people, shall not perish from the earth.[135]

News of the Gettysburg victory reached Washington on July 4, 1863—Independence Day. That same day, the key fortress of Vicksburg, Mississippi finally fell, granting the Union effective control of the Mississippi River. Lincoln rejoiced and exclaimed, "the Father of Waters again goes unvexed to the sea."

For weeks, Ulysses S. Grant had slogged through the swamps in the summer heat, fighting a series of small but brilliant engagements while entirely cut off from his lines of supply and communication. Finally, he succeeded in driving the Confederates into Vicksburg. After several failed assaults and a creative but grueling siege, the defenders were forced to surrender to the relentless pressure of "Unconditional Surrender" Grant, as U.S. Grant had been known since the capture of Fort Donelson.

Although the war would continue for two more carnage-filled years, many consider the concurrent victories at Gettysburg and Vicksburg to be the decisive turning point of the war.

Grant versus Lee

Before the war, no one could have imagined that Ulysses S. Grant would rise to command the Union army and eventually become president of the United States. Despite being a West Point–trained cadre of the officer corps, he had left the army under a cloud of rumors over his alleged alcoholism. As his loyal subordinate William Sherman later expressed it:

> A more unpromising boy never entered the Military Academy.[136]
>
> [T]o me he is a mystery, and I believe he is a mystery to himself.[137]

As for the Confederacy, its most famous general was undoubtedly Robert E. Lee. A so-called "gentleman warrior," he allegedly hated slavery personally but was compelled by honor to defend his beloved home state of Virginia. Brilliant and popular, Lee was offered command of the Union army in April, 1861. Needless to say, he declined:

> I cannot raise my hand against my birth-place, my home, my children.[138]

However, the reality of his character was far from noble, and, in this author's opinion—as well as in Ulysses S. Grant's—he is also overrated as a military commander.

Despite declaring before Fort Sumter that he would free all the slaves if it would save the Union and prevent a war, let us not forget that he ultimately committed treason to preserve the practice.

It is an incontrovertible fact that Lee saw Black people as inferiors requiring the firm, civilizing hand of white people. His opposition to slavery was not due to feelings of solidarity with enslaved humans, but because of its deleterious effect on white society. A white supremacist to the bone, he wrote the following to his wife in 1856:

> In this enlightened age, there are few, I believe, but what will acknowledge that slavery as an institution is a moral and political evil in any Country . . .
>
> I think it, however, a greater evil to the white man than to the Black race . . . The Blacks are immeasurably better off here than in Africa, morally, socially, and physically. The painful discipline they are undergoing is necessary for their instruction as a race, and I hope it will prepare and lead them to better things. How long their subjugation may be necessary is known and ordered by a wise, merciful Providence.[139]

As a plantation owner, Lee separated slave families—a punishment more cruel than physical beatings. There were plenty of those, too. After two of his runaway slaves were recaptured, not only did he have them whipped, but he literally had saltwater poured into the lacerations.

After the war, Lee perpetuated the Lost Cause narrative. When testifying before the congressional Joint Committee on Reconstruction in February 1866, he minimized slavery's role in the conflict and emphasized states' rights, helping to establish the framework that would be used to whitewash history for generations to come. He also doubled down on his white supremacy:

> I think it would be better for Virginia if she could get rid of them [Black people]. That is no new opinion with me. I have always thought so, and have always been in favor of emancipation—gradual emancipation . . .
>
> My own opinion is that, at this time, they [Black people] cannot vote intelligently, and that giving them the [vote] would lead to a great deal of demagogism, and lead to embarrassments in various ways.[140]

As W.E.B. Du Bois wrote of Lee:

> People do not go to war for abstract theories of government. They fight for property and privilege and that was what Virginia fought for in the Civil War. And Lee followed Virginia. He followed Virginia not because he particularly loved slavery (although he certainly did not hate it), but because he did not have the moral courage to stand against his family and his clan. Lee hesitated and hung his head in shame because he was asked to lead armies against human progress and Christian decency and did not dare refuse.[141]

Compare this to Ulysses S. Grant, whose prewar years were marked by a series of financial disasters that left him in desperate poverty. After resigning from the Army in 1854, he attempted to make a living as a farmer on land given to his wife by her father. The farm, which he named "Hardscrabble," was the very opposite of prosperous. Grant cleared the land himself, built a log cabin with his own hands, and worked alongside slaves lent to him by his wife's family.

Sometime in the 1850s, Grant legally acquired an enslaved man named William Jones from his father-in-law, who owned a medium-sized plantation and as many as 30 slaves. On March 29, 1859, Grant went to the St. Louis County Courthouse and wrote an act of manumission, legally freeing Jones from slavery. Grant was in dire economic straits at the time and could have sold Jones for $1,000 or more, the equivalent of roughly $40,000 in today's dollars.

To supplement his meager farming income, Grant hauled firewood to St. Louis in a cart to sell on street corners—a humiliating occupation for a West Point graduate. Contemporary accounts describe him standing in the cold, trying to sell cordwood for $4 a load, often going unrecognized by former acquaintances who walked past him.

In 1858, after he was forced to abandon farming due to malaria and economic failure, Grant tried to enter real estate and bill collecting in St. Louis. He failed in these ventures as well. He applied for a position as county engineer but was rejected, despite his military engineering training. To buy Christmas presents for his family, he had to pawn his watch, the only valuable thing he had left.

By 1860, Grant was forced to move his family to Galena, Illinois, where he worked as a clerk in his father's leather goods store, earning just $600 a year—roughly $20,000 in today's money. At age 38, he was working under his younger brothers, who managed the store. It was from this humble position—standing behind a counter, selling leather harnesses and other goods—that Grant would answer the call to arms when Fort Sumter was fired upon in April 1861.

As for their military prowess, Lee certainly exhibited moments of battlefield brilliance. At the Second Battle of Bull Run, in August 1862, he demonstrated his ability to coordinate complex flanking maneuvers. At Chancellorsville, in May 1863, the daring division of his forces in the face of a numerically superior enemy is still studied in military academies as a masterwork of tactical audacity.

However, Lee also made his fair share of mistakes, some of them quite serious. His decision to stand and fight with his back to the Potomac River at Antietam was extremely risky. Only McClellan's characteristic caution saved Lee's army from complete destruction. A more aggressive Union commander might have annihilated the Army of Northern Virginia on that occasion.

At Gettysburg, Lee made several critical errors. Against Longstreet's advice, he ordered Pickett's Charge on the third day—a direct frontal assault across open ground against the well-fortified Union position on Cemetery Ridge. The infamous attack was a catastrophic failure, with the troops involved suffering approximately 50 per cent casualties and gaining nothing. Perhaps this is why the British general, J. F. C. Fuller, accused Lee of being "one of the most incapable Generals-in-Chief in history."[142]

But most importantly, Lee had a far more limited vision than Grant when it came to broad strategic thinking. Lee's invasion of the North in 1863, which led to Gettysburg, was itself a strategic mistake. The campaign overstretched his supply lines and placed his army in unfamiliar territory, far from its base of support.

Lee's approach throughout the war, while producing impressive tactical victories, was strategically unsound. His aggressive campaigns resulted in casualties the South could ill afford. The South's best chance for victory was to fight a defensive war and wear down Northern public opinion, but Lee's temperament drove him toward costly offensive operations, always looking for a spectacular knockout blow.

It is also an irony of history that Lee's bold victory in the Seven Days' Battles, which repelled McClellan's invasion of Virginia in the summer of 1862, marked the end of the North's reformist attempt to end the rebellion while keeping slavery intact. Far from defending slavery, his success actually made its destruction inevitable, though this was hardly Lee's fault or intention.

As for Grant, his relentless, grinding style of warfare has been compared to Russian generals like Kutuzov and Bagration, whose armies wore down Napoleon's finest through relentless pressure and a willingness to sustain as many casualties as it took. It was this tenacity that won Lincoln over. As Ron Chernow wrote in his excellent biography, *Grant*:

> Grant was the antithesis of everything Lincoln had deplored in his predecessors—as eager to fight as they were reluctant; as self-reliant as they were dependent; as uncomplaining as they were petulant. Grant did not badger or connive for more troops or scapegoat others. There would be no more grumbling from Lincoln about dilatory generals as Grant converted the Union army into a scene of ceaseless activity. With his zest for combat, Grant was itching for a fight.[143]

Grant would pursue a policy of "desperate and continuous hard fighting," inflicting massive casualties and applying unrelenting pressure.' "I look upon the conquering of the organized armies of the enemy as being

> of vastly more importance than the mere acquisition of their territory," he instructed his generals.' Gone was the gentility of his predecessors. Adopting a modern style of combat, Grant would speed up the war's tempo, following up on victories and creating a sense of unending activity. By concentrating his forces, he would create two or three large armies so that his soldiers would never be, in Rawlins's words, "whipped in detail." Most important, Grant would use his scattered forces simultaneously so the enemy could not shift troops to one threatened point without jeopardizing another. Union forces would pin down Confederate units that might otherwise have succored their colleagues. "Oh, yes! I see that," Lincoln responded gleefully to this strategy. "As we say out West, if a man can't skin he must hold a leg while somebody else does."[144]
>
> Abraham Lincoln delighted in Grant's uncommon tenacity. In mid-August, fearful that a new draft would stoke more unrest in northern cities, Halleck urged Grant to send troops to deal with this eventuality. Grant balked from reluctance to relax his tight hold on Petersburg or give Lee a chance to send men to Georgia against Sherman. When Lincoin saw this response, he rejoiced in Grant's grit and wired him: "I have seen your despatch expressing your unwillingness to break your hold where you are. Neither am I willing. Hold on with a bull-dog gripe, and chew & choke, as much as possible."[145]

The case can be made that differences in Lee's and Grant's strategic outlook reflected, at least in part, the different class interests they represented, as well as their personal backgrounds.

Lee was about as blue-blooded as you can get in the United States. The plantation-owning son of a Revolutionary War hero, he married the daughter of George Washington's adopted son. He had never known want and commanded his armies from the perspective of the planter aristocracy.

Grant, on the other hand, had experienced extreme hardship, stuck to his principles, and persevered. His lack of pretension and his ability to connect with common soldiers was influenced by those difficult years when he had been pushed nearly to the bottom of American society. When on campaign, he ate simple food, slept in modest quarters when such were even available, and more often than not slept on the ground with his men.

In stark contrast to the polished, aristocratic bearing of Robert E. Lee, Ulysses S. Grant cut an unremarkable, even shabby figure. At just 5 feet 8 inches tall and around 135 pounds, he lacked the commanding stature one might expect of a conquering general. He habitually wore a private's uniform, often mud-splattered and rumpled from days in the field, with only his shoulder straps indicating his rank.

As Colonel Theodore Lyman of the Army of the Potomac wrote in his diary:

> [Grant] is rather under middle height, of a spare, strong build; light-brown hair, and short, light-brown beard. His eyes are of clear blue; forehead high; nose aquiline; jaw squarely set. His face had three expressions: deep thought; extreme determination; and great simplicity and calmness . . .
>
> Grant is a man of a good deal of rough dignity; rather taciturn; quick and decided in speech. He habitually wears an expression as if he had determined to drive his head through a brick wall, and was about to do it. I have much confidence in him.[146]

General Horace Porter, who served on Grant's staff, described his first encounter with the future war hero:

> In an arm-chair facing the fireplace was seated a general officer, slight in figure and of medium stature, whose face bore an expression of weariness. He was carelessly dressed, and his uniform coat was unbuttoned and thrown back from his chest. He held a lighted cigar in his mouth, and sat in a stooping posture, with his head bent slightly forward. His clothes were wet, and his trousers and top-boots were spattered with mud. General Thomas approached this officer, and, turning to me and mentioning me by name, said, "I want to present you to General Grant." Thereupon the officer seated in the chair, without changing his position, glanced up, extended his arm to its full length, shook hands, and said in a low voice, and speaking slowly, "How do you do?" This was my first

> meeting with the man with whom I was destined afterward to spend so many of the most interesting years of my life.[147]

Lincoln himself was astonished upon first meeting Grant in person. Having grown accustomed to the bombast and bluster of a long string of pretentious but lackluster generals, he had expected someone far more imposing, given his military achievements.

In his recollections, Major General Grenville Dodge painted this picture of his former commander:

> The great distinguishing qualities of General Grant were truth, courage, modesty, generosity and loyalty. He was loyal to every work and every cause in which he was engaged—to his friends, his family, his country and to his God, and it was these characteristics which bound to him with hooks of steel all those who served with him.
>
> He absolutely sunk himself to give to others honor and praise to which he, himself, was entitled. No officer served under him who did not understand this. I was a young man and given much larger commands than my rank entitled me to. General Grant never failed to encourage me by giving me credit for whatever I did, or tried to do. If I failed, he assumed the responsibility; if I succeeded, he recommended me for promotion. He always looked at the intention of those who served under him, as well as to their acts. If they failed in intention, he dropped them so quickly and efficiently that the whole country could see and hear their fall.[148]

Even the vice president of the Confederacy, Alexander Stephens, was taken aback:

> General Grant is a remarkable man, and if he lives and continues in good health, will figure largely in the future history of this country. I consider him one of the most remarkable men I ever saw. He is modest, unassuming, and possesses a wonderful degree of common sense, a thing uncommon in his day amongst men of position and station.
>
> I was never more surprised in any person than in General Grant when I saw him at City Point last February. Very soon after being in his

> company, I was deeply impressed with his genius and character. What is to be his future, time will determine. But the measure of his deeds and fame, whether for good or evil, is very far from being felt yet. The impression he made on me was favourable in every respect. In manners he is simple, natural, and unaffected; in intercourse, frank and explicit; in thought, perception, and action, quick; in purpose, fixed, decided, and resolute. His ambition, if such may be termed his aspirations, is high, honourable, and noble. Such is the opinion I formed of General Grant in my first acquaintance with him. Such is my present opinion . . .
>
> Every man is more or less the creature of circumstances. He is no exception to this rule. How far he may hereafter be controlled by circumstances which he cannot control, is a problem in the solution of which the destinies of this country are deeply involved. He is the Great Man of the Continent; great, not in learning, acquirements, or accomplishments, but in conception, thought, and action; one of those master spirits which seldom fail, if life and vigor of faculties continue to impress themselves upon the age in which they live and to mark grand epochs in their country's history.[149]

Unfortunately, most Americans' limited knowledge of Grant is colored by the Lost Cause narrative that he was a drunk, a bad and corrupt president, and a butcher who didn't care about the lives of his own men.

Only recently have historians begun to acknowledge his real qualities and understated genius, as well as his fundamental honesty and human decency. As Thomas Carlyle did with Oliver Cromwell, they have had to drag Grant out from under "a mountain of dead dogs."

Grant takes command

While the armies in the East took a breather after Gettysburg, the fighting in the West raged more brutally than ever. In September 1863, Union forces under William Rosecrans suffered a major defeat at Chickamauga, Georgia, in one of the war's most horrific battles—second only to Gettysburg in total casualties.

After Grant's show of creative tenacity at Vicksburg, Lincoln knew that he had finally found someone he could rely on. On October 16, 1863, he was put in charge of the new Military Division of the Mississippi to oversee all Western armies. After he won the Battle of Chattanooga—a key railroad junction that opened the way to an invasion of Georgia and the Deep South—Lincoln promoted Grant to lieutenant general on March 9, 1864—a rank previously held only by George Washington and Winfield Scott.

As Lincoln told one of his secretaries, William Stoddard, who doubted whether Grant would live up to expectations:

> Grant is the first general I have had. He's a general. I'll tell you what I mean. You know how it's been with all the rest. As soon as I put a man in command of the army, he'd come to me with a plan of campaign and about as much say, "Now, I don't believe I can do it, but if you say so, I'll try on it," and so put the responsibility of failure on me. They all want me to be the general. It isn't so with Grant. He hasn't told me what his plans are. I don't know, and I don't want to know. I'm glad to find a man who can go ahead without me.[150]

Grant was transferred East to take overall command of the Union forces. One commander after another had been awed into inaction by the mystique surrounding Robert E. Lee. But Grant knew that, like every other general he had faced, Lee was a man, and not a god; he had actually met Lee once during the war with Mexico.

As an exasperated Grant later told his officers during the Battle of the Wilderness:

> Oh, I am heartily tired of hearing about what Lee is going to do. Some of you always seem to think he is suddenly going to turn a double somersault and land in our rear and on both of our flanks at the same time. Go back to your command, and try to think what we are going to do ourselves, instead of what Lee is going to do.[151]

Instead of relying on flashy maneuvers and tactical trickery, Grant's military philosophy was straightforward:

> The art of war is simple enough. Find out where your enemy is. Get at him as soon as you can. Strike him as hard as you can, and keep moving on . . .[152]
>
> One of my superstitions had always been when I started to go anywhere, or to do anything, never to turn back or to stop until the thing intended was accomplished . . .[153]
>
> [I]n every battle there comes a time when, with both sides equally exhausted, victory will come to the army that exerts the final last effort.[154]

Ely Parker, a Seneca Indian and friend of Louis Henry Morgan's, served as Grant's military secretary at Appomattox. He had this to say about the dogged nature of his boss:

> It has been a matter of universal wonder in this army that General Grant himself was not killed, and that no more accidents occurred to his staff, for the general was always in the front (his staff with him, of course), and perfectly heedless of the storm of hissing bullets and screaming shell flying around him. His apparent lack of concern does not arise from heedlessness or vain military affectation, but from a sense of responsibility resting upon him when in battle.
>
> When at Ringgold, we rode for half a mile in the face of the enemy, under an incessant fire of cannon and musketry, nor did we ride fast, but upon an ordinary trot, and not once do I believe did it enter the general's mind that he was in danger. I was by his side and watched him closely. In riding that distance we were going to the front, and I could see that he was studying the positions of the two armies, and, of course, planning how to defeat the enemy, who was here making a most desperate stand, and was slaughtering our men fearfully.
>
> Another feature in General Grant's personal movements is that he requires no escort beyond his staff, so regardless of danger is he. Roads are almost useless to him, for he takes short cuts through fields and woods, and will swim his horse through almost any stream that obstructs his way.
>
> Nor does it make any difference to him whether he has daylight for his movements, for he will ride from breakfast until two o'clock in the

> morning, and that too without eating. The next day he will repeat the dose, until he finishes his work. Now such things come hard upon the staff, but they have learned how to bear it.[155]

Grant's mandate as lieutenant general was clear: to pin down and destroy the Army of Northern Virginia.

Unendurable pressure

The Confederates had been at a numerical and logistical disadvantage from the beginning. Despite being more or less surrounded, however, they benefited from interior lines, which allowed them to shift troops from one battlefront to another, as needed. They mainly needed to wage a defensive war and "not lose."

Without coordination, however, the North couldn't fully capitalize on its advantages. In the early stages, the conflict was waged almost as though there were several smaller wars unfolding in different parts of the country: in Missouri, Kentucky, Virginia, on the Atlantic and Gulf coasts, and so on. Instead of a concerted squeeze, as envisioned by Winfield Scott's Anaconda Plan, they did little more than slowly chip away at their adversary.

Lincoln had never served in the armed forces, but once the war broke out, he took it upon himself to study military history, tactics, and strategy. As early as January 1862, he had written the following to one of his generals, Don Carlos Buell:

> [I] state my general idea of this war to be that we have the *greater* numbers, and the enemy has the *greater* facility of concentrating forces upon points of collision; that we must fail, unless we can find some way of making *our* advantage an overmatch for his; and that this can only be done by menacing him with superior forces at *different* points, at the *same* time; so that we can safely attack, one, or both, if he makes no change; and if he *weakens* one to *strengthen* the other, forbear to attack the strengthened one, but seize, and hold the weakened one, gaining so much.[156]

Many Southerners feared what would happen once the North's resources were fully brought to bear. With its larger army and navy, and a rapidly expanding industrial base, the Union had the means to exert relentless pressure on the Confederacy. But Lincoln had a hard time getting his generals to implement a coherent strategy. In addition to weak coordination, there were innumerable instances of corruption, incompetence, petty rivalries, and mistrust within and between the country's military and civilian leaders.

With Grant, however, Lincoln finally had the commander he needed. Grant shared the president's strategic outlook for a coordinated campaign to end the war. Most importantly, he possessed the resolve to press for victory despite the costs in time, money, and lives. Fully aware of the South's limited manpower and woeful industrial capacity, Grant's approach called for the simultaneous advance of multiple Union armies on several fronts, reducing the Confederacy's ability to transfer forces along its interior lines. Combined with the continuing strategy to constrict the Southern economy and logistics, this was a far more aggressive, synchronized use of Union advantages than before.

Along with economic strangulation, emancipation, and the arming of Black troops, Grant knew that the key to destroying Southern morale once and for all was to smash the Army of Northern Virginia. A legend in its own time, Lee's force was the embodiment and pride of the Confederate cause. Once these "bodies of armed men" were off the field, secession would be played out.

The South didn't have to occupy the North or take Washington in order to win. Their probes into Union territory mainly aimed at gaining political leverage. Like the American colonists in the war against Britain, their strategy was to resist the Union armies long enough to wear down Northern morale, force peace negotiations, and, if at all possible, gain recognition and support from one or more of the world's major powers.

But the world's workers and oppressed sided with the Union. Commenting on the *Trent* Affair,* in the *New York Daily Tribune* on January 11, 1862, Marx wrote of the:

> [N]atural sympathy the popular classes all over the world ought to feel for the only popular Government in the world.[157]

He added:

> Under the present circumstances, however, when a great portion of the British working classes directly and severely suffers under the consequences of the Southern blockade; when another part is indirectly smitten by the curtailment of the American commerce, owing, as they are told, to the selfish "protective policy" of the Republicans; when the only remaining democratic weekly . . . week after week exhausts its horse-powers of foul language in appeals to the working classes to urge the Government, for their own interests, to war with the Union—under such circumstances, simple justice requires to pay a tribute to the sound attitude of the British working classes, the more so when contrasted with the hypocritical, bullying, cowardly, and stupid conduct of the official and well-to-do John Bull . . .
>
> There was an influential war party in England, which, what for commercial, what for political reasons, showed eager for a fray with the United States. The *Trent* affair put that party to the test. It has failed. The war passion has been discounted on a minor issue, the steam has been let off, the vociferous fury of the oligarchy has raised the suspicions of English democracy, the large British interests connected with the United States have made a stand, the true character of the civil war has been

* Diplomatic incident between the United States and Britain during the American Civil War. The US Navy intercepted a British Royal Mail steamer, the RMS Trent, and detained two Confederate envoys on their way to Britain and France to argue for diplomatic recognition of the Confederate States. The British accused the US of violating British neutrality. In the Union, the public initially celebrated the capture. In the Confederate States, the hope was that the incident would lead to a breakdown in relations between Britain and the US and possibly even war, or at least diplomatic recognition of the Confederacy by Britain. Lincoln ended the crisis by releasing the two envoys.

> brought home to the working classes, and last, not least, the dangerous period when Palmerston rules single-headed without being checked by Parliament, is rapidly drawing to an end. That was the only time in which an English war for the slaveocrats might have been hazarded. It is now out of question.[158]

After emancipation, British or French recognition of the slave power became virtually impossible, as the authorities faced even more intense pressure from workers. At a meeting called by the London Trades' Council at St. James' Hall on March 26, 1863, more than 3,000 workers gathered to declare solidarity and "sympathy with the Northern States of America, and in favor of Negro emancipation." This, despite the severe deprivation caused by the Southern cotton shortage, which hit the textile mills and led to mass layoffs.

"Hard war"

Following the internal logic of revolution, the conflict between the sections had been transformed from a war to preserve the Union into a war to uproot slavery, and the Union enjoyed the moral high ground. To accelerate the war's end, the Southern economy had to be brought to its knees.

Now that Lincoln had audacious and resolute field commanders willing and able to carry out his policies in a concerted way, the economic and demographic might of the North was all but unstoppable. Union generals including Grant, Sherman, and Philip Sheridan believed that the South must be made to feel the "hard hand of war."

After wearing down the perimeter of the rebellious states and liberating the Mississippi River, the war was taken deep into the heart of the Confederacy. Slaves were freed *en masse*, railroads and other property destroyed, and plantations and foodstuffs expropriated. While the economy in the North was booming, the Southern economy was now in free fall, and both its armies and civilians suffered terrible privations.

Generally speaking, civilians were not targeted by either side for mass oppression or wholesale massacre. In so many other civil wars, from Antiquity to the present day, the victors rounded people up, executed them, sold them into slavery, and so on.

It would be absurd, of course, to argue that there were no abuses as hundreds of thousands of troops crisscrossed the country. As we've seen, particularly in the border states, there were vicious reprisals against civilians by paramilitary partisans on both sides. Sherman's "bummers"* weren't always genteel to the local plantation owners whose goods they expropriated. And it's not an unimportant detail that during the Gettysburg campaign, Black residents of Pennsylvania were hunted down by Lee's army, to be sent South into slavery—even if they hadn't previously been slaves.

Generally speaking, it is fair to say that the American Civil War differed from the wholesale massacres committed by the White Armies during the Russian Civil War, and from the ways Roman armies treated defeated opponents in civil wars and foreign conquests. The literature on the American Civil War abounds with examples of fraternization and of acts of kindness toward wounded or captured enemy soldiers.

Nevertheless, this emerging "total war" approach targeted not only the South's armies, forts, and other strategic points, but also the material foundations of Confederate war-making, including its economy and slave system. In the end, it helped exhaust the Confederacy's capacity to keep armies in the field. This was not the "total war" of the twentieth century, with industrialized killing and mass civilian casualties. But it was a decisive escalation in the scale and scope of warfare never seen in US history up to that point.

In May 1864, Grant embarked on the Overland Campaign, an overpowering, continuous push toward Richmond. In his words, "I propose to fight it out on this line if it takes all summer."[159]

Grant kept doggedly after Lee through a series of savage battles at the Wilderness, Spotsylvania Court House, the North Anna,

* Nickname for Sherman's troops, who expropriated provisions from plantations in Georgia and the Carolinas.

and Cold Harbor. The Union suffered roughly 55,000 casualties, while Confederate losses were about 33,000. Grant then brought relentless pressure to bear on the besieged defenders of Petersburg and Richmond. It was a long and brutal grind, and many in the North doubted whether he could pull it off.

Then, on September 2, 1864, after an extended siege, Sherman captured Atlanta, whose burning was later immortalized in the film *Gone With the Wind*. He then marched across Georgia to the coastal city of Savannah, cutting a wide swath of destruction as tens of thousands of soldiers tore up railways and lived off the land. On December 22, Sherman wrote to Washington:

> His Excellency President LINCOLN:
>
> I beg to present you, as a Christmas gift, the city of Savannah, with 150 heavy guns and plenty of ammunition, and also about 25,000 bales of cotton.[160]

His troops then did the same as they marched through the Carolinas to link up with Grant. They were particularly rough on the Palmetto State, as it had been the chief instigator of the rebellion. As historian Anne J. Bailey wrote in the *New Georgia Encyclopedia*:

> Confederate president Jefferson Davis had urged Georgians to undertake a scorched-earth policy of poisoning wells and burning fields, but civilians in the army's path had not done so. Sherman, however, burned or captured all the food stores that Georgians had saved for the winter months. As a result of the hardships on women and children, desertions increased in Robert E. Lee's army in Virginia. Sherman believed his campaign against civilians would shorten the war by breaking the Confederate will to fight, and he eventually received permission to carry this psychological warfare into South Carolina in early 1865. By marching through Georgia and South Carolina, he became an archvillain in the South and a hero in the North.[161]

James McPherson commented on Sherman's qualities as a commander and on the aims of his famous "march to the sea" and up through the Carolinas in an article written for *The New York Review*:

> [A]s a battlefield commander Sherman lacked the killer instinct. Despite his reputation in the South as a ferocious ogre of vengeance and spoliation, Sherman was actually sparing of the lives of his own soldiers, of the enemy's soldiers, and of civilians. He preferred to accomplish his strategic goals by maneuver rather than by all-out combat. After the battle of Shiloh in 1862, he wrote to his wife: The scenes on this field would have cured anybody of war. Mangled bodies, dead, dying, in every conceivable shape, without heads [or] legs." Sherman tried to conduct his campaigns to avoid another Shiloh. Of seventeen Civil War army commanders on both sides, Sherman's armies suffered the second-lowest percentage of casualties (Robert E. Lee's army had the highest).
>
> Sherman's march from Atlanta to Savannah in November–December 1865 has become the stuff of legend. But the campaign of his army northward from Savannah to North Carolina in February–March 1865 was an even more stunning achievement. In both campaigns Sherman's 60,000 men lived off the land they marched through. But the Georgia march covered 285 miles in a direction parallel to the principal rivers in relatively dry fall weather against token enemy opposition. The march through the Carolinas covered a distance 50 per cent greater and crossed many rain-swollen rivers and swamps in an unusually wet winter against increasing opposition as the Confederates scraped together a small army in a futile effort to stop Sherman. General Joseph Johnston, whom Jefferson Davis reluctantly restored to command in February, believed that it would be "absolutely impossible for an army to march across lower portions of [South Carolina] in winter." But, he later wrote:
>
>> When I learned that Sherman's army was marching through the Salk swamps, making its own corduroy roads at the rate of a dozen miles a day and more, and bringing its artillery and wagons with it, I made up my mind that there had been no such army in existence since the days of Julius Caesar.

The mobility and logistics of these marches were part of Sherman's strategy of the indirect approach. Without any large battles, they devastated Confederate resources and undermined the will of the Southern people to continue fighting. Sherman had long pondered the nature of this war . . .

At first Sherman, like many professional officers, believed that the war was a conflict solely between armies that should scrupulously respect the rights and property of enemy civilians. But by 1862 he had become convinced by the fierce resistance of the whole Southern white population that "we are not only fighting hostile armies, but a hostile people, and must make old and young, rich and poor, feel the hard hand of war." The Union array must act "on the proper Rule that all in the South are Enemies of all in the North . . . The whole Interior is alive with Guerrillas . . . The entire South, man, woman, and child, is against us, armed and determined." Sherman thus told the Southern people that an invading army:

> May take your house, your fields, your everything, and turn you all out, helpless, to starve. It may be wrong, but that don't alter the case. In War you can't help yourselves, and the only possible remedy is, to stop war . . . Our duty is not to build up, it is rather to destroy both the Rebel Army and whatever of wealth or property it has founded its boasted strength upon.

In his actions, Sherman showed that he preferred to destroy wealth and property that sustained the enemy army rather than that army itself. This was the strategy that underlay the legendary ruin wreaked by his "bummers" in the marches through Georgia and South Carolina . . . In another respect, also, Sherman anticipated twentieth-century ideas of psychological warfare. The terror and destruction spread by his soldiers, he wrote, "was a power, and I intended to utilize it . . . to humble their pride, to follow them to their inmost recesses, and to make them fear and dread us."

At the outset of his march through Georgia, Sherman vowed to show Southerners that "we have a power which Davis cannot resist. This may not be war, but rather Statesmanship."[162]

At the same time, Philip Sheridan was smashing the economy of the Shenandoah Valley in Virginia, which had long been the breadbasket of the Confederacy. According to Grant:

> The Shenandoah Valley was very important to the Confederates, because it was the principal store-house . . . for feeding their armies . . . It was well known that they would make a desperate struggle to maintain it. It had been the source of a great deal of trouble to us . . . I determined to put a stop to this. I started Sheridan at once for that field of operation, and on the following day sent another division of his cavalry.[163]

As historian Mark Neely, Jr. explained:

> Grant's relentless pressure and Sherman's destructive marches were not acts of barbarism but calculated strategies to end the war by exhausting the Confederacy's capacity to continue fighting. The target was the South's ability to wage war.[164]

In Georgia alone, Sherman estimated he had inflicted $100 million in damages, equivalent to around $1.6 billion in today's dollars. Around one-fifth of this "inured to our advantage," while the "remainder [was] simple waste and destruction."[165]

His troops wrecked 300 miles of railroad, numerous bridges, and miles of telegraph lines. They seized 5,000 horses, 4,000 mules, and 13,000 head of cattle, and confiscated 9.5 million pounds of corn and 10.5 million pounds of fodder, as well as destroying an untold number of cotton gins and mills.

Nearly 20,000 self-emancipating slaves followed in his army's wake. Many were targeted for murder by vengeful Southerners who couldn't stand up against the Union army itself.

"40 acres and a mule"

As we've seen, the Confiscation Acts and Emancipation Proclamation authorized the seizure of property belonging to Confederate supporters, including slaves, and allowed the president to arm freed people to help suppress the rebellion.

As the Southern economy began to implode, tens of thousands more slaves joined the exodus from the plantations, or, in many cases occupied them. Many crowded in squalid conditions near Union encampments, seeking refuge and protection from marauding Confederate guerrillas.

Thousands were put to work to help the Union war effort—doing the same kinds of heavy labor they had been forced to do as slaves. In theory, they were now wage workers. But after deductions for clothing and food, many received no actual money for their efforts. Many even worked on their former plantations—now operated by the Union Army or leased to Northern entrepreneurs—for little more than room and board.

After centuries of slave revolts and resistance, this was hardly the paradise of "free labor" they had envisioned. Unsurprisingly, their chief aspiration was to become independent farmers. Thousands got a tantalizing taste of this when they spontaneously occupied and worked plantation lands abandoned by their owners.

Sherman's Special Field Orders No. 15, issued in Savannah in January 1865, set aside 400,000 acres of coastal lands in Georgia and South Carolina. The idea was that "each family [of former slaves could] have a plot of not more than forty acres of tillable ground."[166] Some also received old army mules. This was the origin of the concept of "40 acres and a mule" as a form of reparations for slavery.

In these and other lands confiscated by the military, sections were parceled out to freedpeople, who received possessory title to work them independently. Their burning desire to make this the permanent status quo was summed up in a moving letter sent to President Andrew Johnson on October 28, 1865, by the Committee of Freedmen on Edisto Island, South Carolina:

> We have been encouraged by the government to take up these lands in small tracts, receiving certificates of the same. We have thus far taken 16,000 acres of land here on this island.
>
> We are ready to pay for this land when the government calls for it, and now, after what has been done, will the good and just government take

> from us all this right and make us subject to the will of those who have cheated and oppressed us for many years?
>
> God forbid!
>
> We, the freedmen of this island and of the state of South Carolina, do, therefore, petition to you as the President of these United States, that some provisions be made by which every colored man can purchase land and hold it as his own.
>
> We wish to have a home, if it be but a few acres.
>
> Without some provision being made, our future is sad to look upon.
>
> Yes, our situation is dangerous.
>
> We therefore look to you in this trying hour as a true friend of the poor and neglected race for protection and equal rights with the privilege of purchasing a homestead—a homestead right here in the heart of South Carolina.
>
> We pray that God will direct your heart in making such provision for us as freedmen, which will tend to unite these states together stronger than ever before.
>
> May God bless you in the administration of your duties as the President of these United States, is the humble prayer of us all.[167]

As we will see in Part Three, Johnson was no "true friend of the poor and neglected race," and all of this was eventually undone.

During the heady days of the war, however, even Confederate President Jefferson Davis's farm in Mississippi was operated by a self-governing colony of freedmen, complete with elected sheriffs and justices of the peace. Due to their collective efforts, they turned a tidy profit of $159,000 on the 1865 cotton crop.

But Northern capital was already intruding on these idyllic dreams of self-sufficient yeomanry. Although freedmen managed to buy 5,000 acres of land in the South Carolina islands between 1863 and 1864, corporate investors bought four times as many acres to lease or flip for a quick profit.

Union-occupied Louisiana offered another example of what was to come. In January 1863, General Nathaniel P. Banks issued General Order No. 12. While ostensibly intended to protect the rights of freedpeople, it required them to sign annual labor contracts with plantation owners, effectively making wage labor compulsory.

The regulations declared that "labor is a public duty" and mandated that freedpeople had to work on plantations, unless they could prove employment elsewhere. Vagrancy and homelessness were considered "a crime," and those found "idle" could be forced to work on public projects or assigned to plantations against their will. Workers could be fined or otherwise punished for "insolence," "disobedience," or breaking contracts, and written passes were required to move from one place to another.

Frederick Douglass and other Black leaders protested that the Banks system violated the principle of free labor, as it used state power to coerce labor rather than allowing workers to negotiate terms and move freely between employers, in accordance with the law of supply and demand. Banks's justification was that to revive Louisiana's cotton economy and maintain order, freedpeople needed to be taught "habits of industry."

The beginning of the end—and the end of the beginning

Unable to gain recognition from the major European powers, the Confederates pinned their hopes on the 1864 elections. Lincoln's former top general, George B. McClellan, ran against him as a "peace" candidate on the Democratic Party ticket.

McClellan's reactionary campaign slogans included: "McClellan and Peace" and "The Union As It Was, The Constitution As It Is." He called for an immediate cessation of hostilities and a negotiated settlement with the Confederacy.

The election was, without a doubt, a referendum on the war and emancipation. Even Lincoln himself didn't think he stood much of a chance. However, he had far more support than he knew—especially among the rank-and-file soldiers. Carl Schurz, a prominent '48er, made the following prediction just weeks before election day:

> I will make a prophecy that may now sound peculiar. In fifty years, perhaps sooner, Lincoln's name will be inscribed close to Washington's on this American Republic's roll of honor.[168]

Tens of thousands of troops were granted leave to return to their hometowns to cast their votes. The fall of Atlanta in early September buoyed the national mood. In the words of the diarist George Templeton Strong:

> Glorious news this morning—Atlanta taken at last!!! . . . it is (coming at this political crisis) the greatest event of the war.[169]

Lincoln was reelected in a landslide, winning 55 per cent of the popular vote and 212 of 233 electoral votes. 78 per cent of the Union Army voted his way. The message was clear: after so much suffering and sacrifice, the soldiers wanted the war seen through to victory.

At his Second Inaugural Address, given on March 4, 1865, Lincoln delivered yet another eloquent masterpiece:

> Fellow-Countrymen:
>
> At this second appearing to take the oath of the Presidential office, there is less occasion for an extended address than there was at the first. Then a statement, somewhat in detail, of a course to be pursued seemed fitting and proper. Now, at the expiration of four years, during which public declarations have been constantly called forth on every point and phase of the great contest which still absorbs the attention and engrosses the energies of the nation, little that is new could be presented. The progress of our arms, upon which all else chiefly depends, is as well known to the public as to myself, and it is, I trust, reasonably satisfactory and encouraging to all. With high hope for the future, no prediction in regard to it is ventured.
>
> On the occasion corresponding to this four years ago, all thoughts were anxiously directed to an impending civil war. All dreaded it, all sought to avert it. While the inaugural address was being delivered from this place,

devoted altogether to saving the Union without war, insurgent agents were in the city seeking to destroy it without war, seeking to dissolve the Union and divide effects by negotiation. Both parties deprecated war, but one of them would make war rather than let the nation survive, and the other would accept war rather than let it perish, and the war came.

One-eighth of the whole population were colored slaves, not distributed generally over the Union, but localized in the southern part of it. These slaves constituted a peculiar and powerful interest. All knew that this interest was somehow the cause of the war. To strengthen, perpetuate, and extend this interest was the object for which the insurgents would rend the Union even by war, while the Government claimed no right to do more than to restrict the territorial enlargement of it.

Neither party expected for the war the magnitude or the duration which it has already attained. Neither anticipated that the cause of the conflict might cease with or even before the conflict itself should cease. Each looked for an easier triumph and a result less fundamental and astounding. Both read the same Bible and pray to the same God, and each invokes His aid against the other. It may seem strange that any men should dare to ask a just God's assistance in wringing their bread from the sweat of other men's faces, but let us judge not, that we be not judged. The prayers of both could not be answered. That of neither has been answered fully.

The Almighty has His own purposes. "Woe unto the world because of offenses; for it must needs be that offenses come, but woe to that man by whom the offense cometh." If we shall suppose that American slavery is one of those offenses which, in the providence of God, must needs come, but which, having continued through His appointed time, He now wills to remove, and that He gives to both North and South this terrible war as the woe due to those by whom the offense came, shall we discern therein any departure from those divine attributes which the believers in a living God always ascribe to Him? Fondly do we hope, fervently do we pray, that this mighty scourge of war may speedily pass away.

Yet, if God wills that it continue until all the wealth piled by the bondsman's two hundred and fifty years of unrequited toil shall be

> sunk, and until every drop of blood drawn with the lash shall be paid by another drawn with the sword, as was said three thousand years ago, so still it must be said "the judgments of the Lord are true and righteous altogether."
>
> With malice toward none, with charity for all, with firmness in the right as God gives us to see the right, let us strive on to finish the work we are in, to bind up the nation's wounds, to care for him who shall have borne the battle and for his widow and his orphan, to do all which may achieve and cherish a just and lasting peace among ourselves and with all nations.[170]

The work yet to be finished, of course, was a revolutionary war to liberate four million humans from bondage. Long gone was the firm yet nonetheless conciliatory tone of his first inauguration. The presidency had taken a terrible toll on Lincoln's health. Not only did the stress and strain of the war leave its mark, but he had also suffered the death of his 11-year-old son Willie while in the White House. But the Great Emancipator saw the war through to the end.

Just a few weeks later, on April 2, 1865, after a long and debilitating siege, the Confederates succumbed to Grant's merciless pressure at the Third Battle of Petersburg. Richmond had to be abandoned. True to form, Grant sought only a decisive military victory and not personal glory. Instead of marching triumphantly into the enemy capital he immediately continued his pursuit of the Army of Northern Virginia,

On April 4, 1865, Lincoln made an unprecedented and symbolic visit to the Confederate capital. With minimal security—accompanied only by his young son Tad, a small group of officers, and a dozen sailors—Lincoln walked through the still-smoldering streets of the city.

At the Confederate White House, he sat in Jefferson Davis's chair and met with Union officers and local officials, already eager to discuss the process of bringing Virginia back into the Union.

As word spread that "Father Abraham" was in the former Confederate capital, thousands of recently enslaved people poured into the streets to see him with their own eyes. In a scene right out of the Bible, they surrounded him, straining to touch him, some falling to their knees in reverence. Lincoln, visibly moved and uncomfortable with such adulation, is reported to have told them:

> Don't kneel to me. That is not right. You must kneel to God only, and thank Him for the liberty you will enjoy hereafter.[171]

The end for Lee and the main force of the Confederate military came on April 9, at the tiny crossroads of Appomattox Courthouse in Virginia. To prevent the war from devolving into a prolonged guerrilla struggle and to accelerate the process of national healing, Grant offered Lee and his men extraordinarily lenient terms of surrender, allowing the officers to keep their sidearms and horses.

On April 11, 1865, Abraham Lincoln delivered a speech from the White House balcony. He publicly suggested for the first time that some Black men—specifically the educated and those who had served in the Union Army—should be given voting rights. The renowned actor and proslavery zealot, John Wilkes Booth, was in the crowd, and he allegedly sneered to a friend:

> Now, by God, I'll put him through. That is the last speech he will ever make.[172]

Less than a week later, on April 14, Booth shot Lincoln in the back of the head while Lincoln was watching a play at Ford's Theatre. "Uncle Abe" died the next morning. Vice President Andrew Johnson and Secretary of State William H. Seward were also targeted for assassination; Seward was attacked but survived, while the attempt on Johnson was not carried out.

Lincoln's death at that stage of the struggle was a historical accident of epic proportions. It is impossible to say how Reconstruction might have unfolded if Lincoln had lived. As we've seen, he favored remarkably lenient terms for the South's reintegration. However, that didn't mean he had warm feelings for the former Confederate leaders. Given his towering authority and experience dealing with complex and contradictory interests and personalities, he would undoubtedly have done a better job than his successor.

Instead, Andrew Johnson of Tennessee would preside over the first phase of postwar Reconstruction, with dire consequences for the freed people.

The costs of war

The scale and human toll of Civil War battles were hair-raising. In total, the fighting raged for four years across more than 10,000 battlefields, with some 237 major named battles. The human costs were appalling. Casualty rates ran as high as 30 per cent or more in some clashes. At Antietam, more soldiers were killed, wounded, or went missing than in the entire First Revolution—23,000 in a single day. For comparison, that's four times the number of US casualties during the D-Day invasion of Normandy during WWII.

Approximately 2.2 million men served in the Union Army and Navy during the Civil War, including 46,000 conscripts and 118,000 substitutes raised by the draft. This represented around 12 per cent of the Northern population of 18.5 million. By contrast, the Confederacy mobilized a total of 1.2 million soldiers, or around 20 per cent of the white population. This dramatic difference helps illustrate the North's demographic advantage.

An estimated 624,511 soldiers and sailors died due to battlefield injuries, accidents, or disease during the war. That's around 2.4 per cent of the 1860 population and would be equivalent to roughly *eight million* Americans killed today. Hundreds of thousands more were wounded and maimed. On top of this, untold numbers of civilians were killed, wounded, and driven from their homes.

In the Union Army, your chance of dying was about one in four, more often from illness than from battle. For every one killed in battle, two died from disease. Records for the Confederacy are less precise, but some states suffered a 25 per cent death rate among military-age males. Incredibly, in 1866, 20 per cent of Mississippi's entire state budget was spent on artificial limbs for dismembered veterans.

The war devastated the Southern economy in ways that still affect the region today. Total property damage in the South was estimated at $1.5 billion in 1865 dollars—equivalent to $28 billion today. This included not only the destruction of cities, farms, and infrastructure, but also the complete collapse of the region's banking system, not to mention the loss of the country's number one capital asset, the slaves themselves.

The war created approximately 200,000 widows and left more than 400,000 children fatherless. The federal government's pension system, established to care for Union veterans and their families, became one of the largest welfare programs in American history. By 1893, Union pension expenditures accounted for an incredible 43 per cent of the federal budget. Some Confederate veterans received pensions from their state governments, but these were neither generous nor easy to come by.

The Confederacy suffered from devastating inflation during the war. By 1865, the Confederate currency had depreciated to less than 2 per cent of its original value, rendering the life savings of countless Southern families worthless. A barrel of flour that cost $7 in Richmond in 1861 cost $1,000 by early 1865.

The war also created the country's first large-scale refugee crisis. Approximately 500,000 formerly enslaved people ended up internally displaced during the war, fleeing to Union lines and "contraband camps." These overcrowded camps often lacked adequate food, shelter, and medical care, leading to outbreaks of disease that killed thousands.

As we've seen, Confederate apologists fabricated the myth of the "Lost Cause," arguing that the South's cause was noble but doomed due to the North's economic and demographic superiority. It should go without saying that the cause of perpetuating slavery was by no means noble. However, the population figures presented above show that there is a small grain of truth in their argument. As Engels explained:

> Force, nowadays, is the army and navy, and both, as we all know to our cost, are "devilishly expensive." Force, however, cannot make any money; at most it can take away money that has already been made . . .
>
> In the last analysis, therefore, money must be provided through the medium of economic production; and so once more force is conditioned by the economic situation, which furnishes the means for the equipment and maintenance of the instruments of force.[173]

As for economic production, in 1860, the South produced less than 10 per cent of US-manufactured goods. Meanwhile, New York state's industrial output alone was four times greater than the entire Confederacy. The South had tried to industrialize in the 1840s to avoid being overwhelmed by Northern manufactured goods. However, as explained in the section "Political economy in the antebellum South," slave labor and mono-exports of cotton were too lucrative and entrenched for this to take off.

During the war, the South not only lost access to Northern markets, but the Union's increasingly effective naval blockade also cut it off from much of the world. There was some smuggling and blockade-running, including trade across the lines with the North and commerce through neutral ports, but it was not enough to offset the blockade's broader economic impact.

This was the age of the railroad, and the "iron horses" had become the backbone of the economy. As a result, they are also a reliable indicator of relative economic development and industrialization. At the start of the war, the North had 24,000 miles of tracks; another 4,000 miles were built during the war. The South had just 9,000 miles at the start, and they built just 400 miles more. They simply didn't have the resources to do any more than that. Furthermore, and as the war entered its final stages, much of what they did have was destroyed or twisted into "Sherman's neckties."*

---

* A Civil War nickname for railroad rails torn up and twisted (often around trees) by Union troops during Sherman's campaigns to destroy Confederate infrastructure and supply lines.

All told, Confederate war spending in 2026 dollars was roughly $27 billion, whereas the Union spent over $80 billion—nearly three times as much.

It's therefore fair to say that as long as the North's will to continue remained, it was all but guaranteed to win in the long run—as Marx pointed out.

Another unfinished revolution

The total market value of enslaved people in the United States in 1860 was enormous. Economic historians estimate that the aggregate value of the nearly four million chattels was equivalent to roughly $12 billion or more in today's dollars. This made slaves the largest single financial asset in the United States on the eve of the Civil War—more than the combined value of the country's banks, railroads, and factories.

With this in mind, it is clear why Marxists consider the emancipation of the slaves as one of the greatest revolutionary expropriations without compensation in the whole of human history. It was the mass action of the slaves themselves that forced the hand of Lincoln and his generals. Hundreds of thousands risked their lives to escape, join the Union army, or otherwise resist, sabotage, and hobble the Southern economy in what W.E.B. DuBois famously called a slave "general strike." And it was their heroism in battle that further radicalized Northern public opinion in favor of all-out abolition.

Millions of ordinary Northerners, as well as Southerners, mobilized in an attempt to change their destinies—even though for most Confederates, it was in a distorted, counterrevolutionary direction. As during the First Revolution, the question of what to do with Indian lands in the West remained central both during and after the fighting, as we will see in Part Three.

In short, the Civil War and the period of Reconstruction that followed represented the last great push of the bourgeoisie as a historically progressive class. In fact, the American Civil War and its aftermath could be considered the most classical bourgeois revolution of all, insofar as in previous revolutions, the capitalists didn't play as conscious and direct a role *as a class* in imposing their preferred class and property relations on the nation-state as a whole.

Just a few years later, in 1871, the world would witness the Paris Commune, the first seizure of power by the working class. All major revolutionary movements since then have had at least one foot in the camp of proletarian revolution.

Both the Union and the Confederacy claimed to be fighting for "freedom"—but what kind? Their definitions ultimately reflected the class interests that prevailed in each section of the country. Did they mean personal freedom and free labor? The freedom to own property? What kind of property? Property in slave plantations and human chattels? Or in commercial farms and industrial capital?

As with all bourgeois revolutions, though historically progressive, the Civil War couldn't eradicate exploitation and oppression. In fact, it depended on it. To paraphrase Malcolm X, you can't have capitalism without racism—and you can't have racism without capitalism.

Given the level of development of the means of production and of the working class, it could go no further than to privilege one class of property owners over another. Northern capitalism emerged victorious, and the former members of the slavocracy had to adapt to the new ways or lose their political and economic power altogether.

As we will see in Part Three, the North used the war and its aftermath to break up, or accelerate the breakup of, noncapitalist forms of exploitation and production throughout the country. It also consolidated the state institutions that established the political and legal framework for largely unimpeded capitalist accumulation and expansion in the century that followed.

The war led to an unprecedented centralization of finance capital and the mobilization of vast human and material resources to secure victory. For all intents and purposes, the compromises and constraints of the Hamiltonian-Jeffersonian era were dead and buried. Federal power was consolidated at an entirely new level.

In short, the Civil War helped forge the country as we know it today. Although regional differences are still evident, it transformed people's understanding of the country: from "the United States are" to "the United States is."

In the final analysis, the historical purpose of the Civil War was to enhance capital's capacity to exploit labor on an even higher level than after the First Revolution.

Major General Gordon Granger's General Order No. 3, better known as the Juneteenth Declaration, epitomized the new reality. Issued when federal authority finally reached Galveston, Texas, on June 19, 1865, it reads as follows:

> The people of Texas are informed that, in accordance with a proclamation from the Executive of the United States, all slaves are free. This involves an absolute equality of personal rights and rights of property between former masters and slaves, and the connection heretofore existing between them becomes that between employer and hired labor. The freedmen are advised to remain quietly at their present homes and work for wages. They are informed that they will not be allowed to collect at military posts and that they will not be supported in idleness either there or elsewhere.[174]

As one former plantation owner succinctly put it:

> Emancipated slaves own nothing, because nothing but freedom has been given to them.[175]

Welcome to wage slavery.

Capital never sleeps, and it was eager to gain untrammeled access to both Western and Southern land and labor. Imposing the wage-labor–capital relation on the greatest number of humans is its historic mission. However, achieving this without backsliding into the social norms of the old order would prove devilishly difficult.

Frederick Douglass understood the nature of exploitation and oppression all too well. In an address delivered in New York City on May 10, 1865, he warned:

> Slavery has been fruitful in giving itself names. It has been called "the peculiar institution," "the social system," and the "impediment," as it was called by the General Conference of the Methodist Episcopal Church. It has been called a great many names, and it will call itself by yet another name; and you and I and all of us had better wait and see what new form this old monster will assume, in what new skin this old snake will come forth next.[176]

America's Second Revolution represented a tremendous national-democratic leap forward. However, the end of the shooting war was only the beginning of a new phase of struggle. In a modified form, revolution and counterrevolution would continue to rage for another decade in the fiery cauldron of Reconstruction.

"[F]or a whole half-century—since the Civil War over slavery in 1860–65—two bourgeois parties have been distinguished there by remarkable solidity and strength. The party of the former slave-owners is the so-called Democratic Party. The capitalist party, which favored the emancipation of the Negroes, has developed into the Republican Party.

Since the emancipation of the Negroes, the distinction between the two parties has been diminishing. The fight between these two parties has been mainly over the height of customs duties. Their fight has not had any serious importance for the mass of the people. The people have been deceived and diverted from their vital interests by means of spectacular and meaningless duels between the two bourgeois parties.

This so-called bipartisan system prevailing in America and Britain has been one of the most powerful means of preventing the rise of an independent working-class, i.e., genuinely socialist, party."

— Vladimir Lenin, "The Results and Significance of the US Presidential Elections"
November 1912

Part Three: Reconstruction

The US Civil War marked a decisive turning point in world history. For four bloody years, Northern capitalism went to war with the Southern slavocracy in a high-stakes fight for control of Western territories and the federal government.

At first, Lincoln viewed the conflict as a kind of "special military operation." He aimed to restore the Union by clearing out the reactionary rebels who had hijacked eleven Southern states. But, under growing pressure from hundreds of thousands of self-emancipating slaves, many of whom eventually served in the Union Army, the conflict was transformed. It became a revolutionary war to abolish chattel slavery and impose free labor on the entire American nation-state.

However, the violence and class struggle didn't end with the Civil War. It merely changed focus. The military defeat of the Confederate armies was only the beginning of a messy, painful, and in many ways, still unfinished process.

Many tragic decades would be necessary before capitalism was fully embedded throughout the continent. It took years before the promise of Lincoln's Emancipation Proclamation was fulfilled—

even in states that had stayed in the Union. In fact, a careful reading of the 13th Amendment reveals that, to this day, slavery has not been abolished altogether.

Reconstruction was the name given to the convulsive period of revolution and counterrevolution that began even before the Second American Revolution had ended. Now that the "wolf's ear" of slavery had been let go, the status of roughly four million landless, homeless, stateless freedpeople was the nation's central political, economic, and moral problem. For nearly a century, the declaration that "all men are created equal" had rung hollow. Reconstruction was a golden opportunity to right the colossal perversion of justice flowing from the First American Revolution, which had enshrined slavery in the Constitution.

Southern devastation

Overturning centuries of chattel slavery had come at a terrible cost. By the war's end, all classes and races in the country had suffered unimaginable death, disfigurement, and dislocation. But the desolation was orders of magnitude worse in the South. As historian Stephanie McCurry described it:

> All wars have postwar periods that are perhaps more uncertain than the conflict itself. But this was far more than that. The term Reconstruction doesn't begin to cover it.[1]

The South's economy was in tatters and its infrastructure in ruins. Hundreds of plantations had been burned, and their livestock had been decimated. Hundreds of miles of rail lines and much of its rolling stock had been wrecked. Most of its factories and more than half of its farm machinery, including cotton gins, had been destroyed. Hundreds of thousands of people, Black and white alike, were hungry, homeless, and dying of disease.

Currency devaluation and hyperinflation eviscerated purchasing power—when there were even any commodities to be had. By early 1865, the Confederate "grayback" was worth a mere fraction of the Union dollar. When Jefferson Davis's government collapsed altogether, the currency became literally worthless. War bondholders and other lenders to the Confederate cause were plum out of luck.

A standard price index of commodities in the Eastern Confederacy rose from 100 at the start of the war to over 9,125,200 by April 1865. In other words, goods costing $1 in 1861 required roughly $92 or more to purchase in 1865.

The shock and shame felt by Southerners at the scope and scale of their defeat cannot be overstated. As the young daughter of a planter told a Northern newspaper, she had nothing to look forward to but:

> A joyless future of probable ignominy, poverty, and want [with] God alone knowing where any of us will end a life robbed of every blessing and already becoming intolerable.[2]

In 1867, the farmer and preacher A. C. Ramsey of Alabama wrote an extremely interesting and revealing letter to a friend in South Carolina:

> The war ruined me. Before it, the children and I were worth $45,000 in Negroes and lands. We had on the place about 65 Negroes, after giving Janie and Mary their share. The children had 35, and I had 30 of my own, besides eight or ten which my wife had; perfectly independent as we thought. I was, however, owing some money which I could easily have paid had the war not come on.
>
> But alas! the war came, I bent all my energies to its support, made nothing but provisions, all went to support the soldiers and their families, had no cotton on hand at the surrender, debts accumulating all the time, Negroes gone, and here I was left with land and nothing else, and it greatly depreciated in value, and in fact could not sell it at all. My children left with nothing but a piece of land—320 acres—and I not able to help them to a dollar; and besides a debt hanging over me now, that my land, if it had been sold, would not pay. So I saw nothing ahead but ruin . . .
>
> There will be in this Country great distress and destitution; hundreds of men who were in good circumstances before the war are completely ruined. Suing and being sued is the order of the day, and probably not

> more than one in ten will be able to survive the crash that awaits us. And what the Radicals will do can only be judged by their former acts and propositions now in their Congress. I believe they intend to give us a Territorial government and place the negroes over us in point of privilege. I hope, however, the good Lord may intervene and thwart their designs.[3]

These glimpses into the mindset of a handful of defeated Southerners give a flavor of the emotionally charged minefield the advocates of Reconstruction had to navigate.

One young planter, burning with anger and humiliation, summed it up in just a few words:

> They've [Northerners] left me one inestimable privilege—to hate 'em. I get up at half-past four in the morning, and sit up till twelve at night, to hate 'em.[4]

The meaning of freedom

Now that the right to buy and sell humans for the purpose of exploiting their labor had been abolished, defining "freedom" gained new urgency. For the freedpeople, true emancipation meant not just freedom *from* slavery, but the freedom *to* control their own labor and to work their own land, embodied in the idea of "40 acres and a mule." They yearned to become self-sufficient producers who would never again feel the lash of a master's whip.

Other Americans envisioned a society in which juridically free individuals could work for themselves or enter freely into wage-labor contracts, choose between employers, and rise through individual effort and merit. This outlook was summed up in the slogan: "free soil, free labor, free men."

Their assumption was that wage labor was merely a stepping stone on the road to small-scale proprietorship by increasingly skilled workers controlling their own labor process. Abraham Lincoln articulated this vision of free labor in a 1859 speech:

> The prudent, penniless beginner in the world, labors for wages a while, saves a surplus with which to buy tools or land for himself; then labors on his own account another while, and at length hires another new beginner to help him.
>
> This, say its advocates, is free labor—the just and generous, and prosperous system, which opens the way for all—gives hope to all, and energy, and progress, and improvement of condition to all.[5]

And earlier in the same speech, he declared:

> By some it is assumed that *labor* is available only in connection with capital—that nobody labors, unless somebody else, owning capital, somehow, by the use of that capital, induces him to do it. Having assumed this, they proceed to consider whether it is best that capital shall *hire* laborers, and thus induce them to work by their own consent; or *buy* them, and drive them to it without their consent. Having proceeded so far they naturally conclude that all laborers are necessarily either *hired* laborers, or *slaves*. They further assume that whoever is once a *hired* laborer, is fatally fixed in that condition for life; and thence again that his condition is as bad as, or worse than that of a slave. This is the "*mud-sill*" theory.
>
> But another class of reasoners hold the opinion that there is no such relation between capital and labor, as assumed; and that there is no *such* thing as a freeman being fatally fixed for life, in the condition of a hired laborer, that both these assumptions are false, and all inferences from them groundless. They hold that labor is prior to, and independent of, capital; that, in fact, capital is the fruit of labor, and could never have existed if labor had not *first* existed—that labor can exist without capital, but that capital could never have existed without labor. Hence they hold that labor is the superior—greatly the superior—of capital.[6]

By no means does this make Lincoln a historical materialist or communist. However, self-ownership, upward mobility, and a safe and prosperous home were virtually synonymous with freedom—and even masculinity. This was an early iteration of the "American dream."

However, other, thornier questions further complicated the meaning of "freedom." For example, did freedom from slavery also include the right to participate in majority-rule political decision-making?

For both freedpeople and the Radical Republicans, genuine freedom required *both* economic autonomy *and* political power, including the right to vote, serve on juries, testify in court, hold elected office, draft and approve legislation, and so on.

As we will see, after the initial resistance of the former slave masters was swept aside, during the revolutionary upswing of Reconstruction, radical democracy blossomed. After centuries of domination by the slavocracy, poor Black and white farmers seized their destinies in their hands and came together to defend their common interests against their mutual enemies: the big planters and capitalists.

Poor whites who collaborated with freedpeople and Northern Radicals in the hopes of bettering their lives were derisively called "scalawags."* However, like the truth, freedom and democracy are concrete questions. As one pro-Republican "scalawag" from Arkansas asked his neighbors:

> Do you want good roads throughout your state? Do you want free bridges? Do you want free schools and the advantages of education for your children?[7]

Unsurprisingly, this incipient grassroots democracy and class unity was seen as a threat to the powers that be on both sides of the Mason–Dixon line†. It threatened not only racial hierarchies, but capitalist property relations themselves, and could not be tolerated.

All of this and more played out in the colossal social experiment of Reconstruction. It was, without a doubt, an exhilarating new dawn.

---

* Pejorative term for white Southerners who supported Republican Reconstruction policies and efforts. They were considered traitors to their region by Southern Democrats.

† A boundary drawn in the 1760s between the British colonies of Pennsylvania, Delaware, Maryland, and Virginia. After Pennsylvania abolished slavery in 1780, it formed the border between the free and slave states, and came to be seen as the political and cultural dividing line between North and South.

And yet, it devolved into the living nightmare of white vigilante terror and Jim Crow segregation. As W.E.B. Du Bois poetically wrote:

> The slave went free; stood a brief moment in the sun; then moved back again toward slavery. The whole weight of America was thrown to color caste.[8]

However, in recognition of Reconstruction's profound revolutionary potential, he added:

> The most magnificent drama in the last thousand years of human history is the transportation of ten million human beings out of the dark beauty of their mother continent into the new-found Eldorado of the West. They descended into Hell; and in the third century they arose from the dead, in the finest effort to achieve democracy for the working millions which this world had ever seen.[9]
>
> The attempt to make Black men American citizens was, in a certain sense, all a failure, but a splendid failure.[10]

In the words of historian Eric Foner:

> The tide of change rose and then receded, but it left behind an altered landscape.[11]

Continental expansion

Uprooting slavery and restructuring the Southern economy were necessary steps toward the emergence of full-fledged US imperialism in the decades that followed. Part Three will therefore focus mainly on events in the South.

However, it is impossible to understand the processes that unfolded without placing them in their broader, deeply interconnected context. As we will see, there was far more to this period than the *re*construction of the seceded state governments. At the same time, the American nation-state as a whole and the foundations of modern industrial and finance capitalism were being *con*structed.

Reconstruction of the seceded states may have taken center stage, but events on the Western frontier were equally dramatic and violent.

As explained in Parts One and Two, duplicity and wars aimed at swindling, subjugating, or exterminating the continent's Indigenous peoples were nothing new and had been smoldering for hundreds of years. Now, after successfully subduing the Southern slavocracy, the Union turned its attention to the Plains and Rocky Mountain tribes.

The Homestead Act of 1862—an essential part of the Republicans' "free soil" program—was a decisive piece of the puzzle. Its purpose was to facilitate settlement of the continent by non-Indians, with expanded capitalist consumer markets following in their wake. It achieved this by granting 160 acres of public land to anyone who improved their holdings by building a dwelling and cultivating crops for at least five years.

This sounds like a win-win, but for many settlers, reality often fell short of the ideal. Much of the best land was claimed by speculators and railroad companies, and in the most arid regions, the plots were often too small to be viable. Many homesteaders lacked the capital needed for equipment, seed, and survival during the first, difficult years.

And for the Indian peoples, it was an unmitigated catastrophe. As federal troops redeployed to take on the Confederates during the war, local militias filled the vacuum, often escalating attacks on Native populations and intensifying pressure on territorial boundaries.

The US–Dakota War of 1862 in Minnesota, often referred to as the "Sioux Uprising," culminated in the largest mass execution in US history. 38 Dakota were hanged at Mankato on December 26, 1862, after perfunctory military trials. Lincoln reviewed the cases personally, and commuted the sentences of 265 others condemned to death.

As during the First Revolution, the Civil War divided many Indigenous polities, especially in Indian Territory. Different factions within the Cherokee, Choctaw, Chickasaw, Creek, and Seminole nations aligned with the Union or the Confederacy for various reasons, and long-running internal disputes often erupted into mini civil wars in their own right.

Between 1865 and 1877, some 400,000 land-hungry families received land grants through the Homestead Act, settling nearly 28 million acres of western territory. Not only did these grants carve out a growing market for Northern manufactured goods, but it also provided a "safety valve" for the revolutionary pressure cooker of overcrowded cities in the Northeast. In order to give some form to the anarchy, Dakota Territory was established in 1861, the states of Nebraska and Colorado were admitted to the Union in 1867 and 1876, and Wyoming Territory was organized in 1868.

The time-honored American pastime of lavish corporate handouts was also on full display, as the federal government granted roughly 130 million acres of public land to private railroad companies. Railroad construction represented the largest single investment in American history up to that time. Between 1865 and 1877, the country's rail network more than doubled, from around 35,000 miles to over 70,000 miles, though the expansion was five times greater in the North than in the South. The completion of the first transcontinental railroad in 1869 accelerated the process of western settlement even further. Instead of months, it now took less than a week to travel from New York to San Francisco.

After the war, the US Army pursued a genocidal scorched-earth campaign as part of capital's relentless drive to aggregate land, resources, and labor. The callous and racist attitude of many white Americans toward the aboriginal inhabitants of the continent was summed up in a quote attributed to General Philip Sheridan:

> The only good Indians I ever saw were dead.[12]

The discovery of gold and silver in Nevada, Colorado, Montana, and the Black Hills of Dakota Territory sparked new waves of westward migration. This led to rising tensions and concerted military campaigns against the region's Indigenous tribes.

The Red River War of 1874–75 aimed to break Comanche, Kiowa, Southern Cheyenne, and Arapaho resistance on the southern Plains and force these nations onto reservations by destroying villages, horse herds, and food supplies. As had been happening for centuries, settler encroachment into Indigenous lands drove the conflict. The Plains nations were under extreme pressure as the buffalo herds collapsed, accelerated by commercial hunting, part of a deliberate government policy to dispossess Indians of their lands.

At the Battle of the Little Bighorn in 1876, General George Armstrong Custer and his men were wiped out after his infamous "last stand." Despite their courage and tactical victories, however, the Indigenous resistance could not indefinitely withstand the US military's superior resources and numbers.

The postwar period saw a series of "Reconstruction treaties" that forced Indigenous nations—especially in Indian Territory—into a new political economy after the Civil War. Nations the federal government deemed to have aided the Confederacy were compelled to accept sweeping land cessions, tighter federal supervision, and governmental reorganization dictated by Washington.

This period also saw the shameful expansion of the Indian boarding school system. Under the genocidal banner of "civilization" and "education," federal and church-run institutions removed Indigenous children from their families—sometimes through overt coercion, sometimes by withholding rations or other essentials from populations that resisted.

Children were often transported far from home, renamed, and punished for speaking their languages or practicing their traditional rituals. Their hair was cut, and traditional clothing was confiscated or burned. Kinship ties and cooperative behavior were mocked and undermined. Forced assimilation and cultural destruction were used to prepare them to accept dispossession, individualism, and of course, wage labor.

Conditions were frequently brutal: overcrowding, malnutrition, hard labor, and military-style discipline were common. Physical and sexual abuse was widespread. Mortality rates were often staggering as untreated diseases tore through dormitories. Even when children survived, they often returned traumatized for life, estranged from their families, and often unable to communicate with their own people.

Over the centuries, countless treaties had been signed with the British or US governments, and virtually every one of them was violated. Hundreds of Indian peoples were systematically decimated and forced onto reservations. As Red Cloud of the Oglala Lakota reportedly put it in 1870:

> They made us many promises, more than I can remember, but they never kept but one; they promised to take our land, and they took it.[13]

And as the legendary Hunkpapa Lakota, Sitting Bull, is alleged to have expressed in 1877:

> What treaty that the whites have kept has the red man broken? Not one. What treaty that the whites ever made with us red men have they kept? Not one.[14]

To top off the country's preparations for bona fide imperialist ignition, the US acquired Alaska from Russia in 1867. Alaska Native peoples were not consulted or recognized in the transaction, even though they laid claim to most of the land. As Eric Foner explains:

> Even as the struggle between President Andrew Johnson and Congress reached its climax, the United States acquired Alaska, one part of an imperial agenda long advocated by Secretary of State William H. Seward. Under President Grant, the government attempted to annex the Dominican Republic.[15]

Of course, much more will have to be said about all of this. But suffice it in this volume to note that the Wild West was raging—and we haven't even touched on the murderous pogroms that were also unleashed against Mexicans and Chinese immigrants.

The Gilded Age

Meanwhile, in the North, which had experienced a wartime economic boom, industrial and finance capital continued to rocket ahead. This was the beginning of the Gilded Age, which saw the "robber barons" wage vicious class war against the emboldened working class.

The war had been a pivotal tipping point in the rise of monopoly capital, as the government worked hand in glove with the big financiers to transform the American economy. Lincoln's Secretary of the Treasury had been none other than Salmon P. Chase—the namesake of today's Fortune 500 bank.

All things being equal, capital prefers the largest markets and fewest restrictions to its circulation. Like Hamilton before him, Chase played the role of a jackhammer on behalf of big capital. He was busy as a beaver behind the scenes during the war, ratcheting the financial architecture of American capitalism forward by any means necessary.

Before the war, the only currency issued by the federal government was specie, i.e., gold and silver coins. There were hundreds of different banknotes issued by private banks, exchangeable for specie in limited areas serviced by those specific banks. The Legal Tender Act of 1862 authorized the US Treasury to issue paper currency not backed by gold or silver. These became the first widely circulated "greenbacks." The National Banking Acts of 1863 and 1864 created a uniform national currency and a network of banks to accelerate the aggregation of capital and facilitate financial transactions.

In 1800, there were just 28 state-chartered banks in the United States, each issuing its own unreliable currency. By 1865, the National Banking System included 1,644 nationally chartered banks. By the end of the war, approximately $450 million of these dollars were in circulation. Between 1860 and 1900, total banking assets grew from approximately $1 billion to over $10 billion.

Senator John Sherman of Ohio—William Tecumseh's brother—worked closely with Chase to navigate the labyrinthine halls of Congress. As he later wrote in his memoirs:

> This system of national banks has furnished to the people of the United States a currency combining the national faith with the private stock and private credit of individuals. They have a currency that is safe, uniform, and convertible.[16]

To sell large amounts of debt, the Treasury relied on big financiers—Jay Cooke in particular—who coordinated bond sales to banks and middle-class households.

Chase was also instrumental in the creation of the Bureau of Internal Revenue in 1862, which oversaw the country's first sustained federal income tax. A permanent tax apparatus gave the federal debt credibility and helped bolster confidence in federal credit by expanding the state's capacity to raise revenue on a schedule. It also helped normalize the idea that the national state could routinely mobilize resources on a massive scale, especially during national crises and war.

The result was not just money for the war effort. It also created a national market in public debt and a core of capitalists committed to strong federal credit and reliable interest payments, even as it lined the pockets of insiders. The links that Chase helped forge between Wall Street and the federal government went beyond anything Hamilton could have imagined.

To top it all off, Chase became Chief Justice of the Supreme Court in 1864. His court's rulings tended to reinforce the sanctity of contracts, the stability of public credit, and the centrality of national markets, all to support the expansion of finance capital. However, he himself is alleged to have recognized that he had helped unleash an uncontrollable monster. As he reportedly said:

> My agency in promoting the passage of the National Banking Act was the greatest mistake of my life. It has built up a monopoly which affects every interest in the country.

Major financial institutions were formed at this time. J.P. Morgan's father, Junius Spencer Morgan, energetically expanded his banking operations, laying the groundwork for what would become one of the country's most powerful financial dynasties. Investment banks grew in prominence as intermediaries for railroad finance. Regional and municipal banks proliferated under the new national system, while increasingly complex networks of correspondent banking tied local credit to New York's all-powerful money markets.

New York City became the country's undisputed financial center, channeling capital from across the country and around the world into industrial development, railroads, and, of course, speculation.

The total value of capital invested in manufacturing increased from around $1 billion in 1860 to $2.1 billion by 1870. Manufacturing output in the North rose from $1.9 billion in 1860 to over $3.4 billion by 1870—an increase of nearly 80 per cent in a single decade. Over 440,000 patents were issued between 1865 and 1877, more than the total number issued in all previous American history.

Unsurprisingly, the North led the country in patent registrations and technological innovation, with advances in manufacturing processes, agricultural machinery, and transportation infrastructure. Northern and Midwestern agriculture became increasingly mechanized and commercialized, producing enormous surpluses for export and to feed growing urban populations.

Major Northern cities experienced rapid population growth and urbanization as they became centers of industrial production, attracting both domestic migrants from rural areas and Europeans seeking a new life in the "land of opportunity." In reality, of course, things weren't always rosy. As one anonymous Italian immigrant put it:

> I came to America because I heard the streets were paved with gold. When I got here, I found out three things:
>
> First, the streets were not paved with gold.
>
> Second, they weren't paved at all.
>
> Third, I was expected to pave them.[17]

Between 1865 and 1900, some 14 million immigrants entered the country. Coming mainly from Ireland, Germany, Italy, and Eastern Europe, this transformed the country's demographics and intensified the ethnic-and-racial-identity politics that plague us to this day.

Between 1860 and 1870, coal production, essential for powering steam engines and blast furnaces, rose nearly threefold from about 14 million to over 40 million tons. Iron production doubled from approximately 920,000 tons to 1.7 million tons, laying the groundwork for the steel revolution. The textile industry, then centered in New England, saw the value of its output grow from around $115 million to over $177 million during that same decade.

All told, real GDP increased by approximately 50 per cent during the Reconstruction era. However, the disparity between the two sections was only exacerbated in the postwar period. It is an astonishing fact that between 1860 and 1870, Northern wealth increased by 50 per cent, whereas Southern wealth decreased by 60 per cent. The top 10 per cent of Southern wealth holders saw their personal wealth drop by 90 per cent. This was fertile soil for bitterness and revenge.

Class struggle and corruption

Naturally, all of this was accompanied by the rise of a powerful working class and growing class consciousness. Between 1860 and 1880, the number of industrial wage workers in the country nearly doubled, from around 1.5 to over 2.7 million. The expansion of railroads, coal, steel, textiles, and the mechanization of agriculture drove this explosive growth.

Working conditions were brutal and straight out of Marx's *Capital.* Ten- to twelve-hour workdays were the norm, child labor was widespread, workplace accidents were common, and wages barely kept pace with inflation. In response, the number of strikes rose dramatically, from an average of 15 to 20 per year in the early 1860s to over 500 every year by the mid-1870s.

The National Labor Union, founded in 1866, was the first attempt to organize workers across craft lines on a national scale, reaching a peak membership of around 600,000 by 1868. The movement for the eight-hour workday was also born at this time. As Marx wrote in 1867:

> In the United States of North America, every independent movement of the workers was paralyzed so long as slavery disfigured a part of the Republic. Labor cannot emancipate itself in the white skin, where in the Black it is branded. But out of the death of slavery, a new life at once arose.

> The first fruit of the Civil War was the eight-hour agitation that ran with the seven-league boots of the locomotive from the Atlantic to the Pacific, from New England to California.[18]

As might be expected, the decades following the Civil War were marked by an intensification of the class war. By 1886, the Knights of Labor had reached its peak of 700,000 members. That same year saw the Haymarket Riot in Chicago, which launched May Day as a global workers' holiday, as well as the founding of the American Federation of Labor (AFL) by Samuel Gompers.

Despite his narrow craft-unionism and economism—not to mention his racism and social conservatism—Gompers could talk a good talk, especially when both he and the labor movement were more raw and unvarnished:

> Our enemies would like to see this movement thrust into hades, they would like to see it in a warmer climate, but I say to you that this movement has come to stay. Like Banquo's ghost, it will not down. I say the labor movement is a fixed fact. It has grown out of the necessities of the people, and, although some may desire to see it fail, still the labor movement will be found to have a strong lodgment in the hearts of the people, and we will go on until success has been achieved.
>
> We want eight hours and nothing less. We have been accused of being selfish, and it has been said that we will want more; that last year we got an advance of ten cents and now we want more. We do want more. You will find that a man generally wants more. Go and ask a tramp what he wants, and if he doesn't want a drink he will want a good, square meal. You ask a workingman, who is getting two dollars a day, and he will say that he wants ten cents more. Ask a man who gets five dollars a day and he will want fifty cents more. The man who receives five thousand dollars a year wants six thousand a year, and the man who owns eight or nine hundred thousand dollars will want a hundred thousand dollars to make it a million, while the man who has his millions will want everything he can lay his hands on and then raise his voice against the poor devil who wants ten cents more a day.

> We live in the latter part of the Nineteenth century. In the age of electricity and steam that has produced wealth a hundred fold, we insist that it has been brought about by the intelligence and the energy of the workingmen, and while we find that it is now easier to produce it is harder to live. We do want more, and when it becomes more, we shall still want more. And we shall never cease to demand more until we have received the results of our labor.[19]

With all of that wealth sloshing around, Reconstruction was also marked by widespread corruption and insider dealmaking at every level of business and government. This was the heyday of party patronage machines like Boss Tweed's Tammany Hall in New York City. In exchange for votes, Tweed provided social services, extracted tribute from local businesses, and distributed thousands of city jobs, contracts, and licenses. Ballot stuffing, voter registration and intimidation, and naturalization fraud were his goons' bread and butter.

Then there was the Crédit Mobilier railroad construction scandal of 1872, involving several members of Congress and the vice president. And the Whiskey Ring tax evasion scandal of 1875, which deeply damaged Ulysses S. Grant's presidency, even though he wasn't directly involved.

However, all good things must come to an end, and the boom years came to a screeching halt with the "Long Depression" of 1873–79. Triggered by rampant financial and railroad speculation and punctuated by the collapse of major financial houses such as Jay Cooke & Company, fortunes were lost, and millions were thrown out of work. By 1875, the economy experienced a modest uptick, and with it came an explosion of class struggle, culminating in the Great Railroad Strike of 1877—followed by a renewed plunge into depression.

Sparked in Martinsburg, West Virginia, the strike spread like wildfire via the country's extensive rail network. Workers seized control of rail yards and battled state militia and federal troops in cities from Baltimore to San Francisco. In St. Louis, the strike took on insurrectionary proportions when the general strike committee—led by socialists of the Workingmen's Party and including both Black and white workers—effectively ran the city for several days. This marked the coming-out party of the American working class, and was brutally suppressed by state and federal forces, resulting in over 100 deaths.

Internationally, this was the era of the Franco-Prussian War, the Paris Commune, German unification, the First International, and the rise of Narodnism in Russia. It also saw the Meiji Restoration in Japan, the opening of the Suez Canal, the Third Carlist War in Spain, the Russo-Turkish War, the Great Eastern Crisis in the Balkans, and the "Scramble for Africa," kicked off by Belgian King Leopold II's brutal invasion of the Congo.

All of this was the chaotic backdrop of the country as a whole as it worked to untangle centuries of chattel slavery. Not only the South, but the entire American nation-state was dramatically reforged, economically, politically, and socially. In the words of historian David Blight:

> The American experiment died [with the Civil War] but was then reborn.[20]

Land and freedom

To make sense of Reconstruction, we must be clear about the economic and class relations that prevailed in different parts of the country before the war. The baseline for understanding these dynamics can be found in Parts One and Two of this volume, in the sections on political economy.

To summarize briefly: before the war, both regions of the country were deeply connected to world capitalism via trade networks and financial markets. However, the ruling class of each section based itself on very different modes of exploitation, and as a result, had increasingly divergent political priorities and expectations.

At a certain stage, there were only two possible outcomes. Either the centrifugal tendencies would lead to the Union's dissolution, or it would be forcibly held together and "become all one thing," to paraphrase Lincoln. After the Union victory, the "one thing" it would have to become was a full-fledged capitalist power, based on the exploitation of free labor.

However, in the words of Mephistopheles in Goethe's *Faust*: "All theory, dear friend, is gray, but the golden tree of life springs ever green." Putting theory into practice would prove a monumental task, and many adjustments would have to be made on the fly.

Now that they had won on the battlefield, the Northern capitalists aimed to impose their preferred economic relations on the entire continent. As for the Southern planters, they had to conform to the new ways or lose everything, so they worked to fuse capitalism with the old social forms. Nearly everyone's overriding concern—whether rich or poor, white or Black, Indigenous or immigrant—was land, which was the basis for both freedom and prosperity.

As we've seen, over the course of the war, Lincoln had been transformed into an enthusiastic supporter of the expropriation of private property in slaves. However, he rejected doing the same with the South's big landed estates. As a defender of capitalism, this was too great an infringement on the rights of private property. He saw it as a violation of the Constitution's ban on bills of attainder and the "corruption of blood," which prohibits the permanent forfeiture of property beyond an offender's lifetime. Most importantly, this wasn't big capital's program. The vast plantation-capitalist estates formerly operated by slaves were ripe to be converted into vast capitalist plantations operated by wage laborers.

This stymied the plans of the petty-bourgeois Radical Republicans, who favored mass expropriation and redistribution of the planters' land, much of which had been taken into federal receivership out of military necessity during the war. As far as the *Boston Commonwealth* was concerned, if the secessionists' lands were to be reinstated, "The war will have been a gigantic failure." It added:

> To be safe, peaceable, and permanent, [Reconstruction] must be primarily economical and industrial; it must commence by planting a loyal population in the South, not only as its cultivators but as its rightful

> and actual owners . . . No such thing as a free, democratic society can exist in any country where all lands are owned by one class of men and cultivated by another.[21]

And according to the abolitionist paper, *The Liberator:*

> By all the laws and usages of civilized nations, rebels against a government forfeit their property . . .[22]

Many Radicals considered the South a seceded country, viewing it as an occupied and unincorporated territory. "The Great Commoner," Thaddeus Stevens—who some have compared to Oliver Cromwell, Sam Adams, or Robespierre—didn't mince words. In his view, the Confederate states were "conquered provinces" that had committed "political suicide," and should be treated as such:

> The Southern states have been despotisms, not governments of the people. It is impossible that any practical equality of rights can exist where a few thousand men monopolize the whole landed property . . .
>
> The whole fabric of southern society must be changed, and never can it be done if this opportunity is lost. Without this, this government can never be, as it has never been, a true republic . . .
>
> The property of the chief rebels should be seized and appropriated to the payment of the national debt, caused by the unjust and wicked war which they instigated . . .
>
> Strip a proud nobility of their bloated estates; reduce them to a level with plain republicans, send them forth to labor, and teach their children to enter the workshops or handle the plow, and you will thus humble the proud traitors.[23]

In an 1865 article for the *Westliche Post,* the most widely read German newspaper of St. Louis, Missouri, Joseph Weydemeyer wrote:

> Why not transfer all the lands that have been abandoned, confiscated, or forfeited through tax default to free Negroes to cultivate independently? [In order to end a costly military occupation, it is necessary to] give

> the new representatives of free labor the political power to protect their newly acquired rights . . .
>
> The more allies they gain for the great fight between labor and monopolizing capital . . . the more certain and speedy their victory. But where else in the South will they find these allies, if not among the workers themselves, regardless of what ancestry they have to thank for their skin color?[24]

To this end, Congressman George Julian proposed extending the Homestead Act's provisions to include confiscated lands in the South, with 40–80 acres allocated per head of family.

However, big capital had spent decades squeezing out small producers while aggregating land, labor, and capital to expand production and systematize distribution across the North. Now that the historically regressive slave mode of exploitation had been mostly abolished, the victorious bourgeoisie was not about to let huge swaths of the country be dominated by an equally outmoded economic model in which small plots of land were worked by mules and people with rudimentary tools.

Thus, divisions emerged within the Republican Party, which, like all political parties, contained not only radicals, but conservatives and moderates. While some wanted to use the power of the state to deliberately reshape the South, others preferred a laissez-faire approach, trusting the "invisible hand of the market" to sort things out.

In an attempt to manage this vast and chaotic transition, the Bureau of Refugees, Freedmen, and Abandoned Lands, better known as the Freedmen's Bureau, was created in March 1865. It was authorized to provide emergency relief, establish schools, draft and supervise labor contracts, and, initially, to distribute confiscated Confederate lands to freed families.

Under its auspices, the region's first public schools were established, and the South was flooded with well-intentioned Northern abolitionists, including thousands of women, who sought to bring education and Protestant values including industry and self-discipline to the freedpeople. In the words of one starry-eyed teacher, the goal was "to make a New England of the whole South."

Not all the teachers were white, of course. Many schools were built and supported by resources raised by the freedpeople themselves. During the 1860s, an estimated 20 per cent of the region's 4,000 teachers were Black. The process started even before the war was over. As explained by Eric Foner:

> Black troops helped construct schools, churches, and orphanages, organized debating societies, and held political gatherings where "freedom songs" were sung and soldiers delivered "speeches of the most inflammatory kind."[25]

By the end of 1865, however, many of these policies were already being reversed by the new president, Andrew Johnson. On his watch, the federal government largely shifted toward restoring white Southern landowners' control over plantations and promoting a free-labor order based on wage work and labor contracts, rather than pursuing large-scale confiscation and redistribution of land to former slaves. Though historically progressive from the perspective of capitalism, this clashed head on with the expectations of the Radical Republicans and freedpeople.

Andrew Johnson and the Black Codes

Lincoln's assassination changed the tone, trajectory, and rhythm of Reconstruction. It was always going to be a violent and messy process, but having a vindictive white supremacist in charge only compounded the chaos.

A Jacksonian Democrat, Tennessee's Andrew Johnson was opportunistically added to the 1864 presidential ticket to secure votes from the border states. Although he hated the arrogant airs of the big planters, he hated Black people even more. As Frederick Douglass famously observed after encountering the new vice president at Lincoln's second inauguration:

> Whatever Andrew Johnson may be, he certainly is no friend of our race.[26]

Johnson is reported to have confirmed this once he was in the White House. According to the Cincinnati *Enquirer*, the new president wrote the following to governor Thomas C. Fletcher of Missouri:

> This is a country for white men, and by God, as long as I am President, it shall be a government for white men.[27]

Under Johnson, Presidential Reconstruction followed Lincoln's relatively easy policy of reincorporating the seceded states. But Johnson made it personal. He enjoyed watching former Confederate bigwigs beg for pardons to recover their lands. In September 1865, he granted an average of 100 pardons a day.

To be sure, some Confederate diehards preferred military occupation to any form of cooperation with the federal authorities. But now that emancipation was a fact, most big planters were desperate to get back into politics and have a say in the postwar order. With former slaves now counted fully in the census—instead of as three-fifths of a person—the Southern states could potentially have even greater representation in Congress than before the war.

Whether they were for or against making nice with Washington, however, they all agreed that Black people shouldn't be allowed to rise to their full stature. Nor were they interested in allowing the market to operate freely. They clearly preferred a landless, propertyless, and thus, more easily exploitable population. The more farsighted among them adopted the same attitude as Italy's big landowners during the Risorgimento. To paraphrase Giuseppe di Lampedusa in his masterpiece novel, *Il Gattopardo*: Everything must change for everything to remain the same.

The planters used every trick in the book, both legal and illegal, including bribery, torture, and murder, to whip the freedmen into line. To this end, the original Black Codes were introduced across the South. These state and local statutes limited the kinds of jobs that were open to Blacks, as well as the kinds of property and businesses they could own. They imposed restrictions on freedom of movement, assembly, and speech. They also established separate public facilities and legal systems with harsher punishments for Black people.

In South Carolina, white employers were legally defined as "masters," while the Black workers they employed were classified as "servants."

Vagrancy laws allowed the authorities to arrest and fine Black people who couldn't prove they had a job. Those who couldn't pay the fines could effectively be auctioned off to employers who would pay their fine for them—in exchange for a commitment to work—thus reestablishing a form of bonded labor. There were even provisions allowing the courts to take Black children away from "indigent" parents against their will. These children could then be assigned to white employers as unpaid "apprentices."

For his part, Johnson granted those he pardoned significant autonomy in Reconstruction in their respective areas, and almost all of their lands were returned. But the freedpeople weren't about to roll over without a fight, and in many places, they clashed with the federal troops tasked with kicking them off lands they had occupied during the war.

Nor were the Radical Republicans going to make it easy for Johnson and the planters to have their way. In a historic first, they overrode his veto of the Civil Rights Act of April 1866. This was a predecessor to the 14th Amendment and the first federal law to define citizenship and affirm that all citizens are equally protected by the law, regardless of race, color, or previous condition of slavery or involuntary servitude. They also transformed the 1866 midterm elections into a referendum on Johnson's scandalous Reconstruction policies.

In May and July of that year, white mobs rampaged through Memphis and New Orleans, burning Black churches, schools, and homes. Dozens were killed, and hundreds were wounded. These events shocked Northern voters and helped galvanize support for Radical Republicans in the midterms.

Johnson urged Southern legislatures to refuse to ratify the 14th Amendment, which Congress had approved in June. Hoping to maintain control of Congress, he went on a "Swing Around the Circle" speaking tour in August–September 1866, trying to rally support for candidates who backed his policies. Unfortunately for the increasingly reviled president, his gambit backfired spectacularly, as he was repeatedly drawn into undignified shouting matches with hecklers.

The whip of racist reaction was met by a new upsurge of radicalism, and Northern public opinion leaned toward greater federal intervention in Southern affairs. On election day, the Republicans won veto-proof majorities in both houses of Congress. As many historians have noted, if ever a party won a mandate, the Republicans did so in the 1866 congressional elections.

While rejoicing, Frederick Douglass urged renewed resolve in an article in the *Atlantic Monthly*:

> Whether the tremendous war so heroically fought and so victoriously ended shall pass into history a miserable failure, barren of permanent result . . . or whether, on the other hand, we shall, as the rightful reward of victory over treason, have a solid nation, entirely delivered from all contradictions and social antagonisms, based upon loyalty, liberty, and equality, must be determined one way or the other by the present session of Congress . . . All that is necessary to be done is to make the government consistent with itself, and render the rights of the States compatible with the sacred rights of human nature.
>
> The arm of the Federal government is long, but it is far too short to protect the rights of individuals in the interior of distant States. They must have the power to protect themselves, or they will go unprotected, spite of all the laws the Federal Government can put upon the national statute-book . . .
>
> The true way and the easiest way is to make our government entirely consistent with itself, and give to every loyal citizen the elective franchise,—a right and power which will be ever present, and will form a wall of fire for his protection.
>
> One of the invaluable compensations of the late Rebellion is the highly instructive disclosure it made of the true source of danger to republican government. Whatever may be tolerated in monarchical and despotic governments, no republic is safe that tolerates a privileged class, or

denies to any of its citizens equal rights and equal means to maintain them. What was theory before the war has been made fact by the war.

. . . In every considerable public meeting, and in almost every conceivable way, whether at court-house, school-house, or cross-roads, in doors and out, the subject has been discussed, and the people have emphatically pronounced in favor of a radical policy. Listening to the doctrines of expediency and compromise with pity, impatience, and disgust, they have everywhere broken into demonstrations of the wildest enthusiasm when a brave word has been spoken in favor of equal rights and impartial suffrage. Radicalism, so far from being odious, is now the popular passport to power.

. . . Let there be no hesitation. It would be a cowardly deference to a defeated and treacherous President, if any account were made of the illegitimate, one-sided, sham governments hurried into existence for a malign purpose in the absence of Congress. These pretended governments, which were never submitted to the people, and from participation in which four millions of the loyal people were excluded by Presidential order, should now be treated according to their true character, as shams and impositions, and supplanted by true and legitimate governments, in the formation of which loyal men, Black and white, shall participate.[28]

Radical Reconstruction

When the new session of Congress opened in March 1867, Radical, or Congressional Reconstruction, was off to the races. The indomitable Thaddeus Stevens had made his intent clear for decades:

Every humane and patriotic heart must grieve to see a bloody and causeless rebellion, costing thousands of human lives and millions of treasure. But as it was predetermined and inevitable, it was long enough delayed. Now is the appropriate time to solve the greatest problem ever submitted to civilized man . . .

What an opportunity is presented to this Republic to vindicate her consistency and become immortal. The occasion is forced upon us, and the invitation presented to strike the chains from four million of

> human beings, and create them *men*; to extinguish slavery on this whole continent; to wipe out, so far as we are concerned, the most hateful and infernal blot that has ever disgraced the escutcheon of man; to write a page in the history of the world whose brightness shall eclipse all the records of heroes and of sages.[29]

Congress quickly passed several Reconstruction Acts over Johnson's veto. One of these, the first Military Reconstruction Act, was formally titled "An act to provide for the more efficient government of the Rebel States." This law divided the former Confederacy into five districts under martial law, each led by a Union general. Tennessee was the only exception, as it had already rejoined the Union on July 24, 1866.

Congress set stricter conditions for seceded states to return. These included ratifying the 14th Amendment and ensuring Black men could vote. Anyone who had sworn to support the US Constitution but then joined the rebellion was barred from voting or holding office. Stevens and other Radicals, known as the "Committee of Fifteen," refused to seat former Confederate congressmen.

However, we should be under no illusions. At the time these conditions were being imposed on the South, only eight Northern states allowed Black men full voting rights. Black male suffrage was only achieved nationwide in 1870 through the 15th Amendment. So by no means had the Northern population moved beyond the racial enmity consciously cultivated since Bacon's Rebellion. As the future president, James Garfield, expressed it in 1865:

> I have a strong feeling of repugnance when I think of the Negro being made our political equal. And I would be glad if they could be colonized, sent to heaven, or got rid of in any decent way.[30]

As for the South, emancipation only exacerbated racial tensions, as the former slaves were now free to compete for jobs and land in an economically devastated landscape. In 1865 and 1866, the novelist John T. Trowbridge traveled across eight southern states.

Historian Gary Gallagher described Trowbridge's impressions in a book review for *The Civil War Monitor:*

> Trowbridge noted simmering tensions between former Confederates and white unionists but described antipathy toward African Americans that transcended wartime political divisions. "East Tennesseeans," he wrote bluntly, "though opposed to slavery and secession, do not like Negroes." Although pro-secession slaveholders had been "a bitter and violent minority" in this part of the state, there was "more prejudice against color among the middle and poorer classes—the 'Union' men of the South, who owned few or no slaves—than among planters who owned them by scores and hundreds." . . .
>
> Trowbridge closed with a mixed message concerning the region's future. He believed the White South had no stomach for renewed warfare, but of "*unarmed* rebellion, of continued sectional strife, stirred up by Southern politicians, there exists very great danger." The goal would be "to obtain the exclusive control of the freedmen and to make such laws for them as shall embody the prejudices of the late slave-holding society."[31]

Racism cannot be abolished by decree or force. It is a deeply ingrained social poison cultivated over centuries of exploitation and division. Only a fundamental transformation of society can lay the material basis for expunging this vile legacy of class society from the planet. In a world of superabundance, where no group needs to fight for survival at the expense of another, the economic substrate of racism would be eradicated.

However, this was not the outlook of the morally outraged Radical Republicans. They were determined to punish the South. Furthermore, they sought to remake it in their own image, with Lincoln's hometown of Springfield, Illinois, as their model. In the words of Congressman George Julian of Indiana, all that was needed was to establish:

> Small farms, thrifty tillage, free schools, social independence, flourishing manufactures and the arts, respect for honest labor, and equality of political rights.[32]

However, given the country's dramatically different regional histories, economies, cultures, and climates, it wasn't as simple as snapping one's fingers.

In an attempt to speed up the process, federal troops were stationed throughout the South to protect Black voters and enforce the new order. Disgruntled Confederates derided the occupation as "bayonet rule."

Nonetheless, the result of these measures was an inspiring blossoming of Black engagement in political life. After everything they had been through, the freedpeople had the least to lose and the most to win.

Immediately after emancipation, freedpeople had organized "colored conventions" in both the South and the North to push for their rights. Despite their efforts, however, at the beginning of 1867, fewer than 1 per cent of Black men in the US had the franchise. By the end of that year over 80 per cent could vote.

Between 1870 and 1877, fifteen Black congressmen from former Confederate states were elected to the US House of Representatives. Two US senators were elected from the Black-majority state of Mississippi. All told, over 1,500 Black Americans were elected to state and federal office.

Things were even more dramatic at the local level, as hundreds of Black legislators, sheriffs, and other officials were elected across the South. This stunning inversion of political power turned Southern society on its head. Former slaves now determined electoral outcomes, while many former Confederate leaders were unable to vote at all.

Grassroots Union Leagues popped up across the former Confederacy to provide mutual aid and mobilize Black voters. Electoral coalitions uniting Black Republicans with populist poor white farmers contested elections to defend their mutual interests. Mass political meetings were convened, with some participants walking 25 miles or more to attend. In port cities like New Orleans and Charleston, Black and white longshoremen united to organize labor unions and staged successful strikes for better wages and conditions.*

The response was an intensification of racist vigilante terror. According to an official of the Freedmen's Bureau in Sherman, Texas:

> The freedmen here have been kept in perfect terror of their lives by the desperate men of the County who are hostile and active in abusive assailing and murdering this inoffensive people all over the County for any and every pretext that human ingenuity can devise and often without any plea whatever.[33]

However, this, too, elicited an equal and opposite reaction, as Black militias sprang up to provide armed self-defense, often led by Union veterans.

The 1868 election

In February 1868, Congressional Radicals impeached Johnson—the first use of this provision against a president. The effort to remove him from office fell one vote short of the required two-thirds Senate majority,. Nonetheless, it sent a clear message in the run-up to the first presidential contest since Lincoln's murder.

Serving as a *de facto* plebiscite on Radical Reconstruction, the 1868 election was also the first time newly enfranchised Black men were eligible to vote in seven states that had recently been readmitted to the Union.

War hero Ulysses S. Grant ran on the Republican ticket against the former Democratic governor of New York, Horatio Seymour. As commanding general of the Union armies, Grant had overseen the occupation of the South in the war's aftermath. Initially, he had favored a lenient approach to Reconstruction to hasten the country's healing. However, he was deeply disturbed by the unhinged brutality he witnessed during the Memphis and New Orleans riots of 1866.

---

* During the antebellum period, slave labor was used to load port cargo. Freedmen formed the Longshoremen's Protective Union Association of Charleston (LPUA) in March 1869, and Black longshoremen were at the center of several militant strikes during the Reconstruction period.

By 1868, he was convinced that only strong federal intervention could protect the rights of the freedpeople. His campaign slogan was simple: "Let us have peace."

In an 1868 address calling for "Equal Rights for All"—including women—Frederick Douglass explained what was at stake:

> Since the termination of the war the popular sentiment is crying, "Down with the Rebellion!" and advocating the freedom of the slave, but they do not want them quite so free as themselves; they are willing to leave upon their limbs a few links of their chains to remind them of the rock out of which they have been hewn. There is no such thing as instantaneous emancipation; true, the links of the chain may be broken in an instant, but it will take not less than a century to obliterate all traces of the institution . . .
>
> There is some difference between the Republican and the Democratic Parties . . . The Democratic Party has, during the whole war, been in sympathy with the rebellion, while the Republican Party has always supported the Government. The Democratic Party opposes impeachment [of Andrew Johnson] and desires a "white man's government." . . . The Democratic Party opposes suffrage to both, but the Republican Party is in favor of enfranchising the Negro, and is largely in favor of enfranchising women . . . The Negro needs suffrage to protect his life and property, and to receive an education. He needs it for the safety of reconstruction and the salvation of the Union; for his elevation from the position of a drudge to that of an influential member of society.[34]

What followed was perhaps the most racist campaign in US history—and that's not hyperbole. The Democrats ran on an openly white-supremacist platform denouncing Black suffrage and Reconstruction as "Negro supremacy." They called openly for "a white man's government." As one leading conservative newspaper bluntly put it: "Shall Negroes or white men rule North Carolina?" As James McPherson writes:

> The Democratic platform branded the Reconstruction Acts "a flagrant usurpation of power . . . unconstitutional, revolutionary, and void," and demanded "the abolition of the Freedmen's Bureau, and all political

> instrumentalities designed to secure negro supremacy." This became the party's battle cry. Vice-presidential candidate Frank Blair of Missouri set the tone for the campaign with a public letter that became famous as the Brodhead Letter. "There is but one way to restore the Government and the Constitution, and that is for the President-elect to declare these acts null and void, compel the army to undo its usurpations at the South, disperse the carpet-bag State Governments, [and] allow the white people to reorganize their own governments."[35]

Terrorist vigilantes, including the Ku Klux Klan, suppressed Republican votes. Freedpeople had to arm themselves and travel in large groups to reach polling sites safely. More than 200 political murders were reported in Arkansas alone, and nearly a thousand people, most of them Black, were killed in Louisiana.

The campaign of terror was so effective that Republican candidates received a grand total of zero votes in eleven Georgia counties. Nonetheless, the state was initially called for the Republicans. After the state legislature expelled its Black members, however, the state's Electoral College delegates were awarded to the Democrats.

Despite this campaign of violence and intimidation, 500,000 Black men voted in the historic election, and Grant carried most Southern states. He was elected with 214 electoral votes to Seymour's 80, with a solid 53 per cent of the popular vote. It was a clear mandate for continuing Reconstruction under the protection of the federal government.

Dozens of Black men were elected to office, and Republicans dominated most Southern state governments. Some state legislatures were majority Black—an astounding turnaround after centuries of slavery. However, the racist violence that reared its head during the campaign served as an ominous warning for the future.

Bodies of armed men

Ulysses S. Grant was a consistent revolutionary democrat. He understood the role, strengths, and limits of the state's "bodies of armed men." He saw Reconstruction as an extension of the war to uproot slavery He was committed to bringing bourgeois-republican democracy to the South, and this necessarily included voting rights for the freedmen. As he put it:

> It became an absolute necessity [to extend the franchise], however, because of the foolhardiness of the President and the blindness of the Southern people to their own interest. As to myself, while strongly favoring the course that would be the least humiliating to the people who had been in rebellion, I gradually worked up to the point where, with the majority of the people, I favored immediate enfranchisement.[36]

Unfortunately, Grant was far too trusting, verging on naïveté, both in politics and in his personal relations. Historian Elizabeth Varon notes that neither Robert E. Lee nor a majority of Confederate veterans conceded moral defeat, despite submitting on the battlefield. They still saw theirs as an honorable cause, attributing their failure only to the North's superior resources.

They portrayed Reconstruction as a corrupt "foreign invasion" by Northern "carpetbagger"* adventurers, aided and abetted by collaborationist "scalawag" traitors and "uppity" freedpeople. And when racism and peer pressure weren't enough to cut across the class solidarity emerging organically between poor Blacks and whites, they turned to terror.

Throughout Reconstruction, the most vicious violence was used against Black enclaves and their white Republican allies, especially during election campaigns. The Ku Klux Klan, founded in Pulaski, Tennessee, in 1866, was the most notorious of the white terrorist organizations that took up the mantle of the former slave patrols, posing as defenders of Southern honor and virtue. Other, similar groups also mushroomed, including the White Leagues, Red Shirts, and Knights of the White Camelia.

---

* Term used by white Southerners to disparage Northerners who migrated South during Reconstruction. In their view, carpetbaggers—so-named because of the type of luggage they typically carried—were unscrupulous opportunists taking advantage of the unstable situation for personal economic and political gain.

As part of their campaign of violent intimidation, torch-bearing "night riders" in ceremonial robes would surround Black homes. They would erect burning crosses, throw firebombs, and whip, shoot, rape, mutilate, and hang Black people for perceived violations of racial etiquette or political activism. The sexual violence was intended to deny Black people their humanity. They would humiliate the men in particular for not being "real men" able to defend their homes, women, and children. Unsurprisingly, the freedpeople refused to go down without a fight.

The right to bear arms is a basic Constitutional right for a reason, and the freedpeople understood that any right you can't exercise in practice isn't really a right at all. They knew that to counter the armed bodies of men of the counterrevolution, they would need similar bodies of their own. As Engels explained in relation to progressive revolutionary violence in his 1872 article, "On Authority":

> A revolution is certainly the most authoritarian thing there is; it is the act whereby one part of the population imposes its will upon the other part by means of rifles, bayonets and cannon—authoritarian means, if such there be at all; and if the victorious party does not want to have fought in vain, it must maintain this rule by means of the terror which its arms inspire in the reactionists. Would the Paris Commune have lasted a single day if it had not made use of this authority of the armed people against the bourgeois? Should we not, on the contrary, reproach it for not having used it freely enough?[37]

With the Confederate leaders out of power, the ranks of many state militias swelled with thousands of Black men, often led by Black officers who had served during the war. At its peak, South Carolina's state militia included over 90,000 men, a majority of them Black. In other areas, or to supplement the official militias, mobile volunteer defense units were formed to protect against Klan raids and other vigilante attacks. In Texas, the state police organized by Governor Edmund Davis included many Black officers, who worked to suppress Klan violence in rural areas.

Due to their cowardice, the Klansmen hid under hoods and tended to target isolated individuals instead of armed militias. When they managed to get the upper hand against the Black militias, however, they were particularly ruthless.

During the Colfax, Louisiana, Massacre of 1873, approximately 150 Black militiamen were murdered when they surrendered after a three-week siege. During the Hamburg, South Carolina, Massacre of 1876, seven Black militia members, including a state legislator, were murdered after they too surrendered. From New Orleans to Charleston to Memphis, pogroms against Black people during Reconstruction previewed the horrifying events that would rain upon Tulsa, Oklahoma, in 1921.

Let's be crystal clear: the paramilitary violence wasn't "racist" in the abstract. There were powerful economic and political interests at stake, and the freedpeople and Radicals' commitment to equality and civic engagement posed a mortal threat to those interests. It was no accident that Klan violence always intensified in the weeks before an election. As the KKK's first "Grand Wizard," Nathan Bedford Forrest starkly declared:

> I have no powder to burn killing Negroes. I intend to kill the radicals . . . There is not a radical leader in this town but is a marked man, and if trouble should break out, not one of them would be left alive.[38]

The laws of the market alone have never been enough to impose capitalist relations on a people or place. Invariably, economic and political subterfuge and coercion have been required to atomize the masses and beat them into submission.

In the postwar South, extrajudicial pressure was meted out liberally to prevent laborers from seeking better wages and working conditions, from buying or renting land to work on their own, from carrying arms, serving on juries, testifying in court, voting, and so on.

Since state and local efforts at self-defense proved insufficient, however, President Grant stepped in with even greater federal assistance. Between 1870 and 1871, he pushed Congress to pass three Enforcement Acts, including the Ku Klux Klan Act, which allowed the suspension of *habeas corpus* and authorized federal prosecution of terrorist organizations to stamp them out.

Grant deployed additional troops throughout the South to protect Black voters and supervise elections, and used counterinsurgency tactics to suppress Klan violence. His Justice Department launched the most aggressive federal prosecution of white supremacist violence in American history. As James McPherson explains:

> The president sent several companies of cavalry South to cope with the fast-riding Klansmen. Because Grant was sensitive to Democratic charges of "military despotism," however, he used his powers sparingly. He suspended the writ of *habeas corpus* in only nine counties of South Carolina. There and elsewhere, especially in North Carolina and Mississippi, federal marshals aided by soldiers arrested thousands of Klansmen. Hundreds of others fled their homes to escape arrest. Federal grand juries handed down more than 3,000 indictments. Several hundred defendants pleaded guilty in return for suspended sentences.[39]

By 1872, the first wave of the KKK had largely been suppressed. However, with the onset of the "Long Depression" of 1873, public interest in "Southern issues" waned in the face of other, more pressing concerns.

Grant may have won the Civil War, but despite his best efforts, he failed to win the peace. By 1877, most Black militias had been disbanded or disarmed—often with the open cooperation, or at the very least, total indifference of federal troops. Nonetheless, the attempts at armed self-defense by the freedpeople during Reconstruction rank among the most heroic and inspiring episodes in American class-struggle history.

The rotten compromise of sharecropping

Everyone had different ideas as to how the Southern economy should be organized after the war.

The freedpeople equated freedom with owning their own land and producing their own means of subsistence. Plantation agriculture on a capitalist basis was seen as the reimposition of a kind of slavery, and they weren't entirely wrong. Understandably, they resisted being transformed into wage laborers.

Many freedpeople experienced an improved quality of life in the early years of Reconstruction, as generalized economic dislocation led to labor shortages and, in turn, higher wages and cotton prices.

Historians Roger Ransom and Richard Sutch estimate that under slavery, only 22 per cent of the wealth created during cotton growing went to the slaves. This mostly came as food, clothing, and shelter after accounting for land, seeds, tools, management, and labor. After emancipation, labor's share from cotton production rose to 56 per cent.

In 1860, over four-fifths of white planters and farmers in the cotton-growing South owned their land. By 1880, it was only two-thirds. Between 1857 and 1879, per capita agricultural income in the Cotton Belt rose by 46 per cent for Blacks and fell by 35 per cent for whites. The average freedperson's economic standing was still only half that of Southern whites. But compared to slavery, this represented the greatest proportionate redistribution of income in American history. These changes led to burning resentment and stoked racial hatred.

For their part, the petty-bourgeois Radical Republicans envisioned a utopian laissez-faire meritocracy of small producers and upwardly mobile wage laborers, with freedpeople in the vanguard.

As for the Southern planters, they desperately needed to restore cotton production to pay off their debts. However, having been deprived of their slaves—the main basis of their former wealth—they lacked the necessary capital to invest in modern machinery or even to pay wages.

And the Northern industrialists sought to impose full-on capitalist production on the region. Big capital's historical mandate wasn't to broaden the base of self-sufficient yeoman farmers working small plots of land. Thus, they opposed the confiscation, redistribution, and parcelization of land, instead urging the rapid resumption of agricultural production by wage labor on large, efficient plantations managed by big landowners, whether or not they had previously formed part of the slavocracy.

Reconciling all of these interests proved impossible, and no one got what they wanted. The outcome was the rotten compromise of sharecropping, a Frankenstein's monster that had reared its head on a smaller scale immediately after the war.

Too broke to invest in mechanization, and given the upward pressure on wages, Southern landowners stopped trying to assemble wage workers into large gangs to work their plantations. Instead, they rented parcels of land to freedpeople and poor whites unable to buy their own plots. The result was a bewildering patchwork of tenancy arrangements.

Tenant farming offered a fixed rent and greater personal autonomy for the farmer.

In the share-renting variant, the landlord typically provided land and housing in exchange for one-quarter of the crop as rent; the tenants controlled the farming operation and kept the rest of the harvest.

With sharecropping, the landlord typically provided the seed, fertilizer, tools, and sometimes draft animals in exchange for a larger share of the crop, usually half. Furthermore, the landlord dictated the mix of crops to be grown—almost always cash crops such as cotton or tobacco rather than food crops.

Since most landless farmers had no savings, and since the harvest only comes in once a year, they were forced to borrow money to purchase many necessities. As it happened, many landlords were also merchants, extending credit for items like food, clothing, and household goods at usurious rates, often as high as 50 per cent or 60 per cent.

After paying half of the crop to the landlord to cover rent, and another 10–20 per cent in interest on loans, many sharecroppers had little left over. To pay off their creditors, they were compelled to grow even more cash crops and fewer subsistence crops, further diminishing the land's productivity, making them even more dependent. Millions fell into an inescapable debt trap.

The crop-lien system meant that debts carried over year after year, binding generations of families to the land almost as effectively as slavery. The only silver lining was that sharecroppers kept day-to-day control over their families' labor and time, which would have been inconceivable under the old system. But this was far from the freedom they had dreamed of.

Sharecropping was, thus, neither independent peasant farming nor capitalist wage labor. Rather, it was a distorted, transitional form between the two. Although it may have offered marginal improvements in labor productivity in some circumstances, it failed to fully unlock the productive potential of the South's land and labor.

From the planters' perspective, the inefficiency of sharecropping and other tenancy arrangements was less than ideal. It fragmented operations, reduced their control over production, and stymied modernization. However, given their economic circumstances and the freedpeople's determined resistance to wage labor, it was the only system they could realistically maintain.

For the Northern capitalists, the compromise was acceptable, though it was far from their preferred outcome. Labor costs were kept low, and cotton flowed to Northern mills and international markets, which was what mattered most for continued capital accumulation. Sharecropping also didn't threaten to spread West to any significant degree, where expanding petty-commodity production was on the order of the day. As Eric Foner writes:

> To some extent, sharecropping "solved" the plantation labor shortage . . . In other ways, however, the system merely shifted the focus of labor conflict . . . For many Blacks, however, the credit system that grew up alongside sharecropping quickly undermined its promise of autonomy.[40]

The Freedman's Bank

Another example of the failed effort to ease the transition from slavery to wage slavery was the Freedman's Savings and Trust Company. More commonly known as the Freedman's Bank, it was established by Congress just before Lincoln's assassination to encourage savings among former slaves and Black soldiers. This would help bind them to capitalist financial markets and the moneyed economy.

By 1872, the bank had established 37 branches across 17 states, mostly in the South and in Washington, DC. At its peak, it held over $3.5 million in deposits from 67,000 depositors—equivalent to roughly $90 million today.

However, the bank's management misled depositors regarding interest payments, the use of deposited funds, and purported government guarantees. Like many other financial institutions, the Freedman's Bank fell victim to the Panic of 1873. In 1874, it collapsed altogether due to mismanagement, speculative investments, and outright fraud by its trustees, including Jay Cooke's brother, Henry.

In a desperate bid to save depositors, Frederick Douglass invested $10,000 of his own money and became the bank's president shortly before it imploded. As historian Walter Fleming noted:

> Some, looking for a scapegoat, were anxious that colored officials be in charge when the bank failed, as they were sure it would. Others thought that a Negro administration would restore the confidence of the depositors and enable the institution to survive until better times.[41]

When the bank finally went bust, Congress reimbursed just 62 per cent of account holders, and even then, only partially. Thousands of freedpeople lost their life savings. Their trust in the federal government and bourgeois financial institutions took a massive hit. It was yet another bitter welcome to the realities of life under capitalism.

The Reconstruction Amendments

The 13th, 14th, and 15th Amendments expanded civil rights and significantly altered the country's founding document.

The 13th Amendment, ratified in 1865, abolished slavery and involuntary servitude throughout the United States and its territories, except as punishment for a crime. This marked a historic victory. However, the Radical Republicans were incensed that it did not also include citizenship for the freedpeople.

This shortcoming was rectified with the 14th Amendment, ratified in 1868, which guaranteed citizenship rights to all persons born or naturalized in the United States, including formerly enslaved people. It codified due process and equal protection under the law, and prohibited states from denying these rights. It would subsequently serve as the basis for the doctrine of corporate personhood. It has been the subject of more litigation than any other part of the Constitution, including cases involving civil rights, abortion rights, same-sex marriage, and countless other issues.

As for voting rights, this was finally addressed in 1870 with the ratification of the 15th Amendment, which prohibited denial of the franchise based on race, color, or previous condition of servitude. In practice, however, this was not an iron-clad right, as various state-level restrictions during the Jim Crow era would keep hundreds of thousands of Black men off the election rolls. And of course, women, Native Americans, and others were still excluded.

Nonetheless, taken together, these amendments represented a "second founding of the American republic," in the words of Eric Foner.

Whereas the Bill of Rights, comprising the first ten amendments, sought to protect the states and "the people," both individually and collectively, from the *federal* government, the Reconstruction amendments assert the federal government's authority to protect "the people" from *state* governments.

The 1872 election

In what is considered by many to be the last real gasp of Reconstruction, Georgia was finally readmitted to the Union, on July 15, 1870, after the state legislature ratified the Fifteenth Amendment and Congress required Georgia to seat Black legislators. However, weariness over the process was already setting in. As the *New York Tribune* opined in April of that year:

> Let us have done with Reconstruction. The country is tired and sick of it. Let us have peace.[42]

The 1872 presidential election was the first in which all former Confederate states were able to participate. On the Republican side, Grant was handily renominated.

The Democrats nominated newspaper editor Horace Greeley, who also received the Liberal Republican Party's nomination. This was a faction that had split from the mainline Republicans over corruption scandals and Radical Reconstruction policies.

The Liberal Republicans opposed continued federal intervention in the South, argued for amnesty for former Confederates, and advocated for civil service reform to combat bribery, graft, and extortion. As far as Frederick Douglass was concerned, the Liberals were "mischievous and dangerous," and in the election of 1872:

> Whatsoever may be the faults of the Republican Party, it has within it the only element of friendship for the colored man's rights.[43]

Despite Greeley's name recognition and creeping Reconstruction fatigue, Grant was reelected in a landslide, with 286 electoral votes and 55.6 per cent of the popular vote—the highest proportion for any candidate between 1828 and 1904. Greeley died before the Electoral College met to formalize the process, making him the only presidential candidate in history to die during the election process.

Grant's decisive victory notwithstanding, the political coalition supporting Reconstruction was already fracturing. For the average voter, support for the process had been predicated more on anti-Southern rather than pro-freedmen sentiment. Grant could see that interest in Southern "nation-building" was waning, despite his best efforts to keep it going. As he stated in his Second Inaugural Address, on March 4, 1873:

> The effects of the late civil strife have been to free the slave and make him a citizen. Yet he is not possessed of the civil rights which citizenship should carry with it. This is wrong, and should be corrected. To this correction I stand committed, so far as Executive influence can avail.
>
> Social equality is not a subject to be legislated upon, nor shall I ask that anything be done to advance the social status of the colored man, except

> to give him a fair chance to develop what there is good in him, give him access to the schools, and when he travels let him feel assured that his conduct will regulate the treatment and fare he will receive.[44]

According to many of his contemporaries, Grant was personally honest and incorruptible. But he was far too credulous, and his loyalty to criminally corrupt cabinet members fatally weakened his administration. By 1874, as racist violence escalated across the South, Grant grew increasingly pessimistic.

"Redemption"

Achieving Reconstruction's most ambitious aims likely would have required decades of sustained federal military presence in the South. Even then, given the epoch's economic and political constraints, as well as mounting pressures from the world capitalist market, the project could only go so far. After more than a decade of open war and its slow-burning sequel, Northern patience had reached its limit.

Just months after Grant's second inauguration, the onset of the "Long Depression" of 1873 sounded the experiment's death knell. Massive unemployment and labor unrest exploded in the North. Northern capitalists and politicians had their hands full and they saw the South's men of property as natural allies against working-class militancy. As Washington's leading Republican paper wrote in January 1874:

> People are becoming tired of . . . abstract questions, in which the overwhelming majority of them have no interest. The Negro question, with all its complications, and the reconstruction of the Southern states, with all its interminable embroilment, have lost much of the power they once wielded.[45]

Congress refused to renew the Enforcement Acts, leaving the freedpeople at the mercy of the white-supremacist terrorists. The Democrats' plan to reclaim power and "redeem" the South was simple:

> I tell you that the white people have organized to carry this election, and intend to do it at all hazards; peaceably if possible and forcibly if necessary.[46]

Between 1873 and 1877, white supremacist Southern Democrats known as the "Redeemers" launched a coordinated campaign of voter intimidation, economic coercion, and murder to wrest political power from the Republicans. In some cases, paramilitary-backed Democrats battled Black militias to seize power, often in broad daylight and with complete impunity.

By 1880, roughly 90 per cent of the South's congressmen had served the Confederacy in some capacity, including eighteen generals and the commander of a notorious prisoner-of-war camp. To add insult to injury, even the Confederacy's vice president, Alexander Stephens, was elected to Congress in 1873 and later served as governor of Georgia.

Using cynical appeals to racial solidarity, the planters had finally succeeded in driving a wedge between poor Blacks and whites—just as they had done after Bacon's Rebellion in 1676. Racist tropes flooded the media, blaming the region's ills on "ignorant" Blacks and "greedy" Northern interlopers who took advantage of Dixie's noble heroes and heroines. These caricatures endured for decades and went mainstream in films such as *The Birth of a Nation** and *Gone With the Wind.*

The final nail in Reconstruction's coffin was the 1876 presidential election. The disputed contest between Republican Rutherford B. Hayes and Democrat Samuel Tilden sparked a serious constitutional crisis. Behind the scenes, Republican power brokers worked out a dirty deal with Southern Democrats. Hayes would be awarded the presidency in exchange for withdrawing all remaining federal troops from the South and ending the enforcement of Reconstruction-era legislation. Wendell Phillips, the abolitionist and

* A 1915 D. W. Griffiths film set during the Civil War and Reconstruction. Based on the novel The Clansman: A Historical Romance of the Ku Klux Klan by Thomas Dixon Jr., the film is infamous for its racist depiction of freedpeople, especially Black men, and its heroic portrayal of the KKK. President Woodrow Wilson hosted a screening at the White House that year. It was a massive commercial success and helped inspire a revival of the Klan later that year. The refounded KKK wore regalia inspired by costumes from the film.

Radical Republican leader, had warned of the danger of not carrying the struggle through to the end in an 1865 speech:

> In that battle the North has conquered. Now comes the question, whether I shall be permitted to organize the southern and rebelling half of the Union on my policy—universal, absolute equality before the law? The idea we fought for, shall we be allowed to carry it out in politics ? The radical members of the Republican party say yes . . . The present policy is worse than an error, it is a crime. Two hundred and fifty thousand loyal graves; three hundred and twenty-five thousand men sacrificed in this war; four billions of dollars, a debt that is to hang over and shorten the comforts of our children. Now comes the crisis . . . And so we say, in the things they are now doing, "The North surrenders to the South, and we shall be governed by the white race of the Southern States."[47]

The inimitable W.E.B Du Bois explained it this way:

> It was not, then, race and culture calling out of the South in 1876; it was property and privilege, shrieking to its kind, and privilege and property heard and recognized the voice of its own.
>
> The bargain of 1876 was essentially an understanding by which the Federal Government ceased to sustain the right to vote of half of the laboring population of the South, and left capital as represented by the old planter class, the new Northern capitalist, and the capitalist that began to rise out of the poor whites, with a control of labor greater than in any modern industrial state in civilized lands. Out of that there has arisen in the South an exploitation of labor unparalleled in modern times, with a government in which all pretense at party alignment or regard for universal suffrage is given up. The methods of government have gone uncriticized, and elections are by secret understanding and manipulation; the dictatorship of capital in the South is complete.[48]

In April 1877, the last federal troops were pulled out of the South, leading to the immediate collapse of the remaining Republican state governments.

Convict leasing and Jim Crow

By the Fall of that year, white supremacist "Redeemer" governments controlled virtually every Southern state. They immediately set about dismantling the progressive achievements of Reconstruction. To ensure white, Democratic control, they replaced elected local officials with appointed ones and rewrote state constitutions to disenfranchise Black voters, using loopholes in the 15th Amendment.

On the labor front, convict leasing expanded dramatically. Vagrancy laws were aggressively enforced, and punishment for petty crimes intensified. Tens of thousands of Black men were imprisoned on minor or fabricated charges and hired out to plantations, mines, and railroad companies. By 1880, convict labor was a significant component of the Southern economy. Some states leased out 90 per cent or more of their overwhelmingly Black prison population.

The system generated massive profits for private companies and steady revenue for cash-strapped Southern states. Condemned "criminals" worked in chain gangs building railroads, mining coal, harvesting timber, and working on plantations under brutal conditions. Mortality rates in convict-lease camps were staggering. Sometimes they exceeded 25 per cent annually in coal mines and turpentine camps. An investigation into a Mississippi convict hospital in 1887 found that:

> [The patients'] backs cut in great wales, scars, and blisters, some with the skin peeling off in pieces as the result of severe beatings . . . They are lying there, dying some of them on bare boards, so poor and emaciated that their bones almost came through their skin.[49]

Northerners denounced it as the "newest and most revolting form of slavery." Nonetheless, the convict-lease system persisted in some forms into the 1940s, laying the groundwork for the mass incarceration and exploitation of prison labor that continues to this day.

After 1876, all that remained of the bright shooting star of Radical Reconstruction was legal equality and citizenship at the federal level. Even then, this was often more abstract than real. In some ways, the conditions faced by many former slaves were even worse than before emancipation. To quote the powerful prose of W.E.B. Du Bois once again:

> To be a poor man is hard, but to be a poor race in a land of dollars is the very bottom of hardships.[50]

Nearly a century of a kind of apartheid lay ahead, as the racial caste system of Jim Crow was systematically rolled out to "divide and rule" the South. State after state passed laws mandating racial segregation in schools, transportation, accommodations, parks, and public facilities. Literacy tests, poll taxes, grandfather clauses, and all-white primaries and parties were used to strip Black citizens of voting rights without technically violating the 15th Amendment.

In 1896, *Plessy v. Ferguson* established the "separate but equal" doctrine, granting constitutional legitimacy to segregation until the Supreme Court overturned its own ruling with *Brown v. Board of Education* in 1954.

By 1900, Black voter registration in the South had plummeted to less than 10 per cent, and in many counties, it was 0 per cent. The courts, police, and legislatures worked hand-in-glove with lynch mobs and night riders, and economic coercion was leveraged to maintain white supremacy.

According to the Equal Justice Initiative, there were 4,075 lynchings of Black people in 12 Southern states between 1877 and 1950. However, no part of the country was safe from the metastasized poison of racism, with another 300 Black people lynched *outside* the South during the same period.

Despite this living nightmare, only around 50,000–70,000 freedpeople left the South altogether during Reconstruction; it wasn't until the First and Second Great Migrations in the 20th century that they moved in their millions to the North, West, and Midwest.

Divide and rule

The main task of the now broadly united American ruling class had been accomplished: preventing the emergence of a united American working class. As the pioneering labor leader William Sylvis put it before his death in 1869:

> Our cause is a common one. It is a war between poverty and wealth . . . This moneyed power is fast eating up the substance of the people. We have made war upon it, and we mean to win it. If we can, we will win through the ballot box; if not, then we shall resort to sterner means[51] . . . If we can succeed in convincing these people [Black workers] to make common cause with us . . . We will have a power in this country that will shake Wall Street out of its boots.[52]

Sylvis represented the most advanced section of the early labor leadership. However, even his efforts could not overcome the pernicious divisions actively injected into the workers' movement by the bosses.

Through Jim Crow and its offshoots, American workers have been cleaved along racial lines for decades—all to serve the interests of the big capitalists and landlords. Far from being "privileged," white workers have been materially harmed by this arrangement. They have accepted lower wages, worse working conditions, and reduced public services in exchange for the dubious satisfaction of not being at the very bottom of the social hierarchy.

Politically, the post-Reconstruction "solid South" was dominated by the Democratic Party for nearly a century until the civil rights movement and thinly veiled racism of Nixon's "Southern strategy" flipped the script. This was reinforced by the reactionary "Lost Cause" narrative, which dominated history books and the minds of Americans on both sides of the Mason-Dixon line for decades.

First coined by Edward Pollard in his 1866 book, *The Lost Cause: A New Southern History of the War of the Confederates*, this was a blatant attempt at saving face while whitewashing a reactionary cause:

> The conquered South has yet its place in history; and that place is to be made by a true and faithful narrative of the war . . .
>
> The war was not a revolt; it was not a rebellion; it was truly a war between two nations—a war of ideas . . .
>
> It would be immeasurably the worst consequence of defeat in this war that the South should lose its moral and intellectual distinctiveness as a people, and cease to assert its well-known superiority in civilization.[53]

As Clement Evans, a former Confederate general, Methodist minister, and one-time commander of the United Confederate Veterans, is reported to have said in a Memorial Day address given in 1896:

> If we cannot justify the South in the act of Secession, we will go down in History solely as a brave, impulsive, but rash people who attempted in an illegal manner to overthrow the Union for our Country.[54]

In his wildly popular early-20th-century works, historian William Dunning painted Reconstruction as a misguided and tragic experiment that failed because unqualified freedmen and corrupt carpetbaggers mismanaged Southern state governments.

Progressive historians like Charles and Mary Beard attempted to push back against this cynical lie with their variant of economic determinism.

But it wasn't until W.E.B. Du Bois published *Black Reconstruction in America* in 1935 that a more fully rounded Marxist interpretation of the era emerged. Du Bois put special emphasis on the role of the slaves in securing their own freedom, both during and after the war. More recent historians, including Eric Foner and James McPherson, have built on Du Bois's work, documenting the unprecedented opportunities Reconstruction opened for Black Americans before everything was systematically dismantled.

Of course, the truth about Reconstruction is that its failure had nothing to do with the racial inferiority of the freedmen, and everything to do with outright betrayal by the new master class—the capitalists.

As Du Bois explained:

> The espousal of the doctrine of Negro inferiority by the South was primarily because of economic motives and the interconnected political urge necessary to support the slave industry. The race element was emphasized in order that property holders could get the support of the majority of white laborers and make it more possible to exploit Negro labor. But the race philosophy came as a new and terrible thing to make labor unity or labor class-consciousness impossible.[55]

Reconstruction's collapse left a cancerous sore on the body of the American working class that remains open and oozing to this day. Incredibly, most Americans know virtually nothing about this period. And yet, understanding the promise and tragedy of Reconstruction is essential if we are to understand the country in which we fight for socialism.

A legacy of backwardness

After the war, cotton prices fell due to international competition, and it was no longer the king of the US economy. And yet, by 1870, the South was producing more of the crop than in 1860.

A significant portion of the South's postwar economic development was shaped by outside capital—especially Northern and British investors—who gained control and influence over railroads, finance, and other key industries to extract profits from the region. This limited locally rooted capital formation and kept the region's economy dependent on low-wage labor and the production of raw materials. In all this, the interests of the freedpeople were barely even considered. As Eric Foner describes:

> By all accounts, the Northern men who leased plantations were "an unsavory lot," attracted by the quick profits seemingly guaranteed in wartime cotton production. In the scramble among army officers illegally engaged in cotton deals and Northern investors seeking to "pluck the golden goose" of the South, the rights of Blacks received scant regard.[56]

Some industrial development took place in urban centers such as Atlanta, Richmond, Birmingham, New Orleans, Charleston, Memphis, Nashville, Savannah, Mobile, and Louisville. But the country's largest geographic region remained predominantly agricultural and economically subordinate to the North.

By the mid 1870s, an estimated 75–80 per cent of Black agricultural workers were sharecroppers. Only a small minority of freedpeople, perhaps 5–8 per cent, managed to acquire their own land. The remaining 10 to 15 per cent moved to Southern cities to work as domestic servants, artisans, dock workers, and above all, in textile mills.

Poor Blacks and whites alike congregated in the mill towns made possible by Northern investment. In 1860, the South had just 10,000 spinning mill workers. By 1880, there were 16,700, and by 1900, the number had ballooned to 97,500. Nonetheless, the pace of development in absolute terms remained paltry compared to the manufacturing boom exploding in other parts of the country.

This legacy of economic underdevelopment persisted for decades. On the eve of the Civil War, Southern per capita income had been two-thirds the Northern average. By 1880, it had fallen to two-fifths and would remain around that level well into the 20th century.

Before the war, Southerners had been largely self-sufficient in food. After the war, they had to import nearly half of it, usually at prices far higher than it would have cost to grow their own.

In 1860, the would-be Confederate states accounted for 10 per cent of the country's manufacturing capital and 30 per cent of its railroads. By 1880, it had just 5 per cent of the manufacturing capital and 17 per cent of its railroads.

In 1880, 20 per cent of Southern whites and 70 per cent of Blacks were illiterate. Fewer than three-fifths of white children and two-fifths of Black children of school age attended school. The South spent less than one-third as much per pupil as the north. In the rural South, the average school term was three months or less.

It wasn't until around 1890 that full-fledged capitalist agriculture was established throughout the South. Even then, tenant farming and sharecropping persisted in some areas well into the 1960s, condemning many areas of the rural South to extreme backwardness.

Only when the chaos of Reconstruction subsided did Northern investors begin to shift their capital south in earnest to take full advantage of the region's low wages and lack of unions. Given these propitious conditions, by the 1930s, the South's textile-producing capacity had surpassed New England's. As historian C. Vann Woodward observed:

> The vision that inspired the Southern businessman was that of a South modeled upon the industrial Northeast. The Richmond banker and railroad president John Skelton Williams, for example, said in 1898 that he was "hoping to see in the South in the not distant future many railroads and business institutions as great as the Pennsylvania Railroad, the Mutual Life Insurance Company, the Carnegie Steel Company or the Standard Oil Company." It was assumed, of course, that as such corporations developed, Southern counterparts of the Morgans, Carnegies, and Rockefellers would rise with them . . .
>
> As the old century drew to a close and the new century progressed through the first decade, the penetration of the South by Northeastern capital continued at an accelerated pace. The Morgans, Mellons, and Rockefellers sent their agents to take charge of the region's railroads, mines, furnaces, and financial corporations, and eventually of many of its distributive institutions. Southern counterparts of the Northeastern masters, however, failed to appear. The number of Southern businessmen increased steadily, and some of them waxed in fortune. But the new men, as well as many of the old, acted as agents, retainers, and executives—rarely as principals. The economy over which they presided was increasingly coming to be one of branch plants, branch banks, captive mines, and chain stores . . .
>
> Other industries, too numerous to examine in detail, increased production in their Southern factories or were established in the South for the first time in those years, and usually for the same reasons. They were

> of one general type—the "low wage, low-value-creating industries." The South seems to have had a fatal attraction for them. They were the industries that gave the first rough processing to the South's chief crops and resources, the physical bulk of which often made it economical to do the manufacturing near the source of the raw material. Manufacturers of these products sought large supplies of cheap, unskilled labor. Cotton yarn and coarse cloth, cane sugar, turpentine and rosin, polished rice, cottonseed oil, fertilizers, wood-distillation products, liquors, lumber and timber, and tobacco products bulked large in the vaunted industrialization of the New South. In general, they were the type of industry which added the lowest value of product per wage earner. Only rarely did the South develop an industry, such as furniture manufacturing in North Carolina, which finished goods for the ultimate consumer.[57]

Thus, in many ways, the so-called "New South" became an internal colony of the capitalist Northeast, with the mineral-rich Mountain states suffering a similar fate.

A revolution betrayed—and the limits of bourgeois democracy

In his 1967 speech, "Three Evils," Martin Luther King, Jr. summed up the betrayal of Reconstruction as follows:

> In 1863 the Negro was granted freedom from physical slavery through the Emancipation Proclamation. But he was not given land to make that freedom meaningful. At the same time, our government was giving away millions of acres of land in the Midwest and the West, which meant that the nation was willing to undergird its white peasants from Europe with an economic floor, while refusing to do it for its Black peasants from Africa who were held in slavery two hundred and forty four years. And this is why Frederick Douglass would say that emancipation for the Negro was freedom to hunger, freedom to the winds and rains of heaven, freedom without roofs to cover their heads. It was freedom without bread to eat, without land to cultivate. It was freedom and famine at the same time. And it is a miracle that the Negro has survived.[58]

Reconstruction represented a heroic attempt to carry the Second American Revolution to its fullest possible conclusion. Its failure is an object lesson in the limits of bourgeois democracy. In the scathing words of Malcolm X:

> [The Black man] doesn't see any progress that he has made since the Civil War. He sees not one iota of progress because, number one, if the Civil War had freed him, he wouldn't need civil-rights legislation today. If the Emancipation Proclamation, issued by that great shining liberal called Lincoln, had freed him, he wouldn't be singing "We Shall Overcome" today. If the amendments to the Constitution had solved his problem, his problem wouldn't still be here today. And if the Supreme Court desegregation decision of 1954 was genuinely and sincerely designed to solve his problem, his problem wouldn't be with us today.[59]

Picking up where the First Revolution left off, the historic tasks of the Civil War and Reconstruction remained national-democratic in nature. One of these tasks is the liquidation of earlier forms of economic organization and the establishment of relations suitable to the full flourishing of capitalism. Abolishing chattel slavery was certainly a tremendous step in that direction. However, the postwar period was a convoluted mess, and it took several decades before capitalist relations were fully embedded throughout the country.

National liberation and unification are another combined national-democratic task. This was also broadly achieved. To be sure, American regionalism still underlies much of American culture and politics. But the Civil War and its aftermath transformed what was still a relatively loose confederation of semi-autonomous former colonies into a genuinely federal state. With the American nation-state largely consolidated, its emboldened ruling class set to work expanding across the continent and, eventually, around the globe.

Another major national-democratic task is the agrarian revolution and redistribution of land. During Europe's Golden Age of Revolution, this meant confiscating royal, noble, and Church estates and distributing land to the peasantry, thus undermining the basis of feudal power and paving the way for the freer development of capitalism.

In the context of post–Civil War America, land redistribution would have meant breaking up the plantations of the defeated slavocracy and giving freedpeople their "forty acres and a mule." By the time of Reconstruction, however, the US was well on its way to becoming an industrial capitalist powerhouse. Micronizing the large agricultural estates into scattered, inefficient plots was at odds with the needs of capitalist agriculture at scale, and was naturally opposed by the big bourgeoisie. With no economic basis for meaningful political participation, the freedpeople's hard-won political rights proved ephemeral and were eventually stripped away.

As for land tenancy and agricultural production, by the mid–20th century, large corporate operations finally dominated Southern agriculture, with a tiny percentage of landowners controlling the vast majority of agricultural acreage.

Then there's the national-democratic task of establishing a democratic republic with broad-based suffrage, civil liberties, and popular sovereignty. This, along with formal legal equality for all citizens regardless of birth, nationality, or religion, was also eventually achieved, at least on paper.

The term "democracy" comes from the Greek words *demos* (people) and *kratos* (power, or rule), literally meaning "rule by the people." In Ancient Athens, however, only a minority of male property owners were considered "people" and included in the democratic process. Across the millennia, the ruling classes have fought tooth and nail to limit the franchise, ceding ground only under overwhelming pressure from below.

As we saw in the aftermath of the First Revolution, the capitalist mode of production is inherently incompatible with genuine rule by the majority. By definition, bourgeois democracy is democracy for the bourgeois—the rest is political theater. If the majority really ruled, it wouldn't allow a minuscule fraction of the population to control the overwhelming majority of the wealth.

In the hopes of preventing the masses from getting any dangerous ideas, the concept that democracy means active citizen participation and majority rule has been thoroughly undermined. Instead, we are told, we should content ourselves with abstract rights that for the majority mean little in practice.

The meaning of freedom has also been twisted to fit the needs of the capitalist class. This lofty goal, for which countless millions have sacrificed their lives over thousands of years, is no longer synonymous with economic autonomy or freedom from others' claims on our bodies and labor. Instead, it is reduced to the ability to compete in the marketplace without too much government intrusion.

However, as Frederick Douglass presciently warned:

> No republic is safe that tolerates a privileged class, or denies to any of its citizens equal rights and equal means to maintain them.[60]

The American republic has long tolerated a privileged class and denied its citizens equal means to maintain their rights.

To put it simply, genuine freedom and equality cannot be fully realized within the limits of capitalism, even in an economically advanced country like the US. Only the socialist revolution and a workers' republic can consummate the deep-seated aspirations still held by the vast majority of its inhabitants.

Class struggle and the legacy of sectionalism

The bitter truth is that in the 1860s and '70s, the objective conditions for building socialism weren't yet ripe, either in the United States or anywhere else. The division of society into two great opposing class camps was still at a relatively early stage of differentiation. Despite its ruthless brutality, capitalism still had a historically progressive role to play in developing the productive forces. Even the most radical of the Radical Republicans weren't about to nationalize the economy or form a workers' government.

But did the earthshaking experiment of Reconstruction really have to end in a miscarriage of racist terror and betrayal? In some form or another, it probably did.

Had he not been killed, it's possible Lincoln could have guided the country through a less frenzied version of Reconstruction. Maybe he could have prevented former Confederate leaders from sitting in Congress, kept a lid on the KKK, or cut across the spread of sharecropping. But in the final analysis, the end result would have been the same: the domination of capital over wage labor throughout the country. And wage labor is a living nightmare for most workers, even in the best of times.

And even if he hadn't used it himself to divide and rule, the miasma of racism was going to be a factor. For all the talk of free labor and democratic rights, the convergence of two interrelated class struggles—the workers in the North, and poor Black and white farmers in the South—was the ruling class's worst nightmare.

They simply couldn't tolerate the harmonious emergence of a united American working class, which would have accelerated the demise of their system. Appetite comes with eating, and the dangerous upsurge of revolutionary democracy and racial unity seen during Reconstruction had to be ruthlessly stamped out if capitalism was to survive unchallenged.

Fortunately, in the decades since the freedpeople were sold down the river, the working class has been immeasurably strengthened, and the objective conditions for socialism are now beyond rotten-ripe.

After decades of marginalization and neglect, the backwardness of the South is also turning into its opposite. It has been transformed from an agrarian backwater into one of the most dynamic industrial regions in the country.

The South now attracts significant investment from both domestic and foreign corporations seeking lower labor costs and low union density—another legacy of the Jim Crow era. Major manufacturing hubs and a fresh working class have emerged across the former Confederacy, particularly in Texas, Tennessee, Alabama, and the Carolinas.

During the Civil War, New York state's industrial output was four times that of the entire South. Today, the state of Texas manufactures more than the state of New York. This is yet another striking example of combined and uneven development. The South shall indeed rise again; not in the racist and reactionary manner of the past, but as an integral part of the American socialist revolution.

"The work to be achieved by the American Opposition has international-historic significance, for in the last historic analysis all the problems of our planet will be decided upon American soil. There is much in favor of the idea that, from the standpoint of revolutionary order, Europe and the East stand ahead of the United States. But a course of events is possible in which this order might be broken in favor of the proletariat of the United States.

Moreover, even if you assume that America which now shakes the whole world will be shaken last of all, the danger remains that a revolutionary situation in the United States may catch the vanguard of the American proletariat unprepared, as was the case in Germany in 1923, in England in 1926, and in China in 1925 to 1927.

We must not for a minute lose sight of the fact that the might of American capitalism rests more and more upon a foundation of world economy with its contradictions and crises, military and revolutionary. This means that a social crisis in the United States may arrive a good deal sooner than many think, and have a feverish development from the beginning. Hence the conclusion: It is necessary to prepare."

—Leon Trotsky, "A Letter to the American Trotskyists"
March 1929

Toward the Third American Revolution

Revolution and counterrevolution are dialectically interrelated phenomena inseparable from the class struggle. Marx and Engels painted a vivid picture of this dynamic in the *Communist Manifesto*:

> Freeman and slave, patrician and plebeian, lord and serf, guild-master and journeyman, in a word, oppressor and oppressed, stood in constant opposition to one another, carried on an uninterrupted, now hidden, now open fight, a fight that each time ended, either in a revolutionary reconstitution of society at large, or in the common ruin of the contending classes.[1]

Every revolutionary process has floodtides and ebbs. In its short 250-year history, the US has experienced multiple revolutionary upswings followed by periods of reactionary retreat. However, as Trotsky explained, even when counterrevolution gains the upper hand, it never hurls society back as far as the revolution's starting point.[2] In this way, American capitalism has ratcheted ever forward over the centuries.

Throughout this process, the social, economic, and numerical weight of the working class has been immeasurably strengthened. The amorphous and fractured class composition of colonial times is a thing of the past. Two great classes now confront each other in a life-and-death struggle over the future of humanity. Once the workers move decisively to seize political and economic power, the material and social basis for counterrevolution will be fatally undermined.

Primed for imperialist lift off

In his farewell address, George Washington warned his countrymen against foreign adventures:

> The Great rule of conduct for us in regard to foreign nations is in extending our commercial relations, to have with them as little *political* connection as possible. So far as we have already formed engagements, let them be fulfilled with perfect good faith . . .
>
> Europe has a set of primary interests, which to us have none, or a very remote relation. Hence she must be engaged in frequent controversies, the causes of which are essentially foreign to our concerns. Hence therefore it must be unwise in us to implicate ourselves, by artificial ties, in the ordinary vicissitudes of her politics, or the ordinary combinations and collisions of her friendships or enmities.
>
> Our detached and distant situation invites and enables us to pursue a different course. If we remain one People, under an efficient government, the period is not far off, when we may defy material injury from external annoyance; when we may take such an attitude as will cause the neutrality we may at any time resolve upon to be scrupulously respected; when belligerent nations, under the impossibility of making acquisitions upon us, will not lightly hazard the giving us provocation; when we may choose peace or war, as our interest, guided by justice, shall Counsel.
>
> Why forego the advantages of so peculiar a situation? Why quit our own to stand upon foreign ground? Why, by interweaving our destiny with that of any part of Europe, entangle our peace and prosperity in the toils of European Ambition, Rivalship, Interest, Humor, or Caprice?

> 'Tis our true policy to steer clear of permanent Alliances, with any portion of the foreign world . . . [I]n my opinion, it is unnecessary and would be unwise to extend them.[3]

In 1821, John Quincy Adams echoed these isolationist sentiments in a famous Fourth of July address delivered in the US Capitol:

> [America] goes not abroad in search of monsters to destroy. She is the well-wisher to the freedom and independence of all. She is the champion and vindicator only of her own. She will recommend the general cause by the countenance of her voice, and the benignant sympathy of her example. She well knows that by once enlisting under other banners than her own, were they even the banners of foreign independence, she would involve herself beyond the power of extrication, in all the wars of interest and intrigue, of individual avarice, envy, and ambition, which assume the colors and usurp the standard of freedom.
>
> The fundamental maxims of her policy would insensibly change from liberty to force. The frontlet upon her brow would no longer beam with the ineffable splendor of freedom and independence; but in its stead would soon be substituted an imperial diadem, flashing in false and tarnished lustre the murky radiance of dominion and power. She might become the dictatress of the world; she would be no longer the ruler of her own spirit.[4]

Unfortunately for the champions of the early American republic, capital's drive to accumulate land, labor, resources, and profits runs roughshod over ideals such as freedom and independence. This self-perpetuating logic has defined capitalism from birth to decay, leaving no room for majority-rule democracy, let alone basic human decency.

Foreign policy is merely an extension of domestic policy, and the foreign policy of capitalism is imperialism. Once the American bourgeoisie conquered or otherwise dominated the North American continent, it turned its attention to the world. The former British colony was transformed into its opposite—the most vicious imperialist power humanity has ever seen. Like the fabled scorpion on the frog, it simply couldn't help itself.

The fight for equality continues

In 2011, the Occupy movement took the country by storm, raising the slogan "we are the 99 per cent!" However, the idea that the majority of Americans are dominated by a tiny minority is not new. As an ordinary Pennsylvanian wrote in a letter published April 5, 1775:

> Do not the mechanics and farmers constitute ninety-nine out of a hundred of the people of America? If these, by their occupations, are to be excluded from having any share in the choice of their rulers, or forms of government, would it not be best to acknowledge the jurisdiction of the British Parliament, which is composed entirely of GENTLEMEN?[5]

Much has changed over the centuries, and yet so much remains the same. Despite the rhetorical promise of the Declaration of Independence and Emancipation Proclamation, we still live in a society divided into exploiters and exploited. Only the socialist transition between capitalism and communism can begin to lay the basis for genuine freedom and equality. As Lenin wrote in *The State and Revolution*:

> Democracy means equality. The great significance of the proletariat's struggle for equality and of equality as a slogan will be clear if we correctly interpret it as meaning the abolition of *classes*. But democracy means only *formal* equality. And as soon as equality is achieved for all members of society *in relation* to ownership of the means of production, that is, equality of labor and wages, humanity will inevitably be confronted with the question of advancing further, from formal equality to actual equality, i.e., to the operation of the rule "from each according to his ability, to each according to his needs."
>
> By what stages, by means of what practical measures humanity will proceed to this supreme aim, we do not and cannot know. But it is important to realize how infinitely mendacious is the ordinary bourgeois conception of socialism as something lifeless, rigid, fixed once and for all, whereas in reality *only* socialism will be the beginning of a rapid, genuine, truly mass forward movement, embracing first the *majority* and then the whole of the population, in all spheres of public and private life.[6]

This is why communists fight for equality in life, or "equality in fact,"[7] as Lenin put it—not mere equality in law. We understand that this will only be possible once the artificial constraints and scarcity of the profit system are replaced by a system in which human needs, comfort, and happiness truly reign supreme. Our confidence in the socialist future is not a pipe dream. It flows from the recognition that the material basis for building a world of superabundance already exists.

Expropriate the expropriators!

For centuries, land and slavery dominated the class struggle in America. These questions have largely been resolved through the revolutions and mass expropriations of the past. Slavery is no longer a recognized form of property, and capitalism unquestionably dominates every aspect of our economic lives, from agriculture to manufacturing, from the media to technology.

The concentration of capital is breathtaking. Just 500 or so companies account for over two-thirds of US GDP. Just four corporations control 85 per cent of beef packing and 70 per cent of pork processing; two control nearly 90 per cent of the tractor and combine market; and four dominate the seed and agrichemical sectors. Six companies control 90 per cent of the media. The "Magnificent Seven" tech companies account for over one-third of the S&P 500's market value.

The kind of property to be expropriated by the Third American Revolution is self-evident: private property in the means of production. By this, we mean the key levers of the economy, not the personal property of individuals. Anything considered "too big to fail" is too big to be left in private hands and the whims of the market. While the power of capital is formidable, its concentration in so few hands actually facilitates our historic task. As Marx explained in *Capital*:

> Along with the constantly diminishing number of the magnates of capital, who usurp and monopolize all advantages of this process

> of transformation, grows the mass of misery, oppression, slavery, degradation, exploitation; but with this too grows the revolt of the working class, a class always increasing in numbers, and disciplined, united, organized by the very mechanism of the process of capitalist production itself.
>
> The monopoly of capital becomes a fetter upon the mode of production, which has sprung up and flourished along with, and under it. Centralization of the means of production and socialization of labor at last reach a point where they become incompatible with their capitalist integument. This integument is burst asunder. The knell of capitalist private property sounds. The expropriators are expropriated.
>
> The capitalist mode of appropriation, the result of the capitalist mode of production, produces capitalist private property. This is the first negation of individual private property, as founded on the labor of the proprietor. But capitalist production begets, with the inexorability of a law of Nature, its own negation. It is the negation of negation. This does not re-establish private property for the producer, but gives him individual property based on the acquisition of the capitalist era: i.e., on cooperation and the possession in common of the land and of the means of production.
>
> The transformation of scattered private property, arising from individual labor, into capitalist private property is, naturally, a process incomparably more protracted, violent, and difficult than the transformation of capitalistic private property, already practically resting on socialized production, into socialized property. In the former case, we had the expropriation of the mass of the people by a few usurpers; in the latter, we have the expropriation of a few usurpers by the mass of the people.[8]

The expropriation of the loyalists and slave lords in the 18th and 19th centuries was epic for its time. However, this will pale in comparison to the expropriation of the Fortune 500 by the American workers' state. Instead of being run for the squanderous indulgence of the few, the commanding economic heights will be democratically and rationally planned in the interests of all.

The earth belongs to the living

Writing from Paris in 1789, Thomas Jefferson sent an extraordinary letter to James Madison:

> The question Whether one generation of men has a right to bind another, seems never to have been started either on this or our side of the water. Yet it is a question of such consequences as not only to merit decision, but place also, among the fundamental principles of every government. The course of reflection in which we are immersed here on the elementary principles of society has presented this question to my mind; and that no such obligation can be so transmitted, I think, is very capable of proof. I set out on this ground, which I suppose to be self-evident, "*that the earth belongs in usufruct to the living;*" that the dead have neither powers nor rights over it. The portion occupied by any individual ceases to be his when himself ceases to be, and reverts to the society . . .[9]
>
> [I]t may be proved that no society can make a perpetual constitution, or even a perpetual law. The earth belongs always to the living generation. They may manage it then, and what proceeds from it, as they please, during their usufruct. They are masters too of their own persons, and consequently may govern them as they please. But persons and property make the sum of the objects of government. The constitution and the laws of their predecessors extinguished them, in their natural course, with those who gave them being. This could preserve that being till it ceased to be itself, and no longer.
>
> Every constitution, then, and every law, naturally expires at the end of 19 years.* If it be enforced longer, it is an act of force, and not of right . . .[10]

It has been several generations since the last American revolution. In the interim, the world has been transformed almost beyond recognition. And yet, we are forced to live under the same basic

---

* Using mortality tables compiled by the French naturalist Comte de Buffon, Jefferson calculated that 19 years was the average time it took for a majority of adults—those "ripe for the exercise of their will"—to be replaced by a new generation.

politico-economic framework. It is high time the living generations had a direct say in the running of society. Humans created the institutions that rule our lives, and it is our right to change them as we collectively see fit.

Nothing lasts forever, including America's bourgeois republic. Just two and a half centuries after a skirmish in Massachusetts helped set the modern world in motion, the edifice of US capitalism is tottering, and a majority have lost all confidence in its political parties, leaders, and institutions.

The capitalist mode of production has exhausted its historically progressive role and has nothing left to offer our species. The incessant economic chaos and political dysfunction merely express the fact that the capitalists are no longer fit to rule over us—and haven't been for over a century.

A new class must take political and economic power. A new society must be built, and classes must be abolished altogether. Just as capitalism was propelled by the labor of millions of slaves, the material basis for socialism has been laid by billions of wage slaves. And just as the divergent interests of the colonial and antebellum societies could no longer coexist, the interests of capitalists and workers cannot be indefinitely maintained within the antiquated confines of capitalism.

Revolutionary epochs are as terrifying as they are exhilarating, and the years ahead will be neither easy nor serene. And yet, given the objective potential for socialism, there has never been a better time to be alive. As Abigail Adams expressed it in the parlance of her time:

> These are the times in which a genius would wish to live. It is not in the still calm of life, or the repose of a pacific station, that great characters are formed.[11]

Whether we are geniuses or not, the pace of history is accelerating and the character of revolutionary Marxists will be severely tested. Armed with the lessons of the past, we will pass that test.

The Third American Revolution will make the betrayed promise of the first two Revolutions and Reconstruction a reality. Through the socialist revolution, we will achieve genuine reparations for centuries of dispossession, exploitation, and oppression. On this basis, we will finally avenge the innumerable martyrs who fought and died in the name of genuine freedom and a world fit for all humankind.

Timeline

1619	First African slaves arrive in the 13 colonies in Virginia
1620	*Mayflower* Pilgrims land at Plymouth
1624	New Amsterdam founded as a trading post by the Dutch
1628	Puritans establish the Massachusetts Bay Colony
March 21, 1630	John Winthrop delivers "City upon a Hill" sermon, calling on colonists to build a Christian model civilization at the expense of the Natives already living in the area
1636 – 38	Pequot War. New England colonists destroy the Pequot nation. As many as 700 Pequot are killed in the 1637 Mystic massacre
1640 – 60	English Revolution. A struggle for political power between King Charles I and Parliament, often expressing itself in religious terms, tips into civil war. This inflicts shattering blows against the old feudal regime to lay the basis for a new capitalist order in England. In 1660, counterrevolutionary forces put Charles II on the throne, sending a new wave of religious dissenters to New England

1651 Navigation Act of 1651. Parliament reinforces the long standing principle that ships carrying goods to England or any of its colonies must be English ships with a majority English crew in an effort to establish more control over the colonies' land and labor

1661 A new Navigation Act takes effect, designating some of the most profitable colonial products—including tobacco, sugar, cotton, and more—as "enumerated goods" which can only be shipped to England or other English colonies

1662 Virginia law makes slave status hereditary

1663 Parliament passes a Navigation Act stipulating that all trade between Europe and the Americas must go through English ports first to be taxed

1664 Under threat of naval bombardment, Dutch New Amsterdam surrenders to the English and is renamed New York

1675 – 78 King Philip's War. Deadliest conflict in American history relative to the population of the time. About half of New England's indigenous population is killed or sold into slavery

1676 – 77 Bacon's Rebellion. Nathaniel Bacon leads a coalition of the disenfranchised and dispossessed, including Black and white indentured servants and Black slaves, in a revolt against Virginia Colonial Governor William Berkeley. Bacon's rebels win control of the colony for several weeks, but are beaten back after Bacon's untimely death

1717 Parliament passes Transportation Act, allowing British courts to sentence convicted criminals to bonded labor in the American colonies for sentences of seven years to life

1730s – 40s The "Great Awakening" gives rise to distinctly American religious practices emphasizing personal religious conversion and experience over ecclesiastical orthodoxy

1739 Stono Rebellion. In South Carolina, a small army of escaped slaves recently arrived from Africa marches south toward the freedom of Spanish Florida. They are intercepted and defeated by the colonial militia

1740 South Carolina enacts Negro Act of 1740, one of North America's harshest slave codes. It severely restricts the movement of slaves and outlaws teaching slaves to read and write

1741 New York Conspiracy. A series of fires across New York City sends the population into a panic. The fires are purportedly set by slaves and poor whites as part of a plot to revolt and level the city. 172 arrested and tried for conspiracy, 34 executed

1750 Iron Act prohibits the construction of new iron mills in the colonies. Instead, raw iron must be exported to England, transformed into manufactured goods, and imported back to the colonies

1751 Currency Act prohibits New England colonies from issuing paper money and establishing new public banks

1754 Benjamin Franklin proposes a "Plan of Union" meeting of colonial delegates and publishes his "Join, or Die" cartoon. Both the colonies andthe British authorities reject Franklin's proposal, the first attempt at creating a unified colonial government

1754 – 63	Seven Years' War, known in North America as the French and Indian War. British victory is catastrophic for the Native Americans. France gives up all North American territories east of the Mississippi River. Britain gains control of Florida from Spain
1760s	"Regulator" movement. In the backcountries of all 13 colonies the masses take up direct action against state institutions to "regulate" the application of the law in the face of crushing debt and rising taxes
April 1763 – July 1766	Pontiac's War. Pontiac leads an alliance of Great Lakes and Ohio Valley nations in an uprising against the British. It is bloodily suppressed
October 1763	Proclamation of 1763. Britain prohibits colonial settlement west of the Appalachian Mountains
April 1764	British parliament passes the Revenue Act, commonly known as the Sugar Act. Hits the bottom line of colonial merchants, distillers, and smugglers while raising prices. Colonists hold mass meetings in opposition and organize merchant boycotts of British goods
1764	Currency Act extends the prohibition on issuing paper money as legal tender to all British colonies in North America
1764	James Otis Jr. publishes *The Rights of the British Colonists Asserted and Proved*, systematically arguing that Parliament has no right to tax colonists without consent
March 22, 1765	Parliament's Stamp Act receives royal assent. The act requires colonists to purchase special stamped paper for all legal documents, newspapers, pamphlets, and more

May 15, 1765	Quartering Act requires colonial legislatures to provide housing and certain provisions for British troops garrisoned in their localities. The financial burden falls on colonial taxpayers who organize boycotts, destroy commercial property, burn tax and government offices, and tar and feather pro-Parliament Tories and officials
August 1765	One-third of Boston's population gathers to behead an effigy of stamp distributor Andrew Oliver as well as destroy his office and vandalize his home. Oliver resigns, making enforcement of the Stamp Act in Boston a dead letter
August 1765	Samuel Adams forms the Sons of Liberty as a response to the Stamp Act
May 1766	Parliament repeals the Stamp Act
1767	Townshend Acts impose duties on imported goods that the colonies cannot produce themselves. The act also suspends the New York Assembly due to its refusal to comply with the Quartering Act
March 5, 1770	Boston Massacre. Five people are killed when overstressed British troops fire into a crowd of rowdy Bostonians throwing snowballs and ice
1770	Parliament repeals nearly all of its taxes on the colonies after gaining little revenue and losing much goodwill. Mass fervor in the colonies dies down
October 1772	Samuel Adams and other Massachusetts colonists establish the first long-standing Committee of Correspondence
May 1773	Tea Act, grants a monopoly on the sale of tea in the colonies to the British East India Company and reasserts Parliament's right to tax the colonies

Dec. 16, 1773	Boston Tea Party. A group of Sons of Liberty members systematically dumps 46 tons of tea into Boston Harbor in full view of the public rather than allow it to be unloaded from British ships. Parliament closes the Port of Boston in response
May 1774	Massachusetts Government Act, the first of the "Intolerable Acts," is passed. It removes the colony's royal charter and gives its Governor, Thomas Hutchinson, unprecedented powers to appoint and remove all government officials, judges, and sheriffs without the colonial legislature's input
June 1774	An expanded Quartering Act now allows Royal governors to compel colonists to house British troops in occupied or unoccupied buildings—including private homes—if suitable quarters are not provided by the colonial legislatures
June 1774	Quebec Act triples the size of the Canadian province, effectively closing off westward expansion
September 1774	First Continental Congress. 56 delegates from 12 colonies gather in Philadelphia. The Congress establishes the Continental Association, a coordinated boycott of British goods, and forms Committees of Observation and Inspection in every colony, county, and town to enforce compliance with the boycott
April 19, 1775	Lexington and Concord. Armed conflict begins as British redcoats march toward towns outside of Boston. They aim to seize critical stores of powder and ammunition from patriot militiamen and to arrest Sam Adams and John Hancock, to prevent them from attending the Second Continental Congress. They are intercepted by colonial Minutemen. Running skirmishes between the two sides leave 49 colonists and 73 redcoats dead

May 10, 1775	Second Continental Congress begins with delegates from all 13 colonies. The Congress is tasked with forming an alternative government and preparing for all-out war. They establish a unified Continental Army under the command of George Washington
May 10, 1775	Militiamen capture Fort Ticonderoga, preventing British reinforcements in Canada from moving down into the colonies
June 17, 1775	Battle of Bunker Hill. British-occupied Boston is besieged by colonists who encircle the city. The British successfully capture some colonial fortifications but fail to break the siege. Both sides suffer heavy casualties
Sept. – Dec. 1775	Invasion of Quebec. Richard Montgomery and Benedict Arnold lead a campaign to invade Canada, with the aim of neutralizing Canada as a military threat and, if possible, annexing it. The adventure ends in disaster for the Continentals
Nov. 7, 1775	Virginia's Royal Governor, Lord Dunmore, offers freedom to slaves who escape their rebel masters and join the British military
January 1776	Thomas Paine's *Common Sense* is published, selling an astounding 500,000 copies
March 17, 1776	Siege of Boston ends with British forces driven out of the city by militiamen. 10,000 British troops along with 1,100 loyalists retreat to Nova Scotia, surrendering the last British garrison in any of the 13 colonies
July 4, 1776	Continental Congress ratifies the Declaration of Independence

August 1776	The war moves to the Mid-Atlantic region with the Battle of Long Island, the largest battle of the war. It ends in a victory for British General William Howe
Nov. – Dec. 1776	Howe pushes Washington out of New York and New Jersey, giving him control of New York City and its harbor at the mouth of the Hudson River
September 19 & October 7, 1777	Battles of Saratoga. American forces under Horatio Gates and Benedict Arnold confront John Burgoyne in the Hudson Valley. While the first engagement is indecisive, the second is a total American victory. Burgoyne surrenders nearly 6,000 troops
Nov. 15, 1777	Continental Congress adopts the Articles of Confederation
December 1777 – February 1778	Washington's army winters at Valley Forge. 2,000 of his 12,000 troops die from starvation, disease, malnutrition, and exposure, and countless others desert
February 6, 1778	Franco-American Treaty of Alliance. France begins supplying troops, naval power, supplies, and financial support to the Continental Army
Summer 1778	Washington's army, freshly trained in European military drill and discipline by Prussian military officer Friedrich Wilhelm von Steuben, resumes its campaign against the British in New Jersey. The fighting forces the British to relinquish their hold on Philadelphia
Dec. 28, 1778	British shift gears toward a "Southern Strategy" beginning with the capture of the port city of Savannah

June 30, 1779	British General Sir Henry Clinton's Philipsburg Proclamation promises freedom to any slaves who escape and flee to British lines
Summer 1779	Washington sends troops under John Sullivan and James Clinton on an expedition to the Finger Lakes region of New York with instructions to "lay waste" to all Indigenous settlements in the area
January 1781	Continental soldiers in Pennsylvania and New Jersey mutiny over unpaid wages and expired enlistments
Sept. – Oct. 1781	Siege and surrender of Yorktown. American and French troops, supported by the French navy, force the surrender of British General Charles Cornwallis in the war's last major engagement. Over 7,000 British and Hessian troops march out of Yorktown and lay down their arms before Washington and Lafayette
March 8, 1782	Gnadenhutten Massacre. American militiamen systematically murder 96 Delaware (Lenape) Indians at a Moravian mission village in Ohio, despite a 1778 alliance negotiated between the United States and the Delawares at the Treaty of Fort Pitt
1783 – 89	The "Critical Period." Turbulent years between the end of the war and the ratification of the Constitution. The country is plagued by an inflationary debt crisis and constrained by the weakness of the Articles of Confederation
Sept. 3, 1783	Treaty of Paris officially ends the war. Britain recognizes American independence, ends its occupation of New York and other positions, and cedes the Northwest Territory to the United States

October 1784	Treaty of Fort Stanwix. British and American negotiators force massive land cessions on the Six Nations including all claims in the Ohio territory
1786 – 87	Shays's Rebellion. Captain Daniel Shays, a former Continental Army officer, leads an insurrectionary uprising of indebted Massachusetts farmers and veterans. The rebellion alarms the new American ruling class, pushing it to adopt a stronger federal government
May – Sept. 1787	Constitutional Convention in Philadelphia. 55 delegates from the thirteen states meet and finalize a draft Constitution for ratification by each state
July 1787	Northwest Ordinance prohibits slavery in the Northwest Territory, encompassing the present-day states of Ohio, Indiana, Illinois, Michigan, Wisconsin, and parts of Minnesota
April 30, 1789	George Washington inaugurated as president under the new Constitution after a unanimous election by the Electoral College. Presides over the eight-year "Federalist era"
Sept. 11, 1789	Alexander Hamilton becomes the country's first Secretary of the Treasury. While in office he establishes a National Bank (as a private corporation), implements protective tariffs, and subsidizes manufacturing, all with the aim of accelerating the growth of American capitalism. His plan to bind the interests of the propertied classes to the federal government is aided by a massive dose of insider trading
Dec. 15, 1791	Bill of Rights, consisting of explicit protections of individual and collective liberties and state powers against federal overreach, is ratified

1791 – 94	Whiskey Rebellion, an uprising among frontiersmen in western Pennsylvania against Hamilton's excise tax on whiskey. Hamilton and Washington personally lead an army of 13,000 to crush it
1792 – 1824	The First Party System. Jefferson's Democratic-Republicans, representing agrarian interests and the slaveocracy, and Hamilton's Federalists, representing commercial and financial capital, dominate federal politics
1793	Eli Whitney invents the cotton gin, revolutionizing cotton production and fueling demand for slave labor
1800	Gabriel's Rebellion. Slave uprising in Virginia is crushed before it can begin
1803	Louisiana Purchase. US government buys roughly 828,000 square miles of North American territory from France, posing the question of whether or not slavery will be legal in the new lands
1820	Missouri Compromise. Missouri is admitted to the Union as a slave state, balanced by the admission of Maine as a free state. With the exception of Missouri, slavery is banned in the remaining Louisiana Purchase territory north of latitude 36°30′
1828 – 54	Second Party System. Whig Party, representing the interests of Northern capitalism, and the Jacksonian Democrats, representing the interests of the southern slave owners, dominate federal politics

1830	Indian Removal Act. Congress authorizes President Andrew Jackson to exchange Indigenous lands in the East for lands in the West and to fund removal, essentially giving him the power and financial resources to carry out mass deportations. Thousands of Indians are walked overland in a horrific death march to the newly created "Indian Territory" in present-day Oklahoma
August 1831	Nat Turner's Rebellion. Over 60 white people are killed in a slave uprising led by Nat Turner in Virginia. Slaveholders unleash vicious repression, hanging, drawing, and quartering Turner and executing as many as 200 other slaves
1832 – 33	Nullification Crisis. South Carolina declares the Tariffs of 1828 and 1832 unconstitutional and, therefore, illegal within its borders. The state government threatens to use military force to prevent federal enforcement of the tariffs, raising the specter of secession. Federal and state governments agree on a Compromise Tariff that gradually lowers rates, easing tensions for the moment
1835	Citywide general strike for the ten-hour day in Philadelphia
1839 – 51	Anti-Rent War. A mass rural insurgency in upstate New York against the quasi-feudal patroon system held over from the Dutch colonial era. Anti-renters resist tax collection, demand land reform, and attack state authorities and landlords
Dec. 29, 1845	US annexes Texas and admits it to the Union as a slave state
April 25, 1846 – February 2, 1848	Mexican-American War. US annexes roughly half of Mexico, adding half a million square miles of territory

January 1848 – October 1849	Revolutions of 1848. A wave of revolutions spread from France across Europe, affecting over 50 countries from Ireland to Walachia. For the first time in history, workers put forward their own independent class demands. Following a continent-wide counterrevolution, many European revolutionaries emigrate to the US
1849	Gold discovered in California, accelerating westward expansion along with industrial and agricultural development. Pressure grows to add California to the Union as a free state
1850	Compromise of 1850 and the Fugitive Slave Act. A series of federal laws are passed aiming to ease tensions between North and South. California is admitted as a free state. The Fugitive Slave Act requires all escaped slaves to be returned to their owner, regardless of which state they were caught in
1854 – 91	Sioux Wars. US government fights a series of wars against the Lakota, Dakota, and Nakota peoples. In December 1890, the Wounded Knee Massacre marks the end of the Sioux Wars and the beginning of the reservation era
March 1854	Republican Party founded in opposition to the expansion of slavery
May 1854	Kansas-Nebraska Act supersedes the Missouri Compromise and implements "popular sovereignty" in the territories
1854 – 59	Bleeding Kansas. Proslavery and antislavery forces flood into the Kansas Territory. They form rival governments and fight a vicious, low-grade guerrilla war

May 24 – 25, 1856	After proslavery forces sack Lawrence, Kansas and destroy the presses and type of two abolitionist newspapers, John Brown and his band execute five proslavery activists in the so-called Pottawatomie Creek "massacre"
March 1857	Supreme Court ruling in *Dred Scott v. Sandford* effectively legalizes slavery nationwide
1857	Panic of 1857. A combination of factors—the bursting of the railroad bubble, the ebb of the California gold rush, and the uncertainty introduced by the Dred Scott decision—sparks an economic panic which, at its root, is a classic capitalist crisis of overproduction
Oct. 16 – 18, 1859	John Brown leads a raid on the federal arsenal at Harpers Ferry. The raid fails to spark a slave uprising, but Brown becomes a revolutionary martyr for the antislavery cause
Nov. 6, 1860	Lincoln elected president, giving Republicans control of the White House for the first time
Dec. 20, 1860	South Carolina secedes from the Union. Other Cotton Belt states follow suit over the next two months
Feb. – March 1861	Provisional Congress of the Confederate States convenes. It adopts a constitution explicitly protecting slavery and elects Jefferson Davis as provisional President of the Confederate States
March 2, 1861	Dakota Territory established by outgoing President James Buchanan. The territory encompasses present-day North Dakota and South Dakota, as well as most of Montana and Wyoming

March 4, 1861	Lincoln sworn into office as President
April 12, 1861	The American Civil War begins. Confederate forces bombard Fort Sumter; the Union surrenders the fort after 34 hours
April 17, 1861	Virginia secedes from the Union
April 19, 1861	Secessionist mob in Baltimore attacks Massachusetts troops en route to Washington, DC. Four soldiers and 12 civilian rioters are killed in the first bloodshed of the war
July 21, 1861	Battle of Bull Run. Union suffers a disastrous defeat in the first major battle of the war, shattering illusions in a quick, easy war
August 6, 1861	First Confiscation Act frees slaves directly engaged in the Confederate war effort
February 25, 1862	Federal government begins issuing greenbacks under the Legal Tender Act
April 1862	Battle of Shiloh. General Ulysses S. Grant leads Union forces to victory in a shockingly bloody battle in southwestern Tennessee
May 20, 1862	Homestead Act opens up millions of acres of land to settlement by US citizens, accelerating westward expansion
July 1862	Second Confiscation and Militia Acts declare escaped slaves "forever free" and allow enlistment of Black soldiers in the Union Army
Sept. 17, 1862	Battle of Antietam. Union forces under General George B. McClellan repel the first Confederate invasion of the North in the bloodiest single day in US military history

Dec. 11 – 15, 1862	Battle of Fredericksburg. The incompetence of newly appointed General Ambrose Burnside leads to a devastating defeat for the Union forces
January 1, 1863	Emancipation Proclamation declares all slaves in the Confederate states "are, and henceforward shall be free"
April 30 – May 6, 1863	Battle of Chancellorsville. A significant victory for the Confederates under General Robert E. Lee emboldens him to attempt a second invasion of the North
May 13, 1863	The 54th Massachusetts Infantry, the Union's first authorized all-Black regiment, is mustered into service
June 20, 1863	Western part of Virginia rejoins the Union as the state of West Virginia
July 1 – 3, 1863	Battle of Gettysburg. Union prevails in the bloodiest battle of the war, ending Lee's second Northern invasion and marking the rebellion's "high-water mark"
July 4, 1863	Fall of Vicksburg. Union gains control of the Mississippi River on the same day that news of Gettysburg reaches Washington
July 13 – 17, 1863	Union troops fresh from Gettysburg put down anti-draft riots in New York City
Nov. 19, 1863	Lincoln delivers the "Gettysburg Address"
Nov. 25, 1863	Chattanooga falls to Grant, opening the way for an invasion of the deep South
Dec. 8, 1863	Lincoln issues the "Ten Percent Plan" establishing a path for states to be readmitted to the Union on very lenient terms. It leaves questions about the future of former slaves unanswered

1863 – 64	National Banking Acts allow for the creation of a uniform national currency and a network of national banks chartered by the federal government through combined effort of the federal government and big financiers
February 1864	Radical Republicans respond to the "Ten Percent Plan" with the Wade-Davis Bill, proposing harsher terms for states rejoining the union. Lincoln pocket-vetoes the bill
Sept – Dec. 1864	Sherman's March to the Sea, aimed at completely crippling the Confederacy, begins with the burning of Atlanta. Sherman and tens of thousands of soldiers then march to the coast to capture Savannah before continuing up through South Carolina and into North Carolina
November 8, 1864	Lincoln reelected in a landslide alongside Andrew Johnson, a white supremacist opportunistically added to the ticket as vice president to secure votes from the border states
January 1865	Sherman issues Special Field Orders, No. 15, allotting 400,000 acres of coastal land from South Carolina to Florida for settlement by freed Black families. Origin of the demand for "forty acres and a mule"
March 1865	US government creates the Freedmen's Bureau and Freedman's Bank. The Bureau is authorized to provide emergency relief, establish the region's first public schools, draft and supervise labor contracts and, initially, distribute Confederate lands to freed families
April 9, 1865	Lee surrenders to Grant at Appomattox Courthouse, effectively ending the American Civil War

April 14, 1865	Lincoln assassinated by John Wilkes Booth
June 19, 1865	Juneteenth Declaration. Major General Gordon Granger declares that the Emancipation Proclamation will be enforced in Texas, freeing the last remaining slaves in the former Confederacy
Dec. 5, 1865	13th Amendment ratified, abolishing slavery in the US except as punishment for a crime
1865 – 67	Black Codes introduced across the South, limiting the kinds of jobs Black people can hold and the kinds of property they can own. The codes restrict basic democratic rights, including freedom of movement, assembly, and speech and the right to bear arms. Vagrancy laws allow authorities to arrest and fine Black people who can't prove they're employed
Dec. 24, 1865	Ku Klux Klan founded in Pulaski, Tennessee
April 1866	Radical Republicans in Congress override Johson's veto of the Civil Rights Act, declaring all people born in the US are citizens with equal rights. The Act gives freedmen equal rights, at least on paper, except for the right to vote
May – July 1866	Memphis and New Orleans riots. White mobs burn Black churches, schools, and homes, killing dozens and wounding hundreds
Aug. 20, 1866	National Labor Union founded in Baltimore. First attempt to organize workers across craft lines on a national scale
November 1866	Republicans win veto-proof majority in both houses of Congress
March 1, 1867	Nebraska admitted to the Union

March 1867	Congress convenes, opening the period of Radical or Congressional Reconstruction. A series of Reconstruction Acts are passed over President Johnson's veto, including four Military Reconstruction Acts
February 1868	Congressional Radicals impeach Johnson. The Senate effort to remove him from office fails by one vote
July 9, 1868	14th Amendment ratified, granting citizenship to all people born or naturalized in the US, along with equal rights, at least on paper
July 25, 1868	Wyoming territory organized
November 1868	Grant wins presidency despite massive suppression of Republican votes in many parts of the South. He has a clear mandate for continuing Reconstruction under the protection of the federal government
May 10, 1869	First transcontinental railroad completed
December 1869	Knights of Labor founded in Philadelphia
Jan. 1870	Hiram R. Revels becomes the first Black man elected to Congress, representing Mississippi. Fourteen more Black Congressmen are elected in the following seven years
Feb 1870	15th Amendment ratified, granting Black men the right to vote
March – May 1871	Paris Commune. The working class seizes power for the first time in history. Inspires millions of revolutionaries and helps shape Marx's and Engels's understanding of what a workers' state will look like
April 1871	Congress passes the Third Enforcement Act, including the Klu Klux Klan Act, authorizing federal prosecution of terrorist organizations

September 1872	Crédit Mobilier Scandal reveals investors and politicians overcharged the government millions for the construction of the first transcontinental railroad
Nov. 5, 1872	Grant wins a decisive reelection victory
1873	Panic of 1873. A post–Civil War boom of railroad construction is brought to a screeching halt by rampant financial speculation and the failure of major banks. The panic starts a worldwide economic recession referred to at the time as the "Great Depression"
1873 – 77	"Redeemer" movement launches a murderous, white supremacist campaign aimed at ending Reconstruction and overthrowing Republican state governments across the South
April 13, 1873	Colfax Massacre. White supremacists murder approximately 150 Black militiamen in Louisiana
July 1874	Freedman's Bank collapses
1874–75	Red River War. US army forces the Comanche, Kiowa, Southern Cheyenne, and Arapaho tribes off of land in the the Southern Plains and forcibly relocates them onto reservations
May 1875	Whiskey Ring, a major tax-evasion and bribery scandal, revealed
June 1876	Battle of Little Bighorn, also known as "Custer's Last Stand." Combined forces of the Lakota Sioux, Northern Cheyenne, and Arapaho tribes defeat the US Army in the most significant engagement in the Great Sioux War
July 1876	Six Black militiamen killed by white supremacists in Hamburg, South Carolina
August 1, 1876	Colorado admitted to the Union

November 1876	Disputed 1876 presidential election. Republican Rutherford B. Hayes is awarded the presidency by the Electoral College in a dirty backroom deal for which he promises to withdraw all remaining federal troops from the South and end enforcement of Reconstruction-era legislation
1877	Great Railroad Strike begins in West Virginia and spreads across the country. In St. Louis, workers launch a citywide insurrectionary general strike under the direction of the Workingmen's Party. All strikes are eventually defeated by intense state repression
May 4, 1886	Haymarket Massacre. Four workers are killed and at least 70 injured when police provoke a riot at a demonstration in favor of the eight-hour day. In the aftermath, eight anarchist leaders are charged as accessories to murder. Four are executed, and another dies by suicide while in prision. Origin of International Workers' Day, also known as May Day
December 8, 1886	American Federation of Labor founded in Columbus, Ohio
1896	*Plessy v. Ferguson* establishes the "separate but equal" doctrine, granting constitutional legitimacy to segregation. Supreme Court does not reverse the decision until *Brown v. Board of Education* in 1954

References

Introduction

1. US Continental Congress, Declaration of Independence, July 4, 1776, National Archives.
2. Leon Trotsky, *Their Morals and Ours* (New York: Pathfinder Press, 1992 [1938]), 48.
3. Friedrich Engels, *Marx and Engels Collected Works Vol. 49* (New York: International Publishers, 2010), 34–36.
4. Trotsky, *My Life* (London: Wellred Books, 2018 [1930]), 75.
5. Karl Marx, *MECW Vol. 29*, 263.
6. Vladimir Lenin, *Lenin Collected Works, Vol. 24* (Moscow: Progress Publishers, 1965), 44.
7. Trotsky, *History of the Russian Revolution, Vol. 1* (London: Wellred Books, 2022 [1932]), 17.
8. Lenin, *LCW Vol. 21,* 213–14.
9. Gore Vidal and C. Vann Woodward, "Gore Vidal's 'Lincoln'?: An Exchange," *The New York Review of Books*, April 28, 1988.
10. Trotsky, "Ultralefts in General and Incurable Ultralefts in Particular (A Few Theoretical Considerations)," September 28, 1937, Internal Bulletin no. 1 (New York: Organizing Committee for the Socialist Party Convention, October 1937).

Part One: The American Revolution

1. Simón Bolívar to General Lafayette, March 20, 1826, in *El Libertador: Writings of Simón Bolívar* (Oxford: Oxford University Press, 2003), 171.
2. Ho Chi Minh, "Declaration of Independence of the Democratic Republic of Viet-Nam," September 2, 1945, in *Ho Chi Minh on Revolution: Selected Writings, 1920–66* (New York: Signet Books, 1968), 141.
3. Jawaharlal Nehru, "The Democratic Way of Life," December 18, 1956, in *Selected Works of Jawaharlal Nehru, Second Series, Vol. 36* (New Delhi: Oxford University Press, 2005), 490–93.
4. Julius K. Nyerere, "Message to America from Tanzania's President Julius K. Nyerere," *Time*, July 26, 1976.
5. Fidel Castro, "History Will Absolve Me," October 16, 1953 in *Revolutionary Struggle 1947–1958: Vol. 1 of the Selected Works of Fidel Castro* (Cambridge: The MIT Press, 1972 [1953]), 217.
6. Lewis Henry Morgan, *Ancient Society* (Gloucester, MA: Meridian Books, 1974 [1877]), 85–86.
7. Friedrich Engels, *The Origin of the Family, Private Property, and the State* (London: Wellred Books, 2020 [1884]), 78.
8. Colin Woodard, *American Nations: A History of the Eleven Rival Regional Cultures of North America* (New York: Penguin Books, 2012).
9. Leon Trotsky, "Europe and America," February 15, 1926, in *Fourth International* vol. 4, no. 4 (April 1943): 120–26.
10. David Galenson, *White Servitude in Colonial America: An Economic Analysis* (Cambridge: Cambridge University Press, 1981).
11. Benjamin Franklin, "Rattle Snakes for Felons," May 9, 1751, in *Franklin: Writings* (New York: The Library of America, 1987), 359.

12. Karl Marx, *Marx and Engels Collected Works vol. 6* (New York: International Publishers, 1976), 167.

13. Mary Elliott and Jazmine Hughes, "A Brief History of Slavery You Didn't Learn In School," nytimes.com, *New York Times Magazine,* August 19, 2019.

14. Alexander Spotswood to the Lords Commissioners for Trade and Plantations, April 5, 1717, in *Collections of the Virginia Historical Society, Vol. 2* (Richmond: Virginia Historical Society, 1885), 227.

15. William Berkeley, quoted in Howard Zinn, *A People's History of the United States* (New York: Perennial Classics, 2015), 40.

16. Herbert Aptheker, *The Colonial Era* (New York: International Publishers, 1959), 65.

17. Eric Foner, *Give Me Liberty!: An American History* (New York: W. W. Norton and Company), 100.

18. Edmund Morgan, *American Slavery, American Freedom* (New York: W. W. Norton and Company), 328.

19. Theodore Allen, *The Invention of the White Race, Vol. 2: The Origin of Racial Oppression in Anglo-America* (New York: Verso Books, 2012), 219.

20. "An act concerning Servants and Slaves," 1705, in *The Statutes at Large; Being a Collection of All the Laws of Virginia from the First Session of the Legislature, in the Year 1619, Vol. 3,* ed. William Waller Hening (Richmond: The Franklin Press, 1823), 447–63.

21. Quoted in Zinn, *A People's History of the United States*, 34.

22. Colonel Byrd to Lord Egmont, in "Colonel William Byrd on Slavery and Indentured Servants, 1736, 1739," *The American Historical Review* 1, no. 1 (1895): 88–89.

23. Frederick Douglass, "Life and Times of Frederick Douglass," in *Douglass Autobiographies* (New York: The Library of America, 1994 [1881]), 627–28.

24. Marx, *MECW Vol. 37,* (New York: International Publishers, 1998), 777–78.

25. Marx and Engels, "The Communist Manifesto," in *The Classics of Marxism Vol. 1*, (London: Wellred Books, 2025), 5.
26. Marx, *MECW Vol. 35*, (New York: International Publishers: 1996), 741.
27. Trotsky, *History of the Russian Revolution Vol. 1*, (London: Wellred Books, 2022 [1930]), 27–28.
28. Marx, *MECW Vol. 35*, 704–06.
29. Ibid., 739.
30. Ibid., 747.
31. Ibid., 706.
32. Ibid., 748.
33. Ibid., 179.
34. Marx, *MECW Vol. 37*, 322–25.
35. Marx, *MECW Vol. 31*, (New York: International Publishers, 1998), 515–16.
36. Vladimir Lenin, *Imperialism: The Highest Stage of Capitalism* (London: Wellred Books, 2019 [1916]), 64.
37. Jacques Lacoursière and Robin Philpot, *A People's History of Quebec* (Montreal: Baraka Books, 2009), 51–52.
38. Fred Anderson, *Crucible of War: The Seven Years' War and the Fate of Empire in British North America*, 1754–1766 (New York: Vintage Books, 2001).
39. Marx, *A Contribution to the Critique of Political Economy* (New York: International Publishers, 1970), 21.
40. Charles Andrews, "The American Revolution: An Interpretation," *The American Historical Review* 31, no. 2 (1926): 231.
41. Adam Smith, *Wealth of Nations* (New York: The Modern Library, 1937 [1776]), 549.
42. Ibid, 540.
43. Ibid, 587–88.

44. Franklin to Lord Kames, February 25, 1767, *The Electric Ben Franklin*, accessed on May 1, 2026, ushistory.org.

45. Franklin, "The Mother Country," December 31, 1765, in *Writings*, 565.

46. John Adams, "'The Thirteen Clocks Were Not Made to Strike Together': To Hezekiah Niles," February 13, 1818, in *John Adams Writings from the New Nation 1784–1826* (New York: The Library of America, 2016), 629.

47. Samuel Adams, "Instructions of the Town of Boston to Its Representatives in the General Court. May, 1764," in *The Writings of Samuel Adams: Vol. 1, 1764–1769* (New York: G. P. Putnam's Sons, 1904), 4–5.

48. Quoted in Richard Samuelson, "Introduction: The Life, Times, and Political Writings of James Otis," in *Collected Political Writings of James Otis*, vii.

49. Franklin, "Franklin: His Examination Before the House of Commons," January 1766, in *The World's Famous Orations: Vol. 8* (New York: Funk and Wagnalls, 1906), 38–39.

50. Carl Van Doren, *Benjamin Franklin* (New York: The Viking Press, 1980 [1938]), 391.

51. Quoted in Jacob Axelrad, *Patrick Henry: The Voice of Freedom*, (New York: Random House, 1947), 111.

52. Quoted in "General Gage's Letters," *The New York Times Book Review*, August 9, 1931, 57.

53. Quoted in Harry Frankel, *Sam Adams And the American Revolution* (New York: Pathfinder Press, 1971), 15.

54. Gouverneur Morris, "New York, January 7th, 1774," in *The Life of Gouverneur Morris, with Selections from His Correspondence and Miscellaneous Papers, Vol. 1*, ed. Jared Sparks (Boston: Gray and Bowen, 1832), 25.

55. Trotsky, *History of the Russian Revolution Vol. 1*, 18.

56. J. Franklin Jameson, *The American Revolution Considered as a Social Movement* (Princeton: Princeton University Press, 1973 [1926]), 11–12.
57. T. H. Breen, *The Marketplace of the Revolution* (Oxford: Oxford University Press, 2004), 308.
58. Alfred F. Young, *Liberty Tree* (New York: New York University Press, 2006), 46–48.
59. Samuel Adams, quoted in Frankel, *Sam Adams And the American Revolution*, 32.
60. Samuel Adams to Samuel Cooper, April 30, 1776, in *Writings: Vol. 3, 1773–1777*, ed. Harry Alonzo Cushing (New York: G.P. Putnam's Sons, 1907 [1776]), 283–85
61. William H. Burnside, "Samuel Adams," *EBSCO*, ebsco.com, 2022.
62. Thomas Jefferson, "Setting the Record Straight: To Samuel Adams Wells," May 12, 1819, in *Jefferson: Writings* (New York: Library of America, 1984), 1422.
63. Thomas Hutchinson, quoted in William V. Wells, *The Life and Public Services of Samuel Adams* (Boston: Little Brown and Company, 1865), 410.
64. Alexander Winston, "Firebrand Of The Revolution," *American Heritage* vol. 18, no. 3 (April 1967): 105–108.
65. Jefferson, *The Writings of Thomas Jefferson, Vol. 1*, ed. Henry Augustine Washington (Philadelphia, PA: J.B. Lippincott and Company, 1871), 5.
66. John K. Alexander, *Samuel Adams: The Life of an American Revolutionary* (Lanham, MD: Rowman and Littlefield Publishers, 2011), 150.
67. George Elliott Howard, "Preliminaries of the Revolution," in *The American Nation: A History, Vol. 8*, ed. Albert Bushnell Hart (New York: Harper and Brothers Publishers, 1905), 256.

68. T. H. Breen, *American Insurgents, American Patriots* (New York: Hill and Wang, 2010), 201.

69. Daniel Leonard, quoted in George Elliott Howard, "Preliminaries of the Revolution," in *The American Nation: A History, Vol. 8*, ed. Albert Bushnell Hart (New York: Harper and Brothers Publishers, 1905), 256.

70. John Adams, "A Dissertation on the Canon and the Feudal Law No. 3," September 30, 1765, in *John Adams: Revolutionary Writings, 1755–1775* (New York: The Library of America, 2011), 122.

71. Dylan Jordan, "Patriotism in Print: How Print Media Inspired the American Revolution," hnoc.org, *The Historic New Orleans Collection*, July 20, 2023.

72. Richard L. Bushman, *King and People in Provincial Massachusetts* (Williamsburg, VA: University of North Carolina Press, 1992), 182.

73. Alexis de Tocqueville, *Democracy in America* (New York: The Library of America, 2004 [1840]), 600.

74. Franklin, "Apology for Printers," in *Writings*, 172.

75. Lenin, *Lenin Collected Works Vol. 5* (Moscow: Progress Publishers, 1961), 22.

76. James Otis Jr., "The Rights of the British Colonies Asserted and Proved," 1764, *Collected Political Writings of James Otis* (Indianapolis: Liberty Fund, 2015), 119.

77. John Dickinson, *Letters From a Farmer in Pennsylvania*, 1767–68, Delaware Historical and Cultural Affairs, accessed on May 1, 2026, history.delaware.gov.

78. Jefferson, "A Summary View of the Rights of British America," 1774, in *Jefferson Writings*, 105.

79. Thomas Paine, "Common Sense," January 10, 1776, in *Paine Collected Writings* (New York: The Library of America, 1995) 5–53.

80. Engels, *Anti-Dühring* (London: Wellred Books, 2017), 200.
81. Samuel Adams, "Resolutions of the Town of Boston," *The Writings of Samuel Adams. Vol. 3*, 67–69.
82. Alfred F. Young, *The Shoemaker and the Tea Party* (Boston: Beacon Press, 1999), 42–45.
83. John Adams, "From the Diary: March 4—December 17, 1773," in *John Adams Revolutionary Writings 1755–1775*, 286.
84. Samuel Adams, "To the Committee of Correspondence of Portsmouth, New Hampshire," in *Writings: Vol. 3*, 106–107.
85. George Washington to George William Fairfax, June 10, 1774, in *George Washington Writings* (New York: The Library of America, 1997), 150.
86. Gordon S. Wood, *The Radicalism of the American Revolution* (New York: Vintage Books, 1993), 213.
87. George Mason, "Fairfax County Committee of Safety Proceedings (January 17, 1775)," Constitutional Sources Project, *The Papers of George Mason.*
88. Gore Vidal, *Inventing a Nation* (Harrisonburg, VA: Yale University Press, 2003), 19.
89. Peter Henriques, "George Washington: America's Atlas," historynet.com, HistoryNet, November 17, 2016.
90. "Friday, June 7, 1776," in *Journals of the Continental Congress 1774–1789: Vol. 5* June 5–October 8 1776 (Washington: Government Printing Office, 1906), 425.
91. Washington to Benjamin Harrison, January 18, 1784, in *Writings*, 552.
92. "Letter from J. Waller to unidentified recipient, 21 June 1775," Massachusetts Historical Society.
93. Washington, "General Orders," July 2, 1776, in *Writings*, 225–26.
94. John Chester Miller, *Origins of the American Revolution* (London, Stanford, CA: Stanford University Press, 1966), 439.

95. Theodore Draper, *A Struggle for Power: The American Revolution* (New York: Vintage Books, 1997), 494–95.

96. Paine, "The American Crisis: Number I," December 19, 1776, in *Collected Writings*, 23.

97. General James Wilkinson, *Memoirs of My Own Times: Vol. 1* (Philadelphia: Abraham Smalls, 1816), 132.

98. Washington to John Augustine Washington, October 18, 1777, in *Writings*, 279.

99. Washington to George Clinton, February 16, 1778, in *Writings*, 292.

100. Paul Lockhart, *The Drillmaster of Valley Forge: The Baron de Steuben and the Making of the American Army* (New York: Smithsonian Books, 2008), 104.

101. James Thacher, *A Military Journal During the American Revolutionary War* (Boston: Cottons and Barnard, 1827), 280–81.

102. Henry Kissinger, quoted in *Quotations on the Vietnam War,* ed. Gregory R. Clark (Jefferson, NC: McFarland and Company), 2001.

103. Engels, *Anti-Dühring*, 220.

104. John Burgoyne, quoted in *The American Revolution*, "An Asylum for Mankind (May 1775 – July 1776)," directed by Ken Burns, Sarah Botstein, and David Schmidt, 0:11:54 to 0:11:59.

105. Act creating the 1st Rhode Island Regiment, also known as the "Black Regiment," 1778, February 14, 1778, Rhode Island State Archives, C#0210 Acts and Resolves of the General Assembly, Vol. 17 #14.

106. Farrell Evans, "America's First Black Regiment Gained Their Freedom by Fighting the British," history.com, *HISTORY,* February 3, 2021.

107. Trotsky, "The Red Soldier's Manual," in *The Daily Worker: Special Magazine Supplement*, November 29, 1924, 5.

108. Richard M. Ketchum, *Saratoga: Turning Point of America's Revolutionary War* (New York: Henry Holt and Company, 1997), 152.

109. Aptheker, *Early Years of the Republic and the Constitution* (New York: International Publishers, 1990 [1976]), 62.

110. Washington to John Jay, in *The Writings of George Washington Vol. 14, January 12, 1779–May 5, 1779* (Washington: Government Printing Office, 1936), 439.

111. John Adams to Abigail Adams, June 26, 1776, in *Adams Family Correspondence. Series II, Vol. 2*, ed. L.H. Butterfield (Cambridge, MA: Belknap Press, 1963), 23.

112. Washington to Governor Patrick Henry, in *Writings Vol. 7, January 13, 1777–April 30, 1777*, 409.

113. Washington, "Instructions to Major General John Sullivan," in *Writings Vol. 15, May 6, 1779–July 28, 1779*, 189–90.

114. Jefferson, "Machiavellian Benevolence and the Indians: To Governor William H. Harrison," February 27, 1803, in *Jefferson Writings*, 1118.

115. Jefferson, "A Hemisphere to Itself: To Alexander von Humboldt," in *Writings*, 1312–13.

116. David M. Kennedy and Lizabeth Cohen, *The American Pageant* (Boston: Wadsworth, 2014), 146.

117. Keith and Rusty McNeil, *Colonial and Revolution Songbook* (Riverside, CA: WEM Records, 1996).

118. Thomas Pownall, *A Memorial: Most Humbly Addressed to the Sovereigns of Europe, on the Present State of Affairs, Between the Old and New World*, 1780, Princeton University Library, 3–4.

119. Edmund Burke, quoted in David Armitage, "The Declaration of Independence in Global Perspective," gilderlehrman.org, *The Gilder Lehrman Institute of American History*.

120. Wood, *Revolutionary Characters: What Made the Founders Different* (New York: Penguin, 2006), 252–53.

121. "A New York Loyalist to Lord Hardwicke," teachingamericanhistory.org, *Teaching American History*.

122. Alan Taylor, *American Revolutions: A Continental History, 1750–1804* (New York: W.W. Norton and Company, 2016), 479.

123. Ordinance for the Government of the Territory of the United States North-West of the River Ohio, July 13, 1787, Miscellaneous Papers of the Continental Congress, 1774–1789, Records of the Continental and Confederation Congresses and the Constitutional Convention, RG 360, National Archives, Washington, DC.

124. Abigail Adams to John Adams, March 31, 1776, in *Adams Family Correspondence, Series II, Vol. 1*, ed. L.H. Butterfield (Cambridge, MA: Belknap Press, 1963), 370.

125. John Adams to Abigail Adams, April 14, 1776, in *Adams Family Correspondence, Series II, Vol. 1*, 382.

126. Abigail Adams to John Adams, May 7, 1776, in *Adams Family Correspondence, Series II, Vol. 1*, 402.

127. Jefferson, "Notes on the State of Virginia," 1785, in *Writings*, 288.

128. Jefferson, "Autobiography," 1821, in *Writings*, 44.

129. Samuel Johnson, *Taxation no Tyranny; An Answer to the Resolutions and Address of the American Congress* (London: T. Cadell, 1775), 89.

130. Abigail Adams to John Adams, September 22, 1774, in *Adams Family Correspondence, Series II, Vol. 1*, 162.

131. Julie Winch, *A Gentleman of Color: The Life of James Forten* (Oxford: Oxford University Press, 2002), 172.

132. Benjamin Rush, "Address to the People of the United States," January 1787, in *The Documentary History of the Ratification of the Constitution Digital Edition,* ed. John P. Kaminski et al. (Charlottesville: University of Virginia Press, 2009).

133. Rush, *An Address to the Inhabitants of the British Settlements in America, Upon Slave-Keeping* (New York: Hodge and Shober, 1773), 29.

134. Douglass, "What to the Slave Is the Fourth of July? An Address," in *Douglass Speeches and Writings* (New York: The Library of America, 2022 [1852]), 174–78.

135. *Voices of A People's History*, ed. Howard Zinn and Anthony Arnove (New York: Seven Stories Press, 2004), 104.
136. Jefferson to William S. Smith, in *Writings*, 911.
137. Jefferson to James Madison, in *Writings*, 882.
138. Washington to Henry Knox, February 3, 1787, in *Writings Vol. 29, September 1, 1786–June 19, 1788*, 153.
139. Washington to James Madison, November 5, 1786, in *Writings Vol. 29, September 1, 1786–June 19, 1788*, 51–52.
140. Abigail Adams to Jefferson, January 29, 1787, in *The Adams-Jefferson Letters* (Chapel Hill, NC: The University of North Carolina Press, 1987), 168.
141. A. Freeman, "Letter to the Editor," *The Worcester Magazine*, Vol. 2, Iss. 28 (Second Week in October, 1786), 337.
142. "Journal Notes of the Virginia Ratification Convention Proceedings (June 7, 1788)," ConSource: Virginia Ratification Debates.
143. Aptheker, *Early Years of the Republic and the Constitution*, 55.
144. Engels, *Anti-Dühring*, 127.
145. U.S. Continental Congress, *Declaration of Independence*, July 4, 1776, National Archives.
146. Marx and Engels, "The Communist Manifesto," in *The Classics of Marxism Vol. 1*, 7.
147. Anatole France, *The Red Lily*, (New York: Dodd, Mead, and Company, 1927 [1894]), 95.
148. Lenin, *LCW Vol. 20* (Moscow: Progress Publishers, 1964), 146.
149. Marx and Engels, *MECW Vol. 5*, 46–47.
150. Trotsky, "The Class, the Party and the Leadership," in *The Spanish Revolution: 1931–39* (New York: Pathfinder Press, 2015 [1940]), 439.
151. George Novack, *Understanding History: Marxist Essays* (New York: Pathfinder, 2011 [1972]), 78.

152. Alexander Hamilton to Robert Morris, April 30, 1781, in *The Papers of Alexander Hamilton, Vol. 2: 1779–1781* (New York: Columbia University Press, 1961 [1781]), 635.

153. Hamilton, "Report on Public Credit," January 14, 1790, in *Hamilton Writings* (New York: The Library of America, 2001), 534.

154. Hamilton to Robert Morris, April 30, 1781, in *Papers Vol. 2: 1779–1781*, 618.

155. Jefferson to Governor William H. Harrison, February 27, 1803, in *Writings*, 1118.

156. Vidal, "The End of Gore Vidal," by Lila Azam Zangane, guernicamag.com, *Guernica Magazine*, August 15, 2012.

157. Hamilton, "Speech in the Constitutional Convention on a Plan of Government: Version Recorded by Yates," June 18, 1787, in *Hamilton Writings*, 164.

158. "Tuesday June 26 in Convention," in *Notes of Debates in the Federal Convention of 1787: Reported by James Madison* (Athens, OH: Ohio University Press, 1985), 196.

159. "Thursday July 5th in Convention," in *Notes of Debates in the Federal Convention of 1787,* 244.

160. James Madison, "No. 10: Madison," in *The Federalist Papers,* (New York: Mentor Books, 1962 [1787]), 79.

161. John Adams, "Defence of the Constitutions of Government of the United States of America, Vol. 3," 1787–88, in *The Works of John Adams Vol. 6,* (Freeport, NY: Books for Free Libraries Press, 1969), 185–86.

162. John Adams, "Discourses on Davila, a Series of Papers on Political History," in *The Works of John Adams Vol. 6,* 279–80.

163. Madison, "No. 51: Madison," in *The Federalist Papers,* 322.

164. "Monday July 2nd in Convention," in *Notes of Debates in the Federal Convention of 1787,* 233–34.

Part Two: The US Civil War

1. William Faulkner, "Requiem for a Nun," in *Faulkner Novels 1942-1954* (New York: The Library of America, 1994), 525.
2. Karl Marx, *The Eighteenth Brumaire of Louis Bonaparte* (London: Wellred Books, 2022), 2.
3. Karl Marx, *The General Council of the First International 1864-1866* (Moscow: Progress Publishers, 1974), 51-53.
4. Marx, *MECW Vol. 19*, 50.
5. Quoted in George Novack, "Marx and Engels on the Civil War," *New International* vol. 4, no. 2 (February 1938): 45-47.
6. Friedrich Engels, *MECW Vol. 19*, 30.
7. Vladimir Lenin, *Lenin Collected Works Vol. 28*, 69.
8. Thomas Jefferson, "'A Fire Bell in the Night': To John Holmes," April 22, 1820, in *Jefferson Writings* (New York: The Library of America, 1984), 1434.
9. Alan D. Watson, *Wilmington, North Carolina, to 1861* (Jefferson, NC: McFarland and Company, 2003), 131.
10. Troy L. Kickler, "Urban Slaves: A Little-Recognized Part of The Southern Economy," *North Carolina History Project*, 2026.
11. Marx, *MECW Vol. 35*, 244.
12. John Lockwood and Charles Lockwood, "First South Carolina. Then New York?," *The New York Times*, January 6, 2011.
13. John C. Calhoun, "Speech on the Slavery Question," March 4, 1850, in *The Papers of John C. Calhoun, Vol. 27 1849–1850 with Supplement* (Columbia, SC: University of South Carolina Press, 2003), 193.
14. Ibid, 195-96.
15. Ibid, 200.
16. Ibid, 209-11.
17. Abraham Lincoln, "'House Divided' Speech at Springfield, Illinois," June 16, 1858, in *Abraham Lincoln: Speeches and Writings 1832-1858* (New York: The Library of America, 1989), 426.

18. Tecumseh, *The Portable North American Indian Reader*, ed. Frederick Turner III (New York: Penguin, 1987), 246.

19. Black Hawk, *Black Hawk: An Autobiography*, ed. Donald Jackson (Urbana, IL: University of Illinois Press, 1964), 101.

20. Ibid, 105.

21. "Report of Henry Knox on the Northwestern Indians," June 15, 1789, in *Documents of United States Indian Policy*, ed. Francis Paul Prucha (Lincoln, NE: University of Nebraska Press, 2000), 12.

22. *Johnson and Graham's Lessee v. William McIntosh*, 21 US 543 (1823).

23. *Cherokee Nation v. Georgia*, 30 US 1 (1831).

24. Andrew Jackson, "President Andrew Jackson's Message to Congress 'On Indian Removal,'" December 6, 1830, in Presidential Messages, 1789–1875, Records of the U.S. Senate, Record Group 46, National Archives Building, Washington, DC.

25. Jackson, "Fifth Annual Message to Congress," December 3, 1833, *Miller Center*, accessed April 28, 2026.

26. John G. Burnett, "The Cherokee Removal Through the Eyes of a Private Soldier," December 11, 1890, in *Voices of a People's History of the United States*, ed. Howard Zinn and Anthony Arnove (New York: Seven Stories Press, 2004), 145.

27. *The Civil War*, "The Cause (1861)," directed by Ken Burns (1990, PBS), 0:18:15 to 0:18:20.

28. Bruce Levine, "The Failure of Compromise," *The Gilder Lehrman Institute of American History*.

29. Calhoun to Frederick W. Symmes, July 26, 1831, in *Papers Vol. 11, 1829–1832* (Columbia, SC: University of South Carolina Press, 1978), 415–16.

30. Jackson, "No. 26 Respecting the Nullifying Laws of South Carolina," December 10, 1832, in *U.S. Statutes at Large, Vol. 11 (1856–1857) 34th and 35th Congress* (Boston: Little, Brown and Company, 1859), 780.

31. Ibid, 776.
32. James L. Crouthamel, *Bennett's New York Herald and the Rise of the Popular Press* (Syracuse, NY: Syracuse University Press, 1989), 57.
33. James K. Polk, Special Message to Congress on Mexican Relations, May 11, 1846, *The American Presidency Project.*
34. Amy S. Greenberg, *A Wicked War: Polk, Clay, Lincoln, and the 1846 U.S. Invasion of Mexico* (New York: Knopf Doubleday Publishing Group, 2012), 6.
35. Ulysses S. Grant, "Personal Memoirs of U. S. Grant, Vol. I," 1885, in *Ulysses S. Grant Memoirs and Selected Letters* (New York: The Library of America, 1990), 41.
36. Ralph Waldo Emerson, *Journals of Ralph Waldo Emerson with Annotations* (Boston: Houghton Mifflin Company, 1912 [1846]), 206.
37. Henry Clay, "Henry Clay: On the Compromise of 1850," February 1850, in *The World's Great Speeches: Fourth Enlarged Edition* (Mineola, NY: Dover Publications, 1999), 289–90.
38. Salmon P. Chase, "Union and Freedom, without Compromise" (speech, US Senate, Washington, DC, March 26–27, 1850).
39. "Ralph Waldo Emerson on the Fugitive Slave Law," Concord Free Public Library, Special Collections, accessed April 30, 2026.
40. William Lloyd Garrison, "No Compromise with the Evil of Slavery" (speech, Broadway Tabernacle, New York, February 14, 1854).
41. Douglass, "Call for a Colored National Convention," in *Proceedings of the Colored National Convention held in Rochester, July 6–8, 1853* (Rochester: Frederick Douglass' Paper, 1853), 4.
42. Douglass, "What to the Slave Is the Fourth of July? An Address," July 4, 1852, in *Douglass Speeches and Writings* (New York: The Library of America, 2022), 182.

43. Douglass, "The Fugitive Slave Law, speech to the National Free Soil Convention at Pittsburgh," August 11, 1852, in *Frederick Douglass: Selected Speeches and Writings*, ed. Philip S. Foner (Chicago: Lawrence Hill Books, 1999), 208.

44. Nicole Etcheson, "Review of The Border between Them: Violence and Reconciliation on the Kansas-Missouri Line, by Jeremy Neely," *Great Plains Quarterly* 28, no. 2 (Spring 2008): 154–55.

45. Shearer Davis Bowman, *At the Precipice: Americans North and South During the Secession Crisis*, Chapel Hill, NC: The University of North Carolina Press, 2010, 239.

46. "The Caning of Senator Charles Sumner," *US Senate*, accessed on April 30, 2026.

47. *Dred Scott v. Sandford*, 60 US 393 (1857).

48. Herman Melville, "The Portent," 1859, in *Melville Complete Poems* (New York: The Library of America, 2019), 1.

49. Ira Berlin, *The Long Emancipation: The Demise of Slavery in the United States* (Cambridge, MA: Harvard University Press, 2015), 37.

50. Douglass, "West India Emancipation, speech delivered at Canandaigua, New York," August 3, 1857, in *Selected Speeches and Writings*, 367.

51. Quoted in David Blight, "The Election of 1860 and the Secession Crisis" (lecture, Yale University, New Haven, CT, Spring 2008).

52. Quoted in W.E.B. Du Bois, *John Brown*, (Oxford: Oxford University Press, 2007 [1909]), 151.

53. "John Brown's Last Speech," November 2, 1859, in *Voices of a People's History of the United States*, 187–88.

54. Quoted in Richard Josiah Hinton, *John Brown and his Men* (New York: Funk and Wagnalls Company, 1894), 397.

55. "John Brown's Holy War: The Hanging," *PBS American Experience*, accessed on April 30, 2026.

56. Henry David Thoreau, "Lecture by Henry D. Thoreau," in *Echoes of Harper's Ferry* (Boston: Thayer and Eldridge, 1860), 21–22.

57. Ibid, 41–42.

58. Douglass, "John Brown, speech delivered at Storer College, Harper's Ferry, West Virginia," May 30, 1881, in *Selected Speeches and Writings*, 636–37, 648.

59. Hans J. Massaquoi, "Mystery of Malcolm X," *Ebony*, September 1964.

60. Quoted in *Brink of Destruction: A Quotable History of the Civil War*, ed. Randal Bedwell (New York: Gramercy Books, 1999), 20.

61. Marx, *MECW Vol. 41*, 4–5.

62. Duncan McDonald to John W. Ellis, November 17, 1859, in *The Papers of John Willis Ellis, Vol. 1 1841-1859*, ed. by Noble J. Tolbert (Raleigh, NC: State Department of Archives and History, 1964), 319.

63. John W. Ellis to John B. Floyd, December 10, 1859, in *The Papers of John Willis Ellis Vol. 1*, 331.

64. U.S. Const. art. IV, § 2, cl. 3.

65. *The Civil War*, "A Very Bloody Affair / Forever Free (1862)," directed by Ken Burns, 0:23:31 to 0:23:34.

66. "Declaration of the Immediate Causes Which Induce and Justify the Secession of South Carolina from the Federal Union," December 24, 1860, Avalon Project, Yale Law School, accessed April 30, 2026.

67. "A Declaration of the Immediate Causes which Induce and Justify the Secession of the State of Mississippi from the Federal Union," January 9, 1861, Avalon Project, Yale Law School, accessed April 30, 2026.

68. Alexander H. Stephens, "The 'Cornerstone' Speech," in *Alexander H. Stephens, Public and Private: With Letters and Speeches, Before, During, and Since the War*, ed. Henry Cleveland (Philadelphia: National Publishing Company, 1866), 721.

69. Marx, *MECW Vol. 19*, 34.

70. George Fitzhugh, *Canniballs All! or Slaves Without Masters*, ed. C. Vann Woodward (Cambridge, MA: The Belknap Press, 1988 [1857]), 18.

71. Ibid, 17.

72. "'The Mudsill Speech': Speech to the US Senate by James H. Hammond," March 4, 1858, allenbolar.com, accessed on April 30, 2026.

73. Charles Francis Adams, quoted in James M. McPherson, *This Mighty Scourge: Perspectives on the Civil War* (Oxford: Oxford University Press, 2009), 9–10.

74. James Buchanan, "Fourth Annual Message to Congress on the State of the Union," December 3, 1860, *The American Presidency Project.*

75. Lincoln, "Speech on the Kansas-Nebraska Act at Peoria, Illinois," October 16, 1854, in *Speeches and Writings 1832–1858*, 315.

76. Lincoln, "Speech at Chicago, Illinois," July 10, 1858, in *Speeches and Writings 1832-1858*, 447–48.

77. Marx, *MECW Vol. 19*, 41.

78. *Declaration of the Immediate Causes Which Induce and Justify the Secession of South Carolina from the Federal Union; and the Ordinance of Secession* (Charleston, SC: Evans and Cogswell, 1860), 9.

79. Lincoln, "First Inaugural Address," March 4, 1861, in *Speeches and Writings 1859–1865*, 215.

80. Ibid, 224.

81. Ibid, 218.

82. Ibid, 218.

83. Bruce Catton, *The Coming Fury: The Centennial History of the Civil War, Vol. 1* (London: Phoenix Press, 1988), 216.

84. Mary Boykin Chesnut, *A Diary from Dixie* (Cambridge, MA: Harvard University Press, 1980), 36-38.

85. Quoted in Eric H. Walther, *William Lowndes Yancey and the Coming of the Civil War* (Chapel Hill, NC: The University of North Carolina Press, 2006), 295.

86. William W. Freehling, *The Road to Disunion, Volume 2: Secessionists Triumphant, 1854–1861,* (New York: Oxford University Press, 2007), 400.

87. Leo Tolstoy, *War and Peace*, trans. George Gibian (New York: W.W. Norton and Company, 1996), 537–38.

88. Lincoln to Albert G. Hodges, April 4, 1864, *The American Presidency Project.*

89. Marx, *MECW Vol. 19*, 178.

90. Doris Kearns Goodwin, *Team of Rivals: The Political Genius of Abraham Lincoln* (New York: Penguin, 2005), xvii.

91. Lincoln, "Lucius E. Chittenden (1824-1902)," in *Recollected Words of Abraham Lincoln*, ed. Don E. Fehrenbacher and Virginia Fehrenbacher (Stanford, CA: Stanford University Press, 1996), 100-101.

92. Trotsky, *Their Morals and Ours* (New York: Pathfinder Press, 1992 [1938]), 38.

93. US War Department, *The War of the Rebellion: A Compilation of the Official Records of the Union and Confederate Armies, Series 1, Vol. 51, Part 1* (Washington, DC: Government Printing Office, 1897), 369–70.

94. George Ticknor to Sir Edmund Heath, April 28, 1861, in *Life, Letters and Journals of George Ticknor*, ed. George Hillard (Boston: J. R. Osgood and company, 1876), 434.

95. Quoted in Lloyd Lewis, *Sherman: Fighting Prophet* (Lincoln: University of Nebraska Press, 1993), 138.

96. Foner, "Why the North Fought the Civil War," *History News Network*, April 29, 2011.

97. Ulysses S. Grant, *Personal Memoirs of U. S. Grant: Vol. I*, 238, 246.

98. Ron Chernow, *Grant* (New York: Penguin, 2017), 211.

99. Gary Bloomfield and Michael Richards, *Mark Twain: His Words, Wit, and Wisdom* (Guilford, CT: Globe Pequot, 2017), 180-81.

100. John C. Waugh, *Lincoln and McClellan* (New York: Macmillan Publishers, 2010), 65.
101. Ibid, 50.
102. Ibid, 115.
103. Ida M. Tarbell, *The Life of Abraham Lincoln, Vol. 2* (New York: Lincoln Memorial Association, 1900), 83.
104. Marx, *MECW Vol. 19*, 226.
105. Ibid, 179.
106. Quoted in Wilmer L. Jones, *Generals in Blue and Gray, Vol. 1* (Westport, CT: Praeger, 2004), 26.
107. Quoted in T. Harry Williams, *McClellan, Sherman and Grant* (Westport, CT: Greenport Press, 1976), 98.
108. Trotsky, *My Life* (London: Wellred Books, 2018), 205–206.
109. Lincoln to Orville H. Browning, September 22, 1861, in *Speeches and Writings 1859–1865*, 269.
110. Michael Fellman, *Inside War* (New York: Oxford University Press, 1989), v.
111. Jeremy Neely, "Review of A Savage Conflict: The Decisive Role of Guerrillas in the American Civil War," *Civil War Book Review* vol. 11, no. 4, (2009).
112. Marx and Engels, *MECW Vol. 19*, 194.
113. Engels, *MECW Vol. 41*, 403.
114. Marx, *MECW Vol. 41*, 399–400.
115. Marx, *MECW Vol. 19*, 226.
116. Marx, *MECW Vol. 41*, 415.
117. Lincoln, "Annual Message to Congress," in *Speeches and Writings 1859–1865*, 292.
118. Lincoln, "Appeal to Border-State Representatives for Compensated Emancipation, Washington, DC," in *Speeches and Writings 1859–1865*, 340–41.

119. Lincoln to Horace Greeley, August 22, 1862, in *Speeches and Writings 1859-1865*, 358.
120. Lincoln, "Preliminary Emancipation Proclamation," in *Speeches and Writings 1859–1865*, 368.
121. Marx, MECW Vol. 19, 250.
122. Grant to Lincoln, August 23, 1863, in *Ulysses S. Grant: Memoirs and Selected Letters*, ed. Mary D. McFeely and William S. McFeely (New York: Library of America, 1990), 1031.
123. Lincoln to Albert G. Hodges, April 4, 1864, in *Speeches and Writings 1859–1865*, 585–86.
124. Foner, *The Fiery Trial: Abraham Lincoln and American Slavery* (New York: W. W. Norton and Company, 2010), 246.
125. Steven Hahn, *A Nation Under Our Feet* (Cambridge, MA: The Belknap Press, 2003), 99.
126. Charles Sumner to Lincoln, November 20, 1864, *US Capitol Visitor Center.*
127. Quoted in Rick Beard, "Lincoln's 10 Percent Plan," *The New York Times*, December 9, 2013.
128. Lincoln, "Proclamation Concerning Reconstruction," December 8, 1863, in *Speeches and Writings 1859–1865*, 605.
129. Quoted in James Albert Woodburn, "The Attitude of Thaddeus Stevens Toward the Conduct of the Civil War," *The American Historical Review* 12, no. 3 (April 1907): 572.
130. Douglass, "Men of Color, To Arms!," March 1863, in *Speeches and Writings,* 517–18.
131. Paul D. Escott, *Paying Freedom's Price: A History of African Americans in the Civil War* (Lanham, MD: Rowman & Littlefield, 2017), 59.
132. Ethan S. Rafuse, *McClellan's War* (Bloomington, IN: Indiana University Press, 2005), 118.
133. Ibid, 124.
134. Gary W. Gallagher, *Lee and His Army in Confederate History* (Chapel Hill, NC: University of North Carolina Press, 2001), 68.

135. Lincoln, "Address at Gettysburg, Pennsylvania," November 19, 1863, in *Speeches and Writings 1859–1865*, 536.

136. Quoted in Allie Stuart Povall, *Union Warriors at Sunset* (Jefferson, NC: McFarland and Company, 2022), 84.

137. W.T Sherman, "General Sherman's Opinion of General Grant, November 18, 1879," in *The Century Illustrated Monthly*, Vol. 53, New Series Vol. 31, Nov. 1896 to April 1897 (London: MacMillan & Co., 1897), 821.

138. Quoted in Allen C. Guelzo, *Robert E. Lee: A Life* (New York: Knopf, 2021), 193.

139. Robert E. Lee to Mary Randolph Custis Lee, December 27, 1856, Lee Family Digital Archive, Stratford Hall Historic Preserve.

140. Quoted in the Report of the Joint Committee on Reconstruction at the First Session Thirty-Ninth Congress (Washington, DC: Government Printing Office, 1866), 135–36.

141. Du Bois, "Robert E. Lee," 1928, in *Writings* (New York: Library of America, 1986), 1222–23.

142. Quoted in Allen C. Guelzo, *Robert E. Lee: A Life* (New York: Knopf, 2021), 424.

143. Chernow, *Grant*, 354.

144. Ibid, 356.

145. Ibid, 438.

146. Theodore Lyman, *With Grant and Meade from the Wilderness to Appomattox* (Lincoln, NE: University of Nebraska Press, 1994), 80-81.

147. Horace Porter, *Campaigning with Grant* (Cabin John, MD: Wildside Press, 2010), 1-2.

148. Grenville Mellen Dodge, *Personal Recollections of President Abraham Lincoln, General Ulysses S. Grant and General William T. Sherman* (Glendale, CA: The Arthur H. Clark Company, 1914), 129.

149. Alexander H. Stephens, *Recollections of Alexander H. Stephens: His Diary* (New York: Doubleday, Page and Company, 1910), 400-402.
150. Quoted in Arnold Blumberg, "Grant Takes Washington," *Civil War Quarterly* vol. 2, no. 4 (Early Winter 2015): 16.
151. Quoted in Horace Porter, *Campaigning with Grant*, 70.
152. Quoted in John H. Brinton, *Personal Memoirs of John H. Brinton, Major and Surgeon USV, 1861–1865* (New York: Neale Publishing Company, 1914), 239.
153. Ulysses S. Grant, "Personal Memoirs of U. S. Grant, Vol. I," 1885, in *Memoirs and Selected Letters,* 38.
154. John Alcott Carpenter, *Ulysses S. Grant* (Ann Arbor, MI: The University of Michigan, 1970), 62.
155. "Gen. Grant in Battle," *The New York Times*, Jan. 17, 1864.
156. Lincoln to Don C. Buell, January 13, 1862, in *Speeches and Writings 1859–1865*, 302.
157. Marx, *MECW Vol. 19,* 138.
158. Marx, *MECW Vol. 19,* 138, 142.
159. Matthew Arnold, *General Grant with a Rejoinder from Mark Twain*, ed. John Y. Simon (Kent, OH: Kent State University Press, 1995 [1886]), 12.
160. Noah Andre Trudeau, *Southern Storm: Sherman's March to the Sea* (New York: Harper Collins, 2009), 508.
161. Anne J. Bailey, "Sherman's March to the Sea," in *New Georgia Encyclopedia*, ed. John C. Inscoe et al. (Georgia Humanities Council and University of Georgia Press, 2004).
162. James M. McPherson, "Blitzkrieg in Georgia," *The New York Review of Books*, November 30, 2000.
163. Grant, "Personal Memoirs of U. S. Grant, Vol. I," 614.
164. Mark E. Neely Jr., *The Civil War and the Limits of Destruction* (Cambridge, MA: Harvard University Press, 2007), xxx..

165. Bruce Catton, *Never Call Retreat: The Centennial History of the Civil War, Vol. 3* (New York: Doubleday, 1965), 416.

166. US War Department, *The War of the Rebellion: A Compilation of the Official Records of the Union and Confederate Armies, Series I, Vol. 47, Part 2* (Washington, DC: Government Printing Office, 1895), 61.

167. *Freedom: A Documentary History of Emancipation, 1861-1867, Series 3, Volume 1, ed. Steven Hahn et al. (Chapel Hill, NC: University of North Carolina Press, 2017), 442–43.*

168. Carl Schurz to Theodor Petrasch, October, 12, 1864 in *Speeches, Correspondence and Political Papers of Carl Schurz, Vol. 1 October 20, 1852–November 26, 1870* (New York: Negro Universities Press, 1969), 251.

169. George Templeton Strong, *The Diary of George Templeton Strong, Vol. 3: The Civil War 1860–1865*, ed. Allan Nevins and Milton Halsey Thomas (New York, Macmillan, 1952), 480–81.

170. Lincoln, "Second Inaugural Address," March 4, 1865, in *Speeches and Writings 1859–1865*, 686–87.

171. Quoted in Michael K. Erickson, "Thank Him for the Liberty You Will Hereafter Enjoy," *Public Square Magazine,* July 1, 2020.

172. William Henry Herndon, *Herndon's Lincoln: The True Story of a Great Life, Vol. 3* (New York: Belford, Clarke and Company, 1889), 579.

173. Engels, *Anti-Dühring* (London: Wellred Books, 2017), 200.

174. US War Department, *The War of the Rebellion: A Compilation of the Official Records of the Union and Confederate Armies, Series 1, Volume 48, Part 2* (Washington, DC: Government Printing Office, 1896), 929.

175. Foner, *Nothing But Freedom: Emancipation and Its Legacy* (Baton Rouge, LA: Louisiana State University Press, 2007), 55.

176. Douglass, "In What New Skin Will the Old Snake Come Forth?," in *The Frederick Douglass Papers, Series 1, Vol. 4: Speeches, Debates, and Interviews* (New Haven, CT: Yale University Press, 1979), 85.

Part Three: Reconstruction

1. Bridget O'Brian, "Historian Stephanie McCurry Explores the Lasting Impact of the U.S. Civil War," *Columbia News*, October 9, 2018.
2. Eva Jones, quoted in Stephanie E. Jones-Rogers, *They Were Her Property: White Women as Slave Owners in the American South* (New Haven: Yale University Press, 2019), 181.
3. Alexander Ramsey to Dr. J.J. Wardlaw, January 3, 1867, in the *Gilder Lehrman Institute of American History.*
4. Quoted in J.T. Trowbridge, *The Desolate South, 1865–1866: A Picture of the Battlefields and of the Devastated Confederacy* (New York: Duell, Sloan, and Pearce, 1956), 311.
5. Abraham Lincoln, "Address to the Wisconsin State Agricultural Society, Milwaukee, Wisconsin," September 30, 1859, in *Abraham Lincoln: Speeches and Writings 1859–1865* (New York: The Library of America, 1989), 97–98.
6. Ibid, 96–97.
7. Quoted in James M. McPherson and James K. Hogue, *Ordeal by Fire: The Civil War and Reconstruction* (Boston: McGraw-Hill, 2010), 600.
8. W.E.B. Du Bois, *Black Reconstruction: An Essay Toward a History of the Part which Black Folk Played in the Attempt to Reconstruct Democracy in America, 1860–1880* (New York: Harcourt, Brace and Company, 2017 [1935]), 30.
9. Du Bois, *Black Reconstruction,* 727.
10. Ibid, 708.
11. Eric Foner, *Reconstruction: America's Unfinished Revolution, 1863–1877* (New York: Perennial Classics, 2014), 602.
12. Dee Brown, *Bury My Heart at Wounded Knee: An Indian History of the American West* (New York: Bantam Books / Holt, Rinehart and Winston, 1972), 166.

13. Quoted in Robert W. Larson, *Red Cloud: Warrior-Statesman of the Lakota Sioux* (Norman, OK: University of Oklahoma Press, 1997), 263.

14. Quoted in W. Fletcher Johnson, *The Red Record of the Sioux: The Life of Sitting Bull and the History of the Indian War of 1890–91* (Philadelphia, PA: Edgewood Publishing Company, 1891), 201.

15. Foner, *Reconstruction*, xxxix.

16. John Sherman, *John Sherman's Recollections of Forty Years in the House, Senate and Cabinet: An Autobiography* (Chicago, New York, London, Berlin: Werner Company, 1896), 246.

17. Ellis Island National Museum of Immigration, New York, NY.

18. Karl Marx, *Marx and Engels Collected Works Vol. 35* (New York: International Publishers, 2010), 305.

19. Gompers, Samuel, "A News Account of an Address in Louisville," May 1, 1890, in *The Samuel Gompers Papers: The Early Years of the American Federation of Labor, Vol. 2 1887–1890* (Urbana, IL: University of Illinois Press, 1987), 313.

20. David Blight, "The Reconstruction of America: Justice, Power, and the Civil War's Unfinished Business," *Foreign Affairs*, January/February 2021.

21. Boston Commonwealth, January 15, 1864, quoted in McPherson, *Ordeal by Fire*, 432.

22. *The Liberator*, February 5, 1864, quoted in McPherson, *Ordeal by Fire*, 432.

23. Thaddeus Stevens, "Reconstruction: Hon. Thaddeus Stevens on the Great Topic of the Hour. An Address Delivered to the Citizens of Lancaster, Sept. 6, 1865," *The New York Times,* September 10, 1865.

24. Joseph Weydemeyer, "On the Negro Vote," Westliche Post, September, 14, 1866, quoted in *Karl Marx and Friedrich Engels, The Civil War in the United States,* trans. Andrew Zimmerman (New York: International Publishers, 2016), 173.

25. Foner, *Reconstruction*, 80.

26. Frederick Douglass, "Life and Times of Frederick Douglass," in *Douglass Autobiographies* (New York: The Library of America, 1994), 802.

27. Cincinnati Enquirer, quoted in Hans Louis Trefousse, *Andrew Johnson: A Biography* (New York: W. W. Norton and Company, 1997), 236.

28. Douglass, "Reconstruction, Atlantic Monthly, December 1866," in *Douglass Speeches and Writings* (New York: The Library of America, 2022), 557–62.

29. Stevens, "On the School Law," (speech, Pennsylvania House of Representatives, Harrisburg, PA, April 11, 1835).

30. James A. Garfield to Jacob Dolson Cox, July 1865, in *Journal of the Civil War Era* vol. 4, no. 2, (June 2014): 254.

31. Gary W. Gallagher, "Reporting on the Defeated South," *The Civil War Monitor,* July 22, 2024.

32. George W. Julian, "Dangers and Duties of Reconstruction and Suffrage," (speech, Indiana House of Representatives, Indianapolis, IN, November, 17, 1865).

33. Letter from Office Sub. Asst. Comr. &c., Sherman, TX, October 6, 1866, "Registered Reports of Murders and Outrages, Sept. 1866–July 1867," in *Records of the Assistant Commissioner for the State of Texas Bureau of Refugees, Freedmen and Abandoned Lands, 1865–1869*, National Archives Microfilm Publication M821, Roll 32.

34. Douglass, "Equal Rights for All," (speech, New York, NY, May 14, 1868).

35. McPherson, *Ordeal by Fire*, 587.

36. Ulysses S. Grant, "Personal Memoirs of U. S. Grant, Vol. I," 1885, in *Ulysses S. Grant Memoirs and Selected Letters* (New York: The Library of America, 1990), 752–53.

37. Engels, *MECW Vol. 23*, 425.

38. "Interview with Nathan Bedford Forrest," *Cincinnati Commercial*, August 28, 1868.

39. McPherson, *Ordeal by Fire*, 615.

40. Foner, *Reconstruction*, 405–406.

41. Walter L. Fleming, *The Freedmen's Savings Bank: A Chapter in the Economic History of the Negro Race* (Chapel Hill, NC: University of North Carolina Press, 1927), 85.

42. David Blight, "Retreat from Reconstruction: The Grant Era and Paths to 'Southern Redemption'" (lecture, Yale University, New Haven, CT, April 2008).

43. Quoted in James M. McPherson, "Grant or Greeley? The Abolitionist Dilemma in the Election of 1872," *The American Historical Review* vol. 71, no. 1 (October 1965): 49.

44. Ulysses S. Grant, "Second Inaugural Address" (speech, Washington, DC, March 4, 1873).

45. McPherson, *Ordeal by Fire*, 642.

46. United States Senate, *Mississippi in 1875: Report of the Select Committee to Inquire into the Mississippi Election of 1875 with the Testimony and Documentary Evidence, Vol. 2* (Washington, DC: US Government Printing Office, 1876), 1758.

47. Wendell Phillips, "Speech of Wendell Phillips," Michigan Argus, July 21, 1865.

48. Du Bois, *Black Reconstruction*, 630.

49. "Mississippi Convict System," *The American Missionary* vol. 41, no. 12 (December 1887): 342.

50. Du Bois, "The Souls of Black Folks," in *Writings* (New York: Library of America, 1986), 368.

51. William Sylvis to the Secretary of the First International, quoted in Emanuel Garrett, "Men and Women of Labor out of the Past: William H. Sylvis," *Socialist Appeal* (US), July 25, 1939.

52. William Sylvis, *The Life, Speeches, Labors, and Essays of William H. Sylvis*, ed. James C. Sylvis (Philadelphia: Claxton, Remsen, and Haffelfinger, 1872), 337.

53. Edward A. Pollard, *The Lost Cause: A New Southern History of the War of the Confederates* (New York: E. B. Treat and Company, 1866), 751–52.
54. Quoted in Gaines M. Foster, *Ghosts of the Confederacy: Defeat, the Lost Cause, and the Emergence of the New South, 1865–1913* (New York: Oxford University Press, USA, 1987), 117.
55. Du Bois, *Black Reconstruction*, 39.
56. Foner, *Reconstruction*, 57.
57. C. Vann Woodward, *History of the South, Vol. 10: Origins of the New South* (Baton Rouge, LA: Louisiana State University Press, 1964), 291–310.
58. Martin Luther King Jr., "The Three Evils of Society," (speech, Chicago, IL, May 10, 1967).
59. Malcolm X, "The Black Revolution" in *Malcom X Speaks* (New York: Pathfinder, 1989 [1964]), 76.
60. Douglass, "Reconstruction," in *Atlantic Monthly*, December 1866, 558.

Toward the Third American Revolution

1. Karl Marx and Friedrich Engels, "The Communist Manifesto," in *The Classics of Marxism Vol. 1* (London: Wellred Books, 2025), 4–5.
2. Leon Trotsky, "Theses on revolution and counterrevolution," in *The Challenge of the Left Opposition (1926-27)* (New York: Pathfinder Press, 2014), 209–18.
3. George Washington, "Farewell Address," in *George Washington Writings*, New York: The Library of America, 1997 [1796], 974–75
4. Quoted in George B. Lockwood, *Americanism* (Washington: National Republican Publishing, 1921) 13.
5. Quoted in Herbert Aptheker, *The American Revolution 1763–1783*, New York: International Publishers, 1969, 50–51.
6. Vladimir Lenin, *The State and Revolution,* in *The Classics of Marxism Vol. 1*, 195.

7. Lenin, *Lenin Collected Works Vol. 30* (Moscow: Progress Publishers, 1965), 371.

8. *MECW Vol. 35*, 750–51.

9. Thomas Jefferson, "The Earth Belong to the Living: To James Madison," 1789, in *Jefferson Writings* (New York: The Library of America, 1984), 959.

10. Ibid, 963.

11. Quoted in Dorothie Bobbé, *Abigail Adams: The Second First Lady* (New York: Minton, Balch & Company, 1929) 191.

Titles by Wellred Books

Wellred Books is a revolutionary Marxist publishing house. Founded in 2013, our focus is to republish classic works of Marxism as well as producing new titles. The majority of our titles are also available in ebook and audiobook formats.

INTRODUCTORY TEXTS

What Is Marxism?, Alan Woods & Rob Sewell, featuring extracts from Karl Marx, Friedrich Engels, Vladimir Ilyich Lenin & Leon Trotsky

The Classics of Marxism: Volume One
— *The Communist Manifesto*, Karl Marx & Friedrich Engels
— *Socialism: Utopian & Scientific*, Friedrich Engels
— *The State & Revolution*, Vladimir Ilyich Lenin
— *The Transitional Programme*, Leon Trotsky

The Classics of Marxism: Volume Two
— *Wage-labour & Capital*, Karl Marx
— *Value, Price & Profit*, Karl Marx
— *'Left-wing' Communism: An Infantile Disorder*, Vladimir Ilyich Lenin
— *In Defence of October*, Leon Trotsky
— *Stalinism & Bolshevism*, Leon Trotsky

The Ideas of Karl Marx, Alan Woods, featuring extracts from Friedrich Engels, Vladimir Ilyich Lenin, Leon Trotsky & Ted Grant

Lenin & Trotsky: What They Really Stood For, Alan Woods & Ted Grant

Reformism or Revolution, Alan Woods

BOLSHEVISM & THE RUSSIAN REVOLUTION

In Defence of Lenin, Rob Sewell & Alan Woods

Bolshevism: The Road to Revolution, Alan Woods

Russia: From Revolution to Counter-revolution, Ted Grant

THE GERMAN REVOLUTION

Germany 1918-1933: Socialism or Barbarism, Rob Sewell

Germany: From Revolution to Counter-revolution, Rob Sewell

The Revolutionary Legacy of Rosa Luxemburg, Marie Frederiksen

THEORY

The History of Philosophy: A Marxist Perspective, Alan Woods

Reason in Revolt: Marxist Philosophy & Modern Science, Alan Woods & Ted Grant

Understanding Marx's Capital: A Reader's Guide, Adam Booth & Rob Sewell

Lenin, Trotsky & the Theory of the Permanent Revolution, John Roberts

The Revolutionary Philosophy of Marxism, compilation, featuring Karl Marx, Friedrich Engels, Vladimir Ilyich Lenin, Leon Trotsky, Georgi Plekhanov, Rosa Luxemburg & Alan Woods

Marxism & Anarchism, compilation, featuring Friedrich Engels, Vladimir Ilyich Lenin, Leon Trotsky, Georgi Plekhanov, Alan Woods & others

KARL MARX & FRIEDRICH ENGELS

Anti-Dühring, Friedrich Engels

The Civil War in France, Karl Marx

The Class Struggles in France: 1848-1850, Karl Marx

Dialectics of Nature, Friedrich Engels

The Eighteenth Brumaire of Louis Bonaparte, Karl Marx

The Origin of the Family, Private Property & the State, Friedrich Engels

VLADIMIR ILYICH LENIN

Imperialism: The Highest Stage of Capitalism

'Left-wing' Communism: An Infantile Disorder

Materialism & Empirio-criticism

The State & Revolution

What Is to Be Done?

On Imperialist War: Lenin Selected Writings 1

The Revolutions of 1917: Lenin Selected Writings 2

On the National Question: Lenin Selected Writings 3

LEON TROTSKY

Democracy, Bonapartism & Fascism, Leon Trotsky & Ted Grant

The First Five Years of the Communist International

History of the Russian Revolution

History of the Russian Revolution to Brest-Litovsk

In Defence of Marxism

My Life

Not Guilty, Report of the Dewey Commission

The Permanent Revolution and Results & Prospects

The Revolution Betrayed

Stalin

Writings on Britain

TED GRANT

Ted Grant Writings: Volumes 1-3

Democracy, Bonapartism & Fascism, Leon Trotsky & Ted Grant

History of British Trotskyism

Lenin & Trotsky: What They Really Stood For, Alan Woods & Ted Grant

Reason in Revolt: Marxist Philosophy & Modern Science, Alan Woods & Ted Grant

Russia: From Revolution to Counter-revolution

Ted Grant: The Permanent Revolutionary, Alan Woods

REVOLUTIONARY HISTORY

The Arab Revolution: A Marxist Analysis (Thawra hatta'l nasr! – Revolution Until Victory!), Alan Woods & others

Chartist Revolution, Rob Sewell

Class Struggle in the Roman Republic, Alan Woods

China: From Permanent Revolution to Counter-revolution, John Roberts

Colossus: The Rise & Decline of US Imperialism, John Peterson

The First World War: A Marxist Analysis of the Great Slaughter, Alan Woods

History of the Paris Commune of 1871, Prosper-Olivier Lissagaray

In the Cause of Labour, Rob Sewell

Ireland: Republicanism & Revolution, Alan Woods

Marxism & the USA, Alan Woods

Permanent Revolution in Latin America, John Roberts & Jorge Martin

Revolution & Counter-revolution in Spain, Felix Morrow

Spain's Revolution Against Franco: The Great Betrayal, Alan Woods

The Venezuelan Revolution: A Marxist Perspective, Alan Woods

Women, Family & the Russian Revolution, John Roberts & Fred Weston

To make an order or for more information, visit marxistbooks.com or email sales@marxistbooks.com.

www.ingramcontent.com/pod-product-compliance
Lightning Source LLC
LaVergne TN
LVHW100501110826
845146LV00002B/476

* 9 7 9 8 2 3 4 0 6 8 4 8 4 *